Angels Hastening

Islamic History and Thought

22

Islamic History and Thought provides a platform for scholarly research on any geographic area within the expansive Islamic world, stretching from the Mediterranean to China, and dated to any period from the eve of Islam until the early modern era. This series contains original monographs, translations (Arabic, Persian, Syriac, Greek, and Latin) and edited volumes.

Angels Hastening

The Karbalāʾ Dreams

Christopher Paul Clohessy

Gorgias Press

2021

Gorgias Press LLC, 954 River Road, Piscataway, NJ, 08854, USA

www.gorgiaspress.com

2021 ,

ISBN 978-1-4632-4408-8 **ISSN 2643-6906**

First paperback edition.

Library of Congress Cataloging-in-Publication Data

A Cataloging-in-Publication Record is available from the Library of Congress.

Printed and bound by CPI Group (UK) Ltd, Croydon, CR0 4YY

Dedicated to the memory of

Arthur Derek Clohessy
19.12.1925 – 21.02.1990
and
Joy Margaret Clohessy
02.12.1928 – 20.05.2019

TABLE OF CONTENTS

QUOTATIONS, TRANSLATIONS AND TRANSLITERATION

Unless otherwise stated, all quotations from the Qur'ān are taken from the English interpretation of Muhammad Marmaduke Pickthall.[1] At times, I have compared his translation with that of other English interpreters of the Qur'ān, and these will be named in the text when they occur.

Unless otherwise stated, all translations of the Arabic texts are my own. All Arabic texts have been reproduced exactly from their sources, even when mistakes are extant in the said texts. The system of transliteration, given below, has been followed throughout the text, except in instances in which other authors have been quoted, in which case the said author's system of transliteration has been respected.

Except when quoting from other works, all dates are given according to the Islamic calendar (*hiğra*), followed by a backslash and the Gregorian equivalent.

---

[1] PICKTHALL M.M., *The Meaning of the Glorious Qur'ān*, Dar al-Kitab Allubnani, Beirut and Dar al-Kitab al-Masri, Cairo (n.d.).

SYSTEM OF TRANSLITERATION

ء	-	ʾ	ض	-	ḍ
ب	-	b	ط	-	ṭ
ت	-	t	ظ	-	ẓ
ث	-	ṯ	ع	-	ʿ
ج	-	ğ	غ	-	ġ
ح	-	ḥ	ف	-	f
خ	-	ḫ	ق	-	q
د	-	d	ك	-	k
ذ	-	ḏ	ل	-	l
ر	-	r	م	-	m
ز	-	z	ن	-	n
س	-	s	ه	-	h
ش	-	sh	و	-	w
ص	-	ṣ	ي	-	y

Short Vowels

أ	-	a, u	إ	-	i

Long Vowels

آ	-	ā	ي	-	ī
و	-	ū			

List of Abbreviations

AD	*Anno Domini*
b.	bin (son)
bb.	*bāb* (chapter)
BC	before Christ
bk.	book
bt.	*bint* (daughter)
c.	*circa*
CE	common era
cf.	confer
ch.	chapter
Col.	The Letter to the Colossians
d.	died
Dan.	The Book of Daniel
Deut.	The Book of Deuteronomy
Eccles.	The Book of Ecclesiastes
ed.	editor
edn.	edition

edns.	editions
eds.	editors
eg.	for example
et al.	and others
etc.	etcetera
Ez.	The Book of Ezekiel
ff.	following
GAL	*Geschichte der arabischen Literatur*
GAS	*Geschichte der arabischen Schrifttums*
Gen.	The Book of Genesis
Heb.	The Letter to the Hebrews
Ibid.	*ibidem*
Is.	The Book of Isaiah
Jdg.	The Book of Judges
Jn.	The Gospel of St. John
I Kgs.	The First Book of Kings
lit.	literally
Lk.	The Gospel of St. Luke
Mt.	The Gospel of St. Matthew
n.	number
n.d.	no date
Num.	The Book of Numbers
nn.	numbers
n.n.	no number
n.p.	no publisher
nt.	footnote
pl.	plural
Q.	Qurʾān
Rev.	The Book of Revelation
Rm.	The Letter to the Romans
I Sam.	The First Book of Samuel
sic	thus

Sir.	The Book of Sirach
St.	Saint
sing.	singular
trans.	translator
v.	verse
vol.	volume
vols.	volumes
vv.	verses
Zech.	The Book of Zechariah

PREFACE

When, on an autumn Medina night in 61/680, the night that saw al-Ḥusayn killed, Umm Salama was torn from her sleep by an apparition of a long-dead Muḥammad, she slipped effortlessly into a progression of her co-religionists who, irrespective of status, gender or standing with God, were the recipients of dark and arresting visions. At the core of those Delphian dreams, peopled by angels or *ǧinn* or esteemed forbears and textured with Iraqi dust and martyrs' blood, was the Karbalāʾ event. Her dream would be recounted by an array of Muslim scholars, from al-Tirmiḏī, stellar pupil of al-Buḫārī, and Ibn ʿAsākir, untiring chronicler of Syrian history, to bibliophile theologian Ibn Ṭāʾūs and Egyptian polymath al-Suyūṭī. But this was not Umm Salama's only otherworldly encounter and she was not the only one to have al-Ḥusayn's fate disturb her nights.

This is their story.

Introduction

«By those who drag forth to destruction,
by the meteors rushing,
by the lone stars floating,
by the angels hastening»[1]

In the spring of 64/685, Sulaymān b. ʿAbd al-Malik b. Marwān succeeded his father Marwān, cousin to Muʿāwiya, as caliph of the restive Umayyad dynasty. He launched into a reign of twenty energetic years, quelling strife, opening Islam to the non-Arabic world, reclaiming lost territory and expanding into new, promoting Arabic language and Islamic currency, restoring Islamic confidence, con-

[1] Q. 79:1–4, with Pickthall's interpretation of the words *fa-l-sābiqāt sabq^{an}*. According to Lane, the *sābiqāt* of Q. 79:4 refers to "the angels that precede the devils with the revelation [that they convey] to the prophets: or the angels that precede the jinn or genii, in listening to the revelation: or the angels that precede with the souls of believers to Paradise or with the souls of the unbelievers to Hell." Cf. LANE E.W., *An Arabic-English Lexicon*, vol. IV, Librairie du Liban, Beirut 1968: 1300.

solidating power and firming up a functional bureaucracy. Periodically, he also had peculiar dreams. Sometime before his death in 85/705, one sleepless night drove him to seek advice from the doleful and abstemious al-Ḥasan al-Baṣrī.[2] A handful of transmitters relay the content of Ibn Marwān's dream:

> Some of them mentioned that Sulaymān b. ʿAbd al-Malik b. Marwān saw the Prophet in a dream as though he was doing good to him and being kind to him. He summoned al-Ḥasan al-Baṣrī and asked him about this, and he said: "Perhaps you have caused some good for his family!" Sulaymān replied: "I found the head of al-Ḥusayn in Yazīd b. Muʿāwiya's treasure house. I clothed it five times with silk brocade, prayed *ṣalāt* for it in a group of my companions and buried it." Al-Ḥasan answered: "For this reason, the Prophet is satisfied with you." So, he acted well towards al-Ḥasan and ordered he be rewarded.[3]

On the oneiric scale, Ibn Marwān's is a positive dream; he can look back with contentment on a deed he has done, an event in his vigorous and animated life that has won the satisfaction of the Messenger of God. This book, however, recalls a markedly different catalogue of dreams and an event so traumatic that even the angels appear to step back in dismay; an incident which gave rise to repercussions of cosmic proportions, the texts relating tales of the heavens darkened, the sun eclipsed, the skies raining blood and all crea-

---

[2] Al-Ḥasan al-Baṣrī (d. 109/728), regarded by some as archetypal in the emergence of that Islamic piety which would devolve into Ṣūfī mysticism, backed the Umayyads but had no hesitancy in reprimanding them; his ascetic lifestyle, eloquent preaching and commitment to social justice shaped the whole of his life into a bruising indictment against Umayyad luxury.

[3] Ibn al-Ǧawzī., *Bustān al-waʿiẓīn wa-riyāḍ al-sāmiʿīn*, bb. 418: 263, al-Maǧlisī, *Biḥār al-anwār*, vol. XLV, bb. 39, n. 1: 145, al-Iṣfahānī., *ʿAwālim al-ʿulūm wa-l-maʿārif al-aḥwāl min al-āyāt wa-l-aḫbār wa-l-aqwāl*, vol. XVII, ch. 16, bb. 5, n. 6: 453.

tion groaning.[4] The murder on the field of Karbalāʾ of Abū ʿAbd Allāh al-Ḥusayn, son of ʿAlī and Fāṭima and grandson of Muḥammad, is an episode that slips beyond the sentries of time and space, giving it a timelessness which allows Shīʿī communities in subsequent generations to gauge themselves against the example of the chief of their martyrs, whose capacity for truth and courage urges them to live their own lives more deeply engaged with justice.

This work explores one fragment of that complex story, a part in which the angels play a singular role. One narrative tells of the angel Ğibrîl,[5] ostensibly the principal entity among Islam's normally impassive angels, descending to the home of Muḥammad, "wings

[4] "The Shīʿa exaggerate the day of ʿĀshūrā," grumbles Ibn Kaṯīr, "and contrive many *aḥādīṯ* and a monstrous falsehood, ranging from the incident of the sun being veiled on the day to the withdrawal of the stars" (Ibn Kaṯīr., *al-Bidāya wa-l-nihāya*, vol. IX, bb. *Iḫbār bi-maqtal al-Ḥusayn*: 239, vol. XI, bb. *al-Iḫbār maqtal al-Ḥusayn b. ʿAlī*: 576). Cf. Ibn Abī Shayba., *al-Muṣannaf*, vol. XIII, *Kitāb al-fitan*, bb. 1, n. 38386: 295 ("the sky remained like blood for days," says al-Ḥusayn's servant), al-Ṭabarānī., *al-Muʿğam al-kabīr*, vol. III, nn. 2836, 2837, 2838, 2839 2840: 113–114, al-Bayhaqī., *Dalāʾil al-nubuwwa*, vol. VI, bb. *Ma ruwiya fī iḫbāri-hi bi-qatli ibn ibnati-hi ʿAbd Allāh al-Ḥusayn*: 471–472, al-Ḫawārizmī., *Maqtal al-Ḥusayn*, Part Two, bb. *Fī bayān ʿuqūba qātil al-Ḥusayn*, nn. 14–17: 101–102, Ibn ʿAsākir *Tārīḫ madīnat Dimashq*, vol. XIV, bb. 1566 (*al-Ḥusayn b. ʿAlī b. Abī Ṭālib b. ʿAbd al-Muṭṭalib b. Hāshim b. ʿAbd al-Manāf*): 225–229, Ibn al-ʿAdīm., *Buġyat al-ṭalab fī tārīḫ Ḥalab*, Part Six: 2596, al-Ṭabarī., *Ḏaḫāʾir al-ʿuqbā*, Part One, bb. 9: 248–249, al-Ḏahabī., *Siyar aʿlām al-nubalāʾ*, vol. III, n. 48 (*al-Ḥusayn al-Shahīd Abū ʿAbd Allāh b. ʿAlī b. Abī Ṭālib*): 312 (who lists some of the phenomena, without comment), al-Suyūṭī., *al-Ḫaṣāʾiṣ al-kubrā*, vol. II: 453–454. Among the Shīʿa cf. for e.g. al-Ṭūsī., *al-Amālī fī al-ḥadīṯ*, *mağlis* 11, n. 106–658: 330.

[5] Throughout the Shīʿī and Sunnī books of *aḥādīṯ*, this angel's name is written in an assortment of ways; sometimes 'Ğibrīl', at other times 'Ğibraʾīl' and occasional 'Ğibrāʾīl'. Jeffery notes the variations in the writing the name (Ğabraʾīl, Ğibrīl, Ğabrīl, Ğabraʾil, Ğabrāʾīl, Ğabrayīl, Ğabrāʾil or even Ğabrīn). Cf. JEFFERY A., *The Foreign Vocabulary of the Qurʾān*, Brill, Leiden 2007: 100.

outstretched, weeping, shouting aloud."[6] Evidently, the angels rarely betray emotions, although they are said to tremble with awe before God,[7] exalting Him with praise,[8] but harsh and severe with the wicked,[9] distinct from all other creatures by their unequivocal obedience to God,[10] which endows them with that enigmatic quality called *ʿiṣma.*[11] And while Ibn al-Ğawzī takes note of angels weeping over al-Ḥusayn,[12] and Ibn Shahrāshūb, al-Baḥrānī and al-Mağlisī have left us accounts of Ğibrīl laughing,[13] al-Suyūṭī, writing in his

---

[6] Ibn Qūlawayh., *Kāmil al-ziyārāt*, bb. 17, n. 7: 131, al-Mağlisī., *Biḥār al-anwār*, vol. XLIII, bb. 30, n. 22: 235, al-Iṣfahānī., *ʿAwālim al-ʿulūm wa-l-maʿārif al-aḥwāl min al-āyāt wa-l-aḫbār wa-l-aqwāl*, vol. XVII, Part Seventeen, ch. 11, bb. 6, n. 1: 124, al-Ğazāʾirī., *Riyāḍ al-abrār fī manāqib al-aʾimma al-aṭhār*, vol. I, Part One: 171.

[7] Q. 13:13. Cf. Abū al-Shayḫ., *al-ʿAẓama*, vol. III, n. 515: 993, al-Bayhaqī., *al-Ğāmiʿ al-muṣannaf fī shuʿab al-īmān*, vol. I, bb. 11, n. 914: 521, al-Baġdādī., *Tārīḫ Baġdād*, vol. XIV, n. 6704: 254, Ibn ʿAsākir., *Tārīḫ madīnat Dimashq*, vol. XL, bb. 5608 (*ʿĀbī b. Arṭaʾa*): 58, 61, al-Suyūṭī., *al-Ḥabāʾik fī aḫbār al-malāʾik*, n. 26: 18, al-Muttaqī al-Hindī, *Kanz al-ʿummāl fī sunan al-aqwāl wa-l-afʿāl*, vol. XI, n. 29836: 366.

[8] Q. 39:75, Q. 42:5.

[9] Q. 6:66.

[10] Cf. Q. 21:19, Q. 66:6.

[11] The term *ʿiṣma* evokes the idea of self-possession, of separation from error, and hence of impeccability. Lane notes that chiefly, the term signifies 'prevention' or 'hindrance' (*manʿ*) and is used to describe the manner in which God preserves His prophets; but theologically, it also connotes the faculty for avoiding disobedience, "an inability to disobey: or a disposition that prevents [disobedience], not such as constrains (to act)." Cf. LANE E.W., *An Arabic-English Lexicon*, vol. V, 1968: 2066–2067.

[12] Ibn al-Ğawzī., *Bustān al-waʿiẓīn wa-riyāḍ al-sāmiʿīn*, bb. 414: 262.

[13] Ibn Shahrāshūb., *Manāqib āl Abī Ṭālib*, vol. II, bb. *ʿInd al-ḫāliq wa ʿind al-maḫlūqīn*: 245, al-Daylamī., *Aʿlam al-dīn fī ṣifāt al-muʾminīn*. 277, al-Baḥrānī., *al-Burhān fī tafsīr al-qurʾān*, vol. V, Part Five, *sūrat al-ʿAlaq*, n. 11752: 697, *Ḥilyat al-abrār fī aḥwāl Muḥammad wa āli-hi al-aṭhār*, vol I, bb. 7, n. 2: 68, *Madīnat al-maʿāğiz fī muʿğizāt al-aʾimma al-aṭhār*, vol. I, bb. 1, n. 54: 106, al-Mağlisī., *Biḥār al-anwār*, vol. XXXIX, bb. 76, n. 10: 97, 102, vol. LXXVIII, bb. 1, n. 52: 194, vol. LXXXIX, bb. 124, n. 23: 354.

al-Ḥabā'ik fī aḫbār al-malā'ik, cautions us that neither Ǧibrīl[14] nor Isrāfīl[15] nor Mīkā'īl have laughed since the creation of the Fire, the suggestion being that perhaps, long before that unprecedented event, angels had indeed expressed emotion with less inhibition. Mīkā'īl's abstinence from mirth especially is referenced in texts by authors as diverse as Ibn Ḥanbal and Ibn Abī Firās,[16] while in his *Tafsīr*, al-Qummī notes that Mālik, the angel who guards Hell, is another angel for whom laughter is an alien emotion.[17]

Foremost among the angels in our narrative – if indeed he is an angel at all, and not some other genus and species – and the chief protagonist is the aforesaid Ǧibrīl who, although only mentioned by name three times in the Qur'ān (Q. 2:97–98, Q. 66:4), is also referred to as «*the Faithful Spirit*» (Q. 26:193), «*the Spirit of holiness*» (Q. 2:87, Q. 16:102) and «*Our Spirit*» (Q. 19:17). In a number of other verses, Ǧibrīl is implied but given neither name nor epithet (Q. 53:5–18, Q. 81:19–25). Conversely, the angel involved in the encounters in this story is not always Ǧibrīl; because Ǧibrīl comes to Muḥammad with what might be termed both public and private revelation, sometimes, as if carefully to differentiate be-

---

[14] al-Suyūṭī., *al-Ḥabā'ik fī aḫbār al-malā'ik*, n. 72: 26, al-Bayhaqī., *al-Ǧāmiʿ al-muṣannaf fī shuʿab al-īmān*, vol. I, bb. 11, n. 195: 521.

[15] al-Bayhaqī., *al-Ǧāmiʿ al-muṣannaf fī shuʿab al-īmān*, vol. I, bb. 11, n. 913: 521, al-Suyūṭī., *al-Ḥabā'ik fī aḫbār al-malā'ik*, n. 100: 33, al-Muttaqī al-Hindī., *Kanz al-ʿummāl fī sunan al-aqwāl wa-l-afʿāl*, vol. III, n. 5895: 1455.

[16] Cf. WENSINCK A.J., "Mīkāl" in C. Bosworth et al., (eds.), *The Encyclopaedia of Islam*, vol. VII, Brill, Leiden 1993: 25. Cf. also Ibn Ḥanbal., *Musnad*, vol. III, *Musnad Anas b. Mālik*: 324, Ibn Abī Firās., *Tanbīh al-ḫawāṭir wa nuzhat al-nawāẓir*, vol. I: 66, 301, al-Hayṯamī., *Maǧmaʿ al-zawā'id wa-manbaʿ al-fawā'id*, vol. X, *Kitāb ṣifat al-nār*: 385, al-Suyūṭī., *al-Ḥabā'ik fī aḫbār al-malā'ik*, n. 82: 29, Abū al-Shayḫ., *al-ʿAẓama*, vol. III, n. 384: 814, al-Maǧlisī., *Biḥār al-anwār*, vol. LVI, bb. 24, n. 32: 260.

[17] Cf. al-Qummī., *Tafsīr*, vol. II, *sūrat al-Isrā'*: 5, al-Fayḍ al-Kāshānī., *Nawādir al-aḫbār*: 144, 374, *Tafsīr al-ṣāfī*, vol. III, *sūrat al-Isrā'*: 169, al-Baḥrānī., *al-Burhān fī tafsīr al-qur'ān*, vol. III, *sūrat al-Isrā'*, n. 6196: 474, vol. V, *sūrat al-Takwīr*, n. 11431: 597, al-Maǧlisī., *Biḥār al-anwār*, vol. VIII, bb. 24, n. 3: 291, vol. XVIII, bb. 3, n. 24: 321. Cf. also Q. 39:71, 73, Q. 40:49, Q. 67:8.

tween the Karbalāʾ dreams and the divine revelation usually associated with Ǧibrīl, the texts introduce as the interlocutor an unnamed angel who has never come to Muḥammad before, or identify the visitor as the 'angel of rain' (*malak al-qaṭr* or, in some texts, *malak al-maṭar*). In Islamic angelology, this is the unsmiling Mikāʾīl[18] (but whom al-Rāwandī erroneously names as Ismāʿīl),[19] mentioned together with Ǧibrīl in Q. 2:98 and who, al-Qummī reminds us, is also called the 'angel of mercy',[20] having relinquished cheer in favour of piteous weeping over sinners and imploring God's forgiveness for them. In the Sunnī texts, both Ibn ʿAsākir and al-Haytamī make this distinction between Muḥammad's visitor; among the Shīʿī, it is made, for example, by al-Ṭūsī, Ibn Shahrāshūb (who notes that in the reports of Sālim b. al-Ǧaʿd it was Mīkāʾīl and in the *musnad* of Abū Yaʿlā, the angel of the rain, traditionally, Mīkāʾīl), al-Shāmī, al-Baḥrānī, al-Maǧlisī and al-Iṣfahānī.[21] It is perhaps no small coincidence that it should be the

[18] His names, al-Maǧlisī notes from al-Zamaḫsharī, could be read Mīkāl, Mīkāʾīl, Mīkāʿīl, Mīkaʾīl, Mīkaʿīl, Mīkāʾīl, Mīkāʿil or Mīkaʿil. Cf. al-Maǧlisī., *Biḥār al-anwār*, vol. LVI, bb. 23: 206, 221, Ṣadr al-Dīn al-Shīrāzī., *Riyāḍ al-sālikīn fī sharḥ saḥīfa sayyid al-sāǧǧidīn*, vol. II: 25, 27 (Brockelmann does not list this work, but another, possibly the same, entitled *Sharḥ saḥīfa al-kāmila*), Muḥammad Riḍā al-Ṭūsī., *Kanz al-daqāʾiq wa baḥr al-ġarāʾib fī tafsīr al-qurʾān*, vol. II, *sūrat al-Baqara*: 96.

[19] Cf. al-Rāwandī., *al-Ḫarāʾiǧ wa-l-ǧarāʾiḥ fī-l-muʿǧizāt*, vol. I, Part One, n. 107: 62, al-Maǧlisī, *Biḥār al-anwār*, vol. XVIII, bb. 6, n. 40: 15.

[20] al-Qummī., *Tafsīr*, vol. I, *sūrat al-Baqara*: 54, al-Ṭūsī., *Miṣbāḥ al-mutahaǧǧid*, vol. II: 808, Ibn Ṭāʾūs., *Kitāb al-iqbāl bi-l-aʿmāl al-ḥasana*, vol. II: 660, vol. III: 243 (it is of note that in the same text Ibn Ṭāʾūs also refers to ʿIzrāʾīl as the 'angel of mercy'), al-Kafʿamī., *al-Balad al-amīn*, n. 16: 181, *Kitāb al-miṣbāḥ*: 531, al-Fayḍ al-Kāshānī., *Tafsīr al-ṣāfī*, vol. I, *sūrat al-Baqara*: 167, al-Maǧlisī., *Biḥār al-anwār*, vol. IX, bb. 1, n. 15: 186, vol. LXIV, bb. 1: 20, vol. XCV, bb. 26, n. 6: 400, *Zād al-maʿād*: 29.

[21] al-Ṭūsī., *al-Amālī fī-l-ḥadīṯ*, *maǧlis* 11, n. 86–638: 314, Ibn Shahrāshūb., *Manāqib āl Abī Ṭālib*, vol. IV, bb. *Fī imāmat Abī ʿAbd Allāh al-Ḥusayn*: 55, Cf. al-Shāmī., *al-Durr al-naẓīm fī manāqib al-aʾimma al-lahāhīm*, bb. 5, *Faṣl fī ḏikr maqtal al-Ḥusayn b. ʿAlī*: 535, al-Baḥrānī., *Ḥilyat al-abrār fī aḥwāl Muḥammad wa āli-hi al-aṭhār*, vol. IV, bb. 7, n. 12: 124, al-Maǧlisī.,

angel of rain who comes to Muḥammad to warn of Karbalāʾ, the land of such torturous thirst, whose tragic history would cause the skies to rain down blood in grief over the killing of al-Ḥusayn.

There are other angels too, unnamed and not always identified by their angelic rank; sometimes, the angel concerned asks God's permission to visit Muḥammad, while in other texts, great battalions arrive together ("Was there an angel left in the heavens who did not descend to the Messenger of God, consoling him for his son al-Ḥusayn informing him of the reward of God granted him and carrying to him its dust on which he was felled, slaughtered, killed, thrown, forsaken?").[22] Ibn Qūlawayh and a sprinkling of transmitters after him carry a *ḥadīṯ* which reads: "The angel who went to Muḥammad to inform him about the death of al-Ḥusayn was the angel of the seas."[23]

Nonetheless, Ǧibrīl and Mīkāʾīl dominate our story, and it is not surprising to find these two heavenly beings mentioned together. In his *al-Ḫabāʾik*, al-Suyūṭī relates a *ḥadīṯ* which holds that

---

Biḥār al-anwār, vol. XLIV, bb. 30, n. 10: 229, vol. XLV, bb. 41, n. 22: 227, al-Iṣfahānī., *ʿAwālim al-ʿulūm wa-l-maʿārif al-aḥwāl min al-āyāt wa-l-aḫbār wa-l-aqwāl*, vol. XVII, ch. 18, bb. 3, n. 1: 506.

[22] al-Ḫawārizmī., *Maqtal al-Ḥusayn*, Part One, bb. *Aḫbār rasūl Allāh ʿan al-Ḥusayn wa-aḥwāli-hi*, n. 12: 237, Ibn Ṭāʾūs., *Kitāb al-luhūf fī qatlā al-ṭufūf*: 13–14, Ibn Qūlawayh., *Kāmil al-ziyārāt*, bb. 17, n. 8: 131–132, al-Maǧlisī., *Biḥār al-anwār*, vol. XLIV, bb. 30, n. 46: 246, vol. XLIII, bb. 30, n. 27: 236, vol. XLV, bb. 46, n. 11: 309.

[23] Ibn Qūlawayh., *Kāmil al-ziyārāt*, bb. 21, n. 3: 143, al-Mūsawī., *Tasliyat al-maǧālis wa zīnat al-maǧālis*, vol. II, Part Two, *maǧlis* 5: 111, al-Maǧlisī, *Biḥār al-anwār*, vol. XLV, bb. 41, n. 5: 221, al-Iṣfahānī., *ʿAwālim al-ʿulūm wa-l-maʿārif al-aḥwāl min al-āyāt wa-l-aḫbār wa-l-aqwāl*, vol. XVII, Part Seventeen, ch. 17, bb. 9, n. 7: 501, al-Ǧazāʾirī., *Riyāḍ al-abrār fī manāqib al-aʾimma al-aṭhār*, vol. I, Part One: 270. In other texts, Ibn Qūlawayh insists that "the angel who came to Muḥammad informing him of the death of al-Ḥusayn was Ǧibraʾīl, the Faithful Spirit" (Ibn Qūlawayh., *Kāmil al-ziyārāt*, bb. 17, n. 1: 127–128, al-Maǧlisī., *Biḥār al-anwār*, vol. XLIII, bb. 30, n. 22: 235, al-Iṣfahānī., *ʿAwālim al-ʿulūm wa-l-maʿārif al-aḥwāl min al-āyāt wa-l-aḫbār wa-l-aqwāl*, vol. XVII, Part Seventeen, ch. 11, bb. 6, n. 1: 124), al-Ǧazāʾirī., *Riyāḍ al-abrār fī manāqib al-aʾimma al-aṭhār*, vol. I, Part One: 171).

Ǧibrīl's name means 'servant (*ʿabd*) of God' and Mīkāʾīl's name means 'servant (*ʿubayd*) of God'.[24] While Burge suggests that the use of the diminutive *ʿubayd* may be an attempt to elevate Ǧibrīl above Mīkāʾīl,[25] al-Mağlisī proposes that Mīkāʾīl is one of the greatest of the angels and may even be the head of the angelic community;[26] a rare and late *ḥadīṯ* suggests that Mīkāʾīl was the first to pronounce the words 'Far be it removed from my Lord the Most High' (*subḥāna rabbī al-aʿlā*),[27] although another *ḥadīṯ* nominates Muḥammad as the first speaker of these word.[28] Both al-Tirmiḏī and al-Suyūṭī narrate a tradition in which Muḥammad claims Ǧibrīl and Mīkāʾīl as his two heavenly ministers,[29] while the eleventh Imām al-ʿAskarī notes that Ǧibrīl and Mīkāʾīl are brothers; whoev-

---

[24] Cf. Abū al-Shayḫ, *al-ʿAẓama*, vol. III, n. 382: 812, Ibn Bābawayh., *Maʿānī al-aḫbār*, bb. *Maʿānī asmāʾ al-anbiyāʾ wa-l-rusul*: 48, al-Suyūṭī., *al-Ḥabāʾik fī aḫbār al-malāʾik*, nn. 81: 29, al-Mağlisī., *Biḥār al-anwār*, vol. XLVI, bb. 24, n. 6: 250, vol. LXXXVII, bb. 8, n. 4: 115, Ṣadr al-Dīn al-Shīrāzī., *Riyāḍ al-sālikīn fī sharḥ saḥīfa sayyid al-sāǧǧidīn*, vol. II: 25.

[25] BURGE S.R., *Angels in Islam*, Routledge, London 2012: 208, 224.

[26] Cf. al-Mağlisī., *Biḥār al-anwār*, vol. LVI, bb. 23: 221.

[27] al-Ḥuwayzī., *Tafsīr nūr al-ṯaqalayn*, vol. V, *sūrat al-Aʿla*, n. 4: 553, al-Ṭabarsī., *Mustadrak al-wasāʾil wa mustanbiṭ al-masāʾil*, vol. IV, bb. 45, n. 4925: 358.

[28] Muḥammad Riḍā al-Ṭūsī., *Kanz al-daqāʾiq wa baḥr al-ġarāʾib fī tafsīr al-qurʾān*, vol. XIV, *sūrat al-Aʿlā*: 231.

[29] Cf. al-Tirmiḏī., *al-Ǧāmiʿ al-ṣaḥīḥ*, vol. VI, bk. 46 (*Abwāb al-manāqib*), n. 3680: 360, where the narration is classified as 'weak' (*ḍaʿīf*), al-Suyūṭī., *al-Ḥabāʾik fī aḫbār al-malāʾik*, nn. 84–85: 29, and who points his readers to al-Ḥākim al-Nīsābūrī., *Kitāb al-mustadrak ʿalā al-ṣaḥīḥayn*, vol. II, bk. 27 (*Kitāb al-tafsīr*), nn. 3105–3106: 317, declared by al-Ḥākim to be *ṣaḥīḥ*, and Ibn ʿAsākir., *Tārīḫ madīnat Dimashq*, vol. XXX, bb. 3398 (*ʿAbd Allāh b. Quḥāfa Abū Bakr*): 119, vol. XLIV, bb. 5206 (*ʿAmr b. al-Ḫaṭṭāb*: 64), al-Muttaqī al-Hindī., *Kanz al-ʿummāl fī sunan al-aqwāl wa-l-afʿāl*, vol. XIII, nn. 36148, 36149: 25. For further encounters between Muḥammad, Ǧibrīl and Mīkāʾīl, cf. al-Buḫārī., *Ṣaḥīḥ*, vol. IV, bk. 59 (*Kitāb badʿ al-ḫalq*), bb. 7, n. 3236: 287, Muslim., *Sunan*, vol. VI, bk. 43 (*Kitāb al-faḍāʾil*), bb. 10, n. 6004 – 46 [2306]: 160, al-Nasāʾī., *al-Sunan al-kubrā*, vol. II, bk. 11 (*Kitāb al-iftitāḥ*), bb. 37, n. 942: 60–61, al-Suyūṭī., *al-Ḥabāʾik fī aḫbār al-malāʾik*, n. 83: 29.

er loves them will be counted among the holy ones (*awliyāʾ*) of God, while those who detest them are God's enemies and anyone who claims to love one and hate the other is a liar.[30] Ultimately, Umm Salama herself claims that Mīkāʾīl too was part of the revelation of Q. 33:33, so crucial to the Shīʿa: "this verse…came down in my house in the company of seven – Ǧabraʾīl, Mīkāʾīl, the Messenger of God, ʿAlī, Fāṭima, al-Ḥasan and al-Ḥusayn."[31]

This same Umm Salama is another key player in our story; Hind bt. Abī Umayya, also known as Hind al-Maḫzūmiyya or Hind bt. Suhayl, and who bore the *kunya* Umm Salama, was one of

---

[30] Cf. Q. 2:98. al-ʿAskarī., *al-Tafsīr al-mansūb ilā al-Imām al-Ḥasan al-ʿAskarī, sūrat al-Baqara*: 407, al-Ṭabarsī., *Kitāb al-iḥtiǧāǧ ʿalā ahl al-liǧāǧ*, vol. I: 43, al-Ḥuwayzī., *Tafsīr nūr al-ṯaqalayn*, vol. I, *sūrat al-Baqara*, n. 290: 104, Muḥammad Riḍā al-Ṭūsī., *Kanz al-daqāʾiq wa baḥr al-ġarāʾib fī tafsīr al-qurʾān*, vol. II, *sūrat al-Baqara*: 92.

[31] Ibn Furāt al-Kūfī., *Tafsīr Furāt b. Ibrāhīm, sūrat al-Aḥzāb*, n. 454: 334, 336, al-Qāḍī al-Nuʿmān., *Sharḥ al-aḫbār fī faḍāʾil al-aʾimma al-aṭhār*, vol. III, Part Eleven, n. 945: 13, Ibn Bābawayh., *Kitāb al-amālī fī-l-aḥādīṯ wa-l-aḫbār, maǧlis* 72, n. 4: 472, *Kitāb al-ḫiṣāl*, vol. II, bb. 7, n. 113: 403, al-Ḥaskānī., *Shawāhid al-tanzīl li-qawāʿid al-tafḍīl*, vol. II, *sūrat al-Aḥzāb*, n. 757: 124–125, n. 762: 131, Ibn ʿAlī al-Fattāl., *Rawḍat al-wāʿiẓīn wa-tabṣirat al-muttaʿiẓīn*, vol. I: 157, al-Astarābāḏī., *Taʾwīl al-āyāt al-ẓāhira fī faḍl al-ʿitra al-ṭāhira, sūrat al-Aḥzāb*: 451 (Brockelmann incorrectly transcribes the work as *al-bāhira* rather than *al-ẓāhira*: cf. GAL S. II: 575), Muḥammad Riḍā al-Ṭūsī., *Kanz al-daqāʾiq wa baḥr al-ġarāʾib fī tafsīr al-qurʾān*, vol. X, *sūrat al-Aḥzāb*: 375, al-Baḥrānī., *al-Burhān fī tafsīr al-qurʾān*, vol. IV, *sūrat al-Aḥzāb*, n. 8598: 450, al-Maǧlisī., *Biḥār al-anwār*, vol. XXV, bb. 7, n. 6: 214, vol. XXXV, bb. 5, n. 9: 209, nn. 21–22: 216, al-Iṣfahānī., *ʿAwālim al-ʿulūm wa-l-maʿārif al-aḥwāl min al-āyāt wa-l-aḫbār wa-l-aqwāl*, vol. XVII, ch. 11, bb. 6, n. 3: 125. Al-Ḥaskānī (d. 490/1096) is believed to have lived in a largely Sunnī area and used copious Sunnī sources, so that in *Taḏkirat al-ḥuffāẓ*, al-Ḏahabī claims him as a follower of Abū Ḥanīfa, giving him the *nisba* 'al-Ḥanafī'. Nonetheless, he manifests a substantial Shīʿī tendency, causing al-Ḏahabī to note: "I found a *maǧlis* of his that proves his *tashayyuʿ*." Since the word *tashayyuʿ* could justifiably mean nothing more than 'tendency' or 'partiality', it is probably accurate to say that al-Ḥaskānī was a Ḥanafī Sunnī with a growing proclivity for Shīʿī Islam. Cf. al-Ḏahabī., *Taḏkirat al-ḥuffāẓ*, vol. III, n. 1032: 1200.

Muḥammad's wives and remains forever venerated both among the Sunnī and the Shīʿa. Her standing among the Shīʿa, a community that regards her as second only to Ḫadīǧa among Muḥammad's wives,[32] is not only on account of her transmission of some of their most crucial *aḥādīṯ*,[33] but also because upon marrying her (after her husband Abū Salama's death from wounds received at the Battle of Uḥud in 3/625), Muḥammad gave his daughter Fāṭima into her care.[34] Umm Salama would go on to play a considerable role in the preparations for the marriage between ʿAlī and Fāṭima, as recounted by al-Maǧlisī,[35] and both al-Ḥasan and al-Ḥusayn spent a significant amount of time playing in her house, which in turn would become the locus for some crucial encounters between Muḥammad and a variety of angels.[36] Two features that shape the narrative are precisely Umm Salama's house as a place of divine intervention and the 'tradition of the glass vial' (*ḥadīṯ al-qārūra*), which almost invariably involves her and, concurrently, places her death after the Karbalāʾ event. Although a number of transmitters (like Ibn al-Aṯīr and Ibn Ḥaǧar al-ʿAsqalānī) omit any reference to a dream or a glass vial in relation to Umm Salama, enough authors carry the narrative to make it of interest.

Her date of death is contested; in al-Ḏahabī, there is a narration from Shahr b. Ḥawshab, who claims that he went to Umm

---

[32] Cf. Ibn Bābawayh., *Kitāb al-ḫiṣāl*, vol. II, bb. 9, n. 13: 419.

[33] These are specifically *ḥadīṯ al-kisāʾ*, *ḥadīṯ al-taṭhīr*, *ḥadīṯ al-ṯaqalayn* and *ḥadīṯ al-manzila*, in which Muḥammad claims that ʿAlī has the same status in relation to him as Hārūn had in relation to Mūsā.

[34] "Umm Salama said: The Messenger of God married me and entrusted to me the instruction of his daughter, but by God, she was more assiduous than me and more knowledgeable in everything." Cf. al-Maǧlisī., *Biḥār al-anwār*, vol. XLIII, bb. 1, n. 16: 10, transmitting from al-Ṭabarī., *Dalāʾil al-imāma*, n. 21: 82. Her guardianship of Fāṭima would have been after the death of ʿAlī's mother, Fāṭima bt. Asad.

[35] Cf. al-Maǧlisī., *Biḥār al-anwār*, vol. XLIII, bb. 5, nn. 1–49: 92–145.

[36] According to al-Ḏahabī, she transmitted 378 *aḥādīṯ*, although this would be specifically through the Sunnī transmitters. Cf. al-Ḏahabī., *Siyar aʿlām al-nubalāʾ*, vol. II, n. 20 (*Umm Salama*): 210.

Salama in Medina to comfort her over the killing al-Ḥusayn.[37] Al-Ḏahabī himself notes that she lived until she had received the news of al-Ḥusayn's death, and over whom she grieved greatly.[38] While proposed dates vary – Ibn Saʿd, al-Ṭabarī and Ibn ʿAbd al-Barr suggest a pre-Karbalāʾ 59/678, while Ibn al-Aṯīr proposes 61/680 and al-ʿAsqalānī ranges between 59/678 and 62/681[39] – it seems more likely that her death was after the 61/680 Karbalāʾ event, since in a number of narrations she is reported as lamenting al-Ḥusayn's killing and hearing the *ǧinn* doing the same. The historian al-Yaʿqūbī (if not a Shīʿa, and this is a moot point, then one who evinces a strong Shīʿī predisposition) and the Shāfiʿī historian and jurist Ibn Abī al-Dam both report her as alive after the death of al-Ḥusayn, living in Medina and the first in that city to grieve over him.[40] If she was indeed a witness to all of al-Ḥusayn's life and mar-

---

[37] Ibid. Cf. also al-Ḥākim al-Nīsābūrī., *Kitāb al-mustadrak ʿalā al-ṣaḥīḥayn*, vol. IV, bk. 31 (*Kitāb maʿrifat al-ṣaḥāba*), n. 6844: 101, Ibn Kaṯīr., *al-Bidāya wa-l-nihāya*, vol. IX, bb. *Iḫbār bi-maqtal al-Ḥusayn*: 240, vol. XI, bb. *al-Iḫbār maqtal al-Ḥusayn b. ʿAlī*: 574–5, al-ʿAsqalānī., *Tahḏīb al-tahḏīb*, vol. II, bb. *al-Ḥāʾ*, n. 615: 355.

[38] al-Ḏahabī., *Siyar aʿlām al-nubalāʾ*, vol. III, n. 48 (*al-Ḥusayn al-Shahīd Abū ʿAbd Allāh b. ʿAlī b. Abī Ṭālib*): 318.

[39] Ibn Saʿd., *Kitāb al-ṭabaqāt al-kabīr*, vol. VIII: 67, al-Ṭabarī., *Kitāb aḫbār al-rusul wa-l-mulūk*, vol. XXXIX, n. 2443: 175–176, Ibn ʿAbd al-Barr., *al-Istīʿāb fī maʿrifat al-aṣḥāb*, vol. IV, n. 4111: 1920–1921, Ibn ʿAsākir., *Tārīḫ madīnat Dimashq*, vol. XIV, bb. 1566 (*al-Ḥusayn b. ʿAlī b. Abī Ṭālib b. ʿAbd al-Muṭṭalib b. Hāshim b. ʿAbd al-Manāf*): 240 ("I heard al-Wāqidī, who said: Umm Salama did not live to attain the killing of al-Ḥusayn, dying in the year 58"), Ibn al-Aṯīr., *Usd al-ġāba fī maʿrifat al-ṣaḥāba*, vol. VI, n. 7464: 351–353, Ibn al-Ǧawzī., *Ṣifat al-ṣafwa*, vol. II: 21, al-ʿAsqalānī., *al-Iṣāba fī tamyīz al-ṣaḥāba*, vol. VII, n. 12054: 327–328 (al-ʿAsqalānī gives her possible dates of death as 59/678 via al-Wāqidī, or 61/680, after the news of al-Ḥusayn's death, via Ibn Ḥibbān, or 62/681 via Abū Nuʿaym or simply 'during the caliphate of Yazīd'). Cf. al-ʿAsqalānī., *Tahḏīb al-tahḏīb*, vol. XII, n. 2905: 455–457, *al-Iṣāba fī tamyīz al-ṣaḥāba*, vol. VIII: 248.

[40] Cf. al-Yaʿqūbī., *Tārīḫ*, vol. II, bb. *Maqtal al-Ḥusayn b. ʿAlī*: 245, Ibn Abī al-Dam., *al-Muḫtaṣar fī tārīḫ al-Islām*: 93, al-Maǧlisī., *Biḥār al-anwār*, vol. XLV, bb. 39, n. 1: 124.

tyrdom, her assessment is unique, making her one of the chief protagonists in the story of the Karbalā᾿ dreams.

In most of the dreams and encounters recounted in this work, Muḥammad is the recipient, visited by a heavenly guest; in a smaller genre, he himself appears to someone in a dream. Other members of the core group of the People of the House dream too; ʿAlī b. Abī Ṭālib, husband to Fāṭima and father to al-Ḥusayn, contributes one rare dream to this compendium, while Fāṭima dreams mostly before and during her pregnancy with al-Ḥusayn. The visions of al-Ḥusayn himself are almost always of his grandfather, except for one series in which he dreams of a viscous animal and thereby learns a secret clue to the identity of his killer.

The disparate medley of night visions and dreams also includes a noteworthy dream of Umm al-Faḍl, a nightmare so bleak that it sends her running to Muḥammad for an explanation; and Umm Ayman, to whom the dream of Umm al-Faḍl is sometimes attributed, a woman beloved of Muḥammad and important enough to be given a distinct place by Ibn ʿAsākir, and so included as part of this compilation. Two of the women who dreamed dreams go by the same name; Hind, mother of Muʿāwiya who has a deeply cosmological dream, not dissimilar to that of young Joseph recorded in the Hebrew Scriptures (Gen. 37:9) and of Yūsuf in the Qur᾿ān (Q. 12:4); and Hind, the wife of Yazīd b. Muʿāwiya who, like the wife of Pontius Pilate, is so disquieted by her dream that she tries to alert her husband. Sukayna, the daughter of al-Ḥusayn, is also found in this anthology, with a dream that chastises a Yazīd already smarting from the tongue-lashing he has received from Sukayna's aunt Zaynab.

Soldiers, guards and camp followers are dreamers too. Against al-Ḥusayn's small band of around seventy-two men was set all the might of the opposing army; at least five thousand, but possibly more, with al-Ṭabarī, Ibn Bābawayh and al-Mufīd mentioning at least five thousand, and others claiming up to twenty or thirty thousand.[41] In amidst this great force there were a number of men who had stark and sobering dreams; all of them would deny ever

[41] Cf. CLOHESSY C., *Half of My Heart. The Narratives of Zaynab, Daughter of ʿAlī*, Gorgias Press, New Jersey 2018: 131.

having been part of the fighting force, and most of them turn out to be merchants, camp followers who formed part of Yazīd's force although thereby, their dreams would insist, increasing the number of al-Ḥusayn's enemies. Their dreams were harbingers of the terrible fate that awaited those who had supported the enemies of Muḥammad's grandson.

The *ǧinn*, who are either seen or heard at night lamenting, are also part of this story. The Arabic noun *ǧinn*, used collectively, refers specifically to spiritual beings, visible at will, who may bring either harm or help, as they meddle and pry into life on the human plain. From their place in the unseen world – for the very word *ǧinn* evokes a sense of concealment – they attempt to enfold themselves persistently and sometimes forcefully into every aspect of life. They appear thirty-three times in the Qur'ān, but only in the earlier chapters, traditionally described as Meccan (c. 610–622).

The lament of the *ǧinn* over al-Ḥusayn, combined with that of the human race – whether Umm Salama or the women of Medina or just some unknown voice on the night air – is part of a cosmic reaction to the Karbalā' event, witnessed not only in a physical reaction in the sun, moon and stars, in blood raining down and animals lamenting, but also in the symbolic grief of these wraithlike creatures, who here represent the spirit world.[42] The two classes (*al-ṯaqalān*) of creation, according to the Qur'ān, are the company (*maʿshar*) of *ǧinn* and the company of human beings (Q. 55:31, 33). Consequently, all of humankind and the whole of creation participates in the grief over al-Ḥusayn's death – as al-Maǧlisī notes, "the *ǧinn* of the level and the wild places mourn for him."[43] The 4th/10th century Ǧaʿfar b. Qūlawayh, student of al-Kulaynī and teacher of al-Mufīd, dedicates substantial space in his *Kāmil al-ziyārāt* to the *ǧinn*, whose voices are heard on the night air in Medina and Karba-

[42] In fact, the angels too are recorded as weeping; Ibn Qūlawayh, for example, records a number of *aḥādīṯ* from Imām Ǧaʿfar al-Ṣādiq, recording the four thousand angels who did not arrive at the field of Karbalā' in time to fight with al-Ḥusayn, and who now weep by his grave. Cf. Ibn Qūlawayh., *Kāmil al-ziyārāt*, bb. 27, nn. 1–4: 171–172, nn. 6–9: 173–174, nn. 11, 13–15: 174–176.

[43] al-Maǧlisī, *Biḥār al-anwār*, vol. XLV, bb. 39, n. 36: 192.

lā', in elegiac verse over the death of al-Ḥusayn. If these reports seem esoteric, Sunnī scholars as disparate as Ibn Ḥanbal, Ibn ʿAsākir, Ibn Kaṯīr and al-Hayṯamī all carry them, either in fragments or in sizeable detail, in their respective texts.

Finally, a medley of other characters, including Ibn ʿAbbās and a passing Byzantine diplomat, had dreams and visions that find a place in this work. The scholarly and pious ʿAbd Allāh b. ʿAbbās, revered as 'the ocean' (*al-baḥr*)[44] for the extent of his knowledge, and the 'scholar' of the community (*ḥabr al-umma*),[45] was himself no

---

[44] Ibn Saʿd., *Kitāb al-ṭabaqāt al-kabīr*, vol. II, (*Ibn ʿAbbās*): 366, al-Ḥākim al-Nīsābūrī., *Kitāb al-mustadrak ʿalā al-ṣaḥīḥayn*, vol. III, bk. 31 (*Kitāb maʿrifat al-ṣaḥāba*), n. 6361: 658–659, nn. 6362, 6364: 659, Abū Nuʿaym., *Ḥilyat al-awliyā' wa-ṭabaqāt al-aṣfiyā'*, vol. I, bb. 45 (*ʿAbd Allāh b. ʿAbbās*), n. 1117: 391, Ibn ʿAbd al-Barr., *al-Istīʿāb fī maʿrifat al-aṣḥāb*, vol. III, n. 1588: 936, Ibn al-Aṯīr., *Usd al-ġāba fī maʿrifat al-ṣaḥāb*, vol. III, n. 3035 (*ʿAbd Allāh b. ʿAbbās*): 186, Ibn Kaṯīr., *al-Bidāya wa-l-nihāya*, vol. XII, bb. *Wa fī-hi tawaffā ʿAbd Allāh b. ʿAbbās*: 78–84, al-ʿAsqalānī., *Tahḏīb al-tahḏīb*, vol. V, n. 474: 276.

[45] While many tend to read this as 'learned man', there is, as Lane notes, some dispute about the correct vowel, and there are a number of variant meanings. Both *ḥabr* and *ḥibr* could refer to a non-Muslim religious authority, suggests Wehr, or, as Lane observes, a learned man of the Jews, or of the Christians, Jews or Sabaeans, either the subject of a Muslim government, or one who has converted to Islam. Alternatively, both could mean simply a 'good' or 'righteous' man. Read as *ḥibr*, the word also means 'ink' (by which writing is beautified), but could also refer to a person of handsome or goodly appearance, or could mean 'gladness' or 'delight'. Some therefore have chosen to understand Ibn ʿAbbās as 'the ink of the community' and others as the community's 'learned man' (or occasionally, 'doctor', which seems less precise); since he was neither non-Muslim nor a convert to Islam, other meanings remain an option. Cf. LANE E.W., *An Arabic-English Lexicon*, vol. II, 1968: 498, WEHR H., *A Dictionary of Modern Written Arabic*, 1980: 180, Ibn Saʿd., *Kitāb al-ṭabaqāt al-kabīr*, vol. II, (*Ibn ʿAbbās*): 370, al-Balāḏurī., *Kitāb ansāb al-ashraf*, vol. IV, bb. *ʿAbd Allāh b. ʿAbbās*: 39, al-Ḥākim al-Nīsābūrī., *Kitāb al-mustadrak ʿalā al-ṣaḥīḥayn*, vol. III, bk. 31 (*Kitāb maʿrifat al-ṣaḥāba*), nn. 6360, 6361, 6363: 658–659, Abū Nuʿaym., *Ḥilyat al-awliyā' wa-ṭabaqāt al-aṣfiyā'*, vol. I, bb. 45 (*ʿAbd Allāh b. ʿAbbās*), n. 1118: 391 (named so by Ǧibrīl himself), n. 1121:

stranger to angelic visits, having claimed to have seen Ǧibrīl on two occasions.[46] However, it is not Ǧibrīl who Ibn ʿAbbās will see in the dream recounted in this collection, but Muḥammad, dust-covered, weeping and holding in his hand the glass vial that will play a central part in this story. It is hardly surprising that about Ibn ʿAbbās, acknowledged in the texts as the interpreter (*turǧumān*) of the Qurʾān[47] and on the day of his death as the 'lord' of the com-

---

391, Ibn ʿAṭiyya., *Muḥarrar al-waǧīz fī tafsīr al-kitāb al-ʿazīz*, vol. I: 15, Ibn ʿAsākir., *Tārīḫ madīnat Dimashq*, vol. XXIX, bb. 3363 (*ʿAbd Allāh b. ʿAbbās*): 285, Ibn al-Aṯīr., *Usd al-ġāba fī maʿrifat al-ṣaḥāb*, vol. III, n. 3035 (*ʿAbd Allāh b. ʿAbbās*): 186, 189, al-Ḏahabī., *Siyar aʿlām al-nubalāʾ*, vol. III, n. 51 (*ʿAbd Allāh b. ʿAbbās*): 339, Ibn Kaṯīr., *al-Bidāya wa-l-nihāya*, vol. XII, bb. *Wa fī-hi tawaffā ʿAbd Allāh b. ʿAbbās*: 78, al-ʿAsqalānī., *al-Iṣāba fī tamyīz al-ṣaḥāba*, vol. III, n. 4779: 229–230: (here, the learned man 'of the Arabs' rather than 'of the/this community'), 231, *Tahḏīb al-tahḏīb*, vol. V, n. 474: 276, 279 (named so by Ǧibrīl himself).

[46] Ibn Ḥanbal., *Kitāb faḍāʾil al-ṣaḥāba*, vol. II, bb. *Faḍāʾil ʿAbd Allāh b. ʿAbbās*, n. 1561: 846, al-Tirmiḏī., *al-Ǧāmiʿ al-ṣaḥīḥ*, vol. VI, bk. 46 (*Abwāb al-manāqib*), bb. 42, n. 3822: 560, Ibn Saʿd., *Kitāb al-ṭabaqāt al-kabīr*, vol. II, (*Ibn ʿAbbās*): 370, al-Balāḏurī., *Kitāb ansāb al-ashraf*, vol. IV, bb. *ʿAbd Allāh b. ʿAbbās*: 41, al-Bazzār., *Musnad*, vol. XI, *Musnad Ibn ʿAbbās*, n. 4921: 180–181, Ibn ʿAbd al-Barr., *al-Istīʿāb fī maʿrifat al-aṣḥāb*, vol. III, n. 1588: 933, Ibn al-Ǧawzī., *Ṣifat al-ṣafwa*, vol. I: 314, Ibn al-Aṯīr., *Usd al-ġāba fī maʿrifat al-ṣaḥāb*, vol. III, n. 3035 (*ʿAbd Allāh b. ʿAbbās*): 185, al-Ṭabarī., *Ḏaḫāʾir al-ʿuqbā*, bb. 3: 378, Ibn Kaṯīr., *al-Bidāya wa-l-nihāya*, vol. XII, bb. *Wa fī-hi tawaffā ʿAbd Allāh b. ʿAbbās*: 83, al-ʿAsqalānī., *al-Iṣāba fī tamyīz al-ṣaḥāba*, vol. III, n. 4779: 229, *Tahḏīb al-tahḏīb*, vol. V, n. 474: 276.

[47] Ibn Ḥanbal., *Kitāb faḍāʾil al-ṣaḥāba*, vol. II, bb. *Faḍāʾil ʿAbd Allāh b. ʿAbbās*, nn. 1556, 1558: 845, n. 1562: 847, Ibn Saʿd., *Kitāb al-ṭabaqāt al-kabīr*, vol. II, (*Ibn ʿAbbās*): 366, Ibn Abī Shayba., *al-Muṣannaf*, vol. X, bb. 27, n. 32817: 515, al-Balāḏurī., *Kitāb ansāb al-ashraf*, vol. IV, bb. *ʿAbd Allāh b. ʿAbbās*: 43, al-Ṭabarānī., *Muʿǧam al-kabīr*, vol. XI, n. 11108: 80, al-Ḥākim al-Nīsābūrī., *Kitāb al-mustadrak ʿalā al-ṣaḥīḥayn*, vol. III, bk. 31 (*Kitāb maʿrifat al-ṣaḥāba*), n. 6370: 661, Abū Nuʿaym., *Ḥilyat al-awliyāʾ wa-ṭabaqāt al-aṣfiyāʾ*, vol. I, bb. 45 (*ʿAbd Allāh b. ʿAbbās*), n. 1120: 391, Ibn ʿAṭiyya., *Muḥarrar al-waǧīz fī tafsīr al-kitāb al-ʿazīz*, vol. I: 15, Ibn ʿAsākir., *Tārīḫ madīnat Dimashq*, vol. XXIX, bb. 3363 (*ʿAbd Allāh b. ʿAbbās*): 285, al-Ṭabarī., *Ḏaḫāʾir al-ʿuqbā*, bb. 3: 376, 381, Ibn Kaṯīr., *al-Bidāya wa-l-nihāya*, vol. XII, bb. *Wa*

munity,[48] and recognised as the most learned of his generation,[49] it was said: if a Persian, Byzantine or Turk were to hear him, he or she would at once convert to Islam.[50] There is a Byzantine in our story too, although he makes a rare and brief appearance, like the 1st/8th century Umayyad caliph with whom we began, and whose dream about Muḥammad was unravelled for him by the ascetic mystic al-Ḥasan al-Baṣrī.

Lastly, a much-recounted vision in or around the precincts of a church and seen by some misbehaving soldiers brings our story to an end and pronounces a final judgment on the generation that saw to the killing of al-Ḥusayn.

Following the death of the man held to be the last and the consummation of God's prophets and equally a decidedly adept and gifted leader, the embryonic Muslim community would have been intensely aware of the resultant vacuum in religious and political guidance. Soon after Muḥammad's death, the notion that dreams could be a fount of spiritual guidance now that prophecy had ended began to take root, not unlike the certitude of the North African theologian Tertullian (d. c. 230), the pioneer among the Church Fathers when it came to writing about dreams, that these could be dependable in terms of offering a certain measure of di-

---

fī-hi tawaffā ʿAbd Allāh b. ʿAbbās: 78, al-ʿAsqalānī., *al-Iṣāba fī tamyīz al-ṣaḥāba*, vol. III, n. 4779: 233, al-Muttaqī al-Hindī., *Kanz al-ʿummāl*, vol. XI, n. 33582: 731.

48 Ibn Saʿd., *Kitāb al-ṭabaqāt al-kabīr*, vol. II, (*Ibn ʿAbbās*): 368, Ibn Abī Shayba., *al-Muṣannaf*, vol. X, bb. 27, n. 32815: 515 ('lord of knowledge'), al-Ḥākim al-Nīsābūrī., *Kitāb al-mustadrak ʿalā al-ṣaḥīḥayn*, vol. III, bk. 31 (*Kitāb maʿrifat al-ṣaḥāba*), n. 6363: 659, al-Ṭabarī., *Ḏaḫāʾir al-ʿuqbā*, bb. 3: 392, al-Ḏahabī., *Siyar aʿlām al-nubalāʾ*, vol. III, n. 51 (*ʿAbd Allāh b. ʿAbbās*): 357.

49 Ibn Saʿd., *Kitāb al-ṭabaqāt al-kabīr*, vol. II, (*Ibn ʿAbbās*): 366–370, al-Balāḏurī., *Kitāb ansāb al-ashraf*, vol. IV, bb. *ʿAbd Allāh b. ʿAbbās*: 43, Ibn ʿAbd al-Barr., *al-Istīʿāb fī maʿrifat al-aṣḥāb*, vol. III, n. 1588: 935, al-ʿAsqalānī., *Tahḏīb al-tahḏīb*, vol. V, n. 474: 276.

50 al-Ḥākim al-Nīsābūrī., *Kitāb al-mustadrak ʿalā al-ṣaḥīḥayn*, vol. III, bk. 31 (*Kitāb maʿrifat al-ṣaḥāba*), nn. 6369, 6371: 660–661, Ibn ʿAbd al-Barr., *al-Istīʿāb fī maʿrifat al-aṣḥāb*, vol. III, n. 1588: 936.

vine information. Ultimately, there would be some foundation for this in the corpus of *aḥādīṯ*, once it was established – "when time draws near," suggests Muḥammad, "the dreams of a believer will hardly ever fail to come true," and will in fact be "all that is left of the prophethood."[51] Another much-transmitted text intimates that a true dream is one of many ways in which a prophetic message can be delivered ("the dream of a Muslim is a portion among the forty-six portions of Prophethood").[52]

Through the 2nd/8th and 3rd/9th centuries, with Muslim authorities under pressure to establish divine revelation as an inimitable category of divine encounter dissimilar to other types of visions and dreams,[53] a number of elements of the Islamic understanding of the nature of visions were determined. The *aḥādīṯ* abound with

---

[51] al-Buḫārī., *Ṣaḥīḥ*, vol. IX, bk. 91 (*Kitāb al-taʿbīr*), bb. 5, n. 6990: 88, bb. 26, n. 7017: 23, Muslim., *Ṣaḥīḥ*, vol. I, bk. 4 (*Kitāb al-ṣalāt*), bb. 41, n. [1074] 207 – (479): 590, [1075] 208: 591, vol. VI, bk. 42 (*Kitāb al-ruʾyā*), n. [5905] 6 – (2263): 119, Abū Dāwud., *Sunan*, vol. I, bk. 2 (*Kitāb al-ṣalāt*), bb. 147–148, n. 876: 517, vol. V, bk. 40 (*Awwal kitāb al-adab*), bb. 8, n. 5017: 364, n. 50198: 365, al-Tirmiḏī., *al-Ǧāmiʿ al-ṣaḥīḥ*, vol. IV, bk. 32 (*Abwāb al-ruʾyā*), bb. 1, n. 2270: 316, n. 2272. 318, bb. 10, n. 2291: 330, al-Nasāʾī., *al-Sunan al-kubrā*, vol. II, bk. 12 (*Kitāb al-taṭbīq*), bb. 8, n. 1046: 112, bb. 62, n. 1121: 151.

[52] al-Buḫārī., *Ṣaḥīḥ*, vol. IX, bk. 91 (*Kitāb al-taʿbīr*), bb. 2, n. 6983: 85, bb. 4, nn. 6987, 6988, 6989: 87, bb. 10, n. 6994: 93, bb. 26, n. 7017: 23, Muslim., *Ṣaḥīḥ*, vol. VI, bk. 42 (*Kitāb al-ruʾyā*), n. [5905] 6 – (2263): 119 (reads 'forty-five' rather than 'forty-six'), n. [5906]: 120, n. [5908]: 121, n. [5909] 7 – (2264): 121, n. [5912]: 121–122, n. [5913]: 122, n. [5916] 9 – (2265): 122–123 (reads 'seventy' rather than 'forty-six'), Abū Dāwud., *Sunan*, vol. V, bk. 40 (*Awwal kitāb al-adab*), bb. 8, n. 5018: 364, al-Tirmiḏī., *al-Ǧāmiʿ al-ṣaḥīḥ*, vol. IV, bk. 32 (*Abwāb al-ruʾyā*), bb. 1, n. 2270: 316, n. 2271: 317, bb. 2, n. 2272: 318, bb. 6, n. 2278: 322, bb. 10, n. 2291: 330.

[53] SIRRIYEH E., *Dreams and Visions in the World of Islam*, I.B. Tauris, London 2015: 49. Karamustafa attributes to Abū Saʿd al-Ḫarǧūshī (d. c. 406/1015) a book of dream interpretation, which is one of the oldest extant dream manuals in Arabic. Cf. KARAMUSTAFA A., *Sufism. The Formative Period*, Edinburgh University Press, Edinburgh 2007: 65, LAMOREAUX J.C., *The Early Muslim Tradition of Dream Interpretation*, State University of New York Press, Albany: 2002.

references to dreams, devoting entire books and chapters to classifying them according to their source, their interpretation, their benefits and their perils. At the heart of this is a straightforward dualism; that good dreams (*ru'yā*) have their origin in God, while bad dreams (*ḥulm*) originate from Shayṭān.[54] Consequently, notes Muḥammad,

> when one of you sees a dream that he likes, then it is from God, so let him praise God for it, and speak concerning what he saw. And when he sees other than that, what he dislikes, then it is from Shayṭān, so let him seek refuge in God from its evil, and not mention it to anyone for, surely, it shall not harm him.[55]

The Qur'ān utilizes three[56] discrete expressions for dreams: the word *ru'yā* (typically rendered as 'vision' or 'dream') occurs six

---

[54] Ibn Abī Shayba., *al-Muṣannaf*, vol. X, bb. 5, n. 3115: 132, al-Buḫārī., *Ṣaḥīḥ*, vol. IV, bk. 59 (*Kitāb badʿ al-ḫalq*), bb. 11, n. 3292: 310, vol. VII, bk. 76 (*Kitāb al-ṭibb*), bb. 39, n. 5747: 353, vol. IX, bk. 91 (*Kitāb al-taʿbīr*), bb. 3, n. 6984: 86 and bb. 14, n. 7005: 97–98 and bb. 46, n. 7044: 116, bb. 4, n. 6986: 86 and bb. 10, n. 6995: 93, Muslim., *Ṣaḥīḥ*, vol. VI, bk. 42 (*Kitāb al-ru'yā*): [5897] 1 (2261): 116, [5900] 2 (…): 117, [5902] 3 (…): 118, [5903] 4 (…): 118–119, [5905] 6 (2263), Abū Dāwud., *Sunan*, vol. V, bk. 40 (*Kitāb al-adab*), b. 88, n. 5021: 366, Ibn Māǧa., *Sunan*, vol. V, bk. 35 (*Abwāb taʿbir al-ru'yā*), bb. 4, nn. 3906, 3907, 3909: 146, 148. The distinction between good and bad (*ḥulm*) dreams reflected in the *aḥādīṯ* corpus is not entirely in harmony with the Qur'ānic concept of *ḥulm*, where such dreams are understood as indecipherable or confused but not necessarily as satanic in origin.

[55] al-Buḫārī., *Ṣaḥīḥ*, vol. IX, bk. 91 (*Kitāb al-taʿbīr*), bb. 3, n. 6985: 86, al-Tirmiḏī., *al-Ǧāmiʿ al-ṣaḥīḥ*, vol. vol. VI, bk. 45 (*Kitāb al-daʿawāt*), bb. 52, n. 3453: 180.

[56] Four, notes Kinberg, who includes the interpretation of *bushrā* ('glad tidings') as 'dream' in Q. 10: 64. Cf. KINBERG L., "Dreams and Sleep" in Jane Dammen McAuliffe et al (eds.)., *Encyclopaedia of the Qur'ān*, vol. I, Brill, Leiden 2001: 546.

times,[57] the designation *manām* which occurs four times, twice in reference to sleep[58] and twice connoting 'dream',[59] and the term *ḥulm*, used twice in its plural form (*aḥlām*), and understood as «*a confused medley of dreams*»,[60] the phrase that the sceptics around Umm Salama would use against her. In Q. 12:44, in the framework of the dreams to be interpreted by Yūsuf, it is this axiom used to designate the king's dreams which, note the editors of 'The Study Qur'an', belong to "the category of mixed-up and false dreams – which stem from the internal chatter of the soul (*nafs*) or from demonic inspiration and are not therefore susceptible to meaningful interpretation."[61] On one occasion, a nightmare sends Fāṭima hurrying to her father; she has seen her two sons being slaughtered and is so distraught that Muḥammad resorts to challenging the very world of dreams itself:

> He said: Vision! It presented itself before him and he said: Did you show Fāṭima this tribulation? It replied: No! Then he said: Confused dreams, did you show Fāṭima this tribulation? They replied: Yes, Messenger of God! He said: And what did you

---

[57] Q. 12:5, 43, 100 (in the context of Yūsuf), Q. 17:60 (in the context of the night journey), Q. 37:105 (in the context of Ibrāhīm), Q. 48:27 (in the context of Muḥammad).

[58] Q. 30:23, Q. 39:42.

[59] Q. 8:43 (in the context of Muḥammad), Q. 37:102 (in the context of Ibrāhīm). Sirriyeh, like Kinberg, suggests that the word *bushrā*, which carries a sense of 'good news', is employed in reference to a dream in Q. 10:64. Although this is less obvious than the other references, it is thus defined by the corpus of *aḥādīṯ*: cf. al-Tirmiḏī., *al-Ǧāmiʿ al-ṣaḥīḥ*, vol. IV, bk. 32 (*Abwāb al-ru'yā*), bb. 3, n. 2273: 319, n. 2275: 320, vol. V, bk. 44 (*Abwāb tafsīr al-qur'ān*), bb. 10, n. (1) 3105: 415. Hence too, the good dreams that convey glad tidings are called *mubāshirāt*. Cf. SIRRIYEH E., *Dreams and Visions in the World of Islam*, 2015: 49.

[60] Q. 12:44 and Q. 21:5.

[61] NASR S.E. et al., (eds.), *The Study Quran*, HarperOne, New York 2015, nt. 44: 603.

desire, doing this? They replied: To make her grieve! Then he said: Fāṭima, listen to me! There was nothing in this![62]

In spite of his declaration, the residue of her dream is a sense of foreboding, the same disquiet left by the dream of Umm al-Faḍl; more dramatically, the reader knows that both al-Ḥasan and al-Ḥusayn will indeed be killed after all. After one of Fāṭima's dreams, in the sixth month of her pregnancy with al-Ḥusayn, and in which "there came to me in my sleep one who rubbed his wings against my back" and "there came to me in my sleep one who made me sit up and made incantations over me and prayed God's protection over me," Muḥammad himself relieves her anxiety by identifying her nocturnal visitors, with whom he is on intimate terms; they are his friend ʿIzrāʾīl, "guardian and opener of the wombs of women", his friend Mīkāʾīl, "guardian of the wombs of the people of my house" and his brother Ǧibraʾīl "to whom God has given care of your child."[63]

While the books of *aḥādīṯ* offer a threefold categorization of dreams ("The righteous dream which is good news from God, dreams in which Shayṭān frightens someone, and dreams about something that has happened to the man himself"),[64] two classes of

[62] al-ʿAyyāshī., *Tafsīr*, vol. II, Part Three, *sūrat Yūsuf*, n. 31: 178–179, Muḥammad Riḍā al-Ṭūsī., *Kanz al-daqāʾiq wa baḥr al-ġarāʾib fī tafsīr al-qurʾān*, vol. VI, *sūrat Yūsuf*: 319, al-Baḥrānī., *al-Burhān fī tafsīr al-qurʾān*, vol. III, Part Three, *sūrat Yūsuf*, n. 5288: 177, al-Maǧlisī., *Biḥār al-anwār*, vol. XLIII, bb. 4, n. 15: 91, vol. LVIII, bb. 44, n. 16: 166, al-Iṣfahānī., *ʿAwālim al-ʿulūm wa-l-maʿārif al-aḥwāl min al-āyāt wa-l-aḫbār wa-l-aqwāl*, vol. II, ch. 19, bb. 4, n. 1: 505, n. 3: 508, al-Ǧazāʾirī., *Riyāḍ al-abrār fī manāqib al-aʾimma al-aṭhār*, vol. I, Part One: 43, al-Ḥuwayzī., *Tafsīr nūr al-ṯaqalayn*, vol. II, *sūrat Yūsuf*, n. 86: 429.

[63] al-Rāwandī., *al-Ḫarāʾiǧ wa-l-ǧarāʾiḥ fī al-muʿǧizāt*, vol. II: 841, al-Maǧlisī., *Biḥār al-anwār*, vol. XLIII, bb. 12, n. 39: 272–273, al-Iṣfahānī., *ʿAwālim al-ʿulūm wa-l-maʿārif al-aḥwāl min al-āyāt wa-l-aḫbār wa-l-aqwāl*, vol. XI, ch. 24, bb. 4, n. 147: 899.

[64] al-Buḫārī., *Ṣaḥīḥ*, vol. IX, bk. 91 (*Kitāb al-taʿbīr*), bb. 26, n. 7017: 103–104, Ibn Māǧa., *Sunan*, vol. V, bk. 35 (*Abwāb taʿbir al-ruʾyā*), bb. 3, n. 3906: 146, n. 3907: 146–147), Abū Dāwud., *Sunan*, vol. V, bk. 40 (*Kitāb al-adab*), b. 88, n. 5019: 365, al-Tirmiḏī., *al-Ǧāmiʿ al-ṣaḥīḥ*, vol. IV, bk. 32

dreams can be individualized in Islam's sacred sources, although many dream encounters contain elements of both. Firstly, there are dreams or visions which relay a message; this might be the announcement of good news (Muḥammad designates as *al-mubāshirāt* those good dreams that convey happy tidings),[65] the harbinger of bad news, warnings, predictions or commandments. Striking in the Christian Scriptures, for example, are the dream sequences in Matthew's Gospel, in which the dominant theme is divine announcement. Five dreams, three of them specifically of angels[66] bearing news, are recounted in the Infancy Narratives.[67] In the same text, the wife of Pontius Pilate, the Rome-appointed Prefect of Judaea, reports having «*suffered much over Him today in a dream*» (Mt. 27:19) and urges her husband to spare Jesus. The dream *motif* is crucial in the narratives of the conception and birth of both Jesus and of al-Ḥusayn; but while a number of Joseph's dreams bring warnings about the child's safety, none of them predict his death.

Secondly, there are the more cryptic or inscrutable dreams, whose symbolism needs disentangling and interpretation; Muḥammad, interested in the dreams of his companions, himself

(*Abwāb al-ru'yā*), bb. 1, n. 2270: 316, bb. 7, n. 2280: 323–324, bb. 10, n. 2291: 330.

[65] al-Buḫārī., *Ṣaḥīḥ*, vol. IX, bk. 91 (*Kitāb al-taʿbīr*), bb. 5, n. 6990: 88, Muslim., *Ṣaḥīḥ*, vol. I, bk. 4 (*Kitāb al-ṣalāt*), bb. 41, n. [1074] 207 – (479): 590, n. [1075] 208: 590–591, vol. VI, bk. 42 (*Kitāb al-ru'yā*), n. [5905] 6 – (2263): 120, al-Tirmiḏī., *al-Ǧāmiʿ al-ṣaḥīḥ*, vol. IV, bk. 32 (*Abwāb al-ru'yā*), bb. 2, n. 2272: 318 ("*al-mubāshirāt* are the Muslim's dreams"), al-Nasā'ī., *al-Sunan al-kubrā*, vol. II, bk. 12 (*Kitāb al-taṭbīq*), bb. 62, n. 1121: 151.

[66] Brown believes that most often in Old Testament usage, 'the angel of the Lord' is not a personal, spiritual being acting as intermediate between God and humanity, but simply a way of describing God's visible presence among people. Cf. BROWN R., *The Birth of the Messiah*, Doubleday, New York 1993: 129.

[67] Mt. 1: 20 (an angel to Joseph); Mt. 2: 12 (a dream of the Magi); Mt. 2: 13 (an angel to Joseph); Mt. 2: 19 (an angel to Joseph); Mt. 2: 22 (to Joseph).

invites whoever has had a dream to let him interpret it,[68] and among numerous examples in the Sunna, one could name his interpreting a dream of people wearing shirts of different lengths as a reference to religion,[69] his deciphering a dream of the consumption of milk that leads to it exuding from the fingernails, as religious knowledge,[70] his unravelling the dream of a broken sword symbolizing the casualties on the day of Uḥud, a dream of the sword fixed again symbolizing the conquest of Mecca, a dream of cows, reminiscent of the dreams interpreted in the Joseph/Yūsuf narratives, symbolizing the faithful believers (who were martyred) on the day of Uḥud,[71] or his explanation a dream of a flowing stream as a reference good deeds.[72] The dream of Umm al-Faḍl, examined in this anthology, is an enigmatic vision that demands elucidation, while

---

[68] al-Buḫārī., *Ṣaḥīḥ*, vol. II, bk. 19 (*Kitāb al-tahaǧǧud*), bb. 1, n. 1121: 139, bk. 23 (*Kitāb al-ǧanāʾiz*), bb. 93, n. 1386: 267, vol. V, bk. 62 (*Kitāb faḍāʾil aṣḥāb al-nabī*), bb. 19, n. 3738: 63, vol. IX, bk. 91 (*Kitāb al-taʿbīr*), bb. 35, n. 7028: 109, bb. 36, n. 7030: 111, bb. 48, n. 7047: 118, Muslim., *Ṣaḥīḥ*, vol. VI, bk. 42 (*Kitāb al-ruʾyā*), bb. 3, n. [5931]: 129, bb. 4, n. [5937] 23 – (2275): 132, bk. 44 (*Kitāb faḍāʾil al-ṣaḥāba*), bb. 31, n. [6369] 139 – (2478): 343, Abū Dāwud., *Sunan*, vol. V, bk. 39 (*Awwal kitāb al-sunna*), bb. 8, n. 4634: 176, bk. X (*Awwal kitāb al-adab*), bb. 8, n. 5017: 364.

[69] al-Buḫārī., *Ṣaḥīḥ*, vol. I, bk. 2 (*Kitāb al-īmān*), bb. 15, n. 23: 65, vol. V, bk. 62 (*Kitāb faḍāʾil aṣḥāb al-nabī*), bb. 6, n. 3691: 35, vol. IX, bk. 91 (*Kitāb al-taʿbīr*), bb. 17, n. 7006: 99, bb. 18, n. 7009: 99–100, al-Tirmiḏī., *al-Ǧāmiʿ al-ṣaḥīḥ*, vol. IV, bk. 32 (*Abwāb al-ruʾyā*), bb. 9, n. 2285: 326–327.

[70] al-Buḫārī., *Ṣaḥīḥ*, vol. I, bk. 3 (*Kitāb al-ʿilm*), bb. 22, n. 82: 104–105, vol. V, bk. 62 (*Kitāb faḍāʾil aṣḥāb al-nabī*), bb. 6, n. 3681: 30, vol. IX, bk. 91 (*Kitāb al-taʿbīr*), bb. 15, n. 7006: 98, bb. 16, n. 7007: 99, bb. 34, n. 7027: 109, bb. 37, n. 7032: 111–112, al-Tirmiḏī., *al-Ǧāmiʿ al-ṣaḥīḥ*, vol. IV, bk. 32 (*Abwāb al-ruʾyā*), bb. 9, n. 2284: 325–326, vol. VI, bk. 46 (*Abwāb al-manāqib*), n. 3687: 365.

[71] al-Buḫārī., *Ṣaḥīḥ*, vol. IV, bk. 61 (*Kitāb al-manāqib*), bb. 25, n. 3622: 494, vol. V, bk. 63 (*Kitāb al-maġāzī*), bb. 27, n. 4081: 249, vol. IX, bk. 91 (*Kitāb al-taʿbīr*), bb. 39, n. 7035: 112–113, bb. 4, n. 7041: 115, Muslim., *Ṣaḥīḥ*, vol. VI, bk. 42 (*Kitāb al-ruʾyā*), bb. 4, n. [5934] 20 - (2272): 129–139.

[72] al-Buḫārī., *Ṣaḥīḥ*, vol. III, bk. 52 (*Kitāb al-shahādāt*), bb. 30, n. 2687: 499, vol. V, bk. 63 (*Kitāb manāqib al-anṣār*), bb. 46, n. 3929: 165–166, vol. IX, bk. 91 (*Kitāb al-taʿbīr*), bb. 13, n. 7004: 97, bb. 27, n. 7018: 104–105.

the appearance of symbolic materials such as red dust in some visits by Ǧibrīl combine a straightforward warning with allusive elements.

While Muslim scholars may attribute these dream divisions and categories to Muḥammad, they existed long before him; the 2nd century Artemidorus Daldianus, from contemporary western Turkey, was an avid chronicler of dreams and their interpretation, producing his famous handbook (*Oneirocritica*), which would eventually find its way into the hands of medieval Islamic scholars.[73] Artemidorus apportions dreams into two essential types, the dream properly called *oneiros*, which forecasts future events, and the *enhypnion*, which exposes the dreamer's state of mind or life. The *oneiros* can predict good or bad things, and may be literal (thus liberating the dreamer from the prerequisite of an interpreter), or allegorical (where assistance would be needed in making sense of the prediction). For his part, the Christian scholar Tertullian determines three possible origins for dreams: God, demons, and the mind or soul.[74]

Notwithstanding their religious significance, dreams are sparser in the Hebrew and Christian Scriptures than they are in the sacred sources of Islam. That God communicates with humanity through dreams is plainly asserted in the Scriptures,[75] and divine revelation through dreams is a recurring theme in the Hebrew and Christian texts, in most cases the dream being said to have come from God.[76] There are certainly some biblical dreams recorded which are not specifically said to have come from Him,[77] although their divine origin is presumed. There are approximately a dozen dreams in the Hebrew Scriptures, but only on rare occasions is

---

[73] Cf. SIRRIYEH E., *Dreams and Visions in the World of Islam*, 2015: 9.

[74] NEIL B., "Studying Dream Interpretation from Early Christianity to the Rise of Islam" in *Journal of Religious History*, vol. 40, n. 1, March 2016: 63, BULKELEY K., *Dreaming in the World's Religions. A Comparative History*, New York University Press, New York 2008: 181.

[75] Cf. Num. 12:6, Job 33:14.

[76] Cf. Gen. 20:3, 28:12, 31:10, I Kings 3:5–15, Dan. 2:19, 7:1, Mt. 1:20, 2:12, 13, 19, 22, Acts 23:11, 27:23.

[77] Gen. 37:6, 30:5, 31:1, Jdg. 7:13, II Mach. 15:11.

God Himself said to appear in a dream (Gen. 20:3, 28:13, I Kgs. 3:5); more usually, He communicates through an angel.

Dreams and visions are embedded into the texts of the Hebrew Scriptures from the outset. Using the Hebrew *ḥălôm* (Gk. *hypnō* or *enupnion*) and its derivatives, the text of Genesis is dominated by the dreams of Jacob (Gen. 28:10ff) and Joseph (Gen. 37–42); but as if to underscore that divine communications in dreams are for the good and bad alike, it is also in a dream that Abimelech, the polytheistic Philistine king, is warned of his death (Gen. 3:20), and the trickster Laban sees God (Gen. 31:24). While the book of Numbers assures its readers that God speaks to people in dreams and visions (Num. 12:6), the Wisdom literature appears to dismiss them; with dreams, warns the author of Ecclesiastes, written up to a millennium before Muḥammad, come many cares, vanities and a multitude of words (Eccles. 5:3, 7). The Book of Sirach believes that «*dreams give wings to fools*» (Sir. 34:1), and «*as one who catches at a shadow and pursues the wind, so is anyone who believes in dreams*» (Sir. 34:2). The author concludes that «*divinations and omens and dreams are unreal*» (Sir. 34:5) and that «*dreams have deceived many*» (Sir. 34:7), while Jeremiah, warning against a danger that would later be taken up by Christian and then Islamic scholars, reminds his readers that «*the difference between dreams and God's word is like the difference between straw and wheat*» (Jer. 23:28). In spite of Sirach's dismissive words, in the Hebrew Scriptures Daniel and Joseph are acclaimed as adroit interpreters, with the enigmatic dreams interpreted by Joseph echoed in the Qurʾānic account of Yūsuf, chosen by God for the «*interpretation of events*»[78] and asked by a variety of persons to make sense of their dreams for them (Q. 12:35–42). As with Muḥammad in the Sunna, the Bible urges the circumspect treatment of dreams; regardless of the presence of skilled unravellers of visions like Daniel and Joseph, warnings against false dreams, visions and interpretations occur frequently in the text (Deut. 13:5, Jer. 23:25, 29:8, Zech.

[78] Q. 12:6, (*taʾwīl al-aḥādīṯ*). The editors of 'The Study Bible' note: "In traditional Islamic psychology this entails knowing the source of dreams" (NASR S.E. et al., (eds.), *The Study Quran*, 2015, nt. 6: 592). This source is either angelic or demonic. Cf. also al-Buḫārī., *Ṣaḥīḥ*, vol. IX, bk. 91 (*Kitāb al-taʿbīr*), bb. 11: 88–89.

10:2). Nonetheless, God continues to appear to dreamers like Solomon (1 Kgs. 3:15) and Daniel (Dan. 1:17) or to test holy people like Job («*you scare me with dreams and terrify me with visions*», Job 7:14), and Saul can still lament over a God gone missing, a God who «*no longer answers me, either by prophets or by dreams*» (I Sam. 28:15), the absence of dreams analogous to the loss of the divine proximity.

The great dreamer of the Christian Scriptures is Joseph, husband of Mary. The annunciation to Mary recorded by Luke and Matthew, and in which Joseph is intimately involved, as with its parallel Qurʾānic accounts (Q. 3:42–47, Q. 19:16–21), is not depicted as a dream; however, visits by Ǧibrīl or other angels, although outside of such a context, cannot be classed as ordinary encounters, but must be considered as meetings with the divine. Five dreams are imputed to Joseph, with the same Greek word (*ónar*) used for each. In three of the dreams Joseph receives instructions (Mt 1:20, 2:13, 19) and in two he is warned about a future difficulty (Mt. 2:12, 22). Only in three of the texts is an angel mentioned, while in the other two the angelic presence is presumed. In Mt. 2:12, the recipient of the dream is understood to be Joseph, although the text fails to mention his name.

The Hebrew and Christian Scriptures use a variety of terms to distinguish between 'dreams' and 'visions' (Heb. *ḥăzôn*, Gk. *órama*), a distinction made in the Book of Numbers,[79] and by reason of which some divine encounters might be classed as 'visions' or a 'waking dreams'. Daniel, for example, most often receives his visions in dream form while asleep (Dan. 2:19, 7:1), but he also has daytime visions (Dan. 10:4–5), while in the Book of Revelation, John receives his revelatory vision while «*in the Spirit*» (Rev. 1:10). This distinction can equally be made in the Islamic texts, underscored by a *ḥadīṯ* averring that what Muḥammad saw during the Night Journey (*isrāʾ*) were not dreams but things actually seen, like visions in broad daylight (*ruʾyā ʿayn*),[80] as opposed to those dreams

---

[79] «*The oracle of one who hears the words of God, who sees the vision of the Almighty, who falls down, but with eyes uncovered*» (Num. 24:4).

[80] al-Buḫārī., *Ṣaḥīḥ*, vol. V, bk. 63 (*Kitāb manāqib al-anṣār*), bb. 42, n. 3888: 137, vol. VI, bk. 65 (*Kitāb al-tafsīr*), bb. 9, n. 4716: 192, vol. VIII, bk.

described by the use of *manām*, with its connotation of sleep. The 'night visions' of Isaiah, Israel, Daniel and Paul might also fall into this category.[81]

Like dreams, such visions occur throughout the Hebrew and Christian texts. Both Abram and Jacob are addressed by God in visions (Gen 15:1, 46:2), in accordance with the assurance, already seen, in Num. 12:6, that God speaks to prophets in such a manner. Although at times, as in the childhood of Samuel, «*visions were not widespread*» (I Sam. 3:1), prophets like Isaiah, Ezekiel, Daniel and Zechariah were recurrent recipients (Is. 6:1, Ez. 1:1, 8:3). In Luke's Gospel, Zechariah sees and converses with an angel in a vision in the sanctuary (Lk. 1:11); at the end of the same text, a group of women would have the same experience at the empty tomb (Lk. 24:23). The Book of Acts, also penned by Luke, abounds with visions; Ananias, Cornelius and Paul all see and converse with angelic visitors in visions (Acts 9:10, 10:3, 18:9). Like the slave-girl Hagar (Gen. 16:7), Peter has an encounter with an angel that is quite patently not a dream or a vision (Acts 12:9). A warning from Paul to those fixated with «*the worship of angels, dwelling on visions*» (Col. 2:18) suggests the same difficulties in the nascent Church as will be seen in emerging Islam, and the subsequent need for orthodox formulations.

Notwithstanding the examples of dreams, dreamers and interpreters in the Hebrew and Christian Scriptures, the early Church took an unreceptive view, endorsed by Church Fathers like Jerome (d. 419) and Augustine (d. 430),[82] denying Baptism to interpreters of dreams and, especially after Constantine,[83] censuring all types of divination. There was a general acceptance that some dreams, espe-

---

82 (*Kitāb al-qadar*), bb. 10, n. 6613: 324–325, vol. IX, bk. 91 (*Kitāb al-taʿbīr*), bb. 1, n. 6982: 83.

[81] Gen. 46:2, Is. 29:7, Dan. 2:19, 7:2, 7, 13, Acts 16:9, 18:9.

[82] BULKELEY K., *Dreaming in the World's Religions. A Comparative History*, 2008: 178.

[83] With the conversion of the Roman Emperor Constantine (d. 337) to Christianity, and his subsequent legitimizing of the Church and its worship, Christianity began its transition into the dominant religion of the Roman Empire.

cially those of the saints or of professional religious people like monks and nuns, might come from God (the 'Shepherd of Hermas' being a rare example, since the recipient was no monk but a herder),[84] but as Neil underscores, dreams of the laity were thought to be beset with hazards, leading to the overarching fear that most of them came from the devil.[85] Although to some extent this view would come to be reflected in the *aḥādīṯ*, the traditional Muslim image of Muḥammad, based on the Qurʾānic data which designates him as one who received from God both dreams and the ability to understand them, is that he is, with God's permission, a master of interpretation (*taʿbīr*). In this way, the Prophet's own life gives credence to a phenomenon already approved by the Qurʾān:

> ʿAmr replied: I heard ʿUbayd b. ʿUmayr saying that the dreams of Prophets were Divine Revelations, and then he recited the verse: «*And when (his son) was old enough to walk with him, (Abraham) said: O my dear son, I have seen in a dream that I must sacrifice thee*».[86]

While the skill of unlocking the cryptic meanings of dreams is reserved to a select, divinely-appointed few, such as Joseph and Daniel in the Hebrew Scriptures and, in the Islamic tradition, Yūsuf and Muḥammad, it is patently clear, as in the Karbalāʾ dream narratives, that the good and the wicked equally can receive divine communications in dreams. In the Hebrew Scriptures, both the Pharaoh and Nebuchadnezzar awake troubled by dreams (although awaking troubled is not in itself indicative of the wickedness of the dreamer's life, since in one famous narrative Muḥammad wakes disturbed

---

[84] A mid-2nd century Christian text, hugely popular among the next two generations of Christians and comprising five didactic visions given to a shepherd called Hermas.

[85] NEIL B., "Studying Dream Interpretation from Early Christianity to the Rise of Islam" in *Journal of Religious History*, vol. 40, n. 1, March 2016: 55.

[86] Q. 37:102. Cf. al-Buḫārī., *Ṣaḥīḥ*, vol. I, bk. 4 (*Kitāb al-wuḍūʾ*), bb. 5, n. 138: 136–137, bk. 10 (*Kitāb al-aḏān*), bb. 161, n. 859: 473.

by what he has dreamt). The Pharaoh[87] has two dreams in succession and awakes with a «*troubled mind*» (Gen. 41:8). Nebuchadnezzar, king of Babylon, has dreams leading to anxiety and an extended period of insomnia. He summons his magicians and astrologers to interpret, demanding that they first tell him what his dreams were. They insist that only the gods could do such a thing and that there are no gods living among them, and Nebuchadnezzar orders that all wise men be executed. In fact, Daniel is hovering on the fringes of Nebuchadnezzar's world, one of the divinely-selected few, (Dan. 2:1–10) and insists that God can interpret the mysterious dreams that the Babylonian gods and wise men cannot, a polemical note that also arises in the context of some of the Karbalāʾ dream texts. The suggestion, notes Sirriyeh, is clear; intuitive, divinely-guided interpretations are superior to human deductive methods.[88]

In many of the dreams of the Hebrew Scriptures, it is the message itself rather than actually seeing the messenger that is crucial, so that the dreamer recalls the words but not the one who brings them. Alternatively, in his dream at Bethel, Jacob certainly sees angels, and also the Lord, standing above them, who addresses him directly. The slave girl Hagar also sees the Lord, in the form of an angel, who speaks to her concerning her pregnancy, causing her to declare: «*I have now seen the One who sees me*» (Gen. 16:7–13). Angels become very prominent in early Christian dreams, sometimes as alluring entities come to bring guidance, at times as alarming harbingers of divine anger. In Islam, the messenger who delivered the dream was no longer some capricious god or goddess of the 'time of ignorance' (*ǧāhiliyya*), but Muḥammad, the trustworthiness of his presence verified by the *ḥadīṯ* ("Whoever sees me in a dream has really seen me, since Shayṭān cannot make himself similar to me in a dream"),[89] or at times an angel, or sometimes other es-

---

[87] Held by scholars almost certainly to be Necho II, a king of the 26th Dynasty (610–595 BC).

[88] SIRRIYEH E., *Dreams and Visions in the World of Islam*, 2015: 13.

[89] Among the Sunnī, cf. Ibn Abī Shayba., *al-Muṣannaf*, vol. X, bb. 2, nn. 31088–31091: 122–123, n. 31093: 123, al-Buḫārī., *Ṣaḥīḥ*, vol. I, bk. 3 (*Kitāb al-ʿilm*), bb. 38, n. 110: 119, vol. VIII, bk. 78 (*Kitāb al-adab*), bb. 109,

teemed Muslim personality. The constancy with which the divine erupted into Muḥammad's own life – from 610 he became recipient of many dreams, asleep and awake, visual and auditory, with ʿĀʾisha narrating that the very beginning of revelation to Muḥammad was in the form of true dreams[90] – made him, like the

---

n. 6197: 122, vol. IX, bk. 91 (*Kitāb al-taʿbīr*), bb. 10, nn. 6993, 6994, 6996, 6997: 92–93, Muslim., *Sunan*, vol. VI, bk. 42 (*Kitāb al-ruʾyā*), bb. 1, nn. [5919] 10 – (2266), [5920] 11, [5923] 12 – (2268), [5924] 13: 123–125, Ibn Māǧa., *Sunan*, vol. V, bk. 35 (*Abwāb taʿbīr al-ruʾyā*), nn. 3900–3905: 144–145, Abū Dāwud., *Sunan*, vol. V, bk. 40 (*Kitāb al-adab*), bb. 88, n. 5023: 366, al-Tirmiḏī., *al-Ǧāmiʿ al-ṣaḥīḥ*, vol. IV, bk. 32 (*Abwāb al-ruʾyā*), bb. 4, n. 2276: 320–321, al-Ḥākim al-Nīsābūrī., *Kitāb al-mustadrak ʿalā al-ṣaḥīḥayn*, vol. IV, bk. 47 (*Kitāb taʿbīr al-ruʾyā*), n. 8266: 547, Ibn al-ʿAdīm., *Buǧyat al-ṭalab fī tārīḫ Ḥalab*, Part Six: 2644. Among the Shīʿa, cf. al-Hilālī., *Kitāb Sulaym b. Qays*, vol. II, n. 4: 823, Ibn Bābawayh., *Man lā yaḥḍuru-hu al-faqīh*, vol. II, n. 3191: 585, *Kitāb al-amālī fī-l-aḥādīṯ wa-l-aḫbār, maǧlis* 15, n. 10: 64, *ʿUyūn aḫbār al-Riḍā*, vol. II, bb. 66, n. 11: 257, al-Ṭūsī., *al-Amālī fī-l-ḥadīṯ, maǧlis* 11, n. 97–650: 324, Ibn ʿAlī al-Fattāl., *Rawḍat al-wāʿiẓīn wa-tabṣirat al-muttaʿiẓīn*, vol. I, *maǧlis fī ḏikr wafāti-hi*: 234, al-Ṭabarsī., *Iʿlām al-warā bi-aʿlām al-hudā*, Part Three, bb. 7: 333, vol. II, Part Three, bb. 2: 71, al-Shuʿayrī., *Ǧāmiʿ al-aḫbar*: 172, al-Irbilī., *Kashf al-ġumma fī maʿrifat al-aʾimma*, vol. II, Part Three: 57, 330, al-Daylamī., *Irshād al-qulūb*, vol. II, bb. *Fī faḍāʾil wa manāqib amīr al-muʾminīn ʿAlī b. Abī Ṭālib wa ġaẓawāti-hi*: 393, al-Bayyāḍī., *al-Ṣirāṭ al-mustaqīm ilā mustaḥaqq al-taqdīm fī al-imāma*, vol. III, bb. 14: 155, al-Mūsawī., *Tasliyat al-maǧālis wa ẓīnat al-maǧālis*, vol. II, *maǧlis* 9: 485, al-Maǧlisī., *Rawḍat al-muttaqīn fī sharḥ man lā yaḥḍuru-hu al-faqīh*, vol. V: 398, al-Māzandarānī., *Sharḥ uṣūl al-Kāfī*, vol. VII, *Abwāb al-tārīḫ*: 377, al-Qazwīnī., *al-Shāfī fī uṣūl al-Kāfī*, vol. II, bb. 15: 251, al-Fayḍ al-Kāshānī., *al-Wāfī*, vol. XIV, bb. 195 (3191/584/2, 17–14645): 1550, al-Baḥrānī., *Madīnat al-maʿāǧiẓ fī muʿǧiẓāt al-aʾimma al-aṭhār*, vol. II, Part Two, bb.1: 94, vol. VII, Part Seven, bb. 8, n. 154/2256: 183, al-Maǧlisī., *Biḥār al-anwār*, vol. XXX, bb. 19: 132, al-Iṣfahānī., *ʿAwālim al-ʿulūm wa-l-maʿārif al-aḥwāl min al-āyāt wa-l-aḫbār wa-l-aqwāl*, vol. XVII, ch. 27, bb. 2, n. 1: 722, vol. XXII, ch. 24, bb. 1, n. 5: 467, al-Ǧazāʾirī., *Riyāḍ al-abrār fī manāqib al-aʾimma al-aṭhār*, vol. I, Part One: 304, vol. II: 415.

[90] Cf. for e.g. al-Buḫārī., *Ṣaḥīḥ*, vol. VI, bk. 65 (*Kitāb al-tafsīr*), bb. 3, n. 4956: 404, vol. IX, bk. 91 (*Kitāb al-taʿbīr*), bb. I, n. 6982: 83, Muslim.,

prophet Yūsuf before him, the archetypal dreamer and, guided by heaven, a skilled unraveller of his own dreams and those of others.

Artemidorus, whose *Oneirocritica* became one of the ways in which the pre-Islamic Near Eastern and Mediterranean region impacted upon Islamic ideas of dreams and dreaming,[91] was also confident that the dreams of ordinary people may affect the lives of others, and notes the likelihood that a dream that has a public affect would probably occur to a number of citizens, something borne out by the variety of people, both good and bad, who dreamt of Karbalāʾ. As noted by Neil, in Judaism, Christianity and Islam, dreams were (and often still are) recognised as having not only personal meanings for the dreamer, but also social and cultural meanings for the dreamer's community.[92] What is clear is that, in spite of certain hesitations, Islam displayed a more optimistic view about dreams than did the first few generations of Christians. All three monotheistic systems acknowledged that God could intervene in lives and situations through dreams, and even though all three groups maintained a wary apprehension about the possibility of Satanic intrusion, Judaism and Islam were more proactive than was Christianity in recognizing that visions and dreams could be a vital aid in the spiritual lives of the faithful.

It is not only dreams that hint at divine activity and intervention; the pages of the Qurʾān are infused, in a vivid and palpable manner, with angelic presence, supernatural creatures, rarely glimpsed, although occasionally manifesting themselves, only ever by divine command, in a form accessible to human capacity, and described by the text more precisely in terms of their function than of their nature. As Lizzini observes, even though belief in angels pertains to the very nature of faith in Islam, with angels only second to God in the list of credal statements in Q. 2:285,[93] the early

---

Ṣaḥīḥ, vol. I, bk. 1 (*Kitāb al-īmān*), bb. 73, n. [403] 252 – (160): 252–253, n. [405] 254: 255.

[91] SIRRIYEH E., *Dreams and Visions in the World of Islam*, 2015: 9.

[92] NEIL B., "Studying Dream Interpretation from Early Christianity to the Rise of Islam", 2016: 45.

[93] «*The messenger believeth in that which hath been revealed unto him from his Lord and (so do) believers. Each one believeth in Allah and His angels and His scrip-*

theological discourse in Islam, concerned with more pressing issues, had little to say about angels.[94] After the 2nd/8th century rise of the ʿAbbāsid dynasty, in territories once possessed by the Hellenic-Christian Byzantines and the Persian-Zoroastrian Sāsānids, civilizations now grown tired, Islamic sages and explorers began to encounter the intellectual and philosophical legacies of Rome, Greece, Persia and India; in spite of the influence of these on Islamic theological definitions, subsequent Islamic theology did not linger too long around the theological question of angels, although this in no way diminishes their importance. It was an encounter that would result in a new Islamic civilization, as Muslims appropriated and adapted a variety of intellectual heritages. The outcome would be seen in Islam's formal ventures in theology (*kalām*), the engagement of its religious expression with Greek philosophy (*falsafa*) and a mystical tradition that hungered after intimacy with God (*taṣawwuf*), three fields in which the concept of angels would be cultivated and refined, especially in terms of angelic names and functions.

Qur'ānic references to angels are rudimentary, with the angels mentioned specifically in relation to their function. One text offers a physiological description («*Praise be to Allah, the Creator of the heavens and the earth, Who appointeth the angels messengers having wings two, three and four*»),[95] while another speaks of an upward movement, as angels «*ascend unto him*».[96] For the rest, the Qur'ān deliberates chiefly on the several functions assigned to them, and primarily, as in Juda-

---

tures and His messengers – We make no distinction between any of His messengers – and they say: We hear, and we obey. (Grant us) Thy forgiveness, our Lord. Unto Thee is the journeying».

[94] LIZZINI O., "Islamic Angelology. Revelation, Tradition and Philosophical Elaboration. Some Brief Observations" in *Encounter* n. 227, August-September 1996, Pontificio Istituto di Studi Arabi e d'Islamistica, Rome: 2.

[95] Q. 35:1. In the Hebrew Scriptures too, we are offered a picture, through Isaiah, of «*seraphim, each with six wings: with two wings they covered their faces, with two they covered their feet, and with two they were flying*» above «*the Lord, high and exalted, seated on a throne*» (Is. 6:1–3).

[96] Q. 70:4.

ism and Christianity, the function of worship and praise; dwelling in the divine presence, they offer obeisance, unwearied in the honour they give (Q. 21:19–20, cf. Dan. 7:10, Rev. 5:11–12, where the number of angels encircling the throne is «*thousands upon thousands, and ten thousand times ten thousand*»), and also exercising a mediatory function in asking forgiveness for humans (Q. 42:5). There are other functions too; their nearness to God (*muqarrabūn*)[97] and bearing of the divine throne[98] does not preclude them from activity on the human plane. Angels, at God's command, distribute either blessing or punishment,[99] acting as people's guardians (*ḥafaẓa* or *ḥāfiẓūn*)[100] and as the scribes who take careful note of human actions, the good and the bad.[101]

This early, simple angelology, characterized in the texts by functionality and thus similar to that of primitive Christianity, would be augmented by the corpus of *aḥādīṯ* and stories from popular piety, creating a more substantial definition of angels, who would come to serve as place markers, clearly marking the borders between the earthly and heavenly realms, leaving the divine realm only by permission (clearly expressed in the Ibn Ḥanbal narratives about the angel of the rain), and in that act of leaving, joining the two territories by their interventions among humans. While they are part of the celestial realm and thus distinct from the *ǧinn* and humans, whose sphere is terrestrial, angels are nonetheless present

---

[97] Q. 4:172; Pickthall renders the Arabic *muqarrabūn* as 'favoured', although the sense is of angels in or near to the presence of God (as in Arberry's rendition, 'near-stationed'). Despite a certain similarity in the terminology, they are not comparable to the cherubim of the Hebrew Scriptures, who have a variety of functions but whose primarily role is never clearly stated.

[98] Q. 39:75, Q. 40:7, Q. 69:17 In the opening verses of the book of Ezekiel, the winged creatures bearing up the throne are eventually, some chapters later, identified as cherubim (Ez. 10:2); and the prayer of King Hezekiah in Is. 37:16 is made to God «*enthroned above the cherubim*».

[99] Q. 51:4, Q. 8:50, Q. 47:27.

[100] Q. 6:61, Q. 13:11, Q. 82:10, Q. 86:4.

[101] Q. 43:80, Q. 50:17–18, Q. 82:11.

when humans perform certain activities, such as prayer and battle.[102]

The Arabic for 'angel', *malak*, sometimes *malāk*, is held by Islamic scholars to be an Arabic word, although they diverge over whether it derives from *malaka* or *alaka* (or even possible *la'aka*, 'to send', as noted by Lane).[103] Jeffery for his part holds it to be borrowed from the Ethiopian, although assimilated into Arabic long before Muḥammad, so that the Qur'ān has no difficulty in assuming that angels are patently known to an Arabic audience.[104] The Arabic *malaka-yamliku* carries a range of meanings, with the underlying sense of power, possession, domination or exercising control. As Jeffery notes, perhaps it is from this root that the angel in charge of Hell, Mālik, gets his name.[105] It is, in some of the texts we will see, the imperative issued by Muḥammad to Umm Salama, to 'take control' of the door while within, he is occupied with an angelic visitor. The second possibility, the Arabic *alaka-yaluku* (under which Lane chooses to define 'angel' noting that *malak* is both singular and plural), carries the sense of acting as a messenger between people, conveying or communicating a message or sending a message or messenger.[106] However, the more usual plural for 'angel' is a present participle in the feminine form, *malā'ika.*

While certainly, in that pre-Islamic period which Islam refers to as 'the time of ignorance' (*ǧāhiliyya*) angels were imagined by some to be God's 'daughters', the Qur'ān sharply rebukes such a concept («*it is those who disbelieve in the Hereafter who name the angels with*

---

[102] Q. 17:78, Q. 9:26, Q. 33:9

[103] LANE E.W., *An Arabic-English Lexicon*, vol. I, 1968: 82, vol. VIII: 3007. Godwin informs his readers that the original Hebrew *mal'akh* meant 'God's shadow side' and only later came to mean 'messenger'. Cf. GODWIN M., *Angels. An Endangered Species*, Boxtree Ltd., London 1990: 7.

[104] JEFFERY A., *The Foreign Vocabulary of the Qur'ān*, 2007: 269–270.

[105] Op. cit.: 257.

[106] LANE E.W., *An Arabic-English Lexicon*, vol. I, 1968: 81–82. Cf. also MACDONALD D.B., "Mala'ika" in C. Bosworth et al., (eds.), *The Encyclopaedia of Islam*, vol. VI, 1991: 216, IBN MANẒŪR., *Lisān al-ʿArab*, vol. I: 111.

the names of females»),[107] so that the feminine form of the plural should not be seen to have any special significance.

Quite patently, many of the texts upon which this study is based have been deemed unreliable or even entirely inauthentic by a succession of academics starting with Gustav Weil (d. 1889) and Aloys Sprenger (d. 1893), seemingly the first Western scholars to suggest that a considerable part of the corpus of *aḥādīṯ* must be regarded as spurious. The Hungarian intellectual Ignaz Goldziher (d. 1921) pioneered the first critical study of veritability, concluding that a large proportion of the *aḥādīṯ* came from a period much later than Muḥammad, and ought to be regarded as unsubstantiated. His argument was developed by Joseph Schacht (d. 1969), who proposed that at the very least, the *aḥādīṯ* dealing with legal concerns should be rejected as false. Goldziher and Schacht would be succeeded by scholars such as John Wansbrough (d. 2002) and Michael Cook (b. 1940), although some, like Nabia Abbott (d. 1981) and Fuat Sezgin (d. 2018) attempted a refutation of the Goldziherian hypothesis, while still others, including Harald Motzki (d. 2019) and Fazlur Rahman (d. 1988) sought a middle path, a synthesis of the two extremes.[108]

I have chosen, for the purposes of this study, to read these texts primarily in the manner in which they have impressed themselves upon the lives of believing Muslims, shaping and instructing faith. Even if, as some scholars propose, the ambiguous epistemological nature of the *aḥādīṯ* works is admitted by Muslim jurists, meaning that the majority engender nothing more than probability,[109] they can be and in reality still are read by countless believers whose faith is structured and informed by their content.

I have attempted, as far as possible, to present a chronological development of the stories recounted, using the primary source texts of both Sunnī and Shīʿī Islam as a way of underscoring not only the importance of dreams in the Islamic tradition, but also the

---

[107] Q. 53:27. Cf. also Q. 17:40, Q. 43:19.

[108] Cf. HALLAQ W., "The Authenticity of Prophetic Ḥadīth: a Pseudo-Problem" in *Studia Islamica* LXXXIX, 1999: 75–76.

[109] Op. cit.: 75–90.

critical impact of the Karbalā' event on Islamic history. A list of the sources will be found in the second appendix to this work.

By the time Sulaymān b. ʿAbd al-Malik b. Marwān was learning in a dream that he had won the satisfaction of the Prophet of Islam, al-Ḥusayn had been dead for only a matter of years, and the memory of Karbalā' was being kept alive in a variety of ways, such as by groups like the 'Penitents' (*tawwābūn*) who, with profound regret for their failure to support him, set out to avenge the martyr. But our story starts long before that, long before the *tawwābūn* stopped at al-Ḥusayn's Karbalā' tomb, in remorseful prayer and weeping, to the dreams al-Ḥusayn's grandfather Muḥammad would begin to have shortly before the birth of his youngest grandson.

The Shade of God. Dreams in the Prophet's Household

Not long after the birth of al-Ḥusayn, firstborn of ʿAlī b. Abī Ṭālib and his wife Fāṭima, a parturition thoroughly encased in accounts of heavenly intervention, the infant triggered a visit to his grandfather Muḥammad by the angel Ǧibrīl, fitting the pattern of a series of encounters and auguries that would continue until the Prophet's death. The stark reality of the suffering that lay ahead was in bleak contrast to the proceedings around al-Ḥusayn's birth; Fāṭima carries him in her womb for a period of only six months,[1] and God

[1] A well-attested *ḥadīṯ*, carried by many of the foremost Shīʿī transmitters, reports that Fāṭima carried al-Ḥusayn in her womb for a period of only six months: "She gave birth to him in six months: the birth of a child in six months is unheard of, except for al-Ḥusayn and ʿĪsā son of Maryam" (al-Ṭabarī., *Dalāʾil al-imāma*: 71–72, al-Kulaynī., *al-Kāfī fī ʿilm al-dīn*, vol. I, *Kitāb al-ḥuǧǧa*, bb. *Mawlid al-Ḥusayn b. ʿAlī*, n. 4: 464, Ibn Qūlawayh., *Kāmil al-ziyārāt*, bb. 16, n. 6: 125, Ibn Bābawayh., *ʿIlal al-sharāʾiʿ wa-l-aḥkām*, vol. I, bb. 156: 205, Ibn Shahrāshūb., *Manāqib āl Abī Ṭālib*, vol. III, bb.

guards her "and the one in her womb from Iblīs."[2] God also gives orders to the angels in heaven suitably to celebrate the birth of a grandson for Muḥammad.[3] However, the travail of the future is captured in a grim narrative transmitted by the Sunnī historian al-Baġdādī and by a small number of the later Shīʿī transmitters:

> On the authority of Abū al-ʿAbbās, who said: I was with the Prophet. On his left thigh he had his son Ibrāhīm and on his right thigh al-Ḥusayn b. ʿAlī. He was kissing, now the one, now the other, when Ğibrīl descended to him with a communication from the Lord of the worlds. When he had gone from him, he said: "Ğibrīl came to me from my Lord and said: Muḥammad, your Lord greets you with peace, and says to you that you cannot have both of them. Ransom one of them for his companion." The Prophet looked at Ibrāhīm and wept, and looked at al-Ḥusayn and wept. Then he said: "The mother of Ibrāhīm is a slave,[4] and when he dies, no one will grieve for

---

Manāqib Fāṭima al-zahrā': 359, vol. IV, bb. *Fī imāmat Abī ʿAbd Allāh al-Ḥusayn*: 50, al-Irbilī., *Kashf al-ġumma fī maʿrifat al-a'imma*, vol. I: 583, al-Ḥurr al-ʿĀmilī., *Tafṣīl wasā'il al-shīʿa ilā taḥṣīl masā'il al-sharīʿa*, vol. II, bb. 12, n. 2756: 502, al-Mağlisī., *Biḥār al-anwār*, vol. XIV, bb. 17, nn. 2–3: 207, vol. XXV, bb. 9, n. 15: 254, vol. XXXIX: 71, vol. XLIII, bb. 11, n. 31: 253, n. 44: 258, vol. XLIV, bb. 22: 162, bb. 26, n. 14: 198, bb. 30, n. 17: 232, vol. LXVI, bb 37: 266). Among the Sunnī, cf. al-Ṭabarī., *Ḏaḫā'ir al-ʿuqbā*, bb. 9: 206.

[2] al-Astarābāḏī., *Ta'wīl al-āyāt al-bāhira fī faḍl al-ʿitra al-ṭāhira*: 562, al-Mağlisī., *Biḥār al-anwār*, vol. XXIII, bb. 15, n. 23: 272, vol. XXXVI, bb. 39, n. 137: 108.

[3] Ibn Bābawayh., *Ikmāl (kamāl) al-dīn wa-itmām (tamām) al-niʿma fī iṯbāt al-ġayba wa-kashf al-ḥayra*, vol. I, bb. 24, n. 36: 282, al-Mağlisī., *Biḥār al-anwār*, vol. XLIII, bb. 11, n. 24: 248.

[4] All of Muḥammad's children, except for the short-lived Ibrāhīm who was born of his Coptic wife Māriyya, were born of Ḫadīğa. Cf. Ibn Saʿd., *Kitāb al-ṭabaqāt al-kabīr*, vol. X, *Ḏikr Ḫadīğa*, n. 4926: 19, al-Ḫawārizmī., *Maqtal al-Ḥusayn*, Part One, ch. 5, *Faḍā'il Fāṭima al-Zahrā' bt. rasūl Allāh*, n. 77: 130; al-Ğawzī., *Ṣifat al-ṣafwa*, vol. I, *Ḏikr awlād (Muḥammad)*: 57, al-Ḏahabī., *al-ʿIbar fī aḫbār al-bashar muntaḫab al-ta'rīḫ al-*

> him except me. But the mother of al-Ḥusayn is Fāṭima and his father is ʿAlī, son of my uncle, my flesh and blood, and when he dies my daughter will grieve, and so will ʿAlī and so will I. I prefer my grief to theirs. Ǧibrīl, take Ibrāhīm!" Thus, he ransomed (al-Ḥusayn) with Ibrāhīm. He said: He died after three days, and whenever the Prophet saw al-Ḥusayn coming, he would kiss him, hug to him to his chest, suck his teeth and say: "I have ransomed the one I have ransomed with my son Ibrāhīm."[5]

The text resonates with themes that course deeply through religious literature, like the status of a slave's offspring against that of a freeman and the ransoming of a beloved son. However, a century before al-Baġdādī, al-Masʿūdī told the story with a different accentuation; Muḥammad is to choose between the life of Ibrāhīm, who will inherit the prophecy (*nubuwwa*) after him but be killed by his community, leading God to conduct the entire community into the Fire, or al-Ḥusayn, who will be *imām* after Muḥammad and will also be killed, but this time by half of a community at odds. "I would hate the whole of my community to enter the Fire," laments

---

kabīr, vol. I: 10. When Ibrāhīm, who was born c. 9/630, died in 11/632, al-Ḥusayn, born in 4/626, would have been six years old.

[5] Among the Sunnī, cf. al-Baġdādī., *Tārīḫ Baġdād*, vol. II, n. 635: 20, Ibn al-Ǧawzī., *Kitab al-mawḍūʿāt*, vol. I, bb. *Fī faḍl al-Ḥusayn*: 406 (where he condemns it as a fiction). Cf. also Ibn Ḥanbal., *Kitāb faḍāʾil al-ṣaḥāba*, vol. II, bb. *Faḍāʾil al-Ḥasan wa-l-Ḥusayn*, n. 1409: 789 for mention of Ibrāhīm. Among the Shīʿa, cf. al-Masʿūdī., *Iṯbāt al-waṣiyya*: 165, Ibn Shahrāshūb., *Manāqib āl Abī Ṭālib*, vol. IV, Part Four, bb. *Fī imāmat Abī ʿAbd Allāh al-Ḥusayn*: 81, Ibn Namā al-Ḥillī., *Muṯīr al-aḥzān wa munīr subul al-ashğān*: 21, Ibn Ṭāʾūs., *al-Ṭarāʾif fī maʿrifat maḏāhib al-ṭawāʾif*, vol. I, Part One, n. 289: 202, al-Shāmī., *al-Durr al-naẓīm fī manāqib al-aʾimma al-lahāhīm*, bb. 5, *Fī ḏikr al-Ḥusayn b. ʿAlī*: 489, al-Ḥillī al-ʿAllāma., *Nahǧ al-ḥaqq wa-kashf al-ṣidq*: 256, *Kashf al-yaqīn fī faḍāʾil amīr al-muʾminīn*, Part Three, bb. 2: 321, al-Aḥsāʾī., *ʿAwālī al-laʾālīʾ al-ʿazīziyya fī al-aḥādīṯ al-dīniyya*, vol. IV, n. 127: 92, al-Baḥrānī., *Madīnat al-maʿāǧiz fī muʿǧizāt al-aʾimma al-aṭhār*, vol. IV, Part Four, n. 137/1084: 57, al-Maǧlisī., *Biḥār al-anwār*, vol. XXII, bb. 1, n. 7: 153, vol. XLIII, bb. 12, n. 2: 26, al-Iṣfahānī., *ʿAwālim al-ʿulūm wa-l-maʿārif al-aḥwāl min al-āyāt wa-l-aḫbār wa-l-aqwāl*, vol. XVII, ch. 17, bb. 5, n. 1: 36.

Muḥammad, "and I would love al-Ḥusayn to remain, so that Fāṭima is not bereft of him." So Ibrāhīm, son of a servant, is ransomed.

This was not Muḥammad's first engagement with Ǧibrīl over the fate of his grandson al-Ḥusayn.[6] Both al-Ḫawārizmī and Ibn Ṭā'ūs carry a rare *ḥadīṯ* describing an incident within a year of al-Ḥusayn's birth:

> A full year after the birth of al-Ḥusayn, twelve angels came down to the Messenger of God. One of them was in the form of a lion, the second in the form of a bull, the third in the form of a dragon, the fourth in the form of a human, and the remaining eight in various forms. Their faces were red, their eyes wet with tears, and having spread their wings they said: "Muḥammad, what befell Hābīl (Abel) through Qābīl (Cain) will befall your child al-Ḥusayn, son of Fāṭima; he will receive the same recompense as Hābīl, and his killers will bear the same responsibility as Qābīl." There was not in the heavens an angel drawn near[7] who did not come down to the Prophet, each of them greeting him and consoling him about al-Ḥusayn. They informed him about the reward he would receive and showed him his tomb, and the Prophet said: "God, forsake those who forsake him and kill those who kill him."[8]

In his *Muṯīr al-aḥzān*, Ibn Namā al-Ḥillī describes another encounter which, going by the dates of Ibrāhīm's ransoming, had taken place a full four years before Ibrāhīm's death:

---

[6] As noted by Ibn Isḥāq in his *Sīra*, there were encounters outside of an Ḥusaynian context too, such as Muḥammad's dream of Ǧibrīl holding a horse's rein on the eve of the Battle of Badr, a vision which helped to lift the gloom of Abū Bakr: cf. GUILLAUME A., *The Life of Muhammad. A Translation of Ishāq's Sīrat Rasūl Allāh*, Oxford University Press, Oxford 2006: 300.

[7] The 'angels drawn near' are named in the Qur'ān as the *muqarrabūn*. Cf. Q. 4: 172, where Pickthall renders the word as 'favoured'.

[8] al-Ḫawārizmī., *Maqtal al-Ḥusayn*, Part One, bb. *Aḫbār rasūl Allāh ʿan al-Ḥusayn wa-aḥwāli-hi*, n. 12: 237, Ibn Ṭā'ūs., *Kitāb al-luhūf fī qatlā al-ṭufūf*: 13–14, al-Maǧlisī., *Biḥār al-anwār*, vol. XLIV, bb. 30, n. 46: 246.

> When [al-Ḥusayn] was two years old, the Prophet left on a journey. He stopped on the way and proclaimed «*Lo! we are Allah's and lo! unto Him we are returning*»[9] and his eyes filled with tears. He was questioned about this, and he said: "Ǧabra'īl informs me about a land on the bank of the Euphrates, called Karbalā' and in which my son al-Ḥusayn will be killed. It is as if I am seeing him and the site of his death and place of his burial in it. It is as if I am seeing the captured on the humps of mounts and the head of my son al-Ḥusayn presented to Yazīd, may God curse him. By God, no one will look at the head of al-Ḥusayn and rejoice, but that God will cause divergence between his heart and his tongue and torture him with a painful torment."[10]

This narrative continues at length; a distraught Muḥammad returns from his journey, mounts the pulpit with al-Ḥasan and al-Ḥusayn and, praising them as the finest of his descendants, makes reference to the information he has received from Ǧibrīl about both being murdered. He prays that their martyrdom will be a blessing, but that no blessing will accrue to those who fail them; rather, he asks the deepest part of Hell for the perpetrators. When the gathering responds with weeping, he chastises the people for their failure to act, in spite of their display of grief. In most narratives, the martyrdom of al-Ḥusayn clearly overshadows the murder (and thus martyrdom) of his older brother al-Ḥasan; on this occasion, the two brothers are held up together by their grandfather. At this point, the famous *ḥadīṯ al-ṯaqalayn* (the 'two weighty matters'), so crucial to the Shīʿa, is introduced into the narrative. This *ḥadīṯ* has been narrated through a number of rigorously authenticated chains among

---

[9] Q. 2:156, the famous *al-istirǧāʿ*, traditionally recited upon hearing of someone's death.

[10] Ibn Ṭā'ūs., *Kitāb al-luhūf fī qatlā al-ṭufūf*: 14–15, Ibn Namā al-Ḥillī., *Muṯīr al-aḥzān wa munīr subul al-ashǧān*: 18, al-Maǧlisī., *Biḥār al-anwār*, vol. XLIV, bb. 30, n. 46: 248–249, al-Iṣfahānī., *ʿAwālim al-ʿulūm wa-l-maʿārif al-aḥwāl min al-āyāt wa-l-aḫbār wa-l-aqwāl*, vol. XVII, ch. 11, bb. 2, n. 1: 117. This is a fate similar to the one with which Ǧibrīl will threaten al-Ḥusayn's killers (cf. Ibn Qūlawayh., *Kāmil al-ziyārāt*, bb. 17, n. 7: 131).

the Shīʿa and the Sunnī, although, granted that all the narrations are basically the same in their essentials, the wording and setting differs from narrator to narrator.[11] The setting is usually at ʿArafāt during Muḥammad's 'Farewell Pilgrimage', or at Ġadīr Ḫumm on the way back from that Pilgrimage. Sometimes, the setting changes to the mosque at Medina or Muḥammad's bedroom during his last illness. Shīʿī scholars insist upon at least four occasions, all within the space of ninety days and pertaining to Muḥammad's last days, on which he publicly proclaimed the *ḥadīṯ*, so that it does not fit comfortably into this narrative, which, going by al-Ḥusayn's age, occurs some four years before the death of the Prophet.

More precise information is given about Karbalāʾ in the course of a long account of an encounter with Ǧibrīl that takes place while Muḥammad is eating a meal served by Fāṭima in her house. It is narrated by Umm Ayman, but unlike other transmis-

---

[11] Muslim., *Ṣaḥīḥ*, vol. IV, bk. 44 (*Kitāb faḍāʾil al-ṣaḥāba*), bb. 4 *Faḍāʾil ʿAlī b. Abī Ṭālib*, n. 36: 1873. Cf. also Ibn Ḥanbal., *Musnad*, vol. IV, *Musnad Abī Saʿīd al-Ḫudarī*, n. 11104: 30, n. 11131: 26–27, n. 11212: 54, vol. V, *Ḥadīṯ Zayd b. Arqam*, n. 19285: 75, al-Tirmiḏī., *al-Ǧāmiʿ al-ṣaḥīḥ*, vol. IX, bk. 50 (*Kitāb al-manāqib*), *Manāqib ahl bayt al-nabī*, bb. 77, n. 3788: 340–341, n. 7390: 342, al-Nasāʾī., *al-Sunan al-kubrā*, bk. 76 (*Kitāb al-manāqib)*, bb. 4, *Faḍāʾil ʿAlī*, n. 8148, al-Ḥākim al-Nīsābūrī., *Kitāb al-mustadrak ʿalā al-ṣaḥīḥayn*, vol. III, Part Three, bk. 31 (*Kitāb maʿrifat al-ṣaḥāba*), *Manāqib ahl bayt rasūl Allāh*, n. 4774: 173–174, vol. III, Part Three, bk. 31 (*Kitāb maʿrifat al-ṣaḥāba*), *Manāqib amīr al-muʾminīn ʿAlī b. Abī Ṭālib*, n. 4641: 126–127, al-Baġdādī., *Taʾrīḫ Baġdād*, vol. VIII, n. 4551: 442, Ibn ʿIyāḍ., *Ikmāl al-muʿlim sharḥ ṣaḥīḥ Muslim*, vol. VII, bk. 44 (*Kitāb faḍāʾil al-ṣaḥāba*), bb. 4, *Min faḍāʾil ʿAlī b. Abī Ṭālib*, nn. 36–37: 416–418, al-Ḫawārizmī., *Maqtal al-Ḥusayn*, Part One, ch. 6, *Faḍāʾil al-Ḥasan wa-l-Ḥusayn*, n. 47: 156, Ibn Taymiyya., *Minhāǧ al-sunna al-nabawiyya fī naqḍ kalām al-shīʿa wa-l-qadariyya*, vol. IV: 85, al-Tibrīzī., *Mishkāt al-maṣābīḥ*, vol. III, bk. 30 (*Kitāb al-manāqib*), bb. 10 *Manāqib ʿAlī b Abī Ṭālib*, n. 6131: 1732, al-Mizzī., *Tahḏīb al-kamāl fī asmāʾ al-riǧāl*, vol. X, n. 2098: 50–51, Ibn Kaṯīr., *al-Bidāya wa-l-nihāya*, vol. VII, bb. *Faṣl fī ḫurūǧ al-nabī*: 668, al-Hayṯamī., *Maǧmaʿ al-zawāʾid wa-manbaʿ al-fawāʾid*, vol. IX, Part Nine, bb. *Fī faḍl ahl al-bayt*: 162–163, al-ʿIṣāmī., *Simṭ al-nuǧūm al-ʿawālī*, vol. II, bb. 7, Part Three: 503, al-Ṣabbān., *Isʿāf al-rāġibīn* in the margins of *Nūr al-abṣār fī manāqib āl bayt al-nabī al-muḫtār*: 143.

sions of this intersection between Ǧibrīl and Muḥammad, the food is cooked by Fāṭima. Muḥammad eats, washes, looks penetratingly at the members of the family (ʿAlī, Fāṭima, al-Ḥasan and al-Ḥusayn), falls into prayer and prostration, weeps, expresses his delight in them and then, in answer to Fāṭima's puzzlement, explains the rendezvous with an angel no one else had seen. Amid dire predictions of al-Ḥusayn's death, Ǧibrīl speaks of the place of his martyrdom; it is, he says, a land on the bank of the Euphrates, named Karbalāʾ "because distress (*karb*) and tribulation (*balāʾ*) will increase on the part of your enemies and the enemies of your descendants, on that day distress of which will never cease, and the grief of which will never be extinguished." The angel goes on to extol the merits of the place; Karbalāʾ is, he says, "the purest of the places of the earth and its sanctity the greatest, and certainly it is part of the valley (*al-baṭḥāʾ*) of the Garden."[12]

From the time that Fāṭima conceives her son al-Ḥusayn until the time of his own death, Muḥammad will find himself on numerous occasions accosted by angels, concerned that he know his grandson's standing and fate. A number of these, as we shall see, have as their locus the home of Umm Salama; but they take place in other situations too. At the very moment of his grandson's conception, Muḥammad is the recipient of grave tidings which he must pass on to his daughter:

> When Fāṭima became pregnant with al-Ḥusayn, Ǧibraʾīl went to the Messenger of God and said: "Fāṭima will give birth to a boy, whom your community after you will kill." When Fāṭima was pregnant with al-Ḥusayn, she was reluctant in carrying him and when she gave birth to him, she was reluctant at his birth. Then Abū ʿAbd Allāh said: "Never in the world has a mother been seen to give birth to a boy with such reluctance, but she was reluctant after having learned that he will be killed." He continued: "And this verse came down about her: «*And We*

---

[12] Ibn Qūlawayh., *Kāmil al-ziyārāt*, bb. 88: 447 (although the narrative is not part of the original text, but an addendum put there by one of the author's students, al-Ḥusayn b. Muġīra), al-Maǧlisī., *Biḥār al-anwār*, vol. XLV, bb. 39, n. 30: 181–182.

> *have commended unto man kindness toward parents. His mother beareth him with reluctance, and bringeth him forth with reluctance, and the bearing of him and the weaning of him is thirty months*»."[13]

In a more detailed version of the narrative, Muḥammad remonstrates with Ğibrīl, and Fāṭima with Muḥammad:

> Ğibraʾīl descended to Muḥammad and said to him: "Muḥammad, God extends peace to you and announces to you a child who will be born of Fāṭima and whom your community after you will kill." He replied: "Ğibraʾīl, peace to my Lord, I have no need of a child who will be born of Fāṭima, and whom my community after me will kill!" The narrator went on: Ğibraʾīl ascended: then he descended and said the same thing to him. He replied: "Ğibraʾīl, peace to my Lord, I have no need of a child who will be born of Fāṭima, and whom my community after me will kill!" Ğibraʾīl ascended to heaven: then he descended and said to him: "Muḥammad, your Lord extends peace to you and announces to you that He is the one who sets in his descendants the Imamate (*imāma*), the sovereignty (*walāya*) and the testament (*waṣiyya*)." He replied: "I am satisfied." Then he sent word to Fāṭima: "God has announced to me a child who will born of you, and whom my community after me will kill." Fāṭima sent word back to him: "I have no need of a child born of me, whom your community after you will kill." He sent word to her: "God has placed in his descendants the Imamate, the sovereignty and the testament." She sent word back to him: "I am satisfied." And «[she] *beareth*

---

[13] Q. 46:15, although only part of the verse is quoted. I have followed Pickthall in rendering the verb *karaha-yakrahu* as 'reluctance' although in reality it carries a much stronger sense of 'to loathe', 'to hate' or 'to feel disgust'. Cf. al-Kulaynī., *al-Kāfī fī ʿilm al-dīn*, vol. I, *Kitāb al-ḥuǧǧa*, bb. *Mawlid al-Ḥusayn b. ʿAlī*, n. 3: 464, Ibn Qūlawayh., *Kāmil al-ziyārāt*, bb. 16, n. 4: 122, Ibn Shahrāshūb., *Manāqib āl Abī Ṭālib*, vol. IV, bb. *Fī imāmat Abī ʿAbd Allāh al-Ḥusayn*: 57, al-Astarābādī., *Taʾwīl al-āyāt al-ẓāhira fī faḍl al-ʿitra al-ṭāhira*: 563, al-Mağlisī., *Biḥār al-anwār*, vol. XLIII, bb. 11, n. 21: 246, n. 31: 253, vol. XLIV, bb. 30, n. 16: 231, vol. LIII, bb. 29, n. 126: 102, vol. LXVI, bb. 37: 266.

> *him with reluctance, and bringeth him forth with reluctance, and the bearing of him and the weaning of him is thirty months, till, when he attaineth full strength and reacheth forty years, he saith: My Lord! Arouse me that I may give thanks for the favour wherewith Thou hast favoured me and my parents, and that I may do right acceptable unto Thee. And be gracious unto me in the matter of my seed».*[14]

A third version of the narrative[15] expresses a flurry of movement on the part of Ǧibrīl in response to Muḥammad's baulking at the prospect of a murdered child; the angel ascends swiftly to heaven, and returns a second time with a comparable announcement. Meeting with the same dissent, Ǧibrīl speeds away a second time and then swoops down a third time with a disclosure akin to the first two, but now qualified by the decisive concept of *waṣiyya* (but not, as in other versions, *walāya* or *imāma*).[16] Muḥammad finally assents

---

[14] Q. 46:15, although only part of the verse is quoted. Cf. al-Kulaynī., *al-Kāfī fī ʿilm al-dīn*, vol. I, *Kitāb al-ḥuǧǧa*, bb. *Mawlid al-Ḥusayn b. ʿAlī*, n. 4: 464, Ibn Qūlawayh., *Kāmil al-ziyārāt*, bb. 16, n. 6: 123–124, Ibn Bābawayh., *ʿIlal al-sharāʾiʿ wa-l-aḥkām*, vol. I, bb. 156, n. 3: 205, Ibn Shahrāshūb., *Manāqib āl Abī Ṭālib*, vol. IV, bb. *Fī imāmat Abī ʿAbd Allāh al-Ḥusayn*: 62–63, al-Astarābāḏī., *Taʾwīl al-āyāt al-ẓāhira fī faḍl al-ʿitra al-ṭāhira*: 562–563, al-Maǧlisī., *Biḥār al-anwār*, vol. XXIII, bb. 15, n. 23: 272, vol. XXV, bb. 9, n. 15: 254, vol. XLIII, bb. 11, n. 20: 245, vol. XLIV, bb. 30, n. 17: 232.

[15] Ibn Qūlawayh., *Kāmil al-ziyārāt*, bb. 16, n. 5: 122–123, al-Baḥrānī., *al-Burhān fī tafsīr al-qurʾān*, vol. V, Part Five, *sūrat al-Aḥqāf*, n. 9776: 41, al-Maǧlisī., *Biḥār al-anwār*, vol. XLIV, bb. 30, n. 18: 233, al-Iṣfahānī., *ʿAwālim al-ʿulūm wa-l-maʿārif al-aḥwāl min al-āyāt wa-l-aḫbār wa-l-aqwāl*, vol. XVII, Part Seventeen, ch. 11, bb. 1, n. 3: 115.

[16] Three frustratingly difficult to synopsize technical terms from Shīʿī theology. Simply put, the term *imāma* signifies the Imamate, that divinely-appointed line of leaders over the House of Islam who succeed Muḥammad in a sort of apostolic succession, but whose legitimacy is rejected outside of Shīʿī Islam (and whose number is disputed among the various groupings within Shīʿī Islam). According to Haider, the term *walāya* makes reference to the bond that Shīʿī Muslims feel with that line of leaders, while *wilāya* refers to the leaders' exercise of authority (HAIDER N., *Shīʾi Islam: An Introduction*, Cambridge University Press, New York 2014: 32). Finally, *waṣiyya* indicates the 'bequest' or 'testament'

and takes the news to Fāṭima, who refuses it on its first telling but acquiesces the second time at the explanation of *waṣiyya*. This, notes the text, is the occasion of the revelation of Q. 46: 15.

In recounting Ǧibrīl's first return to heaven, all the transmitters except for al-Maǧlisī employ the 8th form verb *intahaḍa* which, as distinct from the 1st form *nahaḍa-yanhaḍu* (meaning simply 'to rise') has a stronger sense of quitting a place, of rising and hastening away and, when used of a bird (and so conceivably of an angel) of spreading the wings and flying.[17] Ǧibrīl's second return to heaven is expressed by all the transmitters with the 7th form verb *inʿaraǧa*, with its sense of turning from something, of leaving and forsaking it.[18] Ǧibrīl's third descent to Muḥammad is illustrated with the verb *inqaḍḍa*, also in 7th form and the verb which al-Maǧlisī alone uses for the angel's first ascent to heaven; the word means 'to swoop down', 'to rush', 'to hurl oneself' or 'to drop suddenly'.[19] The use of these verbs rather than the more usual ones to describe Ǧibrīl's movements between heaven and earth provides the text with the sense of an angel hastening, of Ǧibrīl's alertness to a message not fully delivered until consent is given to its contents (consonant with sentiments expressed in Q. 5:67: «*O Messenger! Make known that which hath been revealed unto thee from thy Lord, for if thou do it not, thou wilt not have conveyed His message*»).

There is a further occasion on which Muḥammad engages Ǧibrīl in conversation, pleading with him rather than merely responding to his questions or asking to see some physical evidence of Karbalāʾ. The encounter in chronicled by Ibn ʿAsākir:

> On the authority of Muḥammad b. Ṣāliḥ, that the Messenger of God, when Ǧibrīl informed him that his community would kill

---

to which ʿAlī and his descendants, as Muḥammad's appointed successors, are the heir.

[17] Cf. WEHR H., *A Dictionary of Modern Written Arabic*, 1980: 117, LANE E.W., *An Arabic-English Lexicon*, vol. VIII, 1968: 2860.

[18] Cf. WEHR H., *A Dictionary of Modern Written Arabic*, 1980: 704, LANE E.W., *An Arabic-English Lexicon*, vol. V, 1968: 1996.

[19] Cf. WEHR H., *A Dictionary of Modern Written Arabic*, 1980: 902, LANE E.W., *An Arabic-English Lexicon*, vol. VII, 1968: 2536.

Ḥusayn b. ʿAlī, said: "Ǧibrīl, can I not countermand it for him?" He answered: "No, it is a command already written by God."[20]

Ibn Qūlawayh transmits a shorter tradition, with scant detail, concerning Fāṭima's reaction to her father's encounter with Ǧibrīl; going to him, she finds his eyes full of tears and upon asking the reason is informed of Ǧibrīl's descent and his dire foretelling of al-Ḥusayn's fate. "She became anxious and it was burdensome for her," reads the text, "but he informed her of who among her offspring would exercise power, and she felt happy and was at peace."[21]

It is in the house of ʿAlī and Fāṭima that a significant encounter takes places, on the occasion of a family meal with food (usually a plate of traditional soup called *ḥarīra*) provided by Umm Ayman or cooked by Fāṭima herself. It is found twice in al-Mağlisī,[22] while in *Kāmil al-ziyārāt* it appears as an addendum to the chapter entitled *Karbalāʾ wa ziyārat al-Ḥusayn.*[23] The context is an *apologia* by the fourth Imām ʿAlī b. al-Ḥusayn in favour of visitation of the tombs of the holy ones (*ziyāra*). He is relating a story that Umm Ayman told to Zaynab bt. ʿAlī. In his *Kāmil al-ziyārāt*, Ibn Qūlawayh presents two versions aside from the addendum, both narrated by ʿAlī

[20] Ibn ʿAsākir., *Tārīḫ madīnat Dimashq*, vol. XIV, bb. 1566 (*al-Ḥusayn b. ʿAlī b. Abī Ṭālib b. ʿAbd al-Muṭṭalib b. Hāshim b. ʿAbd al-Manāf*):197.

[21] Ibn Qūlawayh., *Kāmil al-ziyārāt*, bb. 16, n. 8: 125, al-Mağlisī., *Biḥār al-anwār*, vol. XLIV, bb. 30, n. 19: 233–234.

[22] al-Mağlisī., *Biḥār al-anwār*, vol. XXVIII, bb. 2, n. 23: 58–60, vol. XLV, bb. 39, n. 30: 180–181. Cf. also al-Iṣfahānī., *ʿAwālim al-ʿulūm wa-l-maʿārif al-aḥwāl min al-āyāt wa-l-aḫbār wa-l-aqwāl*, vol. XVII, Part Seventeen, ch. 16, bb. 2, n. 2: 363.

[23] Ibn Qūlawayh., *Kāmil al-ziyārāt*, bb. 88: 444–445: "An augmentation of the text which we have transmitted as we found it," remarks the editor. As al-Mağlisī's editor notes, this *ḥadīṯ* was acquired in Egypt (on the authority of Muzāḥim b. ʿAbd al-Wāriṯ al-Baṣrī) by al-Ḥusayn b. Aḥmad al-Muġīra, the pupil of Ibn Qūlawayh, the same who added an addendum to his teacher's work containing a *ḥadīṯ* about a threefold descent of Ǧibrīl. Al-Muġīra had attempted to persuade Ibn Qūlawayh to insert it this *ḥadīṯ* into his book, but he would not.

b. Abī Ṭālib, one going back to the fifth Imām and one to the fourth. Both take place in the house of ʿAlī and Fāṭima, and in both it is al-Ḥusayn who interrogates his grandfather about his deportment. In the following version, Umm Ayman is present and narrating, at times inserting herself into the text, and it is ʿAlī and Fāṭima, rather than the boy al-Ḥusayn, who interrogate Muḥammad:

> (Zaynab) said: Umm Ayman told me that the Messenger of God visited the house of Fāṭima one day, and she made *ḥarīra* for him, while ʿAlī brought him a plate of dates. Then Umm Ayman said: I brought them a bowl of milk and butter; the Messenger of God, ʿAlī, Fāṭima, al-Ḥasan and al-Ḥusayn all ate of the *ḥarīra*. Then the Messenger of God drank, and they all drank the milk, and the Messenger of God ate and they all ate of the dates with the butter.

The precursory lines establish the presence of the five core members of the People of the House (Muḥammad, ʿAlī, Fāṭima, al-Ḥasan and al-Ḥusayn) for an important disclosure, reminiscent of the crucial 'tradition of the cloak' (*ḥadīṯ al-kisāʾ*) and the revelation of Q. 33:33. In some narrations of that *ḥadīṯ*, the five core members are in the house of Umm Salama; Umm Salama narrates the tradition, but remains carefully differentiated from the five.[24] Here, the house is Fāṭima's and the narrator is Umm Ayman, who is not a core member of the family:

> After that, the Messenger of God washed his hands with water poured by ʿAlī; having washed his hands, he wiped his face and then looked ʿAlī, Fāṭima, al-Ḥasan and al-Ḥusayn with a look

---

[24] Cf. for e.g. Ibn Ḥanbal., *Musnad*, vol. I, *Musnad ʿAbd Allāh b. al-ʿAbbās b. ʿAbd al-Muṭṭalib*, n. 3062: 708–709, vol. VI, *Ḥadīṯ Wāṯala b. al-ʿAsqaʿ*, n. 16985: 45, vol. X, *Ḥadīṯ Umm Salama*, n. 26570: 177, n. 26612: 186–187, n. 26659: 197, n. 26808: 228, al-Ṭabarī., *Ǧāmiʿ al-bayān ʿan taʾwīl al-qurʾān*, vol. XXII, Part Twenty-Two, *Sūrat al-aḥzāb*, v. 33: 6–7, Ibn al-Aṯīr., *Usd al-ġāba fī maʿrifat al-ṣaḥāba*, vol. V, bb. *Ḥarf al-fāʾ*: 521–522, al-Suyūṭī., *al-Durr al-manṯūr fī al-tafsīr bi-l-maʾṯūr*, vol. V, *Sūrat al-aḥzāb*, v. 33: 376.

> in which we plainly recognized the joy on his face. He gazed towards the heavens for a long time, and then turned his face towards the *qibla* and extended his hands in supplication. Then he sunk down, choked with weeping, in prostration, and prolonged the sobbing, his voice ringing out and his tears flowing. He lifted his head and bowed towards the ground, his tears flowing like pouring rain.

The angel, approaching Muḥammad during a post-meal prayer, is unseen by the others; only in rare cases, such as that of Ibn ʿAbbās, is the angel's visitation witnessed by others present at the time:

> Fāṭima, ʿAlī, al-Ḥasan and al-Ḥusayn grieved, and I grieved with them, when we saw the Messenger of God, but we were too afraid to question him until this had lasted for some time. Then ʿAlī and Fāṭima said to him: "What is causing you to weep, Messenger of God? May God not cause your eyes to weep! But seeing you in this state has wounded our hearts!" He answered: "My brother, I was so happy with you all" – Muzāḥim b. ʿAbd al-Wārīt said at this point in his *ḥadīṯ*: He said: "My beloved! I was happy with you with a happiness the likes of which I have never felt before! I looked at you and praised God for His favour to me through you."

Umm Ayman's words "and I grieved with them" once again carefully differentiates her from the immediate family. Here, ʿAlī and Fāṭima interrogate Muḥammad together; in the other two versions, it is the boy al-Ḥusayn who crawls into his grandfather's lap and asks the reason for his tears:

> Assuredly I was looking at you and praising God for His favour to me through you, when Ǧibrīl descended to me and said: "Muḥammad! God, Blessed and Most High is acquainted with what is in your soul and knows your delight in your brother, your daughter and your grandsons, and has completed the favour for you and gladdened you with this gift; that He has put them and their descendants and those who love them and their *shīʿa* with you in the Garden, with no distinction between you and them. They will live as you live, receive as you

> receive until you are more than satisfied.[25] In the world they will be dealt much tribulation, with adversities afflicted upon them at the hands of a people who arrogate to themselves your faith community (*milla*) and pretend that they are of your community (*umma*), although removed from God and from you. Beaten and killed, the places where they are killed will be scattered, their graves remote, a favour from God for them and for you in them. Praise God, great and powerful for His choice and be satisfied with His divine decree!" I praised God and consented to His divine decree in what He had chosen for them. Then Ǧibraʾīl said: "Muḥammad! Your brother will be oppressed after you, defeated by your community, worn out by your enemies and them murdered after you, killed by the most evil of creatures and of the universe and the most wretched of creation, like the slaughtering of the camel,[26] in a land to which he will emigrate and which will be the place in which his *shīʿa* and the *shīʿa* of his offspring is planted and in which, in every case, their tribulation will increase and their afflictions become greater."

At this point, with a sweep of the hand, the angel turns his attention upon al-Ḥusayn:

> And this grandson of yours – with his hand he gestured at al-Ḥusayn – will be killed among a band of your descendants, of the people of your house and of the best of your community on the bank of the Euphrates, in a land called Karbalāʾ, because distress (*karb*) and tribulation (*balāʾ*) will increase on the

---

[25] al-Mağlisī, *Biḥār al-anwār*, vol. XXVIII, bb. 2, n. 23: 58–60, vol. XLV, bb. 39, n. 30: 180–181, al-Iṣfahānī., *ʿAwālim al-ʿulūm wa-l-maʿārif al-aḥwāl min al-āyāt wa-l-aḫbār wa-l-aqwāl*, vol. XVII, Part Seventeen, ch. 16, bb. 2, n. 2: 363. In *Kāmil al-ziyārāt*, it appears as an appendix to bb. 88 *(Karbalāʾ wa ziyārat al-Ḥusayn)*.

[26] It was to the avaricious and irreligious people of Ṯamūd that God sent the prophet Ṣāliḥ. These demanded a sign, to which God responded with a special camel, and which the people, led by nine especially wicked men, hamstrung and killed, suffering severe consequences for their action. Cf. Q. 7:73–78, Q. 27:45–51, Q. 11:64–65.

> part of your enemies and the enemies of your descendants on the day whose distress will never cease and whose grief will never be extinguished. It is the purest of the places of the earth and its sanctity the greatest, and certainly it is part of the valley (*al-baṭḥāʾ*) of the Garden.

In the other two versions, narrated by ʿAlī b. Abī Ṭālib, it is the young boy al-Ḥusayn who plays a central part and, since the text is a justification of the future visits to the martyrs' tombs, these *ziyārāt* predominate the narrative:[27]

> On the authority of Abū Ǧaʿfar, who said: The Commander of the Faithful said: The Messenger of God visited us and Umm Ayman had presented us with milk, butter and dates. We offered some of it and he ate. Then he went to the corner of the house and prayed some *rakaʿāt*; when he was in the last of his prostrations he wept bitterly, but not one of us questioned him, for the sake of deference and awe of him. Then al-Ḥusayn crawled onto his lap and said to him: "Father, you came to our house, and nothing pleased us as much as your coming; then you wept in a manner that distressed us! What is making you weep?" He replied: "My son, Ǧibraʾīl came to me just now and informed me that you will all be killed, and that the places where you are killed will be scattered." He answered: "Father, what is there for whoever visits our graves, scattered as they are?" He replied: "My son, for those groups from my community who visit you and thereby seek blessing, it is meet that I come to them on the Day of Resurrection and save them from the horrors of the Hour, from their sins, and God will settle them in the Garden."[28]

In the second, the text follows the previous one, but with a slightly expanded ending as Muḥammad addresses al-Ḥusayn:

---

[27] Ibn Qūlawayh., *Kāmil al-ziyārāt*, bb. 16, nn. 9, 10: 125–127, al-Mağlisī., *Biḥār al-anwār*, vol. XLIV, bb. 30, nn. 20, 21: 234–235.

[28] Ibn Qūlawayh., *Kāmil al-ziyārāt*, bb. 16, n. 9: 125–126, al-Mağlisī., *Biḥār al-anwār*, vol. XLIV, bb. 30, n. 20: 234.

"My son, I looked at you all today and I was more delighted with you than I have ever been before. Then Ǧibraʾīl descended to me and informed me that you would all be killed and that the places where you are killed will be scattered. I gave praise to God for that and asked of Him the best for you!" He said: "My father, who will visit our graves and be mindful of them, scattered as they are?" He replied: "Groups from my community will desire, by that means, my charity and my kinship. I will be mindful of them in the place of standing, take them by their shoulders and save them from its horrors and adversities."

Shayḫ al-Mufīd relates the same incident, greatly reduced in detail and with no reference to any angelic visit. Muḥammad is sitting one day with ʿAlī, Fāṭima, al-Ḥasan and al-Ḥusayn, and begins talking to them about their deaths and their graves being isolated from one another. He in turn is interrogated by al-Ḥusayn about the manner of their death, and upon hearing that they will be unjustly killed, asks the identity of the killers. "The most malicious of the people," replies Muḥammad and then assures him, in answer to a further question, that their graves will be visited by a group (*ṭāʾifa*) of his community, seeking the Prophet's charity (*birr*) and kinship (*ṣila*). On the Day of Resurrection, he would take them by the arms and save them from the terrors of that day.[29]

Ibn Qūlawayh traces a further incident in the house back to Ǧaʿfar al-Ṣādiq:

While the Messenger of God was in the house of Fāṭima, with al-Ḥusayn on his lap, he began to weep and fell to the ground prostrating. Then he said: "Fāṭima! Daughter of Muḥammad! The Most High, the Highest appeared to me in your house in this hour in a most beautiful form[30] and most goodly appear-

[29] al-Mufīd., *al-Irshād fī maʿrifat ḥuǧaǧ Allāh ʿalā al-ʿibād*, vol. II, bb. *Tārīḫ al-Imām al-Ḥusayn*: 131.

[30] For a Sunnī discussion of Muḥammad seeing God in 'a most beautiful form' (*fī aḥsan ṣūra*) during his 'night journey', cf. Ibn Kaṯīr., *Tafsīr al-qurʾān al-ʿaẓīm*, vol. VI, *sūrat Ṣād*, vv. 65–70: 84, *sūrat al-Naǧm*, vv.

ance, and said to me: Muḥammad! Do you love al-Ḥusayn? I replied: Yes! The consolation of my eye, my sweet basil,[31] the fruit of my heart and the skin between my eyes! Then he said to me: Muḥammad – and he laid his hand on al-Ḥusayn's head – blessed from birth, upon him My blessings, My benedictions, My mercy, My satisfaction! My curse, My displeasure, My torture, My ignominy and My punishment on whoever killed him, was hostile to him, made an enemy of him, fought him. For he is the master of the martyrs, among the first and the last in the world and the Hereafter, and master, among all the creatures, of the youths among the inhabitants of the Garden. His father is better than him and excellent. Convey peace to him and announce to him that he is the banner of guidance, the lighthouse of My holy ones, mindful of Me, My witness over My creation, the treasurer of My knowledge and My proof over the inhabitants of the heavens and the earths and the two communities[32] of *ǧinn* and mankind."[33]

As already noted, only on rare occasions in the Jewish and Christian Scriptures is God Himself held to appear in a dream; in the Book of Genesis, He is said to have appeared to King Abimelech (Gen. 20:3), to Jacob (Gen. 28:13), and to Laban (Gen. 31:24), while the First Book of Kings records an appearance to Solomon (1 Kgs. 3:5). More commonly, He communicates through an angel. In Gen. 31:11, for example, the same Jacob who had seen God in a

5–18: 448–449, al-Suyūṭī., *al-Durr al-manṯūr fī al-tafsīr bi-l-maʿṯūr*, vol. V, *sūrat Ṣād*, vv. 67–70: 596–597, vol. VI, *sūrat al-Naǧm*, vv. 5–18: 159.

[31] Muḥammad's daughter Fāṭima is named 'the sweet basil of the Prophet' (*rayḥānat al-nabī*), and also 'the mother of the two sweet basils' (*umm al-rayḥānatayn*), pet names given to al-Ḥasan and al-Ḥusayn. Cf. CLOHESSY C., *Fāṭima, Daughter of Muḥammad*, 2018: 298, 300.

[32] Lane notes that *ṯaqalayn* refers to the *ǧinn* and mankind, two communities which, by their acumen, excel all other animate beings. Cf. LANE E.W., *An Arabic-English Lexicon*, vol. I, 1968: 344.

[33] Ibn Qūlawayh., *Kāmil al-ziyārāt*, bb. 21, n. 1: 141–142, bb. 22, n. 6: 147–148, al-Maǧlisī., *Biḥār al-anwār*, vol. XLIV, bb. 30, n. 29: 238, al-Iṣfahānī., *ʿAwālim al-ʿulūm wa-l-maʿārif al-aḥwāl min al-āyāt wa-l-aḫbār wa-l-aqwāl*, vol. XVII, Part Seventeen, ch. 11, bb. 7, n. 2: 132.

dream three chapters earlier, is now said to see God's angel. In Islam, the prevailing opinion among the textual editors is that this 'most beautiful form' spoken of by Muḥammad is in fact Ǧibrīl, the same who, notes the Qur'ān with physiological precision, had assumed for Maryam the likeness of a 'perfect man' (Q. 19:17). "That is, God's messenger Ǧibrīl," notes the editor of *Kāmil al-ziyārāt*, "or some sort of apparition." In his *al-Ǧāmiʿ al-ṣaḥīḥ*, al-Tirmiḏī has two *aḥādīṯ* in which Muḥammad claims to have seen his Lord in the 'most beautiful form';[34] in the same work, al-Tirmiḏī carries a strongly worded *ḥadīṯ* from ʿĀʾisha denying that Muḥammad ever actually saw God, and insisting that what he saw was Ǧibrīl.[35] In spite of those *aḥādīṯ* texts that tell of God appearing to Muḥammad in the 'most beautiful form',[36] and even those that suggest Muḥammad felt the coldness of God's hand on his back,[37] the narratives that speak of Ǧibrīl (rather than God) appearing to Muḥammad in the 'most beautiful form'[38] as well as the Islamic

---

[34] al-Tirmiḏī., *al-Ǧāmiʿ al-ṣaḥīḥ*, vol. I, bk. 44 (*Abwāb tasfīr al-qurʾān*), bb. 38, nn. 3233, 3234, 3235: 540–540.

[35] Op. cit., bb. 6, n. 3068: 378–379.

[36] al-Daylami., *Aʿlām al-dīn fī ṣifāt al-muʾminīn*: 146, al-Māzandarānī., *Sharḥ uṣūl al-Kāfī*, vol. II: 453.

[37] al-Qummī., *Tafsīr*, vol. II, *sūrat Ṣād*: 244, al-Qāḍī al-Nuʿmān., *Sharḥ al-aḫbār fī faḍāʾil al-aʾimma al-aṭhār*, vol. I, Part Four, n. 241: 398, Ibn al-Ḥadīd., *Sharḥ nahǧ al-balāġa*, vol. III, bb. 49: 226, al-Māzandarānī., *Sharḥ uṣūl al-Kāfī*, vol. II: 453, al-Fayḍ al-Kāshānī., *Tafsīr al-ṣāfī*, vol. IV, *sūrat Ṣād*: 309, al-Baḥrānī., *al-Burhān fī tafsīr al-qurʾān*, vol. IV, *sūrat Ṣād*, n. 9135: 682, al-Maǧlisī., *Biḥār al-anwār*, vol. XIII, bb. 16, n. 10: 402, vol. XVIII, bb. 3, n. 79: 373, al-Madanī., *Riyāḍ al-sālikīn fī sharḥ saḥīfa sayyid al-sāǧǧidīn*, vol. I: 162, al-Ḥuwayzī., *Tafsīr nūr al-ṯaqalayn*, vol. IV, *sūrat Ṣād*, n. 84: 470, Muḥammad Riḍā al-Ṭūsī., *Kanz al-daqāʾiq wa baḥr al-ġarāʾib fī tafsīr al-qurʾān*, vol. XI, *sūrat Ṣād*: 263, al-Mūsawī., *Minhāǧ al-baraʿa fī sharḥ nahǧ al-balāġa*, vol. XIII: 416.

[38] al-Daylami., *Aʿlām al-dīn fī ṣifāt al-muʾminīn*: 277, al-Baḥrānī., *al-Burhān fī tafsīr al-qurʾān*, vol. V, Part Five, *sūrat al-ʿAlaq*, n. 11752: 697, *Ḥilyat al-abrār fī aḥwāl Muḥammad wa āli-hi al-aṭhār*, vol I, bb. 7, n. 2: 68, al-Maǧlisī., *Biḥār al-anwār*, vol. LXXVIII, bb. 1, n. 52: 194, vol. LXXXIX, bb.

theological stress on God's transcendence, must persuade us that this beautiful form is in fact angelic.

Although, as we shall see, the house of Umm Salama becomes the locus for angelic encounters, a selection of narratives containing, even in rudimentary form, many of the elements which become the markers for these meetings, record Muḥammad's engagements with Ǧibrīl in other places. Furthermore, the angel in question is not always Ǧibrīl – in the following narrative, not only is the angelic visitor not the usual Ǧibrīl, but the red dust is described by its odour, a rare addition to the story:

> On the authority of Anas b. Mālik, that one of the greatest of the angels sought permission of his Lord, powerful and great, to visit the Prophet and He gave him permission. While he was with him, al-Ḥusayn came in to him. The Prophet kissed him and made him sit on his lap. The angel said to him: "Do you love him?" He replied: "Certainly! And with an intense love! He is my son!" He went on: "Your community will kill him!" He answered: "My community will kill my son?" The angel said: "Yes, and if you wish I can show you some of the dust upon which he will be killed." "Yes," he said: So he showed him red dust, pleasant of smell, and said: "When this dust becomes fresh blood, it is a sign that this son of yours has been killed." Sālim b. Abī al-Ǧaʿd said: I was informed that the angel was Mīkāʾīl.[39]

124, n. 23: 354 (in which Ǧibrīl appears to Muḥammad 'in the most beautiful form', 'laughing' [*ḍāḥiq*] and 'rejoicing' [*mustabshir*]).

[39] al-Ṭūsī., *al-Amālī fī-l-ḥadīṯ*, *maǧlis* 11, n. 86–639: 315, al-Maǧlisī., *Biḥār al-anwār*, vol. XLIV, bb. 30, n. 10: 228–229, al-Iṣfahānī., *ʿAwālim al-ʿulūm wa-l-maʿārif al-aḥwāl min al-āyāt wa-l-aḫbār wa-l-aqwāl*, vol. XVII, Part Seventeen, ch. 11, bb. 6, n. 3: 125. In one *ḥadīṯ*, al-Ṭūsī names Ǧibrīl as the angel asking permission to visit (al-Ṭūsī., *al-Amālī fī-l-ḥadīṯ*, *maǧlis* 11, n. 85–638: 314), while in another he names the visitor as 'one of the loftiest of the angels' (bb. 11, n. 86–639: 314). He ends the *ḥadīṯ* by noting Sālim b. al-Ǧaʿd's declaration that this angel was, in fact, Mīkāʾīl.

In an uncommon and lengthy *ḥadīṯ*, which introduces a number of novel characteristics, al-Maǧlisī proposes another unnamed angelic visitor:

> It is also reported in some reports that one of the angels of the highest level of heaven[40] ardently desired to see the Prophet, and sought permission from his Lord to descend to earth to visit him. This angel had never before descended to earth since it was created;[41] and when he wanted to descend, God Most High inspired him saying: "Angel! Inform Muḥammad that a man from his community named Yazīd will kill his young one,[42] the pure son of the one who is pure like Maryam bt. ʿImrān." The angel said: "I descended to the earth, glad to see your Prophet Muḥammad; but how to inform him of this

---

[40] Iblīs himself had been one of the angels of *al-ṣafīḥ al-aʿlā*, the 'highest level of heaven' (cf. al-Baḥrānī., *al-Burhān fī tafsīr al-qurʾān*, vol. III, *sūrat al-Ḥiǧr*, n. 5843: 3459), which is defined as 'the heaven of the heavens' (Ibn Manẓūr., *Lisān al-ʿarab*, vol. II: 516, al-Zabīdī., *Tāǧ al-ʿarūs min ǧawāhir al-qāmūs*, vol. IV: 122).

[41] In al-Tirmiḏī, for example, there is a *ḥadīṯ* of an angel, who has 'never descended before', seeking permission from God to announce to Muḥammad that Fāṭima is the leader of the women of Paradise, and that al-Ḥasan and al-Ḥusayn are the leaders of the youths of among the inhabitants of the Garden. It is, as already noted, a useful literary device for separating divine revelation brought by Ǧibrīl, from other heavenly angelic messages. Cf. for e.g. Ibn Ḥanbal., *Musnad*, vol. II (*Musnad ʿUmar b. al-Ḫaṭṭāb*): 231, vol. VI (*Ḥadīṯ Umm Salama*): 296, Muslim., *Ṣaḥīḥ*, vol. II, bk. 3 (*Kitāb faḍāʾil al-qurʾān*), bb. 43, n. [1877] 254 – (806): 325–326, al-Tirmiḏī., *al-Ǧāmiʿ al-ṣaḥīḥ*, vol. VI, bk. 46 (*Kitāb al-manāqib*), bb. 30, n. 3781: 432–3. Cf. also al-Ḥākim al-Nīsābūrī., *Kitāb al-mustadrak ʿalā al-ṣaḥīḥayn*, vol. III, bk. 31 (*Kitāb maʿrifat al-ṣaḥāba*), nn. 4784, 4785: 177.

[42] Lane holds that the primary signification of *farḫ* is the young of a bird or of an egg-laying creature, and sometimes the young of any animal. Cf. LANE E.W., *An Arabic-English Lexicon*, vol. VI, 1968: 2362. Steingass adds a young 'plant' or 'shoot'. STEINGASS F., *Learner's Arabic English Dictionary*, 1993: 782. The text places ultimate responsibility for al-Ḥusayn's death upon Yazīd b. Muʿāwiya, rather than whoever it was who actually struck the death-blow.

shameful news? I felt ashamed in front of him that he be distressed by the killing of his son. Would that I had not descended to the earth!" The narrator continued: Then, from above his head, the angel was summoned to do what he had been ordered. The angel went in to the Messenger of God, spread his wings in front of him, and said: "Messenger of God! Know that I sought permission from my Lord to descend to the earth, yearning to see you and visit you. Would that my Lord had broken my wings[43] and I had not come to you with this

[43] The theme of angels with broken wings evokes the memory of a narrative around the conception and birth of al-Ḥusayn, about an angel named Fuṭrus or, in one account by al-Maǧlisī, Ṣalṣā'īl (al-Maǧlisī., *Biḥār al-anwār*, vol. XLIII, bb. 11, n. 47: 258–259). God orders Ǧibrīl to descend with a crowd of angels in congratulations at al-Ḥusayn's birth. They pass an island on which dwells Fuṭrus, banished there with broken wings for having delayed to obey God. Fuṭrus begs Ǧibrīl to carry him with them in the hope of Muḥammad's intercession. Muḥammad subsequently commands that Fuṭrus should rub against the cradle of al-Ḥusayn, and at once God restores his wings (cf. among others al-Ṭabarī., *Dalā'il al-imāma*: 79, *Bishārat al-muṣṭafā*: 219, al-Ṣaffār al-Qummī., *Baṣā'ir al-daraǧāt fī ʿulūm āl Muḥammad*, vol. I, bb. 6, n. 7: 68, al-Masʿūdī., *Iṯbāt al-waṣiyya*: 164, Ibn Qūlawayh., *Kāmil al-ziyārāt*, bb. 20, n. 1: 140–141, Ibn Bābawayh., *Kitāb al-amālī fī al-aḥādīṯ wa-l-aḫbār*, n. 8: 137–138, al-Ṭūsī., *Miṣbāḥ al-mutahaǧǧid*, vol. II: 827, Ibn ʿAlī al-Fattāl., *Rawḍat al-wāʿiẓīn wa-tabṣirat al-muttaʿiẓīn*, vol. I: 155, al-Rāwandī., *al-Ḫarā'iǧ wa-l-ǧarā'iḥ fī-l-muʿǧizāt*, vol. I: 252, Ibn Shahrāshūb., *Manāqib āl Abī Ṭālib*, vol. IV, bb. *Fī imāmat Abī ʿAbd Allāh al-Ḥusayn*: 63, al-Shāmī., *al-Durr al-naẓīm fī manāqib al-a'imma al-lahāhīm*, bb. 5, *Fī ḏikr al-Ḥusayn b. ʿAlī*: 568, Ibn Ṭā'ūs., *Kitāb al-iqbāl bi-l-aʿmāl al-ḥasana*: 698, al-Ḥillī al-ʿAllāma., *Iṯbāt al-hudāt bi-l-nuṣūṣ wa-l-muʿǧizāt*, vol. IV, bb. 15, n. 30: 45, al-Bayyāḍī., *al-Ṣirāṭ al-mustaqīm ilā mustaḥaqq al-taqdīm fī al-imāma*, vol. II, n. 5: 179 (not in the context of al-Ḥusayn's birth), al-Kafʿamī., *Kitāb al-miṣbāḥ*: 543, *al-Balad al-amīn*: 185, al-Baḥrānī., *Madīnat al-maʿāǧiz fī muʿǧizāt al-a'imma al-aṭhār*, vol. III, n. 8/955: 437–438, al-Maǧlisī., *Rawḍat al-muttaqīn fī sharḥ man lā yaḥḍuru-hu al-faqīh*, vol. IV, Part Fourteen: 33, *Biḥār al-anwār*, vol. XXVI, bb. 8, n. 10: 340, vol. XLIII, bb. 11, n. 18: 243, n. 27: 250, vol. XLIV, bb. 25, n. 7: 182, vol. L, bb. 3, n. 47: 66, vol. XCVIII, bb. 32, n. 9: 367, al-Iṣfahānī., *ʿAwālim al-ʿulūm wa-l-maʿārif al-aḥwāl min al-āyāt wa-l-aḫbār wa-l-aqwāl*, vol. XVII, ch. 11, bb. 6, n. 9: 128, al-

> news; but the discharge of the command of my Lord, powerful and great, is necessary. Know, Muḥammad, that a man from your community whose name is Yazīd, may God increase for him malediction in this world and punishment in the next, will kill your young one, the pure son of the one who is pure. His killer will be little blessed in the world after him; God will seize him in retaliation for him, for the wickedness of his action, and he will be eternally in the Fire." The Prophet wept bitterly and said: "Angel, will a community prosper by the killing of my son, the young one of my daughter?"[44] He replied: "No, Muḥammad, instead, God will reproach them for the disparity of their hearts and their tongues in the house of this world; and there will be painful punishment for them in the Hereafter."[45]

Most of these encounters are taken up and developed into a theme woven around the presence of Umm Salama and the arrival of the boy al-Ḥusayn at her house to visit his grandfather; outside of that context, the pattern rarely varies.[46] Ǧibrīl arrives and informs Muḥammad that after him, his community would kill his grandson; in some narratives the meeting takes place around the time of al-

---

Ǧazā'irī., *Riyāḍ al-abrār fī manāqib al-a'imma al-aṭhār*, vol. I, Part One: 154, al-Ṭabarsī., *Mustadrak al-wasā'il wa mustanbiṭ al-masā'il*, vol. XVI, bb. 42, n. 7: 17–19, n. 9: 19). Cf. CLOHESSY C., *Fāṭima, Daughter of Muḥammad*, 2nd ed., Gorgias Press, New Jersey 2018: 148–149.

[44] In al-Mūsawī's transmission, Muḥammad asks this question of Ǧibrīl, when he comes to Muḥammad bringing consolation and some of the dust of Karbalā' (cf. al-Mūsawī., *Tasliyat al-maǧālis wa zīnat al-maǧālis*, vol. II, Part Three, *maǧlis* 4: 111).

[45] al-Mūsawī., *Tasliyat al-muǧālis wa zīnat al-maǧālis*, vol. II, Part Two, *maǧlis* 5: 113, al-Baḥrānī., *Madīnat al-ma'āǧiz fī mu'ǧizāt al-a'imma al-aṭhār*, vol. III, n. 10/957, al-Maǧlisī., *Biḥār al-anwār*, vol. XLV, bb. 46, n. 14: 314–315, al-Iṣfahānī., *'Awālim al-'ulūm wa-l-ma'ārif al-aḥwāl min al-āyāt wa-l-aḫbār wa-l-aqwāl*, vol. XVII, Part Seventeen, ch. 21, bb. 2, n. 6: 599.

[46] Cf. for e.g. Ibn Qūlawayh., *Kāmil al-ziyārāt*, bb. 17, n. 1: 127–128, n. 6: 130–131, n. 7: 131, n. 8: 131–132, al-Maǧlisī., *Biḥār al-anwār*, vol. XLIV, bb. 30, n. 9: 228, n. 22: 235, nn. 26–27: 236, n. 28: 237.

Ḥusayn's birth,[47] while in others, al-Ḥusayn is present and Ǧibrīl probes Muḥammad about his love for the boy. Muḥammad is tormented by what he is hearing: "Will a nation that killed my young one prosper?"[48] he asks, and another text relates that he "took ʿAlī by the hand and withdrew with him for a substantial part of the day and they were overcome with tears," with Ǧibrīl exhorting them to patience.[49] Ǧibrīl offers to show him dust from the land in which al-Ḥusayn would fall. In the hands of Muḥammad that dust, occasionally described by its musky fragrance,[50] takes on all the attributes of a relic; Ǧibrīl causes the distance between Muḥammad's seat and Karbalāʾ to sink down until the two parts meet (here, Ǧaʿfar al-Ṣādiq illustrates the joining of the two by bringing together his two index fingers) and with his wings grasps some of the dust and gives it to Muḥammad. "The Messenger of God said: Dust, blessed are you and blessed whoever is killed in you!"[51]

Other members of the household of the Prophet also dream dreams. Sometime in the summer of 37/657, near the city of Nine-

[47] Ibn Qūlawayh., *Kāmil al-ziyārāt*, bb. 17, n. 6: 130–131, al-Mağlisī., *Biḥār al-anwār*, vol. XLIV, bb. 30, n. 26: 236, al-Iṣfahānī., *ʿAwālim al-ʿulūm wa-l-maʿārif al-aḥwāl min al-āyāt wa-l-aḫbār wa-l-aqwāl*, vol. XVII, Part Seventeen, ch. 11, bb. 6, n. 15: 131.

[48] Ibn Qūlawayh., *Kāmil al-ziyārāt*, bb. 17, n. 7: 131 (the author notes that he may have said "the young one of my daughter").

[49] Op. cit., bb. 16, n. 1: 121, al-Mağlisī., *Biḥār al-anwār*, vol. XLIII, bb. 30, n. 15: 231.

[50] Ibn Qūlawayh., *Kāmil al-ziyārāt*, bb. 17, n. 1: 127–128, al-Mağlisī., *Biḥār al-anwār*, vol. XLIII, bb. 30, n. 22: 235, al-Iṣfahānī., *ʿAwālim al-ʿulūm wa-l-maʿārif al-aḥwāl min al-āyāt wa-l-aḫbār wa-l-aqwāl*, vol. XVII, Part Seventeen, ch. 11, bb. 6, n. 1: 124, al-Ǧazāʾirī., *Riyāḍ al-abrār fī manāqib al-aʾimma al-aṭhār*, vol. I, Part One: 171 (where it is the angel rather than the dust exuding an odour of musk).

[51] Ibn Qūlawayh., *Kāmil al-ziyārāt*, bb. 17, n. 1: 127–128, n. 5: 129–130, al-Ṭūsī., *al-Amālī fī-l-ḥadīt*, *mağlis* 11, n. 85–638: 314, al-Ṭabarī's *Bishārat al-muṣṭafā*, Part Seven: 214, al-Fayḍ al-Kāshānī., *Nawādir al-aḫbār*, n. 17: 161, al-Mağlisī., *Biḥār al-anwār*, vol. XLIV, bb. 30, n. 9: 228, n. 22: 235.

veh, writes Ibn Ḥanbal in his *Musnad*, a servant traveling to Ṣiffīn[52] with the retinue of ʿAlī b. Abī Ṭālib is puzzled to hear ʿAlī crying out: "Patience, Abū ʿAbd Allāh! Patience, Abū ʿAbd Allāh, on the bank of the Euphrates!" The servant wonders who Abū ʿAbd Allāh might be, and ʿAlī takes up the story:

> I came to see the Messenger of God and his eyes were overflowing with tears. I said: "Prophet of God, did someone make you angry? What is the matter with your eyes that they overflow with tears?" He replied: "No, Ğibrīl just ascended from me, having told me that al-Ḥusayn would be killed on the bank of the Euphrates. And he also said: Would you like me to let you savour the smell of its earth?" The narrator continued: "I said: Yes! He stretched out his hand and seized a handful and gave it to me, and I cannot stop my eyes from shedding tears."[53]

---

[52] The inconclusive battle of Ṣiffīn (37/657), fought by ʿAlī against Muʿāwiya's army on the banks of the Euphrates, was less of battle in the classical sense and more a series of minor and not particularly earnest skirmishes over a period of three days. Part of the problem was that there were members of the same tribe and even the same family on opposing sides, and the dismay at spilling the blood of a fellow Muslim remained a strong deterrent.

[53] Ibn Abī Shayba., *al-Muṣannaf*, vol. XIII, *Kitāb al-fitan*, bb. 1, n. 38383: 294, Ibn Hanbal., *Musnad*, vol. I, *Musnad ʿAlī b. Abī Ṭālib*: 85, Ibn Abī ʿĀṣim., *al-Āḥād wa-l-maṯānī*, vol. I, bb. 36 (*Min ḏikri al-Ḥusayn b. ʿAlī*), n. 427: 308, al-Bazzār., *Kashf al-astār*, vol. III, bb. *Manāqib al-Ḥusayn*, n. 2641: 231–232, al-Āğurrī., *Kitāb al-sharīʿa*, vol. III, bb. *Iḫbār al-nabī bi-qatli al-Ḥusayn*, n. (1109) 1725: 320–321, al-Ṭabarānī., *al-Muʿğam al-kabīr*, vol. III, n. 2811: 105, al-Shağarī., *Tartīb al-amālī al-ḫamīsiyya*, vol. I, bb. *Fī faḍl al-Ḥusayn b. ʿAlī*, n. 771: 210, Ibn ʿAsākir., *Tārīḫ madīnat Dimashq*, vol. XIV, bb. 1566 (*al-Ḥusayn b. ʿAlī b. Abī Ṭālib b. ʿAbd al-Muṭṭalib b. Hashim b. ʿAbd al-Manāf*):187–189, Ibn al-Aṯīr, *Usd al-ġāba fī maʿrifat al-ṣaḥāba*, vol. II, bb. 1173 (*al-Ḥusayn b. ʿAlī*), n. 331: 24, Sibṭ al-Ğawzī., *Taḏkirat al-ḫawāṣṣ al-umma bi-ḏikr ḫaṣāʾiṣ al-aʾimma*, bb. *Ḏikr maqtali-hi*: 250, Ibn al-ʿAdīm., *Buġyat al-ṭalab fī tārīḫ ḥalab*, Part Six: 2596, al-Ṭabarī., *Ḏaḫāʾir al-ʿuqbā*, bb. 9: 252–253, al-Mizzī., *Tahḏīb al-kamāl fī asmāʾ al-riğāl*, vol. VI, n. 1323 (*al-*

Ibn Abī Shayba's editor denounced the chain of transmission as 'extremely weak' and Ibn Ḥanbal too expressed doubts, thereby casting aspersions on the whole narrative; al-Bazzār would also transmit it,[54] as would the eminent Ḥanbalī *muḥaddiṯ* Sulaymān b. Aḥmad al-Ṭabarānī half a century later in his massive compilation *al-Muʿǧam al-kabīr*. Historian Ibn ʿAsākir included the story a number of times in his *Tārīḫ madīnat Dimashq*, with only slight variants, and specified the imprecise location – the bank of the Euphrates – as the narrative progressed:

> Ḥammād b. Zayd, on the authority of Ǧumhān,[55] that Ǧibrīl came to the Prophet with some of the dust of the town in which al-Ḥusayn would be killed. It was said that its name is Karbalāʾ, and the Messenger of God said: Distress (*karb*) and tribulation (*balāʾ*).[56]

These words would be remembered in the future by al-Ḥusayn himself. Writes al-Ṭabarānī:

> When al-Ḥusayn b. ʿAlī was surrounded on all sides, he asked: What is the name of this land? He replied: Karbalāʾ. The narra-

Ḥusayn b. ʿAlī b. Abī Ṭālib): 407, al-Ḏahabī., *Siyar aʿlām al-nubalāʾ*, vol. III, n. 48 (*al-Ḥusayn al-Shahīd Abū ʿAbd Allāh b. ʿAlī b. Abī Ṭālib*): 288 (who transmits it from Ibn Ḥanbal and declares it 'obscure'), *Tārīḫ al-islām*, vol. V: 66, Ibn Kaṯīr., *al-Bidāya wa-l-nihāya*, vol. XI, bb. *al-Iḫbār bi-maqtal al-Ḥusayn b. ʿAlī*: 571–2, al-Hayṯamī., *Maǧmaʿ al-zawāʾid wa-manbaʿ al-fawāʾid*, vol. IX, bk. 37 (*Kitāb al-manāqib*), bb. 95 (*Manāqib al-Ḥusayn b. ʿAlī*), n. 15112: 217–218, al-ʿAsqalānī., *Tahḏīb al-tahḏīb*, vol. II, bb. *al-Ḥāʾ*, n. 615: 347, *al-Iṣāba fī tamyīz al-ṣaḥāba*, vol. II, n. 1729 (*al-Ḥusayn*): 71, al-Suyūṭī., *al-Ḫaṣāʾiṣ al-kubrā*, vol. II: 451–452, al-Maǧlisī., *Biḥār al-anwār*, vol. XLIV, bb. 30, n. 46: 246–248 (and who adds: "The name of the land is Karbalāʾ"), al-Muttaqī al-Hindī., *Kanz al-ʿummāl fī sunan al-aqwāl wa-l-afʿāl*, vol. XIII, n. 37663: 655.

[54] al-Bazzār., *Musnad*, vol. III, *Musnad ʿAlī b. Abī Ṭālib*, n. 884: 101.

[55] The editor notes that in *Siyar aʿlām al-nubalāʾ* the name occurs as 'Saʿīd b. Ǧumhān' (al-Ḏahabī., *Siyar aʿlām al-nubalāʾ*, vol. III, n. 48 (*al-Ḥusayn al-Shahīd Abū ʿAbd Allāh b. ʿAlī b. Abī Ṭālib*): 290).

[56] Ibn ʿAsākir., *Tārīḫ madīnat Dimashq*, vol. XIV, bb. 1566 (*al-Ḥusayn b. ʿAlī b. Abī Ṭālib b. ʿAbd al-Muṭṭalib b. Hāshim b. ʿAbd al-Manāf*): 197, 220.

> tor continued: He answered: The Prophet has spoken the truth, that it is a land of distress and tribulation.[57]

Led by Ibn Bābawayh, the Shīʿī transmitters carry a story, on the authority of Ibn ʿAbbās, in which the content of the dream changes. Standing on the banks of the Euphrates on the way to Ṣiffīn, ʿAlī addresses the man who will come to be known as the 'scholar' of the nation and its 'ocean of knowledge':

> "Ibn ʿAbbās, do you know this place?" I said to him: "Commander of the Faithful, I do not know it!" He replied: "If you knew it as I know it, you would not be able to pass by it without weeping as I weep!" Ibn ʿAbbās continued: He wept at length, until his beard was wet and the tears flowed onto his chest, and we wept together. Then he said: "Alas! Alas! What have I to do with the family of Abū Sufyān? What have I to do with the family of war, the party of Satan and the friends of unbelief? Patience, Abū ʿAbd Allāh! Your father suffered the same as you are suffering because of them." Then he called for water, performed the ablution for the prayer and prayed as God willed that he pray. After that, he spoke in a manner similar to his first speech, except that he dozed for an hour at the end of his prayer and his words. Then he awoke and said: "Ibn ʿAbbās!" I replied: "I am here!" He said: "Should I tell you what I saw in my dream just now while I slept?" I answered: "Your eyes slept and you saw what is good, Commander of the Faithful!" He went on: "I saw as if I was in the presence of men who had descended from heaven with white flags and girded with their swords, all shining white. They had proceeded around this earth a step, when I saw these palm trees strike the earth with their branches, surging with fresh blood. Then it

[57] al-Ṭabarānī., *al-Muʿǧam al-kabīr*, vol. III, n. 2812: 106, n. 2819: 108. Cf. also Ibn Abī ʿĀṣim., *al-Āḥād wa-l-maṯānī*, vol. 1, bb. 36 (*Min ḏikri al-Ḥusayn b. ʿAlī*), n. 424: 307, al-Āǧurrī., *Kitāb al-sharīʿa*, vol. III, bb. *Iḫbār al-nabī bi-qatli al-Ḥusayn*, n. (1108) 1724: 320, al-Ṭabarī., *Ḏaḫāʾir al-ʿuqbā*, bb. 9: 255, al-Hayṯamī., *Maǧmaʿ al-zawāʾid wa-manbaʿ al-fawāʾid*, vol. IX, bk. 37 (*Kitāb al-manāqib*), bb. 95 (*Manāqib al-Ḥusayn b. ʿAlī*), n. 15117: 219, n. 15133: 224.

> was as if I were with al-Ḥusayn, my child,[58] my young one, my embryo,[59] my purest and choicest part; he was submerged in it and appealing for help, but he was not relieved. It was as though the men in white had descended from heaven, calling out to him and saying: Patience, family of the Messenger! You will be killed at the hands of the of the most evil of people, but this is the Garden, Abū ʿAbd Allāh, yearning for you! Then they consoled me, saying: Abū al-Ḥasan, rejoice! God will console[60] you the day the people will be raised before the Lord of the worlds. Then I awoke in this state."[61]

In another dream, transmitted by Ibn Shahrāshūb, ʿAlī catches a glimpse of the things that lie ahead for the family of Muḥammad:

> The Commander of the Faithful saw in a dream a speaker who said: "Whenever the heart recalls the Prophet's band, the women's captivity, the dishonouring of the veil, the slaughter of the youth, the killing of the one entrusted, the killing of

---

[58] According to Lane, the word *saḫl* refers to "an infant that is an object of love to his parents", with the connotation of a newly-born kid or lamb. Cf. LANE E.W., *An Arabic-English Lexicon*, vol. IV, 1968: 1325.

[59] Cf. Q. 22:5 and Q. 23:14. Pickthall, and numerous other English interpreters of the Qurʾān, translate the word *muḍġa* as 'lump of flesh'.

[60] Lit. 'gladden' or 'console' or 'cool' 'the eye'. Cf. Q. 19:26, Q. 20:40, Q. 28:9, 13.

[61] Ibn Bābawayh., *Kitāb al-amālī fī-l-aḥādīṯ wa-l-aḫbār*, *maǧlis* 87, n. 5: 597, *Ikmāl (kamāl) al-dīn wa-itmām (tamām) al-niʿma fī iṯbāt al-ġayba wa-kashf al-ḥayra*, vol. II, bb. 48, n. 1: 533, al-Rāwandī., *al-Ḫarāʾiǧ wa-l-ǧarāʾiḥ fī-l-muʿǧizāt*, vol. III, Part Three, bb. 20, *faṣl* 56: 1145, al-Shāmī., *al-Durr al-naẓīm fī manāqib al-aʾimma al-lahāhīm*, bb. 5, *Fī ḏikr al-Ḥusayn b. ʿAlī*: 538, al-Ḥillī al-ʿAllāma., *Iṯbāt al-hudāt bi-l-nuṣūṣ wa-l-muʿǧizāt*, vol. III, bb. 12, Part Five, n. 33: 443, al-Baḥrānī., *Madīnat al-maʿāǧiz fī muʿǧizāt al-aʾimma al-aṭhār*, vol. II, Part Two, n. 472: 166, vol. IV, Part Four, n. 273/1220: 197, al-Maǧlisī., *Biḥār al-anwār*, vol. XLIV, bb. 31, n. 2: 252–244, al-Iṣfahānī., *ʿAwālim al-ʿulūm wa-l-maʿārif al-aḥwāl min al-āyāt wa-l-aḫbār wa-l-aqwāl*, vol. XVII, n. 2: 144, al-Ǧazāʾirī., *Riyāḍ al-abrār fī manāqib al-aʾimma al-aṭhār*, vol. I, Part One: 176, ʿAbbās Qummī., *Safīnat al-biḥār*, vol. III: 250.

> Shabīr and the poisoning of al-Shabbar,[62] the water of the heart glistens in the eyes, pearls of which flow upon the cheek. O heart, steadfast in spite of their affliction; with tribulations come lessons."[63]

ʿAlī himself would be one who would regularly materialize in people's dreams, there performing a substantial number of tasks, specifically for those who make *ziyāra* to his place of burial. These functions notes Sindawi, include "chastising his enemies, doing battle against those who would desecrate his grave, granting protection to those who seek refuge at his grave, demanding of visitors to fulfil the pledges they have made to his grave, foretelling the visitor's future, divining the identity and religious affiliation of the visi-

---

[62] The names Shabbar and Shabīr recall a strand in the books of *aḥādīṯ* in which the relationship between ʿAlī and Muḥammad is compared to the relationship between Hārūn and Mūsā. Ǧibrīl commands that ʿAlī's two children be named after the children of Hārūn – Shabbar and Shabīr. "My tongue is Arabic," protests Muḥammad, not understanding the names, and Ǧibrīl translates them as al-Ḥasan and al-Ḥusayn. Cf. al-Hilālī., *Kitāb Sulaym b. Qays*: 705, al-Ṭabarī., *Bishārat al-muṣṭafā*: 174, Ibn Bābawayh., *Kitāb al-amālī fī al-aḥādīṯ wa-l-aḫbār*, n. 3: 134, 191, 439, *ʿUyūn aḫbār al-Riḍā*, vol. II, bb. 31, n. 5: 25, *Maʿānī al-aḫbār*, n. 6: 57, *ʿIlal al-sharāʾiʿ wa-l-aḥkām*, vol. I, bb. 116, n. 6: 138, Ibn ʿAlī al-Fattāl., *Rawḍat al-wāʿiẓīn wa-tabṣirat al-muttaʿiẓīn*, vol. I: 123, 153, al-Ṭabarsī., *Iʿlām al-warā bi-aʿlām al-hudā*: 160, 218, al-Rāwandī., *al-Ḫarāʾiǧ wa-l-ǧarāʾiḥ fī-l-muʿǧizāt*, vol. I: 345, Ibn Shahrāshūb., *Manāqib āl Abī Ṭālib*, vol. III, bb. *al-Nukat wa-l-laṭāʾif*: 251, Ibn Ṭāʾūs., *Kitāb al-iqbāl bi-l-aʿmāl al-ḥasana*: 382, al-Maǧlisī., *Biḥār al-anwār*, vol. IX, bb. 2: 298, vol. XIII, bb. 11, n. 11: 331, vol. XXXVI, bb. 50, n. 4: 36, vol. XXXVII, bb. 50: 37, 92, vol. XXXVIII, bb. 63: 190, vol. XXXIX, bb. 72: 33, 62, vol. XLIII, bb. 11, n. 1: 237, nn. 3–4: 238, n. 10: 241, n. 29: 245, vol. XLIX, bb. 4: 77, vol. XCIX, bb. 8: 191, vol. CI, bb. 4, n. 18: 110, al-Ṭabarsī., *Mustadrak al-wasāʾil wa mustanbiṭ al-masāʾil*, vol. I, bb. 8, n. 7–1163: 461, vol. XV, bb. 32, n. 7–17805: 144.

[63] Ibn Shahrāshūb., *Manāqib āl Abī Ṭālib*, vol. II, bb. *Mā tafarrada min manāqibi-hi*: 209, al-Maǧlisī., *Biḥār al-anwār*, vol. XXVII, bb. 9, n. 9: 209. The Arabic plural *ʿibar* is something of a play on words, since it could mean 'tears' but also 'lessons' or 'exhortations'. Cf. WEHR H., *A Dictionary of Modern Written Arabic*, 1980: 686.

tor, returning stolen objects to their owners, demanding of the Shiʾites that they pay their debts and conforming the authenticity of a disputed tradition."[64] The defence of graves and the pledges made their feature prominently in a dream of Muḥammad in the house of ʿAlī and Fāṭima, as well as a dream of the punishment inflicted upon those who desecrate the grave of al-Ḥusayn, both recounted in this text. ʿAlī's appearance in people's dreams, making intercession for them, advising them and particularly forbidding them from doing the wrong and encouraging them to fulfil their duties echoes a theme that is deeply embedded within Shīʿī theology. It is as though he had never died and was there in person.[65]

ʿAlī b. Abī Ṭālib was not the only one to dream dreams of the prophet of Islam. A report taken from *al-Maqātil* tells of Abū Bakr b. ʿAbbās recounting a dream in which he saw Muḥammad and Ibrāhīm *al-ḫalīl* praying at the grave of al-Ḥusayn.[66] Al-Qāḍī al-Nuʿmān's frugally worded report is suffused with the theological impact of linking the figure of Muḥammad with the prophet Ibrāhīm, whose faith he shares,[67] and whom the Qurʾān styles 'most truthful' (*ṣiddīq*, Q. 19:41) and 'gracious' (*ḥalīm*, Q. 9:114, Q.11: 75), portraying him as God's friend (*ḫalīl*, Q. 4:125). The authenticity of

---

[64] SINDAWI K., "The Image of ʿAlī b. Abī Ṭālib in the Dreams of Visitors top his Tomb" in L. MARLOW (ed.)., *Dreaming Across Boundaries. The Interpretation of Dreams in Islamic Lands*, Ilex Foundation, Boston 2008: 179.

[65] Consonant with the words of ʿAlī himself that the Imāms did not die but continue to live. Cf. for e.g. al-Ṣaffār., *Baṣāʾir al-daraǧāt fī ʿulūm āl Muḥammad*, vol. I, Part Six, bb. 5. n. 4: 275, al-Rāwandî., *al-Ḫarāʾiǧ wa-l-ǧarāʾiḥ fī-l-muʿǧizāt*, vol. II, Part Two: 344, Ibn al-Ḥadîd., *Sharḥ nahǧ al-balāġa*, vol. VI, Part Six, n. 86: 373, 373–379, al-Ḥurr al-ʿĀmilî., *Iṯbāt al-hudāt bi-l-nuṣūṣ wa-l-muʿǧizāt*, vol. IV, Part Four, bb. 13, *faṣl* 2, n. 8: 20, vol. IV, Part Four, bb. 16, *faṣl* 8, n. 37: 48, al-Baḥrānī., *Madīnat al-maʿāǧiz fī muʿǧizāt al-aʾimma al-aṭhār*, vol. III, Part Three, n. 740: 76.

[66] al-Qāḍī al-Nuʿmān., *Sharḥ al-aḫbār fī faḍāʾil al-aʾimma al-aṭhār*, vol. III, Part Twelve, n. 1105: 167.

[67] Cf. Q. 22:78 «*And strive for Allah with the endeavour which is His right. He hath chosen you and hath not laid upon you in religion any hardship; the faith of your father Abraham (is yours)*».

Muḥammad's religious standing cannot but be ratified by his being bracketed with Ibrāhīm who, like him, is called 'upright' or 'pure of faith' (*ḥanīf*, Q. 2:135, Q. 3:67, 95, Q. 4:125, Q. 6:79, 161, Q. 10:105, Q. 16:120, 123, Q. 30:30), and who, like him is visited by angelic messengers who announce the impending birth of a son (Q. 11:69–76, Q. 15:51–9, Q. 29:31, Q. 51:24–30) and who, like him, must ransom a son offering him as a sacrifice, although ultimately loosed from the task (Q. 37:99–111).

Ibn ʿAsākir reports a dream in which *muḥaddiṯ* ʿĀmir b. Saʿd al-Bağalī reports:

> When al-Ḥusayn b. ʿAlī was killed, I saw the Messenger of God in a dream, and he said: "I saw al-Barāʾ b. ʿĀzib and greeted him with peace from me, and informed him that the killers of al-Ḥusayn b. ʿAlī are in the Fire, and that God was on the point of exterminating the people of the earth with a painful punishment because of him." He said: I came to al-Barāʾ and informed him, and he said: "The Messenger of God has told the truth. The Messenger of God said: Whoever sees me in a dream, sees me in truth, for Shayṭān does not appear in my form."[68]

Most of all, however, it is Muḥammad's grandson al-Ḥusayn who dreams of his grandfather, and especially as his own life draws to its close. The texts delineate three distinct encounters, all with a variety of embellishments and lacunae among the transmitters: his prayer at the grave of Muḥammad on the eve of his departure to Karbalāʾ, a vision or dream he has, imprecisely dated, in which he receives a command from Muḥammad which he will not reveal, and his dozing off and dreaming in front of his tent shortly before his death in battle.

Among the dictations in his *Kitāb al-amālī*, Ibn Bābawayh relates a detailed account, narrated by the sixth Imām Ğaʿfar al-Ṣādiq,

---

[68] Ibn ʿAsākir., *Tārīḫ madīnat Dimashq*, vol. XIV, bb. 1566 (*al-Ḥusayn b. ʿAlī b. Abī Ṭālib b. ʿAbd al-Muṭṭalib b. Hāshim b. ʿAbd al-Manāf*): 258, al-Shāmī., *al-Durr al-naẓīm fī manāqib al-aʾimma al-lahāhīm*, bb. 5, *Fī ḏikr al-Ḥusayn b. ʿAlī*: 566–567, Ibn al-ʿAdīm., *Buġyat al-ṭalab fī tārīḫ ḥalab*, Part Six: 2644, al-Irbilī., *Kashf al-ġumma fī maʿrifat al-aʾimma*, vol. II, Part Three: 57.

of the days leading up to al-Ḥusayn's leaving for Kūfa and, ultimately, Karbalāʾ, unfolding something of the history of Muʿāwiya, the fateful accession by his son Yazīd, the threat against al-Ḥusayn and his departure for Iraq:

> When night drew near, (al-Ḥusayn) went to the *masǧid* of the Prophet, to take leave of the grave, and when he arrived there, a light from the grave shone upon him and then returned to its place. On the second night he went to take leave of the grave and stood in prayer; it was protracted, and he dozed while he was prostrating. Then the Prophet came to him in a dream; he took hold of al-Ḥusayn, pressed him to his breast and began to kiss him between his eyes, saying: "You are as dear to me as my own father! It is as if I see you soiled with your blood, between a group from this nation which hopes for my intercession. There will be no share for them with God. My son, you are coming to your father, your mother and your brother; they are yearning for you, but for you there are grades in the Garden which cannot be obtained except through martyrdom!" Then al-Ḥusayn awoke, weeping, from his dream; he came to the people of his house, informed them of his vision and bade them farewell.[69]

[69] Ibn Bābawayh., *Kitāb al-amālī fi-l-aḥādīṯ wa-l-aḫbār*, *maǧlis* 30, n. 1: 152, al-Baḥrānī., *Madīnat al-maʿāǧiz fī muʿǧizāt al-aʾimma al-aṭhār*, vol. III, Part Three, bb. 3, n. 54/1001: 486–487, al-Maǧlisī., *Biḥār al-anwār*, vol. XLIV, bb. 44, n. 1: 310–313, vol. LVIII, bb. 44, n. 46: 182, al-Iṣfahānī., *ʿAwālim al-ʿulūm wa-l-maʿārif al-aḥwāl min al-āyāt wa-l-aḫbār wa-l-aqwāl*, vol. XVII, Part Seventeen, ch. 12, bb. 1, n. 1: 160–161. Cf. also al-Ǧazāʾirī., *Riyāḍ al-abrār fī manāqib al-aʾimma al-aṭhār*, vol. I, Part One: 199, al-Ṭabarsī., *Mustadrak al-wasāʾil wa mustanbiṭ al-masāʾil*, vol. III, bb. 14, n. 3816: 374. Cf. also Ibn Abī al-Dam., *al-Muḫtaṣar fī tārīḫ al-islām*: 89. In al-Rabġūzī's Turkish version of *Qiṣaṣ al-anbiyāʾ* (c. 1310), on the night before they died, all of al-Ḥusayn's group had a dream of their forefathers, telling them that they were about to set out to join them in the afterlife. Cf. BOESCHOTEN H.E. & O'KANE J., (eds.), *Al-Rabghūzī. The Stories of the Prophets*, vol. II, Brill, Leiden 2015: 627.

In a tersely worded summary, Ibn Shahrāshūb reports merely that al-Ḥusayn had been praying sleepily one day and had seen Muḥammad in a dream who informed him of all that lay ahead. Ibn Shahrāshūb includes a detail missing from Ibn Bābawayh's account; that al-Ḥusayn addresses his grandfather, saying: "I have no need to return to the world: take me with you [to the grave]." Muḥammad replies: "The return is inescapable until you have undergone martyrdom."[70] In his *Madīnat al-maʿāǧiz*, the 12th/17th century jurist and exegete al-Baḥrānī relates something of al-Ḥusayn's supplication (after an extended *ṣalāt*) at the graveside:

> Lord, this is the grave of Your Prophet, and I am the son of his daughter and I have formed a judgment about the affair according to what I have learned. I enjoin the good and forbid the wrong. I ask You, by rights of the owner of this grave only what You have chosen for me concerning my affair; what is satisfying to you in it, and satisfying to Your Messenger.[71]

It is at this point that al-Ḥusayn begins to weep, remaining at the grave until dawn, when he dozes and sees his grandfather in a dream. Muḥammad comes to him, observes al-Baḥrānī, "in a company of angels on his right and his left," as he provides an expanded account of the Prophet's lament:

---

[70] Ibn Shahrāshūb., *Manāqib āl Abī Ṭālib*, vol. IV, bb. *Fī imāmat Abī ʿAbd Allāh al-Ḥusayn*: 88, al-Mūsawī., *Tasliyat al-maǧālis wa zīnat al-maǧālis*, vol. II, *maǧlis* 6: 156, al-Baḥrānī., *Madīnat al-maʿāǧiz fī muʿǧizāt al-aʾimma al-aṭhār*, vol. III, Part Three, bb. 3, n. 53/1000: 483–485, al-Maǧlisī., *Biḥār al-anwār*, vol. XLIV, bb. 37, n. 1: 328.

[71] In al-Rabġūzī's *Qiṣaṣ al-anbiyāʾ*, as part of the dream, two hands extend from Muḥammad's tomb to embrace al-Ḥusayn; the Prophet kisses him, telling him that he is coming to join his loved ones who have already passed through death, mentioning specifically ʿAlī, Fāṭima and ʿAlī's older brother, Ǧaʿfar al-Ṭayyār ('the flyer', or sometimes called *ḏū al-ǧanāḥayn* – 'possessor of two wings'). Cf. BOESCHOTEN H.E. & O'KANE J., (eds.), *Al-Rabghūzī. The Stories of the Prophets*, 2015: 624.

> It is as if I see you in the near future, soiled with your blood,[72] butchered at your nape, your grey hair smeared with your blood, and you alone and a foreigner in the land of Karbalāʾ amidst a band from my community, appealing for help and not helped and, together with that, thirsty and not given water, parched and not quenched. They regarded your women as fair game and slaughtered your weaned one(s);[73] nevertheless, they hope for my intercession (God will not accept my intercession for them)[74] on the Day of Resurrection.

The lament underscores the great themes of Karbalāʾ; the betrayal and abandonment of al-Ḥusayn by Muḥammad's own community, the tormenting thirst of the day, which al-ʿAbbās b. ʿAlī[75] had given his life trying to alleviate, the ill-treatment of the women and children both during and immediately after the conflict, and the terrible price that the perpetrators would have to pay. With the promise of divine vengeance, the reward is held out to the martyr:

> My beloved! Ḥusayn! Your father and mother and brother have already reached me, and they are yearning for you. And if you are to have the highest rank in the gardens, you will not obtain it except by martyrdom. So, hurry to your rank; I and your father, your brother and your mother anticipate your arrival soon and our gathering together as a single body.

---

[72] The word occurs here, as in a number of other places, in the plural, as 'bloods'. Although unusual in English, this poses little problem for the Semitic languages. In both Hebrew and in Greek, for example, the word 'blood' is used in the plural to describe the discharge of blood after an act of violence, as in murder or battle.

[73] Written so in the transcript, notes the editor, but in the original as the plural *fuṭm* rather than the singular *faṭīm* (which may have been deliberately used in conjunction with *ḥarīm*).

[74] The editor notes that this is not in the transcript.

[75] Half-brother to al-Ḥusayn, and called 'the moon of the Banū Hāshim' (*qamar Banī Hāshim*) and 'the water bearer' (*al-saqqāʾ*), al-ʿAbbās had attempted, with staggering valour, to fetch water for the women and children on the field of Karbalāʾ, the supply cut off by the enemy, and was martyred for his efforts.

Notwithstanding the promise of his rank in Paradise, al-Ḥusayn awakes dismayed and alarmed, and relates his dream to the people of his house. "And on that day," notes al-Baḥrānī, "there was no grief more intense or tears more numerous than among the People of the House."[76]

Two centuries before Baḥrānī, the 10th/16th century writer al-Mūsawī observes in his *maqtal* that it was during al-Ḥusayn's nocturnal prayer at his grandfather's grave that Medinan governor al-Walīd,[77] who would be dismissed for his hesitancy in using force against al-Ḥusayn, sent to al-Ḥusayn's home of to see if he had already moved out of Medina, and not finding him there, praised God for not afflicting him with the blood of the Prophet's grandson. In fact, al-Ḥusayn would return home early in the morning. While al-Baḥrānī repeats in large measure the account of al-Ḥusayn's second night in prayer at the grave given in the *maqtal*, al-Mūsawī records part of al-Ḥusayn's prayer on that first night:

> Peace be with you, Messenger of God! I am al-Ḥusayn, son of Fāṭima, your young one and the son of your young one, and your grandson whom you left behind in your community. I testify of them, Prophet of God, that they abandoned me, thwarted me, and were not heedful of me, and this is my complaint to you until I meet you.[78]

A second, less detailed or clearly defined encounter seems in fact to be al-Ḥusayn referencing the encounter he had at the grave of Muḥammad. It appears to emanate from the same time period, that is, as al-Ḥusayn is beginning the journey that will end at Karbalāʾ:

---

[76] al-Mūsawī., *Tasliyat al-muğālis wa zīnat al-mağālis*, vol. II, *mağlis* 6: 154–156, al-Baḥrānī., *Madīnat al-maʿāğiz fī muʿğizāt al-aʾimma al-aṭhār*, vol. III, Part Three, bb. 3, n. 53/1000: 483–485, al-Mağlisī., *Biḥār al-anwār*, vol. XLIV, bb. 37, n. 1: 328.

[77] al-Walīd b. ʿUtba b. Abī Sufyān (died 65/684) dismissed by Yazīd in 61/680. Cf. also Ibn Abī al-Dam., *al-Muḫtaṣar fī tārīḫ al-Islām*: 89.

[78] al-Mūsawī., *Tasliyat al-muğālis wa zīnat al-mağālis*, vol. II, *mağlis* 6: 154–156.

> ʿAbd Allāh b. Ǧaʿfar[79] came to ʿAmr b. Saʿīd and asked him to write to al-Ḥusayn an assurance of protection, and reassuring him to return from where he was going. ʿAmr b. Saʿīd wrote him a letter in which he reassured him of kinship, and ensuring security for himself. He sent it with his brother Yaḥyā b. Saʿīd, and Yaḥyā and ʿAbd Allāh b. Ǧaʿfar followed after it after sending of his two sons.[80] These two handed him the letter and took pains with him over his return. He said: "I saw the Messenger of God in a dream and he enjoined me to do what I am doing." They said to him: "What was this vision?" He replied: "I have not told anyone about it, nor will I tell anyone until I meet my Lord, great and powerful."[81]

A final encounter tells of al-Ḥusayn sitting in front of his tent on the eve of the battle, legs drawn up and garment around him, ostensibly cleaning his sword and preparing it for the fight, but in fact dozing off, his head dropping drowsily. His sister Zaynab hears the

---

[79] ʿAbd Allāh b. Ǧaʿfar b. Abī Ṭālib b. ʿAbd al-Muṭṭalib, husband of al-Ḥusayn's sister Zaynab.

[80] Ostensibly, ʿAwn and Muḥammad the two sons of ʿAbd Allāh b. Ǧaʿfar are Zaynab's children and therefore al-Ḥusayn's nephews; but cf. CLOHESSY C., *Half of My Heart. The Narratives of Zaynab, Daughter of ʿAlī*, 2018: 221.

[81] Abū Miḫnaf., *Maqtal al-Ḥusayn*: 155, Ibn Aʿṯam., *Kitāb al-futūḥ*, vol. V: 30, 67, al-Mufīd., *al-Irshād fī maʿrifat ḥuǧaǧ Allāh ʿalā al-ʿibād*, vol. II, bb. *Tārīḫ al-Imām al-Ḥusayn*: 69, al-Ṭabarsī., *Iʿlām al-warā bi-aʿlām al-hudā*, Part Three, bb. 2: 230, vol. I, Part Three, bb. 2: 446, Ibn Shahrāshūb., *Manāqib āl Abī Ṭālib*, vol. IV, bb. *Fī imāmat Abī ʿAbd Allāh al-Ḥusayn*: 94, Ibn al-Aṯīr, *Usd al-ġāba fī maʿrifat al-ṣaḥāba*, vol. II, bb. 1173 (*al-Ḥusayn b. ʿAlī*), n. 330: 24, *al-Kāmil fī al-tārīḫ*, vol. III, *Ḏikr maqtal al-Ḥusayn*: 277, al-Ḏahabī., *Siyar aʿlām al-nubalāʾ*, vol. III, n. 48 (*al-Ḥusayn al-Shahīd Abū ʿAbd Allāh b. ʿAlī b. Abī Ṭālib*): 297, Ibn Kaṯīr., *al-Bidāya wa-l-nihāya*, vol. XI, bb. *al-Iḫbār bi-maqtal al-Ḥusayn b. ʿAlī*: 504, al-Maǧlisī., *Biḥār al-anwār*, vol. XLIV, bb. 37, n. 2: 366, al-Iṣfahānī., *ʿAwālim al-ʿulūm wa-l-maʿārif al-aḥwāl min al-āyāt wa-l-aḫbār wa-l-aqwāl*, vol. XVII, Part Seventeen, ch. 13, bb. 1: 216. Al-Maǧlisī also reports al-Ḥusayn telling ʿAbd Allāh b. al-ʿAbbās and ʿAbd Allāh b. al-Zubayr that he is following Muḥammad's orders, but without reference to any dream (al-Maǧlisī., *Biḥār al-anwār*, vol. XLIV, bb. 37, n. 2: 364).

threatening noise of the approaching army, and goes to wake him, since he has not been roused by the clamour that so disturbs his sister – that of an arriving enemy force – to ask if has not heard how near they are. "Do you not hear the sounds coming closer?"[82] she asks. Al-Ḥusayn lifts his head and says: "I saw the Messenger of God while asleep, and he said to me: Truly, you are coming to us!" She strikes her face and cries out: "O my woe!" Al-Ḥusayn replies: "Woe is not for you, my sister. Calm down, and may the Merciful be merciful to you!"[83]

Al-Ḥusayn has other dreams about the fate that lies ahead of him. Transmitting an extensive narrative from Ibn Bābawayh, al-Mağlisī relates a dream which does not involve his grandfather and the interlocutor remains unidentified, but which nonetheless speaks deeply to al-Ḥusayn's fate. It takes place during the journey to Karbalāʾ, at a watering hole between Mecca and Kūfa named al-ʿUḏayb,[84] about thirty-eight miles from al-Qādisiyya:

> Then he travelled until he alighted at al- ʿUḏayb where he proposed a midday siesta. He awoke from his sleep weeping, and his son said to him: "Father, what is making you weep?" He said: "My son, this is an hour in which a vision does not lie. Something intervened in my dream saying: You are hurrying

---

[82] Ibn ʿAlī al-Fattāl., *Rawḍat al-wāʿiẓīn wa-tabṣirat al-muttaʿiẓīn*, vol. I: 183.

[83] Ibn Aʿṯam., *Kitāb al-futūḥ*, vol. V: 97, al-Mufīd., *al-Irshād fī maʿrifat ḥuğağ Allāh ʿalā al-ʿibād*, vol. II, bb. *Tārīḫ al-Imām al-Ḥusayn*: 90, Ibn ʿAlī al-Fattāl., *Rawḍat al-wāʿiẓīn wa-tabṣirat al-muttaʿiẓīn*, vol. I: 183, al-Ṭabarsī., *Iʿlām al-warā bi-aʿlām al-hudā*, vol. I, Part Three, bb. 2: 237, 454, Ibn al-Aṯīr., *al-Kāmil fī al-tārīḫ*, vol. III, *Ḏikr maqtal al-Ḥusayn*: 284–285, Ibn Kaṯīr., *al-Bidāya wa-l-nihāya*, vol. XI, bb. *al-Iḫbār bi-maqtal al-Ḥusayn b. ʿAlī*: 529, al-Mağlisī, *Biḥār al-anwār*, vol. XLIV, bb. 37, n. 2: 391, al-Ğazāʾirī., *Riyāḍ al-abrār fī manāqib al-aʾimma al-aṭhār*, vol. I, Part One: 220 (who does not name Zaynab as the sister involved).

[84] Cf. HOWARD I.K.A., (trans.), *The History of al-Ṭabarī*, vol. XIX, 1990: 95.

the course and the fates are journeying with you to the Garden."[85]

In a second encounter on the road to Karbalāʾ, at Qaṣr Banī Muqātil according to Abū Miḫnaf, and also involving his son ʿAlī, al-Ḥusayn dreams of a cryptic horseman:

> ʿUqba b. Simʿān said: We set out with him at once, and he dropped his head drowsily, dozing while he was on the back of his horse. Then he awoke, proclaiming: «*Lo! we are Allah's and lo! unto Him we are returning*» and «*Praise be to God, Lord of the worlds*». This he did two or three times, and his son ʿAlī b. al-Ḥusayn approached him and said: "For what reason are you praising God and reciting the verse of returning?" He replied: "My son, I dozed off, and a horseman on horseback appeared to me, saying: The people are journeying and the fates are approaching them. I understood that these were our souls, announcing our death to us." He said: "Father, may God show you no evil. Are we not in the right?" He replied: "Certainly, by God, to whom is the journey of the servants."[86]

By the end of the battle of Karbalāʾ al-Ḥusayn, exhausted, all his companions dead, was encircled by enemy soldiers. A number of transmitters like al-Ṭabarī remark on the prevailing reluctance

---

[85] Ibn Bābawayh., *Kitāb al-amālī fī-l-aḥādīṯ wa-l-aḫbār*, *maǧlis* 30, n. 1: 153, al-Maǧlisī., *Biḥār al-anwār*, vol. XLIV, bb. 37, n. 1: 314, vol. LVIII, bb. 44, n. 46: 182, al-Iṣfahānī., *ʿAwālim al-ʿulūm wa-l-maʿārif al-aḥwāl min al-āyāt wa-l-aḫbār wa-l-aqwāl*, vol. XVII, ch. 13, bb. 1, n. 1: 164, al-Ǧazāʾirī., *Riyāḍ al-abrār fī manāqib al-aʾimma al-aṭhār*, vol. I, Part One: 199, al-Ṭabarsī., *Mustadrak al-wasāʾil wa mustanbaṭ al-masāʾil*, vol. V, Part Five, bb. 33, n. 5463: 114.

[86] Abū Miḫnaf., *Maqtal al-Ḥusayn*: 177, Ibn Aʿṯam., *Kitāb al-futūḥ*, vol. V: 71, al-Mufīd., *al-Iršād fī maʿrifat ḥuǧaǧ Allāh ʿalā al-ʿibād*, vol. II, bb. *Tārīḫ al-Imām al-Ḥusayn*: 82, Ibn ʿAlī al-Fattāl., *Rawḍat al-wāʿiẓīn wa-tabṣirat al-muttaʿiẓīn*, vol. I: 180, 183, al-Ṭabarsī., *Iʿlām al-warā bi-aʿlām al-hudā*, vol. I, Part Three, bb. 2: 233, 450, Ibn Namā al-Ḥillī., *Muṯīr al-aḥzān wa munīr subul al-ashǧān*: 47 (a much-reduced version with few of the details included), Ibn Kaṯīr., *al-Bidāya wa-l-nihāya*, vol. XI, bb. *al-Iḫbār bi-maqtal al-Ḥusayn b. ʿAlī*: 526, al-Maǧlisī, *Biḥār al-anwār*, vol. XLIV, bb. 37, n. 2: 379.

among the common soldiery to kill the Prophet's grandson. Ultimately, al-Ḥusayn will be killed because an annoyed and edgy Shimr harangues and intimidates his troops. Whoever it was who ultimately struck the death blow, and Sinān b. Anas seems a prime candidate,[87] there is no one who bears responsibility for al-Ḥusayn's death more than Shimr. It is Shimr, therefore, who takes a central role in our last set of dreams attributed to al-Ḥusayn. Al-Mağlisī recounts an incident at the height of the battle:

> Then Shimr,[88] may God curse him, descended upon him. The cursed one, who was leprous, beat him with his foot, threw him onto his back and then seized him by his beard. Al-Ḥusayn said: "You are the black and white dog which I saw in my dream!" He replied: "Do you compare me with dogs?" He

---

[87] Sibṭ al-Ğawzī, for example, names five possibilities, with Sinān in first place and Shimr in fifth. Cf. Sibṭ al-Ğawzī., *Taḏkirat ḫawāṣṣ al-umma bi-ḏikr ḫaṣā'iṣ al-a'imma*: 214. Both Ibn al-ʿAdīm and Ibn Kaṯīr suggest Sinān, Shimr or ʿUmar b. Saʿd: cf. Ibn al-ʿAdīm., *Buġyat al-ṭalab fī tārīḫ ḥalab*, Part Six: 2571, 2641, Ibn Kaṯīr., *al-Bidāya wa-l-nihāya*, vol. XI, bb. *al-Iḫbār bi-maqtal al-Ḥusayn b. ʿAlī*: 549, while al-Ṭabarī suggests Sinān or Shimr and notes that the latter was a leper; al-Ṭabarī., *Ḏaḫā'ir al-ʿuqbā*, bb. 9: 249–250.

[88] Shimr (or Shamir) b. Ḏī al-Ğawshan b. Shuraḥbīl b. al-Aʿwar b. ʿUmar b. Muʿāwiya al-ʿĀmir had once supported ʿAlī but later switched sides. (Cf. HOWARD I.K.A., (trans.), *The History of al-Ṭabarī*, vol. XIX, 1990, nt. 192: 49). Ibn Ziyād sent Shimr to replace ʿUmar b. Saʿd as military commander at Karbalā'. Abū Miḫnaf in his account twice attributes these words to one ʿAbd Allāh b. Ḥawza (and in Ibn Abī Shayba and al-Ḫawārizmī, al-Ḥuwayza), but not to Shimr. Cf. Abū Miḫnaf., *Maqtal al-Ḥusayn*: 219–220, Ibn Abī Shayba., *al-Muṣannaf*, vol. XIII, *Kitāb al-fitan*, bb. 1, n. 38385: 295, al-Ḫawārizmī., *Maqtal al-Ḥusayn*, Part Two, bb. *Fī bayan ʿuqūba qātil al-Ḥusayn*, n. 30: 106–107, Ibn al-ʿAdīm., *Buġyat al-ṭalab fī tārīḫ ḥalab*, Part Six: 2643. Cf. also al-Ṭabarī., *Ḏaḫā'ir al-ʿuqbā*, bb. 9: 247 (where Shimr is not mentioned), Ibn ʿAsākir., *Tārīḫ madīnat Dimashq*, vol. XIV, bb. 1566 (*al-Ḥusayn b. ʿAlī b. Abī Ṭālib b. ʿAbd al-Muṭṭalib b. Hāshim b. ʿAbd al-Manāf*): 235 (attributing the words to Ḥurayza).

> began to beat al-Ḥusayn's throat[89] with his sword, saying: "Today I kill you, and my soul knows with certain knowledge, in which there is neither falsity nor doubt nor reserve, that your father was the best of speech."[90]

The incident is problematic in its detail, since not all texts record Shimr as striking the death blow, but it hearkens back to a much earlier moment in the battle:

> Then another (man) came and said: "Where is al-Ḥusayn?" He answered: "Here I am!" He continued: "Rejoice in the Fire!" Al-Ḥusayn replied: "Rejoice in a Merciful Lord and an intercessor whose prayer is answered.[91] Who are you?" He answered: "I am Shimr b. Ḏī al-Ğawshan." Al-Ḥusayn said: "God is the greatest! The Messenger of God said: I saw as if a black and white dog was licking the blood of the people of my house." Then al-Ḥusayn said: "I saw as if dogs were biting me, and among them was a black and white dog which was the fiercest of them against me. That dog is you" (for he was a leper).[92]

---

[89] The Arabic *maḏbaḥ*, defined by Lane as the part of the throat below the lower jaw. Cf. LANE E.W., *An Arabic-English Lexicon*, vol. III, 1968: 955.

[90] Ibn Aʿṯam., *Kitāb al-futūḥ*, vol. V: 119, al-Mūsawī., *Tasliyat al-mağālis wa zīnat al-mağālis*, vol. II, *mağlis* 7: 323, al-Mağlisī, *Biḥār al-anwār*, vol. XLV, bb. 37, n. 2: 56, al-Iṣfahānī., *ʿAwālim al-ʿulūm wa-l-maʿārif al-aḥwāl min al-āyāt wa-l-aḫbār wa-l-aqwāl*, vol. XVII, ch. 13, bb. 1: 299.

[91] Lane takes note that *al-muṭāʿ* is an epithet for Muḥammad, meaning 'he whose prayer is answered; whose intercession for his people is accepted'. Cf. LANE E.W., *An Arabic-English Lexicon*, vol. V, 1968: 1892.

[92] Cf. Ibn Namā al-Ḥillī., *Muṯīr al-aḥzān wa munīr subul al-ashğān*: 64, al-Mūsawī., *Tasliyat al-mağālis wa zīnat al-mağālis*, vol. II, *mağlis* 7: 323, al-Suyūṭī., *al-Ḫaṣāʾiṣ al-kubrā*, vol. II: 450 (with fewer details), al-Mağlisī, *Biḥār al-anwār*, vol. XLV, bb. 37, n. 2: 31, al-Iṣfahānī., *ʿAwālim al-ʿulūm wa-l-maʿārif al-aḥwāl min al-āyāt wa-l-aḫbār wa-l-aqwāl*, vol. XVII, Part Twelve, bb. 4, n. 5: 156, Part Thirteen, bb. 1: 274. Ibn ʿAbd al-Barr mentioned that Ğaʿfar al-Ṣādiq was asked about a vision which had taken fifty years to be fulfilled, in which Muḥammad saw a spotted dog lapping his blood, and

What al-Ḥusayn is referring to is a much earlier dream;[93] at times, it is recorded as a dream of Muḥammad,[94] at other times of al-Ḥusayn, but in the narrative quoted above, of both Muḥammad and his grandson. The following account, narrated by Ǧaʿfar al-Ṣādiq and reported by Ibn Qūlawayh, omits Muḥammad as a recipient:

> When al-Ḥusayn b. ʿAlī had gone up to ʿAqabat al-Baṭn,[95] he said to his companions: "I do not foresee myself but being killed." They said: "Why that, Abū ʿAbd Allāh?" He replied: "A vision which I saw in my dream." They asked: "What was it?" He replied: "I saw dogs biting me, and the fiercest towards me was a spotted dog."[96]

Transmitting from Ibn Shahrāshūb, al-Maǧlisī paints a broader picture, adding elements not found in other reports (including the colour green given to the glass vial):

---

understood that a man would kill al-Ḥusayn. The killer of al-Ḥusayn turned out to be Shimr b. Ḏī al-Ǧawshan, who was leprous. Cf. Ibn ʿAbd al-Barr., *Bahǧat al-maǧālis wa uns al-muǧālis*, bb. *Nawādir min al-ruʾyā muḫtaṣar*: 439, al-Maǧlisī., *Biḥār al-anwār*, vol. LXII, bb. 1: 60.

[93] In al-Rabġūzī's text, al-Ḥusayn dreams of Muʿāwiya's death and of a dog, representing Yazīd, taking his place. One of the many crimes with which Yazīd is accused is that of 'playing with dogs at night'. Cf. BOESCHOTEN H.E. & O'KANE J., (eds.), *Al-Rabghūzī. The Stories of the Prophets*, 2015: 623.

[94] Cf. al-Maǧlisī, *Biḥār al-anwār*, vol. XLV, bb. 37, n. 2: 56, al-Iṣfahānī., *ʿAwālim al-ʿulūm wa-l-maʿārif al-aḥwāl min al-āyāt wa-l-aḫbār wa-l-aqwāl*, vol. XVII, ch. 13, bb. 1: 300. Both al-Maǧlisī and al-Iṣfahānī make reference to al-Ḫawārizmī's *al-Manāqib*.

[95] Generally, Baṭn al-ʿAqaba, a stopping point between Mecca and Kūfa. Al-Iṣfahānī calls it ʿĀqabat al-Baṭn.

[96] Ibn Qūlawayh., *Kāmil al-ziyārāt*, bb. 23, n. 14: 75, al-Maǧlisī, *Biḥār al-anwār*, vol. XLV, bb. 37, n. 24: 87, al-Iṣfahānī., *ʿAwālim al-ʿulūm wa-l-maʿārif al-aḥwāl min al-āyāt wa-l-aḫbār wa-l-aqwāl*, vol. XVII, ch. 12, bb. 4, n. 5: 156, ch. 13, bb. 2, n. 14: 319. Cf. Muslim., *Ṣaḥīḥ*, vol. IV, bk. 22 (*Kitāb al-musāqāt*), bb. 10, n. [4021] 47 – (1572): 289 for a *ḥadīṯ* that says that a black dog with white markings is a devil.

> When it was just before daybreak, al-Ḥusayn was dropping his head drowsily. Then he woke up and said: "Do you know what I just saw in my dream?" They replied: "What was it you saw, son of the Messenger of God?" He continued: "I saw as if dogs were charging me to bite me and among them was a black and white dog which I saw was the fiercest of them against me. I believe that whoever is entrusted with my killing will be a leprous man from among these people. Then after that, I saw my grandfather, the Messenger of God, and with him a group of his companions. He said to me: My son, you are a martyr of the family of Muḥammad; the people of the heavens and the people of the highest level of heaven rejoice over you. Your fast breaking will be with me tonight, so hurry, and do not tarry. This angel has descended from heaven to receive your blood in a green glass vial. This is what I saw, and the matter has drawn near[97] and departure from the world has come close; there is no doubt in that."[98]

Sometime after al-Ḥusayn's death, the dog returns to the dreams of a Syrian, although if Shimr is the spotted dog in the dream, then this dream recounts the killer of al-Ḥusayn as a black dog. Its subtext is a story related by al-Buḫārī, Muslim and Abū Dāwud, of a person, sometimes an (Israeli) prostitute, giving water to a thirsty dog and this being counted as a good deed that brings forgiveness

---

[97] The editor notes that the original text reads *anifa al-amr* rather than *azifa al-amr*, which he regards as incorrect. However, if this is indeed an error, it is transmitted by al-Iṣfahānī in his *ʿAwālim al-ʿulūm wa-l-maʿārif al-aḥwāl min al-āyāt wa-l-aḫbār wa-l-aqwāl*, vol. XVII, ch. 13, bb. 1: 247.

[98] Ibn Aʿtam., *Kitāb al-futūḥ*, vol. V: 99–100, al-Ḫawārizmī., *Maqtal al-Ḥusayn*, Part One, bb. *Fī ḫurūǧ al-Ḥusayn min Makka ilā al-ʿIrāq*, n. 7: 356, al-Mūsawī., *Tasliyat al-maǧālis wa zīnat al-maǧālis*, vol. II, *maǧlis* 6: 268–269, al-Maǧlisī., *Biḥār al-anwār*, vol. XLV, bb. 37, n. 2: 3 (from *al-Manāqib*), al-Iṣfahānī., *ʿAwālim al-ʿulūm wa-l-maʿārif al-aḥwāl min al-āyāt wa-l-aḫbār wa-l-aqwāl*, vol. XVII, ch. 13, bb. 1: 247), al-Ǧazāʾirī., *Riyāḍ al-abrār fī manāqib al-aʾimma al-aṭhār*, vol. I, Part One: 222. al-Qummī., *Safīnat al-biḥār*, vol. III: 250.

and reward.[99] Contrarily, a number of transmitters carry reports in which Muḥammad says that a black dog is a *shayṭān*,[100] and that such a dog should be killed.[101] However, in a number of other transmissions, it is vicious rather than merely black dogs that should be killed:[102]

> My grandfather Ṣāliḥ b. Shaḥām – in Aleppo (Ḥalab), may God have mercy on him, for he was upright and pious – saw in a dream a black dog, panting with thirst, its tongue protruding down to its chest. I said: This dog is thirsty! It occurred to me

---

[99] Cf. al-Buḫārī., *Ṣaḥīḥ*, vol. III, bk. 42 (*Kitāb al-musāqāt*), bb. 9, n. 2363: 317, bk. 46 (*Kitāb al-maẓālim*), bb. 23, n. 2466: 373, vol. IV, bk. 59 (*Kitāb badᶜ al-ḫalq*), bb. 17, n. 3321: 322, bk. 60 (*Kitāb aḥādīṯ al-anbiyāʾ*), bb. 55, n. 3467: 423, vol. VIII, bk. 78 (*Kitāb al-adab*), bb. 27, n. 6009: 35, Muslim., *Ṣaḥīḥ*, vol. VI, bk. 39 (*Kitāb al-salām*), bb. 41, nn. [5859] 153 – (2244), [5860] 154 – (2245), [5861] 155: 102–103, Abū Dāwud., *Sunan*, vol. III, bk. 15 (*Kitāb al-ǧihād*), bb. 44, n. 2550: 234.

[100] Muslim., *Ṣaḥīḥ*, vol. I, bk. 4 (*Kitāb al-ṣalāt*), bb. 50, n. [1137] 265 – (510): 616, Abū Dāwud., *Sunan*, vol. I, bk. 2 (*Kitāb al-ṣalāt*), bb. 109, n. 702: 416–417, al-Tirmiḏī., *al-Ǧāmiᶜ al-ṣaḥīḥ*, vol. I, bk. 2 (*Abwāb al-ṣalāt*), bb. 136, n. 338: 356, al-Nasāʾī., *al-Sunan al-kubrā*, vol. I, bk. 9 (*Kitāb al-qibla*), n. 751: 443) and that such a dog should be killed (Abū Dāwud., *Sunan*, vol. III, bk. 17 (*Kitāb al-ṣayd*), bb. 21–22, nn. 2845, 2846: 403–404, al-Tirmiḏī., *al-Ǧāmiᶜ al-ṣaḥīḥ*, vol. I, bk. 2 (*Abwāb al-ṣayd*), bb. 16, n. 1486: 268, bb. 17, n. 1489: 270). However, in a number of other transmissions, it is vicious rather than black dogs that should be killed (Abū Dāwud., *Sunan*, vol. III, bk. 17 (*Kitāb al-ḥaǧǧ*), bb. 9, nn. [2161] 66 – (1198), [2162] 67, [2163] 68, [2165] 69, [2167] 71, [2168] 72 – (1199), [2169] 73 – (1200), [2170] 74, [2171] 75, [2172] 76, [1199], [2173] 77, [2176] 79: 297–302, al-Tirmiḏī., *al-Ǧāmiᶜ al-ṣaḥīḥ*, vol. II, bk. 7 (*Abwāb al-ḥaǧǧ*), bb. 21, nn. 837, 838: 260–261).

[101] Abū Dāwud., *Sunan*, vol. III, bk. 17 (*Kitāb al-ṣayd*), bb. 21–22, nn. 2845, 2846: 403–404, al-Tirmiḏī., *al-Ǧāmiᶜ al-ṣaḥīḥ*, vol. I, bk. 2 (*Abwāb al-ṣayd*), bb. 16, n. 1486: 268, bb. 17, n. 1489: 270.

[102] Abū Dāwud., *Sunan*, vol. III, bk. 17 (*Kitāb al-ḥaǧǧ*), bb. 9, nn. [2161] 66 – (1198), [2162] 67, [2163] 68, [2165] 69, [2167] 71, [2168] 72 – (1199), [2169] 73 – (1200), [2170] 74, [2171] 75, [2172] 76, [1199], [2173] 77, [2176] 79: 297–302, al-Tirmiḏī., *al-Ǧāmiᶜ al-ṣaḥīḥ*, vol. II, bk. 7 (*Abwāb al-ḥaǧǧ*), bb. 21, nn. 837, 838: 260–261.

> that giving him a drink, and by means of it enter the Garden.[103] I was on the point of doing so when with a great shout, one shouted from behind him, saying: "Ṣāliḥ! Do not give him a drink, Ṣāliḥ, do not give him a drink! This is the killer of al-Ḥusayn b. ʿAlī, being tormented by thirst until the day of Resurrection."[104]

On occasion, it is al-Ḥusayn himself who plays the central role in a dream. Transmitting from al-Mufīd and al-Ṭūsī, al-Maǧlisī reports the words of al-Ḥusayn: "There is not a servant whose eyes flow with tears on account of us, or whose eyes water with one tear for us but that God will settle him because of it in the Garden for a long period.[105] He then transmits the dream of Aḥmad b. Yaḥyā al-Awdī, who sees al-Ḥusayn in a dream and asks him to confirm this heavenly assurance, which he does.[106]

Fāṭima, daughter of Muḥammad and mother to al-Ḥusayn, is another member of the Prophet's house whose nights are punctu-

---

[103] The editor notes that the correct phrase is on the authority of Ibn Manẓūr: "It occurred to me that giving him a drink, the Garden would not be prejudiced thereby."

[104] Ibn ʿAsākir., *Tārīḫ madīnat Dimashq*, vol. XIV, bb. 1566 (*al-Ḥusayn b. ʿAlī b. Abī Ṭālib b. ʿAbd al-Muṭṭalib b. Hāshim b. ʿAbd al-Manāf*): 259, Ibn al-ʿAdīm., *Buġyat al-ṭalab fī tārīḫ ḥalab*, Part Six: 2643.

[105] The term *ḥuqub* (pl. *aḥqāb* or *aḥqūb*) is an undefined period of time, although Lane notes that some say seventy or eighty years or more. A *ḥiqba*, notes Wehr, is a long stretch of time or an historical epoch, while Hava suggests a year or eighty years. Penrice too suggests eighty. Cf. WEHR H., *A Dictionary of Modern Written Arabic*, 1980: 226, LANE E.W., *An Arabic-English Lexicon*, vol. II, 1968: 610, HAVA J.G., *Arabic English Dictionary for Advanced Learners*, Goodwood Books, New Delhi 2001: 127, PENRICE J., *A Dictionary and Glossary of the Kor-ān*, Asian Educational Services, New Delhi 1995: 37. In the Qurʾānic text, English interpreters tend to render it as 'years and years' or 'ages' or 'many years'. Cf. Q. 18:60 (*ḥuqub*) and Q. 78:23 (*aḥqāb*).

[106] al-Mufīd., *al-Amālī*, *maǧlis* 4, n. 6: 241, al-Ṭūsī., *al-Amālī*, *maǧlis* 4, n. 35–181: 117, al-Maǧlisī., *Biḥār al-anwār*, vol. XLIV, bb. 34, n. 34: 292, al-Iṣfahānī., *ʿAwālim al-ʿulūm wa-l-maʿārif al-aḥwāl min al-āyāt wa-l-aḫbār wa-l-aqwāl*, vol. XVII, ch. 20, bb. 1, n. 2: 526.

ated by visions and dreams. Extant in al-Rāwandī, and transmitted only by al-Baḥrānī and al-Maǧlisī, Fāṭima's mystical dream is narrated in an *ḥadīṯ* markedly different from all the others concerning al-Ḥusayn's birth, precisely in that in the others, it is Muḥammad who receives angelic announcements of the birth and forewarnings of the death; he then passes this information on to Fāṭima. At other moments of her life, such as in her grief at her father's death, angels certainly do communicate directly with her, earning her the name al-muḥaddaṯa ('the one to whom the angels spoke').[107]

In the narration that follows, it is Fāṭima who is the recipient of an angelic visitation, although no words are actually spoken to her by the angels, and it is for Muḥammad to interpret the meaning for her, in accordance with the books of *aḥādīṯ*, which report that anyone who had a dream would relate it to the Prophet, and he would interpret it.[108] "I see a light shining on your face," he says to his daughter, in a motif of light that runs through many of the reports about Fāṭima, "you will give birth to a proof (*ḥuǧǧa*) of God over this creation." The encounter, in the sixth month of her pregnancy with al-Ḥusayn, is narrated by Fāṭima herself:

> At the completion of the tenth day of the sixth month I was sleeping, and there came to me in my sleep one who rubbed his wings against my back. I was alarmed, and arose, performed the ritual washing and prayed two prostrations. Then I

---

[107] al-Hilālī., *Kitāb Sulaym b. Qays*: 821, al-Mufīd., *al-Iḫtiṣāṣ*: 329, Ibn Shahrāshūb., *Manāqib āl Abī Ṭālib*, vol. III, bb. *Manāqib Fāṭima al-Zahrā'*: 384, al-Irbilī., *Kashf al-ġumma fī ma'rifat al-a'imma*, vol. I: 468, al-Maǧlisī., *Biḥār al-anwār*, vol. XXX, bb. 19: 132, vol. XLIII, bb. 2, n. 1: 10–11, n. 15: 16–17, bb. 3, n. 48: 55, n. 66: 79.

[108] al-Buḫārī., *Ṣaḥīḥ*, vol. II, bk. 19 (*Kitāb al-tahaǧǧud*), bb. 2, n. 1121: 139, bk. 23 (*Kitāb al-ǧanā'iz*), bb. 93, n. 1386: 267, vol. V, bk. 62 (*Kitāb faḍā'il aṣḥāb al-nabī*), bb. 19, n. 3738: 63, vol. IX, bk. 91 (*Kitāb al-ta'bīr*), bb. 35, nn. 7028, 7030: 110–111, Muslim., *Ṣaḥīḥ*, vol. VI, bk. 42 (*Kitāb al-ru'yā*): [5931] 128, bk. 43 (*Kitāb al-faḍā'il*), bb. 31, n. [6369] 139 – (2478): 343, n. [6370] 140 – (2479): 343–344. "A dream hovers over a man so long as it is not interpreted," noted Muḥammad, "then when it is interpreted it is fulfilled": cf. Muslim., *Sunan*, vol. V, bk. 40 (*Awwal kitāb al-adab*), bb. 88, n. 5020: 365.

> slept again, and there came to me in my sleep one garbed in white, who sat at my head and blew in my face and on my neck. I arose, fearful, performed the ritual washing and prayed four prostrations. Then I slept again, and there came to me in my sleep one who made me sit up and made incantations over me and prayed God's protection over me. In the morning I awoke; it was the day of blessed Umm Salama, and I entered in a bathrobe. I came to Umm Salama, and the Prophet looked at my face, and I saw joy on his. All that I had experienced lifted from me and I recounted it to the Prophet. He said: Rejoice! As regards the first, he is my friend ʿIzrāʾīl,[109] guardian and opener of the wombs of women; as regards the second, he is my friend Mīkāʾīl, guardian of the wombs of the people of my house. Did he blow on you? I said, yes! (Fāṭima then said): Then he held me to himself and said: Regarding the third, he is my brother Ǧibraʾīl, to whom God has given care of your child. I returned and delivered him at the completion of the sixth month."[110]

In a narrative suffused with symbolic details, the crucial element is that Fāṭima is visited by three of the chief Islamic angels (*ruʾūs al-malāʾika*), to each of whom is attributed a task not normally associated with that angel. ʿIzrāʾīl (or sometimes ʿAzrāʾīl) is a brooding presence in the narrative, for essentially, he is the angel concerned with death, portrayed, notes Burge, as a functionary without compassion,[111] and far more associated with the end of life than as "guardian and opener of the wombs of women." In fact, the angel of death does play a role in the creation of Ādam, succeeding in obtaining mud from the earth where Ǧibrīl and Mīkāʾīl had failed

---

[109] The angel of death and sometimes angel of the last trumpet, who is alluded to but unnamed in Q. 32:11 and is, by tradition, so overcome by grief when he looks into Hell, that the earth risks being flooded by his tears. Cf. WENSINCK A.J., "Izrāʾīl" in E. van Donzel et al., (eds.), *The Encyclopaedia of Islam*, vol. IV, 1997: 292–293.

[110] al-Rāwandī., *al-Ḫarāʾiǧ wa-l-ǧarāʾiḥ fī-l-muʿǧizāt*, vol. II: 841, al-Maǧlisī., *Biḥār al-anwār*, vol. XLIII, bb. 12, n. 39: 272–273.

[111] BURGE S.R., *Angels in Islam*, 2012: 138.

before him,[112] in an action that conveys the reality that death is an inescapable part of life the moment it begins. However, while al-Suyūṭī deals at length with the 'angels of the womb',[113] he mentions none of the major Islamic angels has having any specific relationship with wombs or childbirth.

Wombs and childbirth also dominate the dream of Lubāba bt. al-Ḥāriṯ (d. 35/655), better known by her *kunya* Umm al-Faḍl,[114] a woman who enjoyed a substantial prominence in the embryonic Islamic community. Two of her sisters, Maymūna bt. al-Ḥāriṯ and Zaynab bt. Ḫuzayma, became wives of Muḥammad,[115] while she herself went on to marry one of Muḥammad's uncles, ʿAbbās b. ʿAbd al-Muṭṭalib al-Hāshimī, producing a number of children for him, including the esteemed ʿAbd Allāh (Ibn ʿAbbās), himself a dreamer like his mother, as well as Quṯam who is, notes al-Ḏahabī, by virtue of suckling, al-Ḥusayn's brother.[116] Umm al-Faḍl is held to have been the second woman to convert to Islam, on the same day as her close friend Ḫadīǧa.[117] She and her sisters were conspicuous in the nascent Muslim community, a factor that did not go unnoticed by Muḥammad, who commented on their faithfulness: "Ibn ʿAbbās transmitted, on the authority of the Messenger of God, that he said: The four faithful sisters are Maymūna bt. al-Ḥāriṯ, Umm al-Faḍl, Salmā and Asmāʾ."[118] It is curious that

---

[112] al-Suyūṭī., *al-Ḥabāʾik fī aḫbār al-malāʾik*, n. 111: 36.

[113] Op. cit., nn. 440–447: 102–104.

[114] al-Ṭūsī., *Kitāb asmāʾ al-riǧāl*: 52, 271.

[115] al-Zabīdī., *Tāǧ al-ʿarūs min ǧawāhir al-qāmūs*, vol. VIII: 376.

[116] al-Ḏahabī., *Siyar aʿlām al-nubalāʾ*, vol. III, n. 82 (*Quṯam b. al-ʿAbbās*): 440–441. Cf. HOWARD I.K.A., (trans.), *The History of al-Ṭabarī*, vol. XXXIX, 1990: 207.

[117] Ibn Saʿd., *Kitāb al-ṭabaqāt al-kabīr*, vol VIII: 204, al-Mizzī., *Tahḏīb al-kamāl fī asmāʾ al-riǧāl*, vol. XXXV, n. 7923: 297, al-Ṭabarī., *Ḏaḫāʾir al-ʿuqbā*, bb. 3: 373, al-Ḏahabī., *Siyar aʿlām al-nubalāʾ*, vol. III, n. 82 (*Quṯam b. al-ʿAbbās*): 440, al-ʿAsqalānī., *al-Iṣāba fī tamyīz al-ṣaḥāba*, vol. VIII, n. 12204: 450, al-Maǧlisī., *Biḥār al-anwār*, vol. CVIII: 82, al-Qummī., *Safīnat al-biḥār*, vol. II: 314.

[118] al-Ṭabarānī., *al-Muʿǧam al-kabīr*, vol. XXIV, n. 360: 131–132, Ibn ʿAbd al-Barr, *al-Istīʿāb fī maʿrifat al-aṣḥāb*, *Kitāb al-nisāʾ wa kunā-hunna*, bb. *al-*

Muḥammad's observation did not encompass their half-sister, Zaynab bt. Ḫuzayma, who was later to become his own wife.

Umm al-Faḍl's dream goes unnoticed by a number of important transmitters: Ibn al-Aṯīr in *Usd al-ġāba fī maʿrifat al-ṣaḥāba* ignores it, as do Ibn Ḥağar al-ʿAsqalānī in his *Tahḏīb al-tahḏīb* and Ibn ʿAbd al-Barr in his *al-Istīʿāb fī maʿrifat al-aṣḥāb*. Even so, the story is carried by a sufficient number of *muḥaddiṯūn* to render it of interest; it is recounted mostly in four strands and is plagued, as will be noted, by two anomalies. Its first narration is marked by a paucity of detail; the 4th/10th century Ismāʿīlī Shīʿī scholar al-Qāḍī al-Nuʿmān, for example, carries a report found also in al-Ṭabarsī and Ibn ʿAsākir:

> On the authority of Umm Faḍl al-Hilāliyya, in the narrative of al-Awzāʿī, that she went to the Messenger of God (and said): "I saw a vision." He replied: "Good!" She continued: "It was ominous!" He answered: "Relate it!" She said: "It was as if one of your limbs was severed and fell into my lap!" He replied: "What you saw is good. Fāṭima will give birth to a boy and he will be placed in your lap."[119]

The son to whom Fāṭima will give birth is unnamed here, and even though Muḥammad offers a wholesome interpretation, there remains something menacing about the dream, even without its later

---

Lām, n. 3381 (*Salmā bt. ʿUmays*): 1861, n. 4081 (*Lubāba al-ṣuġrā*): 1909, al-Mizzī., *Tahḏīb al-kamāl fī asmāʾ al-riğāl*, vol. XXXV, n. 7923: 298, al-Hayṯamī., *Mağmaʿ al-zawāʾid wa-manbaʿ al-fawāʾid*, vol. IX, *Kitāb al-manāqib*, bb. *Manāqib Asmāʾ bt. ʿUmays*: 260, al-ʿAsqalānī., *al-Iṣāba fī tamyīz al-ṣaḥāba*, vol. VIII, n. 12204: 450.

[119] al-Qāḍī al-Nuʿmān., *Sharḥ al-aḫbār fī faḍāʾil al-aʾimma al-aṭhār*, vol. III, n. 1048: 112 (while Fāṭima is pregnant with al-Ḥusayn), al-Ṭabarsī., *Tāğ al-mawālīd*: 86 (This work, while not listed by Brockelmann, is included in a list by Kohlberg. Cf. KOHLBERG E., "al-Ṭabrisī" in P.J. Bearman et al., (eds.), *The Encyclopaedia of Islam*, vol. X, 2000: 40), Ibn ʿAsākir., *Tārīḫ madīnat Dimashq*, vol. XIV, bb. 1566 (*al-Ḥusayn b. ʿAlī b. Abī Ṭālib b. ʿAbd al-Muṭṭalib b. Hāshim b. ʿAbd al-Manāf*): 114 (who names the boy as al-Ḥusayn), al-Iṣfahānī., *ʿAwālim al-ʿulūm wa-l-maʿārif al-aḥwāl min al-āyāt wa-l-aḫbār wa-l-aqwāl*, vol. XVII, ch. 11, bb. 6, n. 7: 127.

accretions. The 'vision' will soon be qualified with the word "were I to relate it to you, it would distress you."[120] Nothing more is added to the story by these transmitters, and based on Muḥammad's construal of things, the reader is left to make up his or her own mind. However, the report is given a second incarnation, now including an account of the boy[121] inadvertently urinating on the Prophet. The fact that Ibn Saʿd reports this story, as does Ibn Māǧa in his *Sunan*, suggests that it is an early development:

> On the authority of Simāk b. Ḥarb, that Umm al-Faḍl, wife of al-ʿAbbās b. ʿAbd al-Muṭṭalib, said: "Messenger of God! I saw in a dream as if one of your limbs was in my house!"[122] He replied: "What you saw was good! Fāṭima will give birth to a boy, and you will suckle him with the milk of your son Quṯam." The narrator continued: al-Ḥusayn was born and Umm al-Faḍl took responsibility for him. She said: "I came with him to the Messenger of God; he was jumping on him and kissing him when he urinated on the Messenger of God. He said: Umm al-Faḍl, hold my son, because he has urinated on me." She went on: "I took him and pinched[123] him so that he cried because of it, and I said: You have troubled the Messenger of God, urinating on him!" When the boy cried, (the Messenger of God) said: "Umm al-Faḍl, you have troubled me in my son, making him

---

[120] Ibn ʿAsākir., *Tārīḫ madīnat Dimashq*, vol. XIV, bb. 1566 (*al-Ḥusayn b. ʿAlī b. Abī Ṭālib b. ʿAbd al-Muṭṭalib b. Hāshim b. ʿAbd al-Manāf*): 196–197.

[121] Although in Ibn Ḥanbal, the culprit could be either al-Ḥasan or al-Ḥusayn, since both boys are with Muḥammad at the time (Ibn Ḥanbal., *Musnad*, vol. VI (*Ḥadīṯ Umm al-Faḍl*): 339. At one point, Ibn Ḥanbal also identifies the boy as al-Ḥasan; cf. Ibn Ḥanbal., *Kitāb faḍāʾil al-ṣaḥāba*, vol. II, bb. *Faḍāʾil al-Ḥasan wa-l-Ḥusayn*, n. 1385: 780.

[122] Or, says Ibn Kaṯīr, "in my lap" (Ibn Kaṯīr., *al-Bidāya wa-l-nihāya*, vol. IX, bb. *Iḫbār bi-maqtal al-Ḥusayn*: 238).

[123] A second narration, close to Ibn Māǧa, on the authority of Qabus b. al-Muḫāriq, has Umm al-Faḍl striking the boy between his shoulders with her hand and Muḥammad saying to her: "You have hurt my son, may God make you good" or "may God have mercy on you." Cf. also al-Ṭabarī., *Ḏaḫāʾir al-ʿuqbā*, bb. 9: 210.

> cry!" Then he called for water and purged[124] it thoroughly and said: "When it is a boy, they should purge it thoroughly and when it is a girl, they should wash it thoroughly."[125]

The text now makes precise the details of the boy being in the lap of Umm al-Faḍl, including the crucial issue of suckling, so that her own son Quṯam will be a foster brother to Fāṭima's son. While it is unusual that Ibn Māǧa should name the older al-Ḥasan after rather than before his younger brother al-Ḥusayn, this is one of a smattering of texts in which the son in question could be either of the two. One of the anomalies is, as we shall see, the identity of the boy, since this impacts profoundly on the meaning of the story.

---

[124] Ibn Saʿd uses the verb *ḥadara-yaḥdiru*, used by few others in transmitting this *ḥadīṯ*, and which I have rendered as 'to purge' (cf. STEINGASS F., *Learner's Arabic English Dictionary*, 1993: 267).

[125] Ibn Saʿd., *Kitāb al-ṭabaqāt al-kabīr*, vol VIII, n. 4225 (*Umm al-Faḍl*): 218, al-Ṭabarī., *Ḏaḫāʾir al-ʿuqbā*, bb. 9: 210, al-Maǧlisī., *Biḥār al-anwār*, vol. XLIV, bb. 30, n. 46: 246–248. "The urine of a baby girl should be washed off and the urine of baby boy should be sprinkled (with water)," declared Muḥammad in a *ḥadīṯ* carried by a number of transmitters: cf. for e.g. Ibn Māǧa., *Sunan*, vol. I, (*Abwāb al-ṭahāra*), bb. 77, n. 522: 365–366, nn. 525–527: 366–368, Abū Dāwud., *Sunan*, vol. I, bk. 1 (*Kitāb al-ṭahāra*), bb. 135, nn. 375, 367, 377: 236–237, al-Tirmiḏī., *al-Ǧāmiʿ al-ṣaḥīḥ*, vol. I, bk. 1 (*Abwāb al-ṭahāra*), bb. 54, n. 71: 97–98, vol. II, bk. 4 (*Abwāb al-safr*), bb. 77, n. 610: 70–71, al-Nasāʾī., *al-Sunan al-kubrā*, vol. I, bk. 1 (*Kitāb al-ṭahāra*), bb. 189, nn. 304, 305: 187. Most of these transmitters carry a variety of transmissions; the boy is not always named, or is sometimes named either as al-Ḥasan or al-Ḥusayn. Al-Tirmiḏī notes that a handful of people, including ʿAlī, ʿĀʾisha, Zaynab, Umm al-Faḍl (Lubāba), Abū al-Samḥ, Abū Layla and Ibn ʿAbbās relate similar stories; but none of these contain the added details about Ǧibrīl. In Ibn Māǧa., *Sunan*, vol. I, (*Abwāb al-ṭahāra*), bb. 77, n. 522: 365–366 and Abū Dāwud., *Sunan*, vol. I, bk. 1 (*Kitāb al-ṭahāra*), bb. 135, nn. 375: 236 is precisely a narration from Umm al-Faḍl about al-Ḥusayn urinating in the lap of Muḥammad, but with none of Ibn Saʿd's details. Likewise, Ibn Māǧa n. 526: 367–368 and Abū Dāwud nn. 376: 237 narrate of either al-Ḥasan or al-Ḥusayn as the culprit, but again without details.

Thirdly, and of most interest, the dream sometimes also includes the prediction of the boy's death. The visit by the angel and the forecast of his martyrdom take place in a substantively brief interval – in most accounts, Umm al-Faḍl leaves the room to wash the urine from Muḥammad's robe and returns to find him in tears: "When I came back, I found him weeping, and said: For what reason is your weeping, Messenger of God? He replied: Ǧibra'īl came to me and informed me that my community will kill this son of mine."[126] In Ibn Kaṯīr's narration, which identifies the boy as al-Ḥusayn, she does not even have time to leave the room:

> I put him in [Muḥammad's] lap, and then I happened to turn around and the eyes of the Messenger of God were pouring tears. I said: "Prophet of God! You are as dear to me as my own father and mother! What is wrong with you?" He replied: "Ǧibrīl came to me and informed me that my community would kill this son of mine." I said: "This one?" He replied: "Yes, and he came to me with some of its red dust."[127]

---

[126] al-Mufīd., *al-Irshād fī maʿrifat ḥuǧaǧ Allāh ʿalā al-ʿibād*, vol. II, bb. *Faṣl fī faḍāʾil al-Imām al-Ḥusayn wa manāqibi-hi*: 129, al-Bayhaqī., *Dalāʾil al-nubuwwa*, vol. VI, bb. *Ma ruwiya fī iḫbāri-hi bi-qatli ibn ibnati-hi ʿAbd Allāh al-Ḥusayn*: 469, al-Ṭabarsī., *Iʿlām al-warā bi-aʿlām al-hudā*, vol. I, Part Three, bb. 2: 218, Ibn Namā al-Ḥillī., *Muṯīr al-aḥzān wa munīr subul al-ashǧān*: 16–17, al-Irbilī., *Kashf al-ġumma fī maʿrifat al-aʾimma*, vol. II: 5 (here, in his fourth transmission, the dream is predicated of al-Ḥusayn rather than of al-Ḥasan), al-Maǧlisī., *Biḥār al-anwār*, vol. XLIV, bb. 30, n. 46: 246–247, al-Iṣfahānī., *ʿAwālim al-ʿulūm wa al-maʿārif al-aḥwāl min al-āyāt wa-l-aḫbār wa-l-aqwāl*, vol. XVII, n. 1: 116, al-Qummī., *Safīnat al-biḥār*, vol. VII: 113.

[127] al-Mufīd., *al-Irshād fī maʿrifat ḥuǧaǧ Allāh ʿalā al-ʿibād*, vol. II, bb. *Faṣl fī faḍāʾil al-Imām al-Ḥusayn wa manāqibi-hi*: 129, al-Ṭabarī., *Dalāʾil al-imāma*: 179, al-Ṭabarsī., *Iʿlām al-warā bi-aʿlām al-hudā*, vol. I: 218, 426, al-Irbilī., *Kashf al-ġumma fī maʿrifat al-aʾimma*, vol. I: 523 (but he posits the same story about al-Ḥasan), Ibn ʿAsākir., *Tārīḫ madīnat Dimashq*, vol. XIV, bb. 1566 (*al-Ḥusayn b. ʿAlī b. Abī Ṭālib b. ʿAbd al-Muṭṭalib b. Hāshim b. ʿAbd al-Manāf*): 196–197, Ibn Kaṯīr., *al-Bidāya wa-l-nihāya*, vol. IX, bb. *Iḫbār bi-maqtal al-Ḥusayn*: 238, al-Mūsawī., *Tasliyat al-maǧālis wa zīnat al-maǧālis*, vol. II, *maǧlis* 6: 110, al-Suyūṭī., *al-Ḫaṣāʾiṣ al-kubrā*, vol. II: 449, al-Maǧlisī., *Biḥār*

This is a late addition to the story, with the Shīʿī transmissions starting with the 5th/11th century al-Mufīd. The text is imprecise; Muḥammad seems not to have the red dust in his possession at that moment, suggesting that the angelic encounter might have occurred at a different time and that something has triggered a memory of the event, resulting in tears. In the Umm Salama narratives, the dust is always seen or presented, suggesting an immediacy that is absent from the Umm al-Faḍl account.

There are, finally, a number of composite reports that include some, but not always all details from the various transmissions:

> Umm al-Faḍl Lubāba bt. al-Ḥāriṯ said: I saw in a dream before [al-Ḥusayn's] birth as if a piece of the flesh of the Messenger of God was cut off and placed in my lap. I recounted the vision to the Messenger of God, and he said: "The vision has spoken truly! Fāṭima will give birth to a boy and I will hand him over to you to suckle him." The matter came to pass in that way, and one day I came with him and placed him in his lap, and he urinated, and some of the drops dribbled onto his robe. So, I pinched him and he cried. He said: "Be slow with such anger, Umm al-Faḍl; this robe of mine can be washed, but you have hurt my son!" She said: I left him and took it to put it in water. When I came back, I found him weeping, and said: For what reason is your weeping, Messenger of God? He replied: "Ǧibraʾīl came to me and informed me that my community will kill this son of mine."[128]

---

al-anwār, vol. XLIV, bb. 30, n. 20: 238, al-Iṣfahānī., *ʿAwālim al-ʿulūm wa al-maʿārif al-aḥwāl min al-āyāt wa-l-aḫbār wa-l-aqwāl*, vol. XVII, n. 7: 127.

[128] al-Mufīd., *al-Irshād fī maʿrifat ḥuǧaǧ Allāh ʿalā al-ʿibād*, vol. II, bb. *Faṣl fī faḍāʾil al-Imām al-Ḥusayn wa manāqibi-hi*: 129, al-Ḥākim al-Nīsābūrī., *Kitāb al-mustadrak ʿalā al-ṣaḥīḥayn*, vol. III, (*Faḍāʾil Abī ʿAbd Allāh al-Ḥusayn*), n. 4884: 210, Ibn Ṭāʾūs., *Kitāb al-luhūf fī qatlā al-ṭufūf*: 12–13, Ibn Namā al-Ḥillī., *Muṯīr al-aḥzān wa munīr subul al-ashǧān*: 16–17, al-Ḥurr al-ʿĀmilī., *Tafṣīl wasāʾil al-shīʿa ilā taḥṣīl masāʾil al-sharīʿa*, vol. III, bb. 8, n. 5–3991: 405, al-Maǧlisī., *Biḥār al-anwār*, vol. XLIV, bb. 30, n. 30: 238–239, n. 46: 246–247, al-Iṣfahānī., *ʿAwālim al-ʿulūm wa al-maʿārif al-aḥwāl min al-āyāt*

The hurt which she has ostensibly caused the boy, and which pales in comparison to the news the Prophet is about to receive, meets with a variety of responses from Muḥammad: "Slowly, Umm al-Faḍl," reports ʿAbbās Qummī, "this spillage of water can be cleaned, but what thing will make this affliction pass from the heart of al-Ḥusayn?"[129] In his *Kitāb al-mustadrak*, al-Ḥākim al-Nīsābūrī also transmits the prediction made to Umm al-Faḍl and the urination incident, but outside the context of the dream narrative.[130]

Two anomalies remain: the first is that sometimes al-Ḥasan rather than his brother is the subject of the dream, in a report transmitted by an unexpectedly large number of Shīʿī transmitters, while at other times, the boy remains unnamed:[131]

> On the authority of Umm al-Faḍl, wife of al-ʿAbbās, that she said: I said: "Messenger of God, I saw in a dream as if one of your limbs was in my lap!" He said: "Fāṭima will give birth to a boy and you will provide for him." Fāṭima gave birth to al-

---

wa-l-aḫbār wa-l-aqwāl, vol. XVII, n. 1: 116, al-Qummī., *Safīnat al-biḥār*, vol. VII: 113.

[129] al-Qummī., *Safīnat al-biḥār*, vol. I: 408.

[130] al-Ḥākim al-Nīsābūrī., *Kitāb al-mustadrak ʿalā al-ṣaḥīḥayn*, vol. III, bk. 31 (*Kitāb maʿrifat al-ṣaḥāba*), nn. 4890, 4895: 213–214. Cf. also al-Qummī., *Safīnat al-biḥār*, vol. I: 408.

[131] Cf. for e.g. Ibn Ḥanbal., *Musnad*, vol. VI (*Ḥadīṯ Umm al-Faḍl*): 340, al-Balāḏurī., *Kitāb ansāb al-ashraf*, vol. IV, bb. *Quṯam b. al-ʿAbbās b. ʿAbd al-Muṭṭalib*: 85, Ibn al-Aṯīr, *Usd al-ġāba fī maʿrifat al-ṣaḥāba*, vol. III, n. 3122: 359. In his *Nūr al-abṣār*, al-Shablanğī carries the story twice, once relating it to al-Hasan and once to al-Ḥusayn. Only in the latter is what she saw described as 'a strange dream' (*ḥulm munkar*); his account omits the urination story but relates the prediction of death. Al-Shablanğī also relates the urination story, but predicated of al-Ḥasan, and outside of the dream and prediction context. Cf. al-Shablanğī., *Nūr al-abṣār fī manāqib āl bayt al-nabī al-muḫtār*, *faṣl fī ḏikr sayyidi-nā al-Ḥasan*: 239–240, *faṣl fī ḏikr sayyidi-nā al-Ḥusayn*: 254–255.

> Ḥasan, and the Prophet handed him to her and she suckled him with the milk of Quṯam b. al-ʿAbbās.[132]

A second anomaly is that sporadically, the dream is predicated of Umm Ayman rather than of Umm al-Faḍl. Ibn ʿAsākir reserves a special place in the fourth volume of his massive history of Damascus, separated by more than sixty volumes from all others, for eight women who were particularly close to Muḥammad.[133] One of these was an Abyssinian[134] servant, long associated with the Prophet's family, Baraka bt. Ṯaʿlaba b. ʿAmr b. al-Nuʿmān, better known by her *kunya* Umm Ayman,[135] whom Muḥammad called 'my mother after my mother'.[136] Umm Ayman would continue to care for

---

[132] al-Shāmī., *al-Durr al-naẓīm fī manāqib al-aʾimma al-lahāhīm*, bb. 5, *Fī ḏikr al-Ḥusayn b. ʿAlī*: 489, Ibn al-ʿAdīm., *Buġyat al-ṭalab fī tārīḫ ḥalab*, Part Six: 2565–6, al-Irbilī., *Kashf al-ġumma fī maʿrifat al-aʾimma*, vol. I: 523, 530, 547 (three times he posits the dream and interpretation of al-Ḥasan), Ibn al-Muṭahhar al-Ḥillī., *al-ʿAdad al qawiyya li-dafʿ al-maḫāwif al-yawmiyya*, bb. 5: 35–36, al-ʿAsqalānī., *al-Iṣāba fī tamyīz al-ṣaḥāba*, vol. V, n. 7096 (*Quṯam b. al-ʿAbbās*): 320, al-Ḥurr al-ʿĀmilī., *Iṯbāt al-hudāt bi-l-nuṣūṣ wa-l-muʿǧizāt*, vol. I, bb. 8, *faṣl* 35, n. 573: 409, al-Maǧlisī., *Biḥār al-anwār*, vol. XLIII, bb. 11, n. 14: 242, n. 33: 255, al-Ǧazāʾirī., *Riyāḍ al-abrār fī manāqib al-aʾimma al-aṭhār*, vol. I, Part One: 76, al-Ṭabarsī., *Mustadrak al-wasāʾil wa mustanbiṭ al-masāʾil*, vol. VIII, n. 2211: 318.

[133] Cf. WINET M., "Female Presence in Biographical Dictionaries: Ibn ʿAsākir's Selection Criteria for Women in his *Taʾrīkh Madīnat Dimashq*" in S. Judd and J. Scheiner (eds.), *New Perspectives on Ibn ʿAsākir in Islamic Historiography*, Brill, Leiden 2017: 103–104.

[134] al-Zuhrī., *al-Maġāzī al-nabawiyya*: 177, al-Ṭabarānī., *al-Muʿǧam al-kabīr*, vol. XXV: 86.

[135] Ibn ʿAsākir., *Tārīḫ madīnat Dimashq*,vol. IV, bb. *Maʿrifat ʿabīda-hu wa imāʾa-hu wa ḏikr ḥadīṯa-hu wa kitāba-hu wa amnāʾa-hu maʿ marāʿāt al-ḥurūf fī asmāʾi-him wa ḏikr baʿḍ ma ḏukira min anbāʾi-him*, n. 1: 302–345.

[136] Ibn Saʿd., *Kitāb al-ṭabaqāt al-kabīr*, vol. VIII: 223, Ibn Kaṯīr., *al-Bidāya wa-l-nihāya*, vol. VIII, bb. *Ḏikr ʿabīdi-hi*: 285, vol IX, bb. *Ḏikr man tawaffa fī haḏā al-sanʿa*: 334, Ibn ʿAbd al-Barr., *al-Istīʿāb fī maʿrifat al-aṣḥāb*, vol. IV, n. 3552: 1794, Ibn al-Aṯīr., *Usd al-ġāba fī maʿrifat al-ṣaḥāba*, vol. VI, n. 7363: 309.

Muḥammad until adulthood,[137] when, upon his marriage to Ḫadīǧa, he arranged for her freedom; despite this, she remained in the service of his household. She would lose a husband and a son (Ayman) in battle, but a later son, Usāma b. Zayd b. Ḥārita, would make a name for himself in emergent Islam.[138] Muḥammad held her in greet esteem,[139] and she is declared to be among the women inhabiting Paradise.[140] Nevertheless, relatively few sources attribute to her the dream more commonly associated with Umm al-Faḍl:

> On the authority of Abū ʿAbd Allāh, who said: Neighbours of Umm Ayman came to the Messenger of God and said: "Messenger of God! Umm Ayman did not sleep last night from weeping. She has not stopped crying since she awoke!" The Messenger of God sent for Umm Ayman, who came to him. He said to her: "Umm Ayman, may God not cause your eye to weep! Your neighbours came to me and informed me that you did not cease to cry the whole night! May God not cause your eye to weep! What is it that is making you cry?" She replied: "Messenger of God, I saw a terribly ominous dream, and I could not stop crying all night!" The Messenger of God said to

---

137 Ibn Saʿd., *Kitāb al-ṭabaqāt al-kabīr*, vol. VIII: 223, al-Balāḏurī., *Kitāb ansāb al-ashrāf*, vol. I: 96, al-ʿAsqalānī., *al-Iṣāba fī tamyīz al-ṣaḥāba*, vol. VIII: 380.

138 al-Balāḏurī., *Kitāb ansāb al-ashrāf*, vol. I: 96, al-Ḏahabī., *Siyar aʿlām al-nubalāʾ*, vol. II, n. 24 (*Umm Ayman*): 224.

139 Ibn Saʿd., *Kitāb al-ṭabaqāt al-kabīr*, vol. VIII: 223–226, al-Ḏahabī., *Siyar aʿlām al-nubalāʾ*, vol. II, n. 24 (*Umm Ayman*): 224.

140 Cf. for e.g. al-Hilālī., *Kitāb Sulaym b. Qays*, vol. I, n. 4: 265, vol. II: 867, al-Qummī., *Tafsīr*, *sūrat al-Rūm*, n. 1: 155, al-Kulaynī., *al-Kāfī fī ʿilm al-dīn*, vol. II, Part Two, n. 6: 405, al-Qāḍī al-Nuʿmān., *Sharḥ al-aḫbār fī faḍāʾil al-aʾimma al-aṭhār*, vol. III, n. 973: 32, al-Rāwandī., *al-Ḫarāʾiǧ wa-l-ǧarāʾiḥ fī-l-muʿǧizāt*, vol. I, bb. I, n. 187: 113, al-Ṭabarsī., *Kitāb al-iḥtiǧāǧ ʿalā ahl al-liǧāǧ*, vol. I, Part One: 91, Ibn Ṭāʾūs., *al-Ṭarāʾif fī maʿrifat maḏhab al-ṭawāʾif*, vol. I, n. 348: 249–250, al-Ḥillī al-ʿAllāma., *Nahǧ al-ḥaqq wa-kashf al-ṣidq*: 270, al-Ḏahabī., *Siyar aʿlām al-nubalāʾ*, vol. II, n. 24 (*Umm Ayman*): 224, al-Baḥrānī., *al-Burhān fī tafsīr al-qurʾān*, vol. II, *sūrat al-nisāʾ*, n. 2674: 157, vol. IV, *sūrat al-Rūm*, n. 8354: 346, al-Maǧlisī *Biḥār*, vol. XVII, bb. 4, n. 46: 379, vol. XXII, bb. 5, n. 8: 265, vol. XXIX, bb. 11, n. 10: 117, n. 27: 128.

> her: "Relate it to the Messenger of God, for God and His Messenger know." She replied: "It is distressing for me to talk about it!" He said to her: "The vision is not what you think. Relate it to the Messenger of God!" She answered: "This is what I saw in my dream; it was as if one of your limbs was found in my house!" The Messenger of God said to her: "Let your eyes rest, Umm Ayman. Fāṭima will give birth to al-Ḥusayn; you will tend him and take charge over him, so that one of my limbs will be in your house." When Fāṭima gave birth to al-Ḥusayn, on the seventh day, the Messenger of God gave the order, and his head was shaven and the weight of his hair was given in silver as alms and an animal slaughtered and sacrificed for him. Then Umm Ayman prepared him and wrapped him in the garment of the Messenger of God. Then she came with him to the Messenger of God, who said: "Welcome, to the bearer and the one borne! Umm Ayman, this is the interpretation of your vision."[141]

Aside from its being predicated of Umm Ayman rather than Umm al-Faḍl, the narrative is somewhat typecast, with Muḥammad's anticipatory counter-prediction that the vision will be good rather than bad, something he fails to do in the case of Umm al-Faḍl, and his theological declaration that 'God and His Messenger know'. The prosaic details of Umm Ayman swaddling the new-born are offset by a singular *ḥadīṯ* which introduces a rush of angelic activity at al-Ḥusayn's birth, ordered by God Himself, suitably to celebrate the birth of a child for Muḥammad. "When al-Ḥusayn b. ʿAlī was born," notes the text, God,

> inspired Mālik, keeper of the Fire, to subdue the fires for its people in honour of the child born to Muḥammad; and He in-

[141] Ibn Bābawayh., *Kitāb al-amālī fī al-aḥādīṯ wa-l-aḫbār*, *maǧlis* 19, n. 1: 82, Ibn ʿAlī al-Fattāl., *Rawḍat al-wāʿiẓīn wa-tabṣirat al-muttaʿiẓīn*, vol. I: 154–155, Ibn Shahrāshūb., *Manāqib āl Abī Ṭālib*, vol. IV, bb. *Fī imāmat Abī ʿAbd Allāh al-Ḥusayn*: 70, al-Maǧlisī., *Biḥār al-anwār*, vol. XLIII, b. 11, n. 15: 242–243, al-Iṣfahānī., *ʿAwālim al-ʿulūm wa al-maʿārif al-aḥwāl min al-āyāt wa-l-aḫbār wa-l-aqwāl*, vol. XVII, n. 3: 23, al-Ǧazāʾirī., *Riyāḍ al-abrār fī manāqib al-aʾimma al-aṭhār*, vol. I: 76.

> spired Riḍwān,[142] keeper of the Gardens, to adorn the Gardens and to perfume them in honour of a child born to Muḥammad on the earth. And God, may He be blessed and exalted, inspired the maidens of Paradise to dress up and to visit each other in honour of a child born to Muḥammad on the earth; and God, powerful and lofty, inspired the angels to perform in ranks the glorification of God (al-tasbīḥ), the praise of God (al-taḥmīd), the exaltation of God (al-tamǧīd) and the proclamation that God is the greatest (al-takbīr) in honour of a child born to Muḥammad on the earth…[143]

But Umm Ayman would have known nothing of this. It is in the home of this woman, so cherished by Muḥammad, that she sees her disquieting vision and in her home that she would help to rear the young al-Ḥusayn; but it is in the house of another woman, no less loved by the Prophet that, his own startling encounters with the angels would play out, and so it is to Umm Salama that we must now turn.

---

142 The angel who looks after Paradise, possibly alluded to in Q. 9: 21 and 57: 20. Cf. MURATA S., "The Angels" in S.H. Nasr (ed.), *Islamic Spirituality. Foundations*, 1997: 325.

143 Ibn Bābawayh., *Ikmāl (kamāl) al-dīn wa-itmām (tamām) al-niʿma fī iṯbāt al-ġayba wa-kashf al-ḥayra*, vol. I, bb. 24, n. 36: 282, al-Maǧlisī., *Biḥār al-anwār*, vol. XLIII, bb. 11, n. 24: 248.

The Odour of Paradise. In the House of Umm Salama

Curiously, important Islamic biographers and historians like Ibn ʿAbd al-Barr and Ibn al-Aṯīr give no indication of any dreams or visions in their short biographies of Umm Salama;[1] and yet, a core narrative, going as far back at least as al-Tirmiḏī,[2] concerns at least one of Umm Salama's important dreams, of Muḥammad after his death, a stark vision of a Muḥammad marked by a harrowing phys-

[1] Ibn ʿAbd al-Barr., *al-Istīʿāb fī maʿrifat al-aṣḥāb*, vol. IV, n. 4111 (Hind bt. Abī ʿUmayya): 1920–1921, Ibn al-Aṯīr., *Usd al-ġāba fī maʿrifat al-ṣaḥāba*, vol. VI, n. 7464: 351–353; nor, for that matter, does Ibn Ḥağar al-ʿAsqalānī (al-ʿAsqalānī., *al-Iṣāba fī tamyīz al-ṣaḥāba*, vol. VII, n. 12054: 325–328, *Tahḏīb al-tahḏīb*, vol. vol. XII, n. 2905: 455), although reference to her dreams is found in some of his other works.

[2] As Karamustafa points out, al-Tirmiḏī was himself no stranger to dreams and visions; nor, for that matter, was his wife, and he often relied upon her dreams to confirm his own. Cf. KARAMUSTAFA A., *Sufism. The Formative Period*, 2007: 44.

ical appearance. This narrative is sometimes from Umm Salama's son ʿUmar, but more often from Umm Salmā, a woman of the *anṣār*,[3] who goes to visit Umm Salama and finds her perturbed and in tears after a dream she has had:

> I said: What is making you cry? She answered: "I saw the Messenger of God – that is, in a dream – and there was dirt on his head and his beard, so I said: What is wrong with you, Messenger of God? He answered: I just witnessed the killing of al-Ḥusayn."[4]

---

[3] al-Irbilī., *Kashf al-ġumma fī maʿrifat al-aʾimma*, vol. II, Part Three: 11.

[4] al-Tirmiḏī., *al-Ǧāmiʿ al-ṣaḥīḥ*, vol. VI, bk. 46 (*Abwāb al-manāqib*), bb. 30, n. 3771: 426 (declared *ḍaʿīf* and, according to Abū ʿĪsā, *ġarīb*. Al-Tirmiḏī's editor notes that Ibn Ḥanbal transmits it, but is in fact referring to the dream that Ibn Ḥanbal transmits concerning Ibn ʿAbbās and not Umm Salama (Ibn Ḥanbal., *Musnad*, vol. I, *Musnad ʿAbd Allāh b. ʿAbbās*: 242, 243), al-Āğurrī., *Kitāb al-sharīʿa*, vol. III, bb. *Iḫbār al-nabī bi-qatli al-Ḥusayn*, n. (1106) 1723: 319–320, al-Qāḍī al-Nuʿmān., *Sharḥ al-aḫbār fī faḍāʾil al-aʾimma al-aṭhār*, vol. III, Part Twelve, n. 1106: 167, al-Ḥākim al-Nīsābūrī., *Kitāb al-mustadrak ʿalā al-ṣaḥīḥayn*, vol. III, Part Three, bk. 31 (*Kitāb maʿrifat al-ṣaḥāba*), *Ḏikr Umm al-muʾminīn Umm Salama*, n. 6843: 101, al-Ṭūsī., *al-Amālī fī-l-ḥadīt, mağlis* 11, n. 87–640: 314–315, al-Ḫawārizmī., *Maqtal al-Ḥusayn*, Part Two, bb. *Fī bayān ʿuqūba qātil al-Ḥusayn*, n. 37: 109, Ibn ʿAsākir., *Tārīḫ madīnat Dimashq*, vol. XIV, bb. 1566 (*al-Ḥusayn b. ʿAlī b. Abī Ṭālib b. ʿAbd al-Muṭṭalib b. Hāshim b. ʿAbd al-Manāf*): 238, Ibn Shahrāshūb., *Manāqib āl Abī Ṭālib*, vol. IV, bb. *Fī imāmat Abī ʿAbd Allāh al-Ḥusayn*: 55, al-Shāmī., *al-Durr al-naẓīm fī manāqib al-aʾimma al-lahāhīm*, bb. 5, *Fī ḏikr al-Ḥusayn b. ʿAlī*: 566–567, Ibn al-Biṭrīq., *al-ʿUmda fī ʿuyūn al-aḫbār fī manāqib amīr al-muʾminīn, faṣl fī manāqib al-Ḥasan wa-l-Ḥusayn*, n. 830: 404, Ibn al-ʿAdīm., *Buġyat al-ṭalab fī tārīḫ Ḥalab*, Part Six: 2644, Ibn Ṭāʾūs., *al-Ṭarāʾif fī maʿrifat maḏāhib al-ṭawāʾif*, vol. I, n. 292: 203, al-Irbilī., *Kashf al-ġumma fī maʿrifat al-aʾimma*, vol. II, Part Three: 11, al-Ṭabarī., *Ḏaḫāʾir al-ʿuqbā*, Part One, bb. 9: 254, al-Ḏahabī., *Siyar aʿlām al-nubalāʾ*, vol. III, n. 48 (*al-Ḥusayn al-Shahīd Abū ʿAbd Allāh b. ʿAlī b. Abī Ṭālib*): 316, Ibn Kaṯīr., *al-Bidāya wa-l-nihāya*, vol. XI, bb. *al-Iḫbār bi-maqtal al-Ḥusayn b. ʿAlī*: 574, al-ʿAsqalānī., *Tahḏīb al-tahḏīb*, vol. II, bb. *al-Ḥāʾ*, n. 615: 356, al-Suyūṭī., *al-Ḫaṣāʾiṣ al-kubrā*, vol. II: 452, al-Baḥrānī., *Ḥilyat al-abrār fī aḥwāl Muḥammad wa āli-hi al-aṭhār*, vol. IV, bb. 7, n. 16: 127, bb. 19, n. 3: 214, *Madīnat al-*

Quite patently, al-Tirmiḏī refrains from any allusion to an angelic encounter, remaining instead in a genre that includes no heavenly entities, but only the materialization of a distraught Muḥammad in a vision. Some might speculate that this is indicative of a reverential desire to separate what is properly called 'revelation' (*waḥy*) from other divine communications, prudently avoiding any intimation that a visit by Ǧibrīl always entails the former. In reality, the Sunnī collection of *aḥādīṯ* transmissions (*al-kutub al-sitta*) is replete with encounters with Ǧibrīl which are not classed on the same level as that revelation he brought down to Muḥammad. In fact, as Rahman[5] underscores, within the Qur'ānic text, Ǧibrīl is given a number of appellations, but never 'angel', suggesting a diversity of rank, vocation and function; it is in the corpus of *aḥādīṯ* that this supernatural being and bringer of revelation is called 'angel'. This is noteworthy even in the famous story of Maryam, and the announcement of her son; in Q 3:43, 45–46 it is accomplished by a group of angels, while in Q 19:17 it is Ǧibrīl appearing, as though different from all other angels, and not as an angel but in the form of a flawless human («*Then We sent unto her Our Spirit and it assumed for her the likeness of a perfect man*»). It seems unlikely therefore that the accounts of Ǧibrīl in the context of revelation would be confused with numerous other messages he brings.

In al-Ḫawārizmī's version, also from Salmā, the dream narrative is preceded by an account of Muḥammad placing before Umm Salama a glass vial containing 'sand' (*raml*) from al-Ṭaff, and telling her that when it changes to fresh blood, al-Ḥusayn will have been killed.[6] The report continues with Salmā hearing a shout ringing out

---

ma'āǧiz fī mu'ǧizāt al-a'imma al-aṭhār, vol. III, Part Three, bb. 3, n. 56/1003: 492, al-Maǧlisī., *Biḥār al-anwār*, vol. XLV, bb. 42, nn. 1–4: 231–232, al-Iṣfahānī., *'Awālim al-'ulūm wa-l-ma'ārif al-aḥwāl min al-āyāt wa-l-aḫbār wa-l-aqwāl*, vol. XVII, ch. 18, bb. 3, nn. 1–3: 506–508, al-Ǧazā'irī., *Riyāḍ al-abrār fī manāqib al-a'imma al-aṭhār*, vol. I, Part One: 273.

[5] RAHMAN F., *Major Themes of the Qur'an*, Bibliotheca Islamica, Chicago 1980: 97.

[6] Ibn al-Aṯīr follows this narrative, with Umm Salama guarding the dust in the same way that eventually she will guard the door of the house, but with no mention of a dream: "It was related that the Prophet gave

from Umm Salama's room; Umm Salama recounts her dream of Muḥammad, who says to her: "The people have fallen upon my son and killed him! I have just witnessed his killing." It is this that drives her to look at the vial, which now contains blood.[7]

The common elements are the dust (*turāb*) on his head and his beard, dust of which, Abū Ǧaʿfar notes, "we have it with us"[8] – this is not merely the dirt associated with a long journey, but rather the dust of Karbalāʾ, whose importance will grow with the narrative, as it develops into dust in his hand given him by Ǧibrīl. A sprinkling of transmitters, beginning with Ibn Bābawayh, omit the traces of dust on the Prophet's head and beard, describing him instead as 'emaciated' (*shāḥib*) and 'distressed' (*kaʾīb*),[9] while others merely remark that he appeared 'dishevelled' (*ashʿaṯ, shaʿiṯ*) and 'dusty' (*aġbar*).[10]

Umm Salama some of al-Ḥusayn's dust which Ǧibrīl had brought to him, and the Prophet said to Umm Salama: When this dust becomes blood, al-Ḥusayn will have been killed. Umm Salama guarded that dust in a glass vial she had with her, and when and when al-Ḥusayn was killed the dust became blood. She also informed the people about his killing" (Ibn al-Aṯīr., *al-Kāmil fī al-tārīḫ*, vol. III, *Ḏikr maqtal al-Ḥusayn*: 303). Cf. also al-Ḏahabī., *Siyar aʿlām al-nubalāʾ*, vol. III, n. 48 (*al-Ḥusayn al-Shahīd Abū ʿAbd Allāh b. ʿAlī b. Abī Ṭālib*): 290, *Tārīḫ al-Islām*, vol. V: 67.

[7] al-Ḫawārizmī., *Maqtal al-Ḥusayn*, Part Two, bb. *fī bayān ʿuqūba qātil al-Ḥusayn*, n. 38: 109–110, al-Iṣfahānī., *ʿAwālim al-ʿulūm wa-l-maʿārif al-aḥwāl min al-āyāt wa-l-aḫbār wa-l-aqwāl*, vol. XVII, ch. 18, bb. 2, n. 3: 508.

[8] al-Maǧlisī., *Biḥār al-anwār*, vol. XLV, bb. 42, n. 2: 231.

[9] Ibn Bābawayh., *al-Amālī*, *maǧlis* 29, n. 1: 139, al-Mufīd., *al-Amālī*, *maǧlis* 38: 319, al-Ṭūsī., *al-Amālī*, *maǧlis* 3, n. 49–130: 90, Ibn ʿAlī al-Fattāl., *Rawḍat al-wāʿiẓīn wa-tabṣirat al-muttaʿiẓīn*, vol. I: 170, al-Maǧlisī, *Biḥār al-anwār*, vol. XLV, bb. 42, n. 1: 230, al-Iṣfahānī., *ʿAwālim al-ʿulūm wa-l-maʿārif al-aḥwāl min al-āyāt wa-l-aḫbār wa-l-aqwāl*, vol. XVII, ch. 18, bb. 3, n. 4: 509.

[10] al-Mufīd., *al-Irshād fī maʿrifat ḥuǧaǧ Allāh ʿalā al-ʿibād*, vol. II, bb. *Tārīḫ al-Imām al-Ḥusayn*: 131 (disheveled and dusty), Ibn ʿAlī al-Fattāl., *Rawḍat al-wāʿiẓīn wa-tabṣirat al-muttaʿiẓīn*, vol. I: 193, al-Ṭabarsī., *Iʿlām al-warā bi-aʿlām al-hudā*, vol. I, Part Three, bb. 2: 219, 428, al-Irbilī., *Kashf al-ġumma fī maʿrifat al-aʾimma*, vol. II, Part Two: 8, al-Maǧlisī., *Biḥār al-anwār*, vol. XLIV, bb. 30, n. 31: 239, vol. XLV, bb. 42, n. 2: 231, al-Iṣfahānī.,

There are others, like al-Qāḍī al-Nuʿmān, who do not specify that Muḥammad actually witnessed the death; rather, the dream takes the form of a prophetic announcement and in the morning, as predicted, news of al-Ḥusayn's death arrives: "I saw the Prophet weeping in my dream," she says, "and I said: Messenger of God, what is making you weep? He said: My son al-Ḥusayn has been killed." The next morning, news of his death comes to Umm Salama.[11] However, in most reports Muḥammad has witnessed the death and in a number, he has been involved the burial of al-Ḥusayn and his companions,[12] often with the words "all night I have been digging the graves for al-Ḥusayn and his companions."[13] *Shayḫ* al-Ṭūsī transmits a narrative from ʿAmr b. Ṯābit[14] whose father had confirmed the details with the fifth Imam:[15]

ʿAwālim al-ʿulūm wa-l-maʿārif al-aḥwāl min al-āyāt wa-l-aḫbār wa-l-aqwāl, vol. XVII, ch. 11, bb. 6, n. 8: 127. al-Ǧazāʾirī., *Riyāḍ al-abrār fī manāqib al-aʾimma al-aṭhār*, vol. I, Part One: 171.

[11] al-Qāḍī al-Nuʿmān., *Sharḥ al-aḫbār fī faḍāʾil al-aʾimma al-aṭhār*, vol. III, Part Twelve, n. 1106: 167, Ibn Ṭāʾūs., *al-Ṭarāʾif fī maʿrifat maḏāhib al-ṭawāʾif*, vol. I, n. 292: 203.

[12] al-Ṭūsī., *al-Amālī fī-l-ḥadīṯ*, *maǧlis* 11, n. 87–640: 314–315, Ibn Ḥamza al-Ṭūsī, *al-Ṯāqib fī-l-manāqib*, bb. 6, *faṣl* 5, n. 272: 332, al-Baḥrānī., *Ḥilyat al-abrār fī aḥwāl Muḥammad wa āli-hi al-aṭhār*, vol. IV, bb. 19, n. 3: 214, al-Baḥrānī., *Madīnat al-maʿāǧiz fī muʿǧizāt al-aʾimma al-aṭhār*, vol. III, Part Three, bb. 3, n. 56/1003: 492, al-Maǧlisī., *Biḥār al-anwār*, vol. XLV, bb. 42, nn. 1–2: 231, al-Iṣfahānī., *ʿAwālim al-ʿulūm wa-l-maʿārif al-aḥwāl min al-āyāt wa-l-aḫbār wa-l-aqwāl*, vol. XVII, ch. 18, bb. 3, n. 3: 509. According to al-Ṭabarī, on the day after the battle, that is, 11th Muḥarram, the bodies of al-Ḥusayn and his companions were buried.

[13] Ibn Bābawayh., *al-Amālī*, *maǧlis* 29, n. 1: 139, al-Mufīd., *al-Amālī*, *maǧlis* 38: 319, al-Ṭūsī., *al-Amālī*, *maǧlis* 3, n. 49–130: 90, Ibn ʿAlī al-Fattāl., *Rawḍat al-wāʿiẓīn wa-tabṣirat al-muttaʿiẓīn*, vol. I: 170, al-Maǧlisī., *Biḥār al-anwār*, vol. XLV, bb. 42, n. 1: 230, al-Iṣfahānī., *ʿAwālim al-ʿulūm wa-l-maʿārif al-aḥwāl min al-āyāt wa-l-aḫbār wa-l-aqwāl*, vol. XVII, ch. 18, bb. 3, n. 4: 509.

[14] Abū Muḥammad ʿAmr b. Abī al-Miqdām Ṯābit b. Hurmuz (d. 172/789): cf. MODARRESSI H., *Tradition and Survival. A Bibliographical Survey of Early Shīʾite Literature*, vol. I, Oneworld, Oxford 2003: 205–206.

[15] Abū Ǧaʿfar Muḥammad b. ʿAlī al-Bāqir (d. between 113/732 and 124/743).

> ʿAmr b. Ṯābit said: My father said: I went to visit Abū Ǧaʿfar Muḥammad b. ʿAlī at his house, and I asked him about this *ḥadīṯ*. I mentioned to him the transmission of Saʿīd b. Ǧubayr of this *ḥadīṯ* on the authority of ʿAbd Allāh b. ʿAbbās, and Abū Ǧaʿfar said: ʿUmar b. Abī Salama told it to me on the authority of his mother, Umm Salama. Ibn ʿAbbās said in the transmission of Saʿīd b. Ǧubayr on his authority: The next night I saw the Messenger of God in my dream, dust covered and dishevelled, and I mentioned this to him and asked him about its significance. He said to me: "Did you not know that I have just finished with the burial of al-Ḥusayn and his companions?"[16]

Closely associated with the dust and the developing theme of the glass vial of blood, the base narrative also tells of Umm Salama seeing Muḥammad not in a dream, but after his return from a journey that is, in its description, something close to the 'night journey' (*isrāʾ*),[17] and which, like that more famous, two-faceted journey of the Prophet, is both physical and spiritual. *Shayḫ* al-Mufīd writes:

> On the authority of Umm Salama, who said: One evening the Messenger of God left us and was away for a long time. When he came back, he was dishevelled and dusty and he was holding (something) in his hand. I said to him: Messenger of God! How is it that I see you dishevelled and dusty? He replied: "I was made to journey by night to a place in Iraq called Karbalāʾ. There I saw the death of my son, al-Ḥusayn, and a group of my children and the members of my family. I could not stop myself from gathering some of their blood and here it is in my

---

[16] al-Ṭūsī., *al-Amālī fī-l-ḥadīṯ*, *maǧlis* 11, n. 87–640: 314–315, al-Maǧlisī., *Biḥār al-anwār*, vol. XLV, bb. 42, n. 2: 231.

[17] In Islamic tradition the 'night journey' and 'ascension' are the two parts of a journey that Muḥammad took during a single night around the year 621. There is a brief outline of the story is in Q. 17:1, and other details come from the books of *aḥādīṯ*.

> hand." He opened his hand and said: "Take it and look after it."[18]

It is, however, within the precincts Umm Salama's own house that the most salient angelic encounters occur, transforming her family home into the locus of divine activity and embedding her deeply into the Karbalāʾ event. It is here that she will, ineffectually, guard a door through which the young al-Ḥusayn will dart, despite her best efforts, into the presence of Ǧibrīl. It is through the crack in that door that Umm Salama will herself be an eyewitness to an angelic visitation; a door which becomes symbolic of another door, thrown open in heaven and though which two other women, worlds apart, will catch a glimpse of something celestial. It is here too, in her own residence, that Umm Salama will receive the dust of Karbalāʾ secreting it in a simple glass vial which becomes a central feature of the narrative.

It is ostensibly a peripatetic religious scholar, born in Herat but found working in Nīsābūr, Baghdad and Mecca, who has left us, in embryonic form, the original narrative. Writing in his 2nd/8th century *Mashyaḫat*, Ibn Ṭahmān, whose chain of transmission is declared 'good' and 'trustworthy', tells us:

> On the authority of Umm Salama: The Messenger of God entered my house and said: "No one must come in to me!" I heard a voice and went in and there was Ḥusayn b. ʿAlī was with him, and he was sorrowing [or she said: He was crying]. I said: Messenger of God, what is wrong with you, that you cry? He replied: "Ǧibrīl informed me that my community would kill this one after me." I said: Who will kill him? He reached for a

---

[18] al-Mufīd., *al-Irshād fī maʿrifat ḥuǧaǧ Allāh ʿalā al-ʿibād*, vol. II, bb. *Tārīḫ al-Imām al-Ḥusayn*: 130.131, Ibn ʿAlī al-Fattāl., *Rawḍat al-wāʿiẓīn wa-tabṣirat al-muttaʿiẓīn*, vol. I: 193, al-Ṭabarsī., *Iʿlām al-warā bi-aʿlām al-hudā*, Part Three, bb. 2: 219, al-Irbilī., *Kashf al-ġumma fī maʿrifat al-aʾimma*, vol. II, Part Two: 8, al-Maǧlisī., *Biḥār al-anwār*, vol. XLIV, bb. 30, n. 31: 239–240.

> clod of earth and said: "The people of this clod of earth will kill him."[19]

All the essential constituents are in place, although the details will vary greatly as the narrative is taken up by the historians, the *muḥaddiṯūn* and the jurists. Unbidden, Umm Salama is at the door, her house about to be established as a site of heavenly intervention. The boy al-Ḥusayn is already inside, although as the account becomes increasingly detailed, his arrival in the midst of an angelic assignation and his darting into the room will become pivotal. The clod of earth too will be given shape and texture, colour and odour to convey the drama. The angel is named as Ǧibrīl, although over the centuries, a variety of names and messages will be imputed to this heavenly visitant.

The 3rd/9th century Kūfa-born Ibn Abī Shayba, who counted Ibn Māǧa among his pupils, includes in his massive *al-Muṣannaf* a report that his contemporary Isḥāq b. Rāhwayh will take up, followed by Ibn Abī ʿĀṣim, al-Bazzār and, a century after Ibn Abī Shayba, by al-Ṭabarānī:

> On the authority of Ṣāliḥ b. Arbada al-Naḫaʿī who said that Umm Salama said: al-Ḥusayn came to see the Prophet, while I was sitting at the door. I looked, and I saw in the hand of the Prophet something that he was turning over and over while he [al-Ḥusayn] was sleeping on his belly. I said: Messenger of God, I looked and saw you turning something over and over in your hand,[20] while the boy was sleeping on your belly, and your tears were streaming! He replied: "Ǧibrīl came to me with

---

[19] Ibn Ṭahmān., *Mashayḫa b. Ṭahmān*, n. 3: 54, al-Qushayrī., *Tārīḫ al-Raqqa*, bb. 27 (*Abū al-Muhāǧir*), n. 153: 98, Ibn ʿAsākir., *Tārīḫ madīnat Dimashq*, vol. XIV, bb. 1566 (*al-Ḥusayn b. ʿAlī b. Abī Ṭālib b. ʿAbd al-Muṭṭalib b. Hāshim b. ʿAbd al-Manāf*): 192, Ibn al-ʿAdīm., *Buġyat al-ṭalab fī tārīh Halab*, Part Six: 2598.

[20] In almost all the texts which deal with Muḥammad holding something in his hand, the verb *qallaba-yuqallibu* ('to turn something over in one's hand') is employed; once, in al-Ḏahabī, Muḥammad is said to 'kiss' (*qabbala-yuqabbilu*) what he is holding, but considering the closeness of the words, this may be a scribal error. Cf. al-Ḏahabī., *Tārīḫ al-Islām*, vol. V: 67.

> the dust on which he would be killed and informed me that my community would kill him."[21]

Ibn Abī Shayba sets forth aspects that will later be amplified; he omits Ibn Ṭahmān's still rather vague command to Umm Salama to prevent access, but proposes an al-Ḥusayn who arrives rather than being there already and inside with Muḥammad. The boy's physical position – sleeping on the stomach of his grandfather – will sometimes change to Muḥammad's back or shoulders or thigh, and whatever it is that the Prophet is fiddling with, and which Umm Salama cannot make out, will itself keep reappearing in subsequent telling, although often in an entirely dissimilar context.

In fact, it is Ibn Abī Shayba's acclaimed fellow-*muḥaddiṯ*, Aḥmad Ibn Ḥanbal, who will reshape the text, delineating the components and introducing a new and unfamiliar angelic personality:

> The angel of the rain[22] sought permission of his Lord to come to the Prophet and it was given him. He said to Umm Salama: "Hold the door for us, no one is to enter in to us!" The narrator said: al-Ḥusayn came in order to go in. She obstructed him, but he made a rush and entered and began to sit on the back of the Prophet, and on his shoulders.[23] The narrator continued: The angel said to the Prophet: "Do you love him?" He replied: "Yes!" He continued: "But your community will kill him, and if you want, I will show you the place where he will be killed." He beat with his hand and brought forth red mud

---

[21] Ibn Abī Shayba., *al-Muṣannaf*, vol. XIII, *Kitāb al-fitan*, bb. 1, n. 38382: 294, Ibn Rāhwayh., *Musnad*, vol. II, bb. 3, n. 1879: 262 (Ibn Rāhwayh's editor points the reader to Ibn Abī Shayba's *al-Muṣannaf* (vol. XIII), n. 38521: 330 from Yaʿlā b. ʿUbayd, but in the 2005 Beirut edition of the *Muṣannaf* this reference does not exist), Ibn Abī ʿĀṣim., *al-Āḥād wa-l-maṯānī*, vol. I, bb. 36 (*Min ḏikri al-Ḥusayn b. ʿAlī*), n. 428: 309, al-Ṭabarānī., *al-Muʿǧam al-kabīr*, vol. III, n. 2820: 115–116 (in a more detailed form).

[22] al-Suyūṭī., *al-Ḥabāʾik fī aḫbār al-malāʾik*: 49.

[23] The text uses two words (*mankib*, *ʿātiq*), both of which are best translated 'shoulder'.

> (*ṭīn*). Umm Salama took it and put it in her robe. Ṯābit said: "It came to our ears that it was Karbalā'".[24]

Over the centuries, Sunnī scholars including al-Ṭabarānī, al-Bayhaqī, Ibn ʿAsākir, Ibn al-ʿAdīm, al-Ḏahabī, Ibn Kaṯīr and al-Haytamī, and their Shīʿī counterparts Ibn Bābawayh, al-Ṭabarsī, Ibn Shahrāshūb, al-Shāmī and al-Baḥrānī would transmit this basic narrative from Ibn Ḥanbal, who offers two further transmissions: in a second rendering,[25] he changes the nature of the command to

---

[24] Ibn Ḥanbal., *Musnad*, vol. III, *Musnad Anas b. Mālik*: 242, 265, al-Bazzār., *Kashf al-astār*, vol. III, bb. *Manāqib al-Ḥusayn*, n. 2641: 233, al-Ṭabarānī., *al-Muʿǧam al-kabīr*, vol. III, n. 2813: 106 (where he changes 'red mud' to 'coarse red sand'), Ibn Bābawayh., *Kitāb al-amālī*, *maǧlis* 11, n. 105657: 330, al-Bayhaqī., *Dalā'il al-nubuwwa*, vol. VI, bb. *Ma ruwiya fī iḫbāri-hi bi-qatli ibn ibnati-hi ʿAbd Allāh al-Ḥusayn*: 469, al-Ṭabarsī., *Iʿlām al-warā bi-aʿlām al-hudā*, vol. I, Part Sixteen, bb. 2: 33, 94, Ibn ʿAsākir., *Tārīḫ madīnat Dimashq*, vol. XIV, bb. 1566 (*al-Ḥusayn b. ʿAlī b. Abī Ṭālib b. ʿAbd al-Muṭṭalib b. Hāshim b. ʿAbd al-Manāf*): 189–190, Ibn Shahrāshūb., *Manāqib āl Abī Ṭālib*, vol. IV, bb. *Fī imāmat Abī ʿAbd Allāh al-Ḥusayn*: 55 (Mīkā'īl or, according to Abū Yaʿla, the angel of the rain), al-Shāmī., *al-Durr al-naẓīm fī manāqib al-a'imma al-lahāhīm*, bb. 5, *Fī ḏikr maqtal al-Ḥusayn b. ʿAlī*: 535–536, Ibn al-ʿAdīm., *Buġyat al-ṭalab fī tārīḫ Ḥalab*, Part Six: 2600, 2601, al-Ṭabarī., *Ḏaḫā'ir al-ʿuqbā*, Part One, bb. 9: 251, al-Mizzī., *Tahḏīb al-kamāl fī asmā' al-riǧāl*, vol. VI, n. 1323 (*al-Ḥusayn b. ʿAlī b. Abī Ṭālib*): 408, al-Ḏahabī., *Siyar aʿlām al-nubalā'*, vol. III, n. 48 (*al-Ḥusayn al-Shahīd Abū ʿAbd Allāh b. ʿAlī b. Abī Ṭālib*): 288–289, *Tārīḫ al-Islām*, vol. V: 66, Ibn Kaṯīr., *al-Bidāya wa-l-nihāya*, vol. IX, bb. *Iḫbār bi-maqtal al-Ḥusayn*: 234–235, vol. XI, bb. *al-Iḫbār bi-maqtal al-Ḥusayn b. ʿAlī*: 570, al-Haytamī., *Maǧmaʿ al-zawā'id wa-manbaʿ al-fawā'id*, vol. IX, bk. 37 (*Kitāb al-manāqib*), bb. 95 (*Manāqib al-Ḥusayn b. ʿAlī*), n. 15111: 217, n. 15121: 221 (who has the angel watching al-Ḥusayn climbing on Muḥammad before posing the question), al-Suyūṭī., *al-Ḥabā'ik fī aḫbār al-malā'ik*, nn. 177, 178: 49, *al-Ḫaṣā'iṣ al-kubrā*, vol. II: 450, al-Baḥrānī *Ḥilyat al-abrār fī aḥwāl Muḥammad wa āli-hi al-aṭhār*, vol. IV, Part Three, bb. 6, n. 12: 124, al-Maǧlisī., *Biḥār al-anwār*, vol. XVIII, bb. 11, n. 14: 124, vol. XLIV, bb. 30, n. 14: 231, al-Iṣfahānī., *ʿAwālim al-ʿulūm wa-l-maʿārif al-aḥwāl min al-āyāt wa-l-aḫbār wa-l-aqwāl*, vol. XVII, Part Sixteen, ch. 11, bb. 6, n. 6: 126–127, ch. 18, bb. 3, n. 1: 507).

[25] Ibn Ḥanbal., *Musnad*, vol. III, *Musnad Anas b. Mālik*: 265.

Umm Salama, omits her attempts to restrain the boy, and changes the red mud back into red dust,[26] while in a third, the angel of the rain becomes an angel who has 'never before descended to Muḥammad':

> On the authority of ʿĀʾisha or Umm Salama [Wakīʿ said that ʿAbd Allāh b. Saʿīd was in doubt], that the Prophet said to one of the two of them: An angel, who had never come to me before, came to see me at the house and said to me: "This son of yours, Ḥusayn, will be killed. If you wish, I will show you some of the dust of the land in which he will be killed." He brought out red dust.[27]

Ibn Ḥanbal underscores five elements in the story not found in the major transmitters before him: he introduces the angel of the rain (traditionally Mīkāʾīl) or an unnamed angel who, unlike Ǧibrīl, has never descended at some previous time to Muḥammad. In this

---

[26] In al-Rabġūzī's text, when al-Ḥusayn reaches Karbalāʾ, he discovers that the earth there is red. Cf. BOESCHOTEN H.E. & O'KANE J., (eds.), *Al-Rabghūzī. The Stories of the Prophets*, 2015: 627

[27] Ibn Ḥanbal., *Musnad*, vol. VI, *Ḥadīṯ Umm Salama zawǧ al-nabī*: 294. The editor judges the chain of transmission as weak on account of its rupture in the person of Ibn Abī Hind (Saʿīd) who was not remembered or mentioned as hearing *aḥādīṯ* from ʿĀʾisha or Umm Salama. Cf. also Ibn Ḥanbal., *Kitāb faḍāʾil al-ṣaḥāba*, vol. II, bb. *Faḍāʾil al-Ḥasan wa-l-Ḥusayn*, n. 1357: 770, Abū Yaʿlā al-Qazwīnī., *Kitāb al-irshād fī maʿrifat ʿulamāʾ al-ḥadīṯ*, n. 47: 307, Ibn ʿAsākir., *Tārīḫ madīnat Dimashq*, vol. XIV, bb. 1566 (*al-Ḥusayn b. ʿAlī b. Abī Ṭālib b. ʿAbd al-Muṭṭalib b. Hāshim b. ʿAbd al-Manāf*): 193–194, Ibn al-ʿAdīm., *Buġyat al-ṭalab fī tārīḫ Ḥalab*, Part Six: 2597 (Ibn al-ʿAdīm says that the Prophet came to see them, weeping, and together they questioned him; he also names the angel as Ǧibrīl and ends by saying: "There was red dust in his hand and he said: This is the dust of that land," leaving a confusion as to whether it is the hand of the angel or the hand of Muḥammad), al-Ḏahabī., *Siyar aʿlām al-nubalāʾ*, vol. III, n. 48 (*al-Ḥusayn al-Shahīd Abū ʿAbd Allāh b. ʿAlī b. Abī Ṭālib*): 290, *Tārīḫ al-Islām*, vol. V: 67, Ibn Kaṯīr., *al-Bidāya wa-l-nihāya*, vol. XI, bb. *al-Iḫbār bi-maqtal al-Ḥusayn b. ʿAlī*: 570, al-Hayṯamī., *Maǧmaʿ al-zawāʾid wa-manbaʿ al-fawāʾid*, vol. IX, bk. 37 (*Kitāb al-manāqib*), bb. 95 (*Manāqib al-Ḥusayn b. ʿAlī*), n. 15113: 218.

manner, Ibn Ḥanbal discreetly detaches the narrative from the revelation with which Ǧibrīl is primarily associated. He articulates a clear and definite command to Umm Salama, giving her an active role in setting the scene for the encounter, and for which command a variety of verbs will be used. While in the earliest texts Umm Salama is merely sitting, or at times standing by the door, Ibn Ḥanbal introduces the directive that she should 'hold' (*masaka-yamsuku*) and, in a second narrative, 'guard' (*ḥafiẓa-yaḥfaẓu*) the door. In al-Hayṯamī's transmission, it is *malaka-yamliku*, which has a stronger sense of 'being in possession or control' of something (and the root from which the very word for angel may be derived). This instruction to safeguard the door, occasionally alternating with 'sit by the door', will persist in the narratives, heightening the tension of the story but creating a false construct; it is essential that the opposite happen, that al-Ḥusayn be permitted to enter, or at the very least be present, if the angel is to address a prediction concerning him to Muḥammad. In al-Kashshī, al-Āǧurrī and Ibn ʿAsākir, Umm Salama guards the door not by reason of an order she has received but because she fears that the boy will awaken Muḥammad from his siesta.[28]

More often than not, the command to guard the door is accompanied by a clarification that 'no one must be allowed to enter in', either in the singular ('to me') or the plural ('to us'). While in Ibn Ḥanbal, and some of the transmissions after him, it is difficult to know whether it is the visiting angel or Muḥammad who gives the order to Umm Salama,[29] others underscore that it is the Proph-

---

[28] al-Kashshī., *Muntaḫab Musnad ʿAbd b. Ḥamīd*, vol. II, bb. 120 (*Ḥadīṯ Umm Salama*), n. 1521: 384, al-Āǧurrī., *Kitāb al-sharīʿa*, Part Five, n. 1662: 2172, Ibn ʿAsākir., *Tārīḫ madīnat Dimashq*, vol. XIV, bb. 1566 (*al-Ḥusayn b. ʿAlī b. Abī Ṭālib b. ʿAbd al-Muṭṭalib b. Hāshim b. ʿAbd al-Manāf*): 194.

[29] al-Ṭabarānī., *al-Muʿǧam al-kabīr*, vol. III, n. 2813: 112, al-Bayhaqī., *Dalāʾil al-nubuwwa*, vol. VI, bb. *Ma ruwiya fī iḫbāri-hi bi-qatli ibn ibnati-hi ʿAbd Allāh al-Ḥusayn*: 469, al-Ḏahabī., *Tārīḫ al-Islām*, vol. V: 66, Ibn Kaṯīr., *al-Bidāya wa-l-nihāya*, vol. XI, bb. *al-Iḫbār bi-maqtal al-Ḥusayn b. ʿAlī*: 570, al-Shāmī., *al-Durr al-naẓīm fī manāqib al-aʾimma al-lahāhīm*, bb. 5, *Fī ḏikr maqtal al-Ḥusayn b. ʿAlī*: 536–537, al-Hayṯamī., *Maǧmaʿ al-zawāʾid wa-manbaʿ al-*

et who issues the command.[30] Both al-Ṭabarānī and al-Bayhaqī use the verb *walağa-yaliğu* ('to enter') in the so-called 'energetic mood' (*nūn al-tawkīd*), with the intensified sense that 'absolutely no one' should be allowed past the door.[31]

Thirdly, Ibn Ḥanbal introduces the haunting question directed to Muḥammad about his love for al-Ḥusayn; this too serves to augment the horror that one so beloved should be killed and that it would be Muḥammad's own community that would perpetrate the act. Next, Ibn Ḥanbal notes the curious action of Ğibrīl beating either the air or the ground with his hand; this action too will vary from text to text. In the earliest transmissions, Ğibrīl merely comes to Muḥammad with some of the dust on which al-Ḥusayn will die, but as the texts are amplified, the angelic action in producing dust from the Karbalā' plain begins to vary substantially between transmitters. Sometimes Ğibrīl simply extends his hand, or reaches into Karbalā' to seize a handful its dust. On other occasions, he beats the air or the ground with his hand, his fist or his wing. The beating of a wing especially evokes motion and flight; there could be a intimation that Ğibrīl journeyed in an instant to Karbalā' (in the 'blinking of an eye' as, in other texts, in lightning speed, he causes the land to sink down, come together and then return to its place) and then, depending on how one translates the verb *ātā*, returns to Muḥammad ("He beat with his wing and came to me with this dust"). In other reports, the angel spreads out his wing over the land of Karbalā' or in the direction of the East, or stretches his wings all the way to Karbalā' to obtain the dust, or simply holds out some of the dust on his wing for Muḥammad.

---

fawā'id, vol. IX, bk. 37 (*Kitāb al-manāqib*), bb. 95 (*Manāqib al-Ḥusayn b. ʿAlī*), n. 15121: 221.

[30] Ibn ʿAsākir., *Tārīḫ madīnat Dimashq*, vol. XIV, bb. 1566 (*al-Ḥusayn b. ʿAlī b. Abī Ṭālib b. ʿAbd al-Muṭṭalib b. Hāshim b. ʿAbd al-Manāf*): 189, 190, al-Mizzī., *Tahḏīb al-kamāl fī asmā' al-riğāl*, vol. VI, n. 1323 (*al-Ḥusayn b. ʿAlī b. Abī Ṭālib*): 408, Ibn Bābawayh., *Kitāb al-amālī*, *mağlis* 29, n. 3: 139.

[31] al-Ṭabarānī., *al-Muʿğam al-kabīr*, vol. III, n. 2820: 115–116, al-Bayhaqī., *Dalā'il al-nubuwwa*, vol. VI, bb. *Ma ruwiya fī iḫbāri-hi bi-qatli ibn ibnati-hi ʿAbd Allāh al-Ḥusayn*: 469.

Finally, Ibn Ḥanbal adds two crucial qualifications to the mud or dust; it is red, and it comes from a place called Karbalāʾ. It is also Ibn Ḥanbal who admits into his text an imprecision between ʿĀʾisha or Umm Salama as narrator. While Abū Yaʿlā and Ibn al-ʿAdīm will solve the problem by putting the two women on an equal footing – "On the authority of ʿĀʾisha and Umm Salama" – and Ibn Kaṯīr will add his laconic 'God only knows', Ibn ʿAsākir and al-Ḏahabī will follow Ibn Ḥanbal's "ʿĀʾisha or Umm Salama" more stringently. In Ibn Ḥanbal's third version of the narrative, the confused narrator is identified as ʿAbd Allāh b. Saʿīd.

Ibn Ḥanbal's contemporary, ʿAbd b. Ḥumayd al-Kashshī,[32] on whose authority Muslim, al-Tirmiḏī and al-Buḫārī transmitted, accentuates the place of encounter as Umm Salama's house and has her guarding the door for fear that al-Ḥusayn would awaken the sleeping Prophet. He also places onto the lips of a distraught Muḥammad a desire for clarity about the killers:

> Saʿīd b. Abī Hind, on the authority of his father, who said: Umm Salama said: The Prophet was sleeping in my house when Ḥusayn came, walking slowly. She continued: I held him back from the door, which I was holding for fear that he would enter and awaken him. She continued: I became distracted by something and he advanced and entered and sat on his belly. She said: I heard the sobbing of the Messenger of God, so I went and said: Messenger of God, by God, what have you found out about him? He replied: "While he was seated on my belly, Ǧibrīl came to me and said to me: Do you love him? I said: Yes! He said: Your community will kill him. Should I show you the dust on which he will be killed?" He continued: "I said: Yes! So, he beat with his wing and produced this dust for me." She said: In his hand was red dust, and he wept, saying: "Would that I knew who would kill you after me!"[33]

---

[32] al-Ḏahabī names him al-Kishshī or al-Kashshī (al-Ḏahabī., *Siyar aʿlām al-nubalāʾ*, vol. XII, n. 81 (*ʿAbd b. Ḥumayd b. Naṣr al-Kishshī*): 235.

[33] al-Kashshī., *Muntaḫab Musnad ʿAbd b. Ḥamīd*, vol. II, bb. 120 (*Ḥadīṯ Umm Salama*), n. 1521: 384, Ibn ʿAsākir., *Tārīḫ madīnat Dimashq*, vol.

While Ibn Ḥanbal's al-Ḥusayn makes a sudden rush for the door, or, in later texts, leaps and darts past Umm Salama, al-Kashshī, using the same imprecise transmitter (ʿAbd Allāh b. Saʿīd) has him advancing slowly or hesitantly (*yadruğu*), pursuing his way with the feeble steps of a small child. Curiously, it is the same root used in some of the visions al-Ḥusayn will have of his grandfather and in which his rank (*daraǧa*) in the Garden will be described. Ǧibrīl's manner of action too is different, beating his wing, and provoking in Muḥammad a verbal response: "Would that I knew who would kill you after me," a response that will soon change into a declaration about God's anger against the killers, so that it is with God, and not with Muḥammad, that they must eventually contend.

Baṣra-born Ibn Abī ʿĀṣim will himself make mention of an important element not found in any major transmitter before him, but that will later be used to enhance the drama of the event:

> On the authority of ʿAbd Allāh b. Wahb, that Umm Salama told him that the Messenger of God lay down one day to sleep, but got up, his soul heavy. Then he lay down, and then got up, in his hand red dust which he was turning over and over. Umm Salama said: Prophet of God, what is this dust? He replied: "Ǧibrīl informed me about al-Ḥusayn, that this one will be killed in the land of Iraq. I said: Ǧibrīl! Show me the dust of the land where he will be killed! And this is it."[34]

This story, in a shortened form in Ibn Abī ʿĀṣim, introduces Muḥammad's agitation, which later transmitters will underscore by reporting that three times he lies down and gets up.[35] Although no

---

XIV, bb. 1566 (*al-Ḥusayn b. ʿAlī b. Abī Ṭālib b. ʿAbd al-Muṭṭalib b. Hāshim b. ʿAbd al-Manāf*): 194, Ibn al-ʿAdīm., *Buġyat al-ṭalab fī tārīḫ Ḥalab*, Part Six: 2599, but cf. also al-Haytamī., *Maǧmaʿ al-zawāʾid wa-manbaʿ al-fawāʾid*, vol. IX, bk. 37 (*Kitāb al-manāqib*), bb. 95 (*Manāqib al-Ḥusayn b. ʿAlī*), n. 15116: 219.

[34] Ibn Abī ʿĀṣim., *al-Āḥād wa-l-maṯānī*, vol. I, bb. 36 (*Min ḏikri al-Ḥusayn b. ʿAlī*), n. 429: 310, al-Ṭabarānī., *al-Muʿǧam al-kabīr*, vol. III, n. 2821: 109, al-Suyūṭī., *al-Ḫaṣāʾiṣ al-kubrā*, vol. II: 450.

[35] al-Ḥākim al-Nīsābūrī., *Kitāb al-mustadrak ʿalā al-ṣaḥīḥayn*, vol. IV, bk. 47 (*Kitāb taʿbīr al-ruʾyā*), n. 8282: 553–554, al-Bayhaqī., *Dalāʾil al-*

direct mention is made of al-Ḥusayn's arriving or of his presence, Muḥammad's words 'this one' or, in other reports, 'this son of mine' hint that he may well have been present. For the first time, we have Muḥammad taking the initiative and asking to see the dust of the land where his grandson will die without waiting for Ǧibrīl's offer to show it to him.

The earliest version of the story among the Shīʿī scholars, even in a most rudimentary form, begins with two problematic personalities. The first represents a confusion of identities between two men with almost exactly the same name: Abū Ǧaʿfar Muḥammad b. Ǧarīr b. Yazīd al-Ṭabarī, by all accounts a Sunnī historian and *mufassir*, and Abū Ǧaʿfar Muḥammad b. Ǧarīr b. Rustam al-Ṭabarī, ostensibly an early Shīʿī scholar. Aside from their names, the two also appear to be close contemporaries. Brockelmann (GAL S. I: 217) gives Ibn Yazīd al-Ṭabarī's date of birth as 224–5/839 but gives no date of death; Sezgin (GAS I: 49, 323) suggests his date of death as 310–11/923. Both Brockelmann and Sezgin impute to him a number of important works, in particular *Kitāb aḫbār al-rusul wa-l-mulūk* and *Ǧāmiʿ al-bayān ʿan taʾwīl al-qurʾān*. However, Brockelmann also ascribes to him, quite erroneously, the work *Bishārat al-muṣṭafā*; Sezgin does not, saying this this work 'is to be deleted' from the list of his works. Instead, Sezgin attributes *Bishārat al-muṣṭafā*, as well as a work entitled *Dalāʾil al-imāma* to Ibn Rustam al-Ṭabarī (GAS I: 540), whose date of death he lists as the first quarter of the 4th/10th century. However, there is now substantial scholarly dispute over his authorship of *Dalāʾil al-imāma*, the introductory essay to the English translation of *Kitāb aḫbār al-rusul wa-l-mulūk* suggesting that *Dalāʾil al-imāma* is written long after Ibn Rustam al-Ṭabarī, possibly nearer to the end of the 4th/10th century

---

nubuwwa, vol. VI, bb. *Ma ruwiya fī iḫbāri-hi bi-qatli ibn ibnati-hi ʿAbd Allāh al-Ḥusayn*: 468, Ibn ʿAsākir., *Tārīḫ madīnat Dimashq*, vol. XIV, bb. 1566 (*al-Ḥusayn b. ʿAlī b. Abī Ṭālib b. ʿAbd al-Muṭṭalib b. Hāshim b. ʿAbd al-Manāf*): 191, 192, al-Shāmī., *al-Durr al-naẓīm fī manāqib al-aʾimma al-lahāhīm*, bb. 5, *Fī ḏikr al-Ḥusayn b. ʿAlī*: 535, al-Ṭabarī., *Ḏaḫāʾir al-ʿuqbā*, Part One, bb. 9: 252, al-Ḏahabī., *Siyar aʿlām al-nubalāʾ*, vol. III, n. 48 (*al-Ḥusayn al-Shahīd Abū ʿAbd Allāh b. ʿAlī b. Abī Ṭālib*): 289–290, *Tārīḫ al-Islām*, vol. V: 67, Ibn Kaṯīr., *al-Bidāya wa-l-nihāya*, vol. IX, bb. *Iḫbār bi-maqtal al-Ḥusayn*: 235–236.

than to its first quarter.[36] Others suggest that the *Dalāʾil* was written by an unknown early 5th/11th century author, a contemporary of *Shayḫ* al-Ṭūsī and living in Baghdad, and still others that *Bishārat al-muṣṭafā* is in fact the work of Muḥammad b. ʿAlī (ʿImād al-Dīn) al-Ṭabarī who lived between the 5th/11th and 6th/12th centuries. Suffice it to say that had Rustam al-Ṭabarī been the author of *Dalāʾil al-imāma*, and were his death to be dated even broadly as the late 3rd/9th or early 4th/10th century (between 250/864–65 and 316/928–29) he would represent the first Shīʿī transmission. As it is, the *Dalāʾil al-imāma* relates the story with an economy of detail, and with no mention of angelic intervention:

> On the day that al-Ḥusayn was killed at Karbalāʾ, Umm Salama, who was in Medina, took out a glass vial containing blood, and said: "By God, al-Ḥusayn has been killed!" Someone said to her: "From where did you learn this?" She replied: "The Messenger of God handed me some of its dust and said to me: When this becomes blood, you will know that my son has been killed." And it was as she said.[37]

A second candidate for the first Shīʿī dispersion of the text is Ibn Ḥamdān, writing in his *al-Hidāya al-Kubrā*. He, however, presents a twofold problem: the first is a twenty-year discrepancy in his given date of birth. The second is that he seems to have been aligned to the ʿAlawiyya, so that his transmissions are distrusted by a sizable number Shīʿī scholars.[38] Nonetheless, his report, going back to the fifth Imām, is of interest for its detailed development of a combination of significant elements. "When al-Ḥusayn had it in mind to depart for Syria," he begins, "Umm Salama sent to him." In setting the scene, Ibn Ḥamdān highlights two key factors about Umm Salama: that she was al-Ḥusayn's guardian (*rabba*), the one who loved him more and was kinder to him than anyone else, and that

---

[36] Cf. ROSENTHAL F., (trans.), *The History of al-Ṭabarī*, vol. I, State University of New York Press, Albany 1989: 118–119.

[37] Ibn Rustam al-Ṭabarī., *Dalāʾil al-imāma*: 180.

[38] Ibn Ḥamdān al-Ḫaṣībī is denounced by al-Nağāshī as having corrupt beliefs (al-Nağāshī., *Kitāb al-riğāl*, n. 159: 67) and seems to have had a substantial connection with the heterodox Nuṣayrī sect.

she has in her possession a sealed glass vial, handed her by Muḥammad and containing dust: " When my son departs for Iraq, place this vial before your eyes," he instructs her, "and when the dust in the vial changes into fresh blood, you will know that my son al-Ḥusayn has been killed." Umm Salama now reminds al-Ḥusayn of this, pleading with him not to go. But al-Ḥusayn is resolute: "Umm Salama, inevitably I will be killed! Where can I flee from destiny (*al-qadr*), from the Divine decree (*al-qaḍāʾ*), from what is determined and from the incumbent order from God Most High, may He be praised?" Umm Salama's anxiety ("where will you go that you will be killed?") is increased not only by the grim finality of the outcome ("If I do not go today, I will go tomorrow, and if I do not go tomorrow, I will go the next day, for there is no escape from death") but also by al-Ḥusayn's foreknowledge of the day and hour of his death, the place of his burial, the one who will strike the fatal blow, and the names, number and family details of his party (*shīʿa*) killed with him. "And if you like," he continues, "I will show you the site of my death." In a mystical vision permitted by God, and similar to a visualization which Ǧibrīl will offer to Muḥammad in later Shīʿī transmitters, the earth yields to al-Ḥusayn and he shows her the place, as yet unnamed, where he and his companions will fall, giving her more of the dust; he then departs, telling her that he will be killed on the day of ʿĀshūrā.[39]

Ibn Ḥamdān continues his narrative by immediately relating a dream of Umm Salama which will be retold by a number of Shīʿī scholars, including al-Masʿūdī, al-Rāwandī, al-Ḥillī al-ʿAllāma and al-Baḥrānī:

---

[39] Ibn Ḥamdān names this day as a Saturday, as does al-Baḥrānī (al-Baḥrānī., *Madīnat al-maʿāǧiz fī muʿǧizāt al-aʾimma al-athār*, vol. III, Part Three, bb. 3, n. 56/1003: 489–492). Actually, it was a Friday. Cf. for e.g. Ibn al-ʿAdīm., *Buġyat al-ṭalab fī tārīḫ Ḥalab*, Part Six: 2571, CLOHESSY C., *Half of My Heart. The Narratives of Zaynab, Daughter of ʿAlī*, 2018: 103. Al-Ḏahabī offers a number of options, ranging between Friday, Saturday and Monday. Cf. al-Ḏahabī., *Siyar aʿlām al-nubalāʾ*, vol. III, n. 48 (*al-Ḥusayn al-Shahīd Abū ʿAbd Allāh b. ʿAlī b. Abī Ṭālib*): 318.

> When it was that night of the morning on which al-Ḥusayn was killed, she saw in her dream someone dishevelled, dust-covered and weeping, who said: al-Ḥusayn and his companions have just been buried! Umm Salama awoke and went out, crying out at the top of her voice. The people of Medina came to her and said to her: "What has happened to you?" She replied: "al-Ḥusayn b. ʿAlī and his companions have been killed!" They said: "Confused dreams!" She answered: "Stop! I have the dust of al-Ḥusayn." She brought the glass vial out for them, and behold, it was fresh blood. They counted the days, and sure enough, al-Ḥusayn had been killed on that day.[40]

The details remain unrefined; the nocturnal visitor is not identified, and nor does he or she claim credit for the actual burial. Umm Salama is already playing a central role, but there is no suggestion yet of the effort she puts into guarding the glass vial and its content; the text suggests that she herself had no idea that the dust had turned to blood, although Ibn Ḥamdān has combined a number of stories that will be related separately by future transmitters. The calculation of the days will come to be associated with the dream of Ibn ʿAbbās rather than that of Umm Salama, while the night visitor will take on a specific identity.

---

[40] Ibn Ḥamdān., *al-Hidāya al-Kubrā*: 203–204, Ibn Ḥamza al-Ṭūsī., *al-Ṯāqib fī-l-manāqib*, bb. 6, n. 272: 331–332, al-Baḥrānī., *Ḥilyat al-abrār fī aḥwāl Muḥammad wa āli-hi al-aṭhār*, vol. III, bb. 19, n. 3: 212–214, *Madīnat al-maʿāǧiz fī muʿǧizāt al-aʾimma al-aṭhār*, vol. III, Part Three, bb. 3, n. 56/1003: 489–492. In shortened form and with a slight change in details, cf. al-Masʿūdī., *Iṯbāt al-waṣiyya*: 262, al-Rāwandī., al-*Ḫarāʾiǧ wa-l-ǧarāʾiḥ fī-l-muʿǧizāt*, vol. I, bb. 4, n. 7: 253, Ibn ʿAbd al-Wahhāb., *ʿUyūn al-muʿǧizāt*: 69, al-Ḥillī al-ʿAllāma., *Iṯbāt al-hudāt bi-l-nuṣūṣ wa-l-muʿǧizāt*: 165, al-Bayyāḍī., *al-Ṣirāṭ al-mustaqīm ilā mustaḥaqqī al-taqdīm fī-l-imāma*, vol. II, n. 6: 179, al-Maǧlisī., *Biḥār al-anwār*, vol. XLV, bb. 37, n. 27: 89 (who transmits numerous variations of the account of the dust in the glass vial), al-Iṣfahānī., *ʿAwālim al-ʿulūm wa-l-maʿārif al-aḥwāl min al-āyāt wa-l-aḫbār wa-l-aqwāl*, vol. XVII, ch. 12, bb. 4, n. 7: 157.

Shāfiʿī[41] jurist and *muḥaddiṯ* Ibn ʿAlī al-Āǧurrī introduces al-Ḥasan into the text, albeit briefly; he will reappear when al-Ṭabarānī takes up the story, but he plays no significant role in the unfolding drama, his presence serving only to underscore the entry by al-Ḥusayn into the room of the sleeping Prophet, a place forbidden to all others but the two boys whom Muḥammad called the 'leaders of the youths of the inhabitants of the Garden'[42] and his 'two sweet basils':

> On the authority of Umm Salama, who said: Whenever he was sleeping, the Messenger of God did not let anyone come to see him except Ḥasan and Ḥusayn. She continued: One day he was sleeping in my house and I was sitting at the door to prevent anyone from entering, when Ḥusayn came, walking; I let him go and he went and dropped down onto his belly. Then the Messenger of God was dismayed, and he wept and embraced

[41] Although Abū Yaʿlā counts him as a Ḥanbalī: cf. *Ṭabaqāt al-Ḥanābila*, vol. I, bb. *al-Sīn*, n. 216: 160.

[42] Cf. Ibn Ḥanbal., *Musnad*, vol. I, *Musnad ʿAlī b. Abī Ṭālib*: 80, *Kitāb faḍāʾil al-ṣaḥāba*, vol. II, bb. *Faḍāʾil al-Ḥasan wa-l-Ḥusayn*, n. 1360: 771, n. 1368: 774, n. 1385: 779, n. 1406: 788, Ibn Māǧa., *Sunan*, vol. I, *al-Muqaddima*, bb. 11 (*Faḍāʾil aṣḥāb rasūl Allāh, Faḍl ʿAlī b. Abī Ṭālib*), n. 118: 44, al-Tirmiḏī., *al-Ǧāmiʿ al-ṣaḥīḥ*, vol. IX, bk. 50 (*Kitāb al-manāqib*), bb. *Manāqib al-Ḥasan wa-l-Ḥusayn*, n. 3771: 331, al-Ṭabarī., *Kitāb aḫbār al-rusul wa-l-mulūk*, vol. XXVIII, n. 210: 168, al-Ḥākim al-Nīsābūrī., *Kitāb al-mustadrak ʿalā al-ṣaḥīḥayn*, vol. III, bk. 31 (*Kitāb maʿrifat al-ṣaḥāba*), nn. 4843, 4844, 4845: 197–198, al-Baġdādī., *Tārīḫ Baġdād*, vol. I: 468, al-Ḫawārizmī., *Maqtal al-Ḥusayn*, Part One, ch. 5, *Faḍāʾil Fāṭima al-Zahrāʾ bt. rasūl Allāh*, n. 42: 108–109, n. 66: 125, Ibn ʿAsākir., *Tārīḫ madīnat Dimashq*, vol. 42: 130, 132, Ibn al-Aṯīr., *al-Kāmil fī al-tārīḫ*, vol. III, *Ḏikr maqtal al-Ḥusayn*: 287, al-Ṭabarī., *Ḏaḫāʾir al-ʿuqbā*, Part One, bb. 9: 224–225, al-Ḏahabī., *Siyar aʿlām al-nubalāʾ*, vol. III, n. 48 (*al-Ḥusayn al-Shahīd Abū ʿAbd Allāh b. ʿAlī b. Abī Ṭālib*): 302, al-ʿAsqalānī., *Tahḏīb al-tahḏīb*, vol. II, bb. *al-Ḥāʾ*, n. 615: 345, al-Hindī., *Muntaḫab*, vol. V: 92; al-Shablanǧī., *Nūr al-abṣār fī manāqib āl bayt al-nabī al-muḫtār*, bb. *Faṣl fī ḏikr manāqib ʿAlī b. Abī Ṭālib*: 43, bb. *Faṣl fī ḏikr sayyidi-nā al-Ḥasan*: 231.

> him.[43] I said: Messenger of God, what is the matter with you, that you weep? You were happy when you went to sleep! He replied: "Ǧibrīl came to me with this dust" (she said the Messenger of God unfolded his hand and in it was red dust) "and he informed me that this son of mine would be killed on this dust." She continued: I said: What is this land? He answered: "It is Karbalā'", and I said: Land of distress (*karb*) and tribulation (*balā'*).[44]

In this report, it is Umm Salama who declares Karbalā' to be a 'land of distress and tribulation'; in many other texts, it is Muḥammad who makes this declaration (leading al-Ḥusayn to declare, "God and His Messenger Prophet have spoken the truth"),[45] although some authors attribute the words to al-Ḥusayn[46] and others to ʿAlī.[47] Al-Āǧurrī expands the words of the angel and so accentuates the divine punishment awaiting the killer – "Ǧibrīl informed me that this son of mine would be killed, and that the

[43] The 8th form of the verb (*iltazama-yaltazimu*) used here is different from the verb used in the other accounts (*laṯama-yalṯimu*, 'to kiss'); I have followed Lane in rendering it as 'to embrace' (cf. LANE E.W., *An Arabic-English Lexicon*, vol. VIII, 1968: 3010).

[44] al-Āǧurrī., *Kitāb al-šarīʿa*, vol. III, bb. *Iḫbār al-nabī bi-qatli al-Ḥusayn*, n. (1105) 1720: 318–319.

[45] al-Ṭabarānī., *al-Muʿǧam al-kabīr*, vol. III, n. 2812: 106, n. 2819: 108. Cf. also Ibn Abī ʿĀṣim., *al-Āḥād wa-l-maṯānī*, vol. I, bb. 36 (*Min ḏikri al-Ḥusayn b. ʿAlī*), n. 424: 307, al-Āǧurrī., *Kitāb al-šarīʿa*, vol. III, bb. *Iḫbār al-nabī bi-qatli al-Ḥusayn*, n. (1108) 1724: 320, al-Hayṯamī., *Maǧmaʿ al-zawā'id wa-manbaʿ al-fawā'id*, vol. IX, bk. 37 (*Kitāb al-manāqib*), bb. 95 (*Manāqib al-Ḥusayn b. ʿAlī*), n. 15117: 219, n. 15133: 224.

[46] Sibṭ al-Ǧawzī., *Taḏkirat al-ḫawāṣṣ al-umma bi-ḏikr ḫaṣā'iṣ al-a'imma*, bb. *Ḏikr maqtali-hi*: 250 (who has al-Ḥusayn weeping as he pronounces the name), al-Ḏahabī., *Siyar aʿlām al-nubalā'*, vol. III, n. 48 (*al-Ḥusayn al-Shahīd Abū ʿAbd Allāh b. ʿAlī b. Abī Ṭālib*): 311.

[47] Ibn Muzāḥim., *Waqʿat Ṣiffīn*, Part Three: 142, al-Qāḍī al-Nuʿmān., *Sharḥ al-aḫbār fī faḍā'il al-a'imma al-aṭhār*, vol. III, Part Twelve, n. 1080: 138, Ibn Kaṯīr., *al-Bidāya wa-l-nihāya*, vol. XI, bb. *al-Iḫbār bi-maqtal al-Ḥusayn b. ʿAlī*: 516.

wrath of God would be vehement against the one who killed him"[48] – and then introduces a novel report from Abū Hurayra:

> On the authority of Abū Hurayra, who said: I went to see the Prophet in his house; he was lying on his back and one of his two sons was on his leg. The Prophet began to say: "Ascend, eye of a mosquito!"[49] Then he raised his leg until he was close to his chest, and opening his mouth, he kissed him. Then he said: "O God, I love him, and loving him, I love whoever loves him!" Then he wept, and I said: Messenger of God, what is making you weep? He answered: "The angel informed me that my community would kill this son of mine that that the wrath of God would be vehement against his killer."[50]

The son, like the angel, is unnamed; and although both al-Ḥasan or al-Ḥusayn would be killed, we must presume that it is the latter of whom Muḥammad speaks. Two very similar narratives are found in Ibn ʿAsākir, where the son involved is said to be either al-Ḥasan or al-Ḥusayn, but without the angelic prediction.[51] Ḥanbalī jurist al-Ṭabarānī, who gathered together a number of versions of the story, himself transmits an account in which both boys are mentioned:

---

[48] al-Āǧurrī., *Kitāb al-sharīʿa*, vol. III, bb. *Iḫbār al-nabī bi-qatli al-Ḥusayn*, n. (1105) 1720: 319. Cf. also Ibn ʿAsākir., *Tārīḫ madīnat Dimashq*, vol. XIV, bb. 1566 (*al-Ḥusayn b. ʿAlī b. Abī Ṭālib b. ʿAbd al-Muṭṭalib b. Hāshim b. ʿAbd al-Manāf*): 193, al-Mizzī., *Tahḏīb al-kamāl fī asmāʾ al-riǧāl*, vol. VI, n. 1323 (*al-Ḥusayn b. ʿAlī b. Abī Ṭālib*): 409.

[49] According to Lane, 'the eye of a gnat' or 'a mosquito' denotes the smallness of the person to whom the words are addressed. Cf. LANE E.W., *An Arabic-English Lexicon*, vol. I, 1968: 330, Ibn Ḥanbal., *Kitāb faḍāʾil al-ṣaḥāba*, vol. II, bb. *Faḍāʾil al-Ḥasan wa-l-Ḥusayn*, n. 1405, 1381: 787, al-Ṭabarī., *Ḏaḫāʾir al-ʿuqbā*, Part One, bb. 9: 213 (in a different context, without any prediction of death).

[50] al-Aǧurrī., *Kitāb al-sharīʿa*, vol. III, bb. *Iḫbār al-nabī bi-qatli al-Ḥusayn*, n. (1105) 1722: 319. Cf. Ibn al-ʿAdīm., *Buǧyat al-ṭalab fī tārīḫ Ḥalab*, Part Six: 2572 for this narrative, but without any reference to the angel or the death prediction.

[51] Ibn ʿAsākir., *Tārīḫ madīnat Dimashq*, vol. XIII, bb. 1383 (*al-Ḥasan b. ʿAlī b. Abī Ṭālib b. ʿAbd al-Muṭṭalib b. Hāshim b. ʿAbd al-Manāf*): 194–195.

> On the authority of Umm Salama, who said: al-Ḥasan and al-Ḥusayn were playing in front of the Prophet in my house, when Ǧibrīl descended and said: "Muḥammad! Your community after you will kill this son of yours" and he motioned with his hand towards al-Ḥusayn. The Messenger of God wept and pressed him to his breast. Then the Messenger of God said: "This dust is entrusted to you." The Messenger of God smelt it and said: Alas,[52] distress and tribulation. She continued: The Messenger of God said: "Umm Salama, when this dust changes into blood, know that my son has been killed!" He said: Umm Salama put it into a glass vial, and started to look at it every day, saying: "A formidable day, the day you turn to blood!"[53]

Once again, inexplicably, al-Ḥasan disappears early in the story, even though he too would be murdered at the hands of his fellow Muslims and thus members, or at least dissident ex-members, of Muḥammad's community. By the time al-Ṭabaranī is writing, the 'Ḥusaynian prototype' is already deeply ascendant; while mourning and grief rituals began almost immediately after Karbalā᾽, spearheaded by al-Ḥusayn's sister Zaynab and his son ʿAlī, it would be the relative stability of the ʿAbbāsid period that would see a growth in public commemorations of Karbalā᾽ and thus of al-Ḥusayn as the chief of the martyrs. Al-Ṭabaranī's own lifetime was witness to

---

[52] This may represent a textual error, since it reads 'alas' (*wayḥa*) whereas most other texts read 'smell' or 'odour' (*rīḥ*), more fitting with the context of Muḥammad smelling the dust. Either he says: "Alas, distress and tribulation" or "the odour of distress and tribulation."

[53] al-Ṭabarānī., *al-Muʿǧam al-kabīr*, vol. III, n. 2817: 198. Cf. al-Shaǧarī., *Tartīb al-amālī al-ḫamīsiyya*, vol. I, bb. *Fī faḍl al-Ḥusayn b. ʿAlī*, n. 785: 215, Ibn ʿAsākir., *Tārīḫ madīnat Dimashq*, vol. XIV, bb. 1566 (*al-Ḥusayn b. ʿAlī b. Abī Ṭālib b. ʿAbd al-Muṭṭalib b. Hāshim b. ʿAbd al-Manāf*): 192–193, Ibn al-ʿAdīm., *Buġyat al-ṭalab fī tārīḫ Ḥalab*, Part Six: 2599, al-Mizzī., *Tahḏīb al-kamāl fī asmā᾽ al-riǧāl*, vol. VI, n. 1323 (*al-Ḥusayn b. ʿAlī b. Abī Ṭālib*): 408–409, al-Hayṯamī., *Maǧmaʿ al-zawā᾽id wa-manbaʿ al-fawā᾽id*, vol. IX, bk. 37 (*Kitāb al-manāqib*), bb. 95 (*Manāqib al-Ḥusayn b. ʿAlī*), n. 15118: 219–220, al-ʿAsqalānī., *Tahḏīb al-tahḏīb*, vol. II, bb. *al-Ḥā᾽*, n. 615: 347, al-Suyūṭī., *al-Ḫaṣā᾽iṣ al-kubrā*, vol. II: 450.

the emergence of a handful of prominent Shīʿī dynasties: the Persian and Iraqi Būyid, the Syrian Ḥamdānid, the massively influential Ismāʿīlī Fāṭimid in Egypt and swathes of North Africa, the Zaydī dominating parts of northern Persia and Yemen and, for a while at least, the north-west African Idrīsid. Consequently, by the middle of the 4th/10th century the Shīʿa were possessed of substantial power. Along with political expansion came the freedom to express the rituals of grief and remembrance more publicly and vividly, so that al-Ḥusayn increasingly dominated the Islamic martyrologies. His father ʿAlī too had been murdered, as had his brother and as would the line of Imāms who followed him; but Karbalāʾ would become one of Shīʿī Islam's chief historical narratives, while remembrance of its martyr would supply Shīʿī faith with its passion and intensity.

The glass vial has already made an appearance in the transmissions of Ibn Rustam al-Ṭabarī, or, if we discount him, of Ibn Ḥamdān; now, for the first time, we are told of Umm Salama's guardianship of the container, as once she held guardianship over a door. She looks at it daily (in the fifty or so years between her being entrusted with the vial of dust and the Karbalāʾ event), addressing it with trepidation about the day what it contains is transformed. The dust of Karbalāʾ now comes to the fore; al-Ṭabarānī has Muḥammad smelling it, noticing the odour of 'distress and tribulation' (*karb wa balāʾ*) emanating from it. Its eventual transmutation into blood, first highlighted by Ibn Rustam al-Ṭabarī and Ibn Ḥamdān, is again underscored in this version, as is the mention of the glass vial; while Ibn Ḥamdān and al-Shağarī have Muḥammad giving Umm Salama the vial, in most texts it is already in her possession and she uses it to seal the dust and store it. Al-Ṭabarānī also transmits three texts on the authority of ʿĀʾisha containing a number of novelties: for example, the dust of Karbalāʾ is now described as white rather than red, and the land in which al-Ḥusayn will be killed is named as al-Ṭaff, losing the impact of the more evocative *karb wa balaʾ*:

> On the authority of ʿĀʾisha, who said: al-Ḥusayn b. ʿAlī came to see the Messenger of God, while he was receiving revela-

tion.[54] He leapt onto the Messenger of God, that is, on a shoulder and played on his back. Ǧibrīl said to the Messenger of God: "Do you love him, Muḥammad?" He replied: "Ǧibrīl, what do I have if I do not love my son?" He continued: "Your community after you will kill him." Then Ǧibrīl extended his hand and presented him with white dust and said: "In this land Muḥammad, this son of yours will be killed. Its name is al-Ṭaff." When Ǧibrīl had left the Messenger of God, he went out with the dust in his hand, weeping, and he said: "ʿĀʾisha! Ǧibrīl informed me that my son Ḥusayn would be killed in the land of al-Ṭaff, and that my community after me would kill him!" Then he went out to his companions, among them ʿAlī, Abū Bakr, ʿUmar, Ḥuḏayfa, ʿAmmār and Abū Ḏarr.[55] He was weeping, so they said: "What is making you weep, Messenger of God?" He replied: "Ǧibrīl informed me that my son al-Ḥusayn would be killed after me[56] in the land of al-Ṭaff. He

---

[54] Ibn Shahrāshūb too situates al-Ḥusayn's arrival at this precise moment (cf. Ibn Shahrāshūb., *Manāqib āl Abī Ṭālib*, vol. IV, bb. *Fī imāmat Abī ʿAbd Allāh al-Ḥusayn*: 55).

[55] A disparate group, headed (curiously, considering the transmitter) by ʿAlī b. Abī Ṭālib rather than by Abū Bakr, ʿĀʾisha's father (although Kohlberg suggests a number of reasons why the name of one of Muḥammad's companions, although in this case it is ʿĀʾisha, even one who is 'avowedly anti-Shīʿa', might appear in a Shīʿī chain of transmission: cf. KOHLBERG E., "Shīʿī *Ḥadīth*" in A F L Beeston et al., (eds.), *Arabic Literature to the End of the Umayyad Period*, Cambridge University Press, Cambridge 1983: 300), Ḥuḏayfa b. al-Yamān (not greatly associated with ʿAlī except perhaps at the 627 Battle of the Ditch), ʿAmmār b. Yāsir b. ʿĀmir b. Mālik Abū al-Yaqzān (who fought and died for ʿAlī at Ṣiffīn, and is revered by the Shīʿa, as is Abū Ḏarr al-Ġifārī al-Kinānī, as one of the 'four companions', early Muslims who were followers of ʿAlī; the other two, not mentioned in this group, are al-Miqdād b. Aswad al-Kindī and Salmān al-Fārsī).

[56] The words 'by my community' are absent here.

> produced this dust for me and informed that that the place he would lie[57] would be on it."[58]

He reproduces this narrative in his *al-Muʿǧam al-awsaṭ*, also on the authority of ʿĀʾisha but with a change of situation; Muḥammad sitting with al-Ḥusayn on his thigh when Ǧibrīl arrives. Ǧibrīl's question is no longer about the Prophet's love for the boy, but about the boy's identity:

> On the authority of ʿĀʾisha, that the Messenger of God sat al-Ḥusayn on his thigh. Then Ǧibrīl came to him and said: "Is this your son?" He replied: "Yes!" He went on: "Your community after you will kill him!" The eyes of the Messenger of God shed tears. Then he said: "If you wish, I will show you the dust of the land in which he will be killed." He replied: "Yes!" So Ǧibrīl produced some of the dust of al-Ṭaff.[59]

The third, almost identical to Ibn Ḥanbal's account, sees al-Ṭabarānī, and Shīʿī transmitter Ibn Namā after him, omit Umm Salama entirely and introduce an ostensibly rhetorical question

---

[57] This is the same word (*maḍǧaʿ*) used in Q. 3:154, and by Zaynab, defending the slain members of the People of the House in her dialogue with Ibn Ziyād (cf. CLOHESSY C., *Half of My Heart. The Narratives of Zaynab, Daughter of ʿAlī*, 2018: 178).

[58] al-Ṭabarānī., *al-Muʿǧam al-kabīr*, vol. III, n. 2814: 107, al-Qāḍī al-Nuʿmān., *Sharḥ al-aḫbār fī faḍāʾil al-aʾimma al-aṭhār*, vol. III, Part Twelve, n. 1074: 134 (in a much-reduced form; it is not in the context of revelation being received, the dust is not described and the account ends with the mention of al-Ṭaff), al-Shaǧarī., *Tartīb al-amālī al-ḫamīsiyya*, vol. I, bb. *Fī faḍl al-Ḥusayn b. ʿAlī*, n. 798: 218, Ibn Shahrāshūb., *Manāqib āl Abī Ṭālib*, vol. IV, *Fī imāmat Abī ʿAbd Allāh al-Ḥusayn*: 55, al-Hayṯamī., *Maǧmaʿ al-zawāʾid wa-manbaʿ al-fawāʾid*, vol. IX, bk. 37 (*Kitāb al-manāqib*), bb. 95 (*Manāqib al-Ḥusayn b. ʿAlī*), n. 15114: 218, al-Isfahānī., *ʿAwālim al-ʿulūm wa-l-maʿārif al-aḥwāl min al-āyāt wa-l-aḫbār wa-l-aqwāl*, vol. XVII, ch. 18, bb. 3, n. 1: 506, but much reduced and with no mention of ʿĀʾisha, but ends at the mention of al-Ṭaff.

[59] al-Ṭabarānī., *al-Muʿǧam al-awsaṭ*, vol. VI, n. 6316: 249, transmitted by al-Shaǧarī., *Tartīb al-amālī al-ḫamīsiyya*, vol. I, bb. *Fī faḍl al-Ḥusayn b. ʿAlī*, n. 798: 218 (with minor changes).

posed to ʿĀʾisha, a question never posed to Umm Salama, the one entrusted with the dust:

> On the authority of ʿĀʾisha, who said: al-Ḥusayn b. ʿAlī came to see the Messenger of God. The Prophet said: "ʿĀʾisha, does it not astonish you that an angel who has never come to see me before came to see me earlier, and he said that this son of mine would be killed? He also said: If you wish, I will show you dust upon which he will be killed. The angel reached out his hand and showed me red dust."[60]

Al-Ṭabarānī transmits two more narratives from Umm Salama, which appropriate elements from a smattering of early transmissions; both the command to Umm Salama and the entry of al-Ḥusayn are simplified and the Prophet, who earlier was clasping the boy to his chest, is now stroking his head in grief. The transmitter adds a clarification of the place by transporting the reader in time to the field of Karbalāʾ, although in most texts, al-Ḥusayn's confirmation of the prophecy occurs upon his arrival at Karbalāʾ rather than at the height of the battle:

> On the authority of Umm Salama, who said: The Messenger of God was sitting one day in my house, and he said: "No one is to come in to me." I was biding my time and then al-Ḥusayn entered, and I heard the sobbing of the Messenger of God, weeping. I looked, and there was Ḥusayn on his lap; the Prophet was rubbing his forehead and weeping.[61] I said: By

---

[60] al-Ṭabarānī., *al-Muʿǧam al-kabīr*, vol. III, n. 2815: 107. Cf. Ibn Namā., *Muṯīr al-aḥzān wa munīr subul al-ashḡān*: 18 (who adds: "Umm Salama took it and concealed it in a glass vial. She brought it out on the day he was killed, and it was blood" and that something similar was reported on the authority of Zaynab bt. Ǧahsh), al-Mağlisī., *Biḥār al-anwār*, vol. XLIV, bb. 30, n. 46: 247 (who omits 'Something similar to this was reported on the authority of Zaynab bt. Ǧahsh'), al-Iṣfahānī., *ʿAwālim al-ʿulūm wa-l-maʿārif al-aḥwāl min al-āyāt wa-l-aḫbār wa-l-aqwāl*, vol. XVII, ch. 11, bb. 2, n. 1: 117).

[61] al-Ṭabarī., *Ḏaḫāʾir al-ʿuqbā*, Part One, bb. 9: 251–252 (in his simplified version, Umm Salama sees Muḥammad rubbing al-Ḥusayn's head and weeping; he tells her of Ǧibrīl's prediction and stretching out his hand,

> God! What have to come to know since he entered? He answered: "Ǧibrīl was with us in the house and asked: Do you love him? I replied: By all that is in the world, yes! He continued: But your community will kill this one in a land called Karbalāʾ." Ǧibrīl reached for some of its dust and showed it to the Prophet. When al-Ḥusayn was surrounded on all sides at the time he was killed, he said: "What is the name of this land?" They replied: "Karbalāʾ!" He answered: "God and His Prophet have spoken the truth, the land of distress and tribulation."[62]

Al-Ṭabarānī's second text is close to Ibn Abī Shayba, although al-Ṭabarānī augments the details of al-Ḥusayn's entry and of Umm Salama's panicky reaction, and returns to the theme of her seeing, from the door, something unidentifiable in the hand of the Prophet:

> On the authority of Umm Salama, who said: The Messenger of God said to me: "Sit by the door; no one is to come in to me."[63] I was standing by the door when al-Ḥusayn came; I was about to reach for him, but the boy outstripped me and went in to his grandfather. I said: Prophet of God, may God make me your ransom! You gave me an order that no one should come to you, but then your son came, and I was about to reach for him but he outstripped me! After a protracted time, I looked from the door and I found you turning something over and over in your hand and your tears flowing, with the boy on

---

shows her red dust, which she puts in a glass vial, and tells her that it will become blood when al-Ḥusayn is killed).

[62] al-Ṭabarānī., *al-Muʿǧam al-kabīr*, vol. III, n. 2819: 108, Ibn al-ʿAdīm., *Buġyat al-ṭalab fī tārīḫ Ḥalab*, Part Six: 2598, al-Hayṯamī., *Maǧmaʿ al-zawāʾid wa-manbaʿ al-fawāʾid*, vol. IX, bk. 37 (*Kitāb al-manāqib*), bb. 95 (*Manāqib al-Ḥusayn b. ʿAlī*), nn. 15116: 219.

[63] al-Ṭabarānī here introduces a different command to Umm Salama: that she should merely 'sit' by the door rather than guard it, but together with the verb *walaǧa-yaliǧu* ('to enter') in the energetic mood (*nūn al-tawkīd*), with, as noted earlier, the sense that absolutely no one should be allowed past the door.

> your belly. He replied: "Yes, Ǧibrīl came to me and informed me that my community would kill him, and he produced for me some of the dust on which he will be killed, and that is what I am turning over and over in my hand."[64]

Contemporary with al-Ṭabarānī is al-Qāḍī al-Nuʿmān, who himself may well qualify as transmitting the earliest Shīʿī version; and while some scholars hold him to have been an *iṯnā ʿasharī*, most evidence suggests that he was an Ismāʿīlī. In his *Sharḥ al-aḫbār fī faḍāʾil al-aʾimma al-aṭhār*, an historical text that enumerates the virtues of the Imāms until the sixth, Ǧaʿfar al-Ṣādiq, he offers four brief texts that are largely different. The first, on the authority of ʿĀʾisha, has already been seen in al-Ṭabarānī, as has the second, with the command to Umm Salama to "sit by the door" and her seeing, from the door, Muḥammad turning something over in his hand. The third places a story far more familiar in other circumstances, onto the lips of Muḥammad's aunt, Umayma bt. ʿAbd al-Muṭṭalib: "The Messenger of God was sleeping in my home," she says, "when al-Ḥusayn, a small boy, wandered into the house." He sits on the stomach of his grandfather, where he urinates. Umayma rushes to grab him, when Muḥammad says: "Give me my son". She releases the boy until he has finished and pours water on Muḥammad to wash him; he then holds the boy in his arms and stands to pray, putting him on the ground as he sits and prostrates in prayer. Then he calls out and raises his hands, and in response to Umayma's query ("I saw you doing something in your prayer I never saw you doing before") Muḥammad replies:

---

[64] al-Ṭabarānī., *al-Muʿǧam al-kabīr*, vol. III, n. 2820: 109, al-Qāḍī al-Nuʿmān., *Sharḥ al-aḫbār fī faḍāʾil al-aʾimma al-aṭhār*, vol. III, Part Twelve, n. 1084: 142. In Ibn al-Ǧawzī, Umm Salama looks from the door to see al-Ḥusayn playing on Muḥammad's chest and, returning to a word used by Ibn Ḥanbal, a lump of mud (*ṭīn*) in the hand of the weeping Prophet. Only when al-Ḥusayn leaves does she enter to ask what has happened. Ǧibrīl has come to give him some on the mud on which al-Ḥusayn will be killed. Ibn al-Ǧawzī omits any details of the perpetrators and the name of the land. Cf. Ibn al-Ǧawzī., *Bustān al-waʿiẓīn wa-riyāḍ al-sāmiʿīn*, bb. 412: 261.

> Ğibraʾīl came to me and informed me that this son of mine would be killed after me. Then he said: If you wish, I can show you some of the dust on which he will be killed. I said: Show me! He showed me red dust.[65]

This is an exceptionally early Shīʿī text; al-Qāḍī al-Nuʿmān is a contemporary of a number of important early scholars, both Sunnī (al-Āğurrī, al-Ṭabarānī) and Shīʿī (Ibn Ḥamdān, Ibn Qūlawayh). What is of particular note in his text is that the words "if you wish, I can show you some of the dust" could easily be read as an invitation from Muḥammad to Umayma, rather than from Ğibrīl to Muḥammad. Nevertheless, his narrative strikes a discordant note here, since it is much closer to the Umm al-Faḍl and Umm Ayman narratives. A tale carried by al-Ṭūsī, al-Haytamī and Ibn ʿAsākir is in comparable form, but substitutes Umayma with Zaynab bt. Ğaḥsh.

> On the authority of Zaynab bt. Ğaḥsh that the Prophet was sleeping with her, when Ḥusayn crept into the house; she paid no attention to him until he came to the Prophet and got up onto his belly, placed his (organ) on his naval, and urinated. The Prophet woke up and I (went to him) and (put him down) from his stomach. The Messenger of God said: "Give me my son!" Then, when his urinating was finished, he took a mug of water and poured it, saying: "It should be poured off when from a baby boy and washed off when from a baby girl." She continued: Then he arose and prayed, and embraced him; when he bowed and prostrated, he put him down and when he stood, he carried him. When he sat, he began to implore and lift his hands and speak. When he finished the prayer, I said: Messenger of God, I saw you do something today I have never seen you do! He replied: "Ğibrīl came to me and informed me

---

[65] al-Qāḍī al-Nuʿmān., *Sharḥ al-aḫbār fī faḍāʾil al-aʾimma al-aṭhār*, vol. III, Part Twelve, n. 1075: 135.

> that my son would be killed. I said: Show me, and he came to me with red dust."[66]

Finally, al-Qāḍī al-Nuʿmān relates an uncommon and composite story found in no major transmitter, on the authority of ʿAlī, about Ǧibrīl informing Muḥammad that al-Raʿd,[67] the angel who drives the clouds, has asked permission of God to visit him and is on his way. They end up at Muḥammad's house, where al-Raʿd stops at the door, refusing to enter because of the pictures owned by some of Muḥammad's wives.[68] This issue dealt with, al-Raʿd enters; then al-Ḥusayn arrives and climbs on Muḥammad's belly, and there follows a conversation usually attributed to Ǧibrīl:

> Then al-Raʿd said: "Messenger of God, who is this?" He replied: "This in my son and the son of my son!" He went on: "Your community after you will kill him. If you wish, I will show you the dust of the country in which he will be killed." The Messenger of God said: "Yes!" So, he spread his wing in the direction of the East and produced a handful of red dust from Karbalāʾ and gave it to the Prophet, who went out weeping.[69]

---

[66] al-Ṭūsī., *al-Amālī fī-l-ḥadīṯ, maǧlis* 11, n. 88–641: 316, Ibn ʿAsākir., *Tārīḫ madīnat Dimashq*, vol. XIV, bb. 1566 (*al-Ḥusayn b. ʿAlī b. Abī Ṭālib b. ʿAbd al-Muṭṭalib b. Hāshim b. ʿAbd al-Manāf*):195–196, al-Hayṯamī., *Maǧmaʿ al-zawāʾid wa-manbaʿ al-fawāʾid*, vol. IX, bk. 37 (*Kitāb al-manāqib*), bb. 95 (*Manāqib al-Ḥusayn b. ʿAlī*), n. 15115: 218–219, al-Maǧlisī., *Biḥār al-anwār*, vol. XLIII, bb. 30, n. 11: 229.

[67] al-Suyūṭī., *al-Ḥabāʾik fī aḫbār al-malāʾik*, nn. 263–273: 68–69. Cf. LANE E.W., *An Arabic-English Lexicon*, vol. III, 1968: 1105.

[68] Angels do not enter houses in which there are images: cf. for e.g. al-Buḫārī., *Ṣaḥīḥ*, vol. III, bk. 39 (*Kitāb al-buyūʿ*), bb. 40, n. 2105: 185–186, Muslim., *Sunan*, vol. V, bk. 37 (*Kitāb al-libās wa-l-zīna*), bb. 26, nn. [5514] 83 (2106), [5515] 84: 471, nn. [5517] 85, [5518] 86: 472, nn. [5519] 87, [5520] (2107): 473, al-Tirmiḏī., *al-Ǧāmiʿ al-ṣaḥīḥ*, vol. V, bk. 41 (*Abwāb al-adab*), nn. 2804, 2805: 163–164.

[69] al-Qāḍī al-Nuʿmān., *Sharḥ al-aḫbār fī faḍāʾil al-aʾimma al-aṭhār*, vol. III, Part Twelve, n. 1082: 140.

Somewhat better known than al-Qāḍī al-Nuʿmān is Ibn Qūlawayh, writing in his handbook of spirituality, *Kāmil al-ziyārāt*. Taught by al-Kulaynī and himself one of al-Mufīd's teachers, Ibn Qūlawayh's text, while in principle a collection of *aḥādīṯ*, is deeply imbued with numinous elements. He proposes a small number of features that are distinctly new. The first is the mystical demonstration of the land; in Ibn Ḥamdān, it is al-Ḥusayn who extends to Umm Salama the invitation that is later found in the mouth of the angel: "If you like, I will show you…" In Ibn Qūlawayh, this mystical vision is accomplished by the angelic visitor:

> On the authority of Abū ʿAbd Allāh: Ǧabraʾīl came to the Messenger of God while al-Ḥusayn was playing in front of him and informed him that his community would kill him. The narrator continued: The Messenger of God grew anxious, and he said: "Should I show you the dust upon which he will be killed?" The narrator said: Then what was between the seat of the Messenger of God and the land in which al-Ḥusayn was killed sank down, until the two pieces met. He took some of it, and then it spread out faster than the blinking of an eye. He emerged saying: "Good betide (*ṭūbā*)[70] you as dust and good betide (*ṭūbā*) whoever is killed in your vicinity!"[71]

In a second, almost identical report, Ibn Qūlawayh qualifies the land in which al-Ḥusayn will be killed as Karbalāʾ, and uses the two index fingers of the narrator, Ǧaʿfar al-Ṣādiq, to illustrate the coming together of the two territories. Of Ǧibrīl he notes that "with his wing, he held out some of the dust and handed it to the Messenger of God."[72]

Against those who have identified the visitor as the angel of the rain or an angel who has never descended before, Ibn Qūlawayh insists, on the authority of Ibn ʿAbbās, that "the angel who

---

[70] Cf. LANE E.W., *An Arabic-English Lexicon*, vol. V, 1968: 1901. While the context suggests a reference to the concept of 'a good final outcome', it could also be an allusion to the mystical tree of Paradise called Ṭūbā.

[71] Ibn Qūlawayh., *Kāmil al-ziyārāt*, bb. 17, n. 1: 127–128.

[72] Op. cit., bb. 17, n. 1: 129–130.

came to Muḥammad to inform him of the killing of al-Ḥusayn was Ǧabra'īl, the Faithful Spirit." Here, Ibn Qūlawayh affixes more additions; Ǧabra'īl arrives "wings outstretched, weeping, shouting aloud," with an emotion rarely seen in angelic beings, and is already carrying with him some of the "dust of al-Ḥusayn."[73] In the same short narrative, Ibn Qūlawayh advances two additional elements. In a significant transformation from Ibn Ṭahmān's 'clod of earth', the dust, which up until this point has exuded the smell of distress (*karb*) and tribulation (*balā'*), now diffuses an aroma like musk. In response to the angel, Muḥammad asks after the fate of his community: "Will a nation that killed my young one[74] prosper (or he said: the young one of my daughter)? Ǧibra'īl replied: God will strike them with disagreement, and their hearts will be at variance."[75]

Previous narrators have detailed the wrath of God and His severe punishment for those who killed al-Ḥusayn; now it is the fate of the whole *umma* of Muḥammad that is brought into question. In two of his reports, Ibn Qūlawayh situates the angelic visit in the house of Umm Salama, noting that Umm Salama kept the dust with her until the day of her death, but failing to mention the glass vial or Umm Salama's anxious vigil. He has Muḥammad asking to see the dust and being the first to mention it, an element already seen almost a century before in Ibn Abī ʿĀṣim, and those who transmit from him.[76]

Finally, Ibn Qūlawayh turns his attention to Fāṭima. "When Fāṭima gave birth to al-Ḥusayn," he writes, "Ǧabra'īl came to the Messenger of God and said to him: Your community after you will kill al-Ḥusayn." He is the first to situate the event at the time of al-

---

[73] Op. cit., bb. 17, n. 7: 131.

[74] Lane holds that the primary signification of the Arabic *farḫ* is the young of a bird or of an egg-laying creature, and sometimes the young of any animal. Cf. LANE E.W., *An Arabic-English Lexicon*, vol. VI, 1968: 2362. Steingass adds a young 'plant' or 'shoot'. STEINGASS F., *Learner's Arabic English Dictionary*, 1993: 782

[75] Ibn Qūlawayh., *Kāmil al-ziyārāt*, bb. 17, n. 7: 131.

[76] Ibn Qūlawayh., *Kāmil al-ziyārāt*, bb. 17, n. 2: 128–129, n. 3: 129, n. 4: 129.

Ḥusayn's birth, but then introduces an even earlier occurrence, a pre-conception prophecy:

> On the authority of al-Muʿallā b. Ḫunays, who said: The Messenger of God arose one morning, and Fāṭima saw him, weeping and grieved. She said: "Messenger of God, what is the matter with you?" But he refused to tell her, so she said: "I will neither eat nor drink until you tell me!" He answered: "Ǧabra'īl came to me with the dust on which a boy, not yet conceived, will be killed" (she was not pregnant with al-Ḥusayn) "and this is his dust."[77]

Twenty years after Ibn Qūlawayh, Ibn Bābawayh, who as a scholar would come to be known as 'the truthful' (*al-ṣadūq*) moves the event forward from al-Ḥusayn's birth to a time when he is 'a child', a factor witnessed in his playful behaviour as it is described by the texts – darting through the door, leaping into the lap of Muḥammad or playing on the Prophet's back and shoulders:

> On the authority of Abū ʿAbd Allāh, who said: The Prophet was in the house of Umm Salama, and he said to her: "No one is to come in to me!" Then al-Ḥusayn, who was still a child, came in and she was unable to restrain him before he went in to the Prophet. Umm Salama went in after him, and al-Ḥusayn was on the chest of the Prophet, who was weeping. There was something in his hand which he was turning over and over. The Prophet said: "Umm Salama, Ǧabra'īl informs me that this one will be killed, and this is the dust upon which he will be killed. Take it with you, and when it becomes blood, my beloved will have been killed."[78]

The details are recognizable: the house of Umm Salama, Muḥammad's request not to be disturbed, the impulsive but nonetheless mandatory arrival of the child who is to be the focal point of the foretelling and Umm Salama's fruitless attempts to hold him back. So too, the boy on the chest of his grief-stricken grandfather, the portentous announcement and Muḥammad fiddling distractedly

[77] Op. cit., bb. 17, n. 7: 132.

[78] Ibn Bābawayh., *Kitāb al-amālī*, *maǧlis* 29, n. 3: 139.

with something Umm Salama cannot make out. Now Ibn Bābawayh's narrative takes an original turn, as Umm Salama speaks up and in response is told something of the destiny of the boy still sleeping on the breast of the Prophet:

> Umm Salama said: Messenger of God, ask God to repel this from him! He replied: "I have already done so, and God, powerful and great, made known to me that he has a rank (*daraǧa*) not given to any other creature, and that he has a party (*shīʿa*) who will intercede and be accepted in intercession. The *Mahdī* will be from his offspring and good betide (*ṭūbā*) whoever was among the friends and the party of al-Ḥusayn. By God, they will be the triumphant[79] on the Day of Resurrection."[80]

Ibn Bābawayh would die a quarter century after the Occultation of the Twelfth Imām; in describing *al-Mahdī* ('the guided one') as one of al-Ḥusayn's offspring, he was giving voice to an already established dogma. In a further narrative and followed by a sprinkling of transmitters, he omits the traces of dust on the Prophet's head and beard, describing him instead as 'emaciated' (*shāḥib*) and 'distressed' (*ka'īb*).

> On the authority of Umm Salama, that she awoke one day weeping. She was asked: "What is the matter with you?" She replied: My son al-Ḥusayn has been killed! I have never seen the Messenger of God since he died, except for this night. I said: You are as dear to me as my own father and mother! Why do I see you emaciated? He replied: "All night I have been digging the graves for al-Ḥusayn and his companions."[81]

The issue of intercession will be taken up afresh by al-Mufīd; but before him, a pupil who was schooled both by al-Mufīd and by Ibn Bābawayh, and who died in the same year as the latter, will make emphatic reference to the rising of *al-Mahdī* from the descendants of the martyred al-Ḥusayn. Unlike al-Bayhaqī and al-Shaǧarī, but

---

[79] Cf. Q. 9:20, Q. 23:111, Q. 24:52, Q. 59:20.

[80] Ibn Bābawayh., *Kitāb al-amālī*, *maǧlis* 29, n. 3: 139–140, al-Maǧlisī., *Biḥār al-anwār*, vol. XLIII, bb. 30, n. 5: 225.

[81] Ibn Bābawayh., *Kitāb al-amālī*, *maǧlis* 29, n. 1: 139.

close to Ibn ʿAsākir, all of whom will later take up the same report, ʿAlī al-Ḫazzāz puts the narrative into the mouth of ʿĀʾisha herself, and then adds a dialogue between Ǧibrīl and Muḥammad about the vengeance that God will take on the killers through *al-Mahdī*, the ninth of al-Ḥusayn's descendants:

> On the authority of Abū Salama, on the authority of ʿĀʾisha, who said: We had an attic room and whenever the Messenger of God wanted to meet with Ǧabraʾīl, he would meet him there. Once, the Messenger of God was meeting him there and he ordered me that no one should come up to him. Then al-Ḥusayn came to see him, and Ǧabraʾīl said: "Who is this?" The Messenger of God replied: "My son," and then the Prophet took him and sat him on his thigh. Ǧabraʾīl said to him: "He will be killed!" The Messenger of God replied: "Who will kill him?" He answered: "Your community will kill him!" The Messenger of God said: "They will kill him?" He answered: "Yes, and if you wish I will inform you of the land in which he will be killed." He motioned towards al-Ṭaff in Iraq, and took from it red dust and showed it to him, saying: "This is from the place where he will lie." The Messenger of God wept.[82]

Ǧabraʾīl urges Muḥammad not to weep, assuring him that "God will avenge the martyrs by the One who will arise for you from the People of the House." Muḥammad asks who this is and is told: "He is the ninth of the descendants of al-Ḥusayn." The one guided by God and who in turn is able to be the authentic guide, *al-Mahdī*

---

[82] al-Ḫazzāz., *Kifāyat al-aṯar fī-l-nuṣūṣ ʿalā al-aʾimma al-iṯnā ʿasharī*, bb. *Ma ǧāʾ ʿan ʿĀʾisha bt. Abī Bakr*: 187, al-Bayhaqī., *Dalāʾil al-nubuwwa*, vol. VI, bb. *Ma ruwiya fī iḫbāri-hi bi-qatli ibn ibnati-hi ʿAbd Allāh al-Ḥusayn*: 470, al-Shaǧarī., *Tartīb al-amālī al-ḫamīsiyya*, vol. I, bb. *Fī faḍl al-Ḥusayn b. ʿAlī*, n. 822: 233, Ibn ʿAsākir., *Tarīḫ madīnat Dimashq*, vol. XIV, bb. 1566 (*al-Ḥusayn b. ʿAlī b. Abī Ṭālib b. ʿAbd al-Muṭṭalib b. Hāshim b. ʿAbd al-Manāf*): 195, al-Suyūṭī., *al-Ḫaṣāʾiṣ al-kubrā*, vol. II: 451 (transmitting from al-Bayhaqī in a simplified form; al-Ḥusayn simply arrives in the room when Ǧibrīl is there and the angel immediately makes the prediction, with few other details).

is also 'the One who will arise' (*al-qā'im*) to avenge all the sufferings that the People of the House and their supporters sustained.

Hailed by al-Ḏahabī,[83] in spite of accusations of crypto-Shīʿī tendencies, as 'the great *ḥāfiẓ* and leader of the transmitters of *aḥādīṯ*', al-Ḥākim al-Nīsābūrī transmits on the authority of Umm al-Faḍl bt. al-Ḥāriṯ, putting the story into her mouth and into the context of her famous dream, as would Ibn ʿAsākir and al-Bayhaqī after him:

> One day I went to visit the Messenger of God and I placed him in my lap. I happened to turn around and behold, the eyes of the Messenger of God were flowing with tears. I said: Messenger of God, you are as dear to me as my own father and mother! What is wrong with you? He replied: "Ǧibrīl came to me and informed me that my community would kill this son of mine!" I said: This one? He answered: "Yes. He came to me with some red dust."[84]

Al-Ḥākim carries a second account, in which Umm al-Faḍl comes to Muḥammad, but without any mention of her ominous dream, and in which Muḥammad tells her: "Ǧibrīl informed me that my community would kill al-Ḥusayn."[85]

One of Ibn Bābawayh's pupils, who would come to be nicknamed 'the instructive' (*al-mufīd*), takes up once again the theme of

---

[83] al-Ḏahabī., *Taḏkirat al-ḥuffāẓ*, Part Three, n. 962– 35/13/1: 162. Both al-Ḏahabī and Ibn Ḥaǧar thought that despite his being truthful as a teaching authority, "in his *Mustadrak* he declared as sound many disreputable *aḥādīṯ*" (al-Ḏahabī., *Mīzān al-iʿtidāl*, Part Three, n. 7804: 608, al-ʿAsqalānī., *Lisān al-mīzān*, vol. VII, n. 7070: 256).

[84] al-Ḥākim al-Nīsābūrī., *Kitāb al-mustadrak ʿalā al-ṣaḥīḥayn*, vol. III, Part Three, bk. 31 (*Kitāb maʿrifat al-ṣaḥāba*), *Awwal faḍā'il Abi ʿAbd Allah al-Husayn*, n. 4884: 210, Ibn ʿAsākir., *Tārīḫ madīnat Dimashq*, vol. XIV, bb. 1566 (*al-Ḥusayn b. ʿAlī b. Abī Ṭālib b. ʿAbd al-Muṭṭalib b. Hāshim b. ʿAbd al-Manāf*): 196–197, al-Bayhaqī., *Dalā'il al-nubuwwa*, vol. VI, bb. *Ma ruwiya fī iḫbāri-hi bi-qatli ibn ibnati-hi ʿAbd Allāh al-Ḥusayn*: 469.

[85] al-Ḥākim al-Nīsābūrī., *Kitāb al-mustadrak ʿalā al-ṣaḥīḥayn*, vol. III, Part Three, bk. 31 (*Kitāb maʿrifat al-ṣaḥāba*), *Awwal faḍā'il Abī ʿAbd Allāh al-Ḥusayn*, n. 4890: 213.

intercession in a passage that will be transmitted from him by al-Ṭabarsī and al-Irbilī:

> On the authority of Umm Salama, who said: While the Messenger of God was sitting one day, with al-Ḥusayn in his lap, his eyes were bathed in tears. I said: Messenger of God! I see you weeping! May I be made your ransom! He replied: "Ǧibraʾīl came to me and consoled me over my son al-Ḥusayn, and informed me that a group from my community would kill him. God will not accord them my intercession."[86]

While in one of his transmissions, Ibn ʿAsākir has Muḥammad describing al-Ḥusayn's killer as "a man from my community, hateful of my progeny; my intercession will not be granted to him,"[87] the loss of the Prophet's intercession is an especially dominant theme in al-Ḥusayn's dream by his father's grave, and again in the writing on the wall, seen by a group of Muslim visitors in a Byzantine church. *Shayḫ* al-Mufīd also permits us a glimpse into the psychology of Umm Salama who, as she does in Ibn Bābawayh, ceases to be a mere cipher and expresses significant emotion. She is the chief narrator of a lengthy text in which Muḥammad returns to the house after a mysterious night-time journey:

> On the authority of Umm Salama, who said: The Messenger of God went out from us one night and stayed away from us a long time. Then he returned to us, dishevelled, dust covered, his hand tightly clasped. I said: Messenger of God, why do I

---

[86] al-Mufīd., *al-Irshād fī maʿrifat ḥuǧaǧ Allāh ʿalā al-ʿibād*, vol. II, Part Two, bb. *Tārīḫ al-Imām al-Ḥusayn*: 130, al-Ṭabarsī., *Iʿlām al-warā bi-aʿlām al-hudā*, vol. I, Part Three, bb. 2: 428–429, al-Irbilī., *Kashf al-ġumma fī maʿrifat al-aʾimma*, vol. II, Part Two: 8 (with both al-Ḥasan and al-Ḥusayn sitting on Muḥammad's lap during this encounter, although Ǧibrīl comforts Muḥammad only on account of al-Ḥusayn), al-Maǧlisī., *Biḥār al-anwār*, vol. XLIV, bb. 30, n. 31: 239–240. Cf. also Ibn Kaṯīr., *al-Bidāya wa-l-nihāya*, vol. IX, bb. *Iḫbār bi-maqtal al-Ḥusayn*: 237, with al-Ḥusayn is in Muḥammad's lap as he talks with Ǧibrīl.

[87] Cf. Ibn ʿAsākir., *Tārīḫ madīnat Dimashq*, vol. XIV, bb. 1566 (*al-Ḥusayn b. ʿAlī b. Abī Ṭālib b. ʿAbd al-Muṭṭalib b. Hāshim b. ʿAbd al-Manāf*): 224.

> see you dishevelled and dust covered? He answered: "I was made to journey by night in this time to a place in Iraq called Karbalāʾ. I was shown the killing of al-Ḥusayn, my son, and a group of my descendants and the people of my house. I have been gathering their blood and here it is in my hand." He presented it to me and said: "Take it and guard it!" I took it, and it was similar to red dust. I put it in a glass vial, plugged its top and guarded it. When al-Ḥusayn left Mecca, heading to Iraq, I would bring out that glass vial every day and night, and would smell it and look at it. Then I would weep for his misfortune. On the 10th day of al-Muḥarram, the day on which he was killed, I took it out at first light and it was as it was. Then I looked at it at the end of the day, and behold, it was fresh blood. I cried out in my house and wept. Then I suppressed my anger, fearing that their enemies in Medina would hear and would be quick to gloat at their misfortune. I never ceased guarding it for the time, until the messenger of his death came to announce it. What I had seen was verified.[88]

He has journeyed to Karbalāʾ and there seen the place where al-Ḥusayn and his companions will be killed; Muḥammad has collected their (not just al-Ḥusayn's) blood in his hand and shows it to Umm Salama, asking her to keep it. In sharp contrast to other accounts, it is not red dust he is carrying, but blood which has the appearance of red dust. The rest is similar to versions where she keeps it in a vial, although an addition here is that she would take the vial out daily and smell it, looking at it and weeping over al-

---

[88] al-Mufīd., *al-Irshād fī maʿrifat ḥuǧaǧ Allāh ʿalā al-ʿibād*, vol. II, bb. *Faṣl fī faḍāʾil Imām al-Ḥusayn wa manāqibi-hi*: 130. The narrative is taken up from al-Mufīd, with small changes, by Ibn ʿAlī al-Fattāl., *Rawḍat al-wāʿiẓīn wa-tabṣirat al-muttaʿiẓīn*, vol. I, *maǧlis fī ḏikr maqtal al-Ḥusayn*: 193. Cf. also al-Ṭabarsī., *Iʿlām al-warā bi-aʿlām al-hudā*, vol. I, Part One, bb. 2: 219, 429, al-Irbilī., *Kashf al-ġumma fī maʿrifat al-aʾimma*, vol. II, Part Three: 8, al-Maǧlisī., *Biḥār al-anwār*, vol. XLIV, bb. 30, n. 31: 239, al-Iṣfahānī., *ʿAwālim al-ʿulūm wa-l-maʿārif al-aḥwāl min al-āyāt wa-l-aḫbār wa-l-aqwāl*, vol. XVII, ch. 11, bb. 6, n. 8: 128), al-Ǧazāʾirī., *Riyāḍ al-abrār fī manāqib al-aʾimma al-aṭhār*, vol. I, Part One: 171.

Ḥusayn's fate. On the day of ʿĀshūrā she takes out the vial and it is unchanged; but that evening when she returns to it, it has turned into blood, supposedly fresh as opposed to appearing like dust, and marking the time of his killing. She cries out and then restrains her grief and anger lest the town citizens react badly; instead, she waits for news of the death to come and confirm what she has seen. The point about restraint lest the other citizens react with a sort of *schadenfreude* suggests some of the societal divisions that existed around the person of al-Ḥusayn.

Another Shīʿī *muḥaddit*, Abū Ǧaʿfar al-Ṭūsī, hailed as the 'scholar of the sect' (*shayḫ al-ṭāʾifa*), has left us a transmission in which Ibn ʿAbbās plays a leading part. This is not his own famous vision of the Prophet, recounted later in this work; instead, Ibn ʿAbbās is resting in his house in Medina when he is disturbed by a loud and distressing cry from the home of Umm Salama. He sets out immediately towards her house, as do numerous fellow citizens:

> When finally, I got to her, I said: Mother of the believers! Why is it that you cry out and call for help? She did not answer me, but turned towards the Hāshimī women and said: "Daughters of ʿAbd al-Muṭṭalib! Help me by weeping with me, because by God, your master and the master of the youths of the inhabitants of the Garden has been killed! By God, al-Ḥusayn, the grandson of the Messenger of God and his sweet basil, has been killed!" Someone said:[89] "Mother of the believers, from where did you learn this?" She replied: "I just saw the Messenger of God in a dream, dishevelled and dismayed, and I asked him the reason for this. He said: My son al-Ḥusayn and the people of his house have been killed today and I have buried them, and have just finished with their burial. She said: I got up and entered the house, and I had scarcely begun to comprehend when I looked, and there was the dust with which Ǧibraʾıl had come from Karbalāʾ, saying: When this dust changes to blood, your son will have been killed. The Prophet had given it to me and said: Put this dust in a glass bottle – or, he said,

[89] al-Iṣfahānī reads: "I said…"

a glass vial – to have with you. When it becomes fresh blood, al-Ḥusayn will have been killed. I saw the glass vial now, and it had become fresh blood, welling forth!" He continued: Umm Salama took some of that blood and splashed her face with it. That day she began to perform a mourning (*ma'tam*) and lamentation (*manāḥa*) for al-Ḥusayn. Then the riders brought news of him, and he had been killed on that day.

ʿAmr b. Ṯābit said: My father said: I went to visit Abū Ǧaʿfar Muḥammad b. ʿAlī at his house, and I asked him about this *ḥadīṯ*. I mentioned to him the transmission of Saʿīd b. Ǧubayr of this *ḥadīṯ* on the authority of ʿAbd Allāh b. ʿAbbās, and Abū Ǧaʿfar said: ʿUmar b. Abī Salama told it to me on the authority of his mother, Umm Salama. Ibn ʿAbbās said in the transmission of Saʿīd b. Ǧubayr on his authority: The next night I saw the Messenger of God in my dream, dust covered and dishevelled, and I mentioned this to him and asked him about its significance. He said to me: "Did you not know that I have just finished with the burial of al-Ḥusayn and his companions?" ʿAmr b. Abī Miqdām said…Gibra'īl came to the Prophet with the dust on which al-Ḥusayn would be killed. Abū Ǧaʿfar added: We have it with us.[90]

Sezgin puts al-Shaǧarī al-Ǧurǧānī among the Imāmī Shīʿa and says that he was "still alive in 420/1029", Brockelmann provides neither dates nor details, and both name only his *Kitāb al-iʿtibār*.[91] According to Ansari and Schmidtke, he was in fact a Zaydī Shīʿa who went by the name of al-Murshad bi-llāh Yaḥyā b. al-Ḥusayn b. Ismāʿīl al-

---

[90] al-Ṭūsī., *al-Amālī fī-l-ḥadīṯ*, *maǧlis* 11, n. 87–640: 314–315, Ibn Shahrāshūb., *Manāqib āl Abī Ṭālib*, vol. IV, bb. *Fī imāmat Abī ʿAbd Allāh al-Ḥusayn*: 55, al-Ḥillī al-ʿAllāma., *Iṯbāt al-hudāt bi-l-nuṣūṣ wa-l-muʿǧiẓāt*, vol. I, Part Seventeen, n. 224: 326, al-Maǧlisī., *Biḥār al-anwār*, vol. XLV, bb. 41, n. 22: 227, bb. 42, nn. 1–2: 230–231, al-Iṣfahānī., *ʿAwālim al-ʿulūm wa-l-maʿārif al-aḥwāl min al-āyāt wa-l-aḫbār wa-l-aqwāl*, vol. XVII, ch. 18, bb. 3, n. 3: 508–509 (with fewer details).

[91] Cf. GAL S. II: 1004, GAS I: 521–522.

Ğurğānī al-Shağarī (d. 479/1086–7 or 499/1106).[92] His transmission includes the presence of al-Ḥasan, and turns the red dust into something a little more solid:

> On the authority of Umm Salama, who said: Ğibrīl came to the Prophet, and al-Ḥasan and al-Ḥusayn came in to him. He said: "Your community after you will kill him" – that is, al-Ḥusayn. Then he said: "Should I show you some of the dust of the place of his killing?" She went on: He produced pebbles for him, which the Messenger of God put into a glass vial.[93]

Umm Salama goes on to describe a lament she hears on the night air on the night al-Ḥusayn was killed, and then says: "I opened the glass vial and there had begun to be blood in it."

While generally the narrative follows the same lines – Umm Salama present and acting as custodian and al-Ḥusayn (with his brother) arriving, necessarily but by surprise – al-Shağarī places Umm Salama away from the immediate precincts for a moment, arriving back just in time to witness the unfolding angelic intervention:

> On the authority of Umm Salama, wife of the Prophet, who said: While Ḥusayn was with the Messenger of God on the house, I had gone out to satisfy a need. Then I entered the

---

[92] ANSARI H. & SCHMIDTKE S., "The Literary-Religious Tradition among 7th/13th Century Yemeni Zaydīs" in D. Hollenberg, C. Rauch et al., *The Yemeni Manuscript Tradition*, Brill, Leiden 2015: 105, "The literary-religious tradition among 7th/13th century Yemenī Zaydīs: The formation of the Imām al-Mahdī li-Dīn Allāh Aḥmad b. al-Ḥusayn b. al-Qāsim (d. 656/1258)" in *Journal of Islamic Manuscripts* 2 (2011): 167.

[93] al-Shağarī., *Tartīb al-amālī al-ḫamīsiyya*, vol. II, bb. *Fī ḏikr ʿĀshūrā*, n. 1800: 115, al-Ḫawārizmī., *Maqtal al-Ḥusayn*, Part Two, bb. *Fī bayān ʿuqūba qātil al-Ḥusayn*, n. 33: 107–108 (omitting mention of al-Ḥasan and al-Ḥusayn), al-Mağlisī., *Biḥār al-anwār*, vol. XLIV, bb. 30, n. 34: 241, al-Iṣfahānī., *ʿAwālim al-ʿulūm wa-l-maʿārif al-aḥwāl min al-āyāt wa-l-aḫbār wa-l-aqwāl*, vol. XVII, ch. 11, bb. 6, n. 9: 128. Notes ʿAbbās Qummī: "In some reports, Umm Salama said: (Muḥammad) came with pebbles and put them in a glass vial, and in others, that he gave her a glass vial in which there was sand from al-Ṭaff" (ʿAbbās Qummī., *Safīnat al-biḥār*, vol. I: 456).

> house; the Messenger of God had taken Ḥusayn and put him to sleep on his belly and he was now wiping the tears from his eyes. I said: Messenger of God, what is making you weep? He answered: "Compassion for this poor one! Ǧibrīl informed me that he would be killed at Karbalāʾ in Iraq, and this is its dust which Ǧibrīl produced for me."[94]

A number of transmitters have al-Ḥusayn already present at the house either playing outside with his brother, or inside and in the care of Umm Salama:

> On the authority of Umm Salama: Ǧibrāʾīl was with the Prophet and al-Ḥusayn was with me and was crying; so I let him be, and he drew near to the Prophet, and Ǧibrāʾīl said: "Do you love him, Muḥammad?" He replied: "Yes!" He continued: "Your community will kill him, and if you wish I will show you some of the dust of the land in which he will be killed." He showed him, and the land is called Karbalāʾ.[95]

Sibṭ al-Ǧawzī[96] makes al-Ḥusayn the narrator in his transmission ("I was informed by Umm Salama, who said: Ǧibraʾīl was with the Messenger of God and you were with me. You were crying...") and has Ǧibrīl spreading his wing over the land of Karbalāʾ as he reveals it to Muḥammad. The al-Ǧawzī text continues with al-

---

[94] al-Shağarī., *Tartīb al-amālī al-ḫamīsiyya*, vol. I, bb. *Fī faḍl al-Ḥusayn b. ʿAlī*, n. 800: 219, n. 831: 237 (in which the narrator adds a question from Umm Salama after she has heard the name Karbalāʾ: "And where is Karbalāʾ?" she asks).

[95] Ibn Ḥanbal., *Kitāb faḍāʾil al-ṣaḥāba*, vol. II, bb. *Faḍāʾil al-Ḥasan wa-l-Ḥusayn*, n. 1391: 782, al-Shāmī., *al-Durr al-naẓīm fī manāqib al-aʾimma al-lahābīm*, bb. 5, *Fī ḏikr al-Ḥusayn b. ʿAlī*: 535–536, al-Ṭabarī., *Ḏaḫāʾir al-ʿuqbā*, Part One, bb. 9: 252, al-Ḏahabī., *Mīzān al-iʿtidāl*, vol I, bb. 12 (Abān b. Abī ʿAyyāsh): 13, al-Shablanğī., *Nūr al-abṣār fī manāqib āl bayt al-nabī al-muḫtār*, *faṣl fī ḏikr sayyidi-nā al-Ḥusayn*: 254–255 (with slightly different wording – Ǧibrīl extends his wing towards the earth, showing Muḥammad a land called Karbalāʾ and producing the red dust of al-Ṭaff).

[96] Grandson of the more famous Ibn al-Ǧawzī, his Shīʿī tendencies are particularly strong in his *Taḏkirat al-ḫawāṣṣ al-umma bi-ḏikr ḫaṣāʾiṣ al-aʾimma*; nonetheless, he is a Sunnī author.

Ḥusayn smelling the land and saying: "This, by God, is the land about which Ǧibrīl informed the Messenger of God, and I will be killed in it." While the narrative contains recognizable elements, the command given to Umm Salama ("let my son be") is the polar opposite of the more typical 'no one must enter'; and although we have other instances of al-Ḥusayn narrating his dialogues with Umm Salama, this particular event is not one of them.[97]

Contrary to their near contemporary Sibṭ al-Ǧawzī, al-Shāmī and Ibn al-ʿAdīm after him have al-Ḥusayn managing to creep past Umm Salama unseen, in spite of her attempts to shield the door:

> On the authority of Umm Salama, who said: The Prophet came to see me and said to me: "Guard the door! No one is to enter in to me." Then I heard his sobbing and I went in, and al-Ḥusayn was in front of him. I said: By God, Messenger of God, I did not see him enter! He replied: "Ǧibrīl was with me just now, and he said to me: Muḥammad! Do you love him? I answered: Ǧibrīl, by all that is in the world, yes! He continued: Your community after you will kill him, and if you wish, Muḥammad, I will show you his dust. Then he handed me this dust!" Umm Salama said: I took it and put it in a glass vial. I poured it out on the day al-Ḥusayn was killed and it had become blood.[98]

Sunnī historian Ibn ʿAsākir includes approximately nine versions of this story in his massive biographical dictionary, in the course of which he presents some novel insights and information. He carries three versions about the angel of the rain seeking permission to visit, all of them slightly different from Ibn Ḥanbal's text; Ibn

---

[97] Sibṭ al-Ǧawzī., *Taḏkirat al-ḫawāṣṣ al-umma bi-ḏikr ḫaṣāʾiṣ al-aʾimma*, bb. *Ḏikr maqtali-hi*: 250. The imperative, although addressed to Umm Salama, is in the masculine form, although this may be an error in transcription.

[98] al-Shāmī., *al-Durr al-naẓīm fī manāqib al-aʾimma al-lahāhīm*, bb. 5, *Fī ḏikr al-Ḥusayn b. ʿAlī*: 536, Ibn al-ʿAdīm., *Buġyat al-ṭalab fī tārīḫ Ḥalab*, Part Six: 2597.

ʿAsākir adds that 'it was the day of Umm Salama'[99] and she is commanded to 'guard' the door rather than just to hold it. He also reports that when al-Ḥusayn enters, Muḥammad reacts by embracing and kissing him, and in his first version he omits all mention of the angel producing mud or dust and Umm Salama secreting it in her robe. In his first two versions, he also omits Ṯābit's declaration that the place being spoken of was Karbalāʾ. In a further transmission, which encompasses some of the elements of al-Ṭabarānī and al-Qāḍī al-Nuʿmān, Ibn ʿAsākir does provide fresh details which augment the prevalent narrative and which will be taken up by al-Hayṯamī and al-Ḏahabī after him, although in a much-reduced form:

> On the authority of Abū ʿUmāma, who said: The Messenger of God said to his womenfolk: "Do not weep over this boy" (that is, Ḥusayn). He continued: It was the day of Umm Salama, and Ǧibrīl descended. The Messenger of God came inside and said to Umm Salama: "Do not invite anyone to come in to me." Then al-Ḥusayn came, and when he noticed the Prophet in the house, he wanted to go in. Umm Salama took him and clasped him in her arms, and began to whisper to him and to soothe him. However, when the weeping became more intense, she let him go and he entered, and sat on the lap of the Messenger of God. Ǧibrīl said to the Prophet: "Your community will kill this son of yours." The Prophet replied: "They will kill him even though they are believers in me?" He replied: "Yes, they will kill him." Then Ǧibrīl took (some) dust and said: "In such and such a place." The Messenger of God went out, Ḥusayn clasped in his arms, grieved and distressed. Umm Salama assumed that he was vexed by the entry of the boy, and she said: "Prophet of God, may I be made your ransom! You said to us 'do not weep over this boy' and ordered me not to invite anyone to call upon you. He came in, and I let him go!" However, he did not respond to her, but went out to his companions

---

[99] As do others; cf. for e.g. al-Shāmī., *al-Durr al-naẓīm fī manāqib al-aʾimma al-lahāhīm*, bb. 5, *Fī ḏikr al-Ḥusayn b. ʿAlī*: 535, Ibn al-ʿAdīm., *Buġyat al-ṭalab fī tārīḫ Ḥalab*, Part Six: 2600.

> who were sitting there and said to them: "My community will kill this one!" Abū Bakr and ʿUmar were among the people and were the boldest of the people (before him), and they said: "Prophet of God, they will kill him even though they are believers?" He replied: "Yes, and this is his dust." And he showed it to them.[100]

Ibn ʿAsākir commences the story with a brief preface; a command 'that they should not weep over the boy' addressed to the women generally, ominous despite its lack of context, and reminiscent of the order given by al-Ḥusayn to the women on the eve of Karbalāʾ, as recorded by al-Ḫawārizmī: "Zaynab! Umm Kulṯūm! Fāṭima! Rubāb! See when I am killed that there is neither ripping of garments for me nor scratching of faces for me, and do not use unseemly language on my behalf!"[101] Ibn ʿAsākir then goes on to underscore that "it was the day of Umm Salama" – not merely a nod in the direction of Muḥammad's domestic arrangements, but a reiteration that Umm Salama's house is a place of divine encounter. She herself is given no particular command, except that she should not invite anyone in, but the boy al-Ḥusayn, in her arms, grows increasingly distressed; omitted is all the youthful playfulness, and, like the dream of Umm al-Faḍl, something menacing hangs over the story. The earliest texts record Muḥammad's almost monosyllabic response to the angel; a simple 'yes' in answer to the angelic enquiries about his love and his desire to see the place where his grandson will be killed. Ibn Abī ʿĀṣim introduces his requesting to see the dust of Karbalāʾ, Ibn Qūlawayh his question about the fate of his community and al-Ḫazzāz his queries about the identity of

---

[100] Ibn ʿAsākir., *Tārīḫ madīnat Dimashq*, vol. XIV, bb. 1566 (*al-Ḥusayn b. ʿAlī b. Abī Ṭālib b. ʿAbd al-Muṭṭalib b. Hāshim b. ʿAbd al-Manāf*): 190–191. Cf. Ibn al-ʿAdīm., *Buġyat al-ṭalab fī tārīḫ Ḥalab*, Part Six: 2601–2602, al-Ḏahabī., *Siyar aʿlām al-nubalāʾ*, vol. III, n. 48 (*al-Ḥusayn al-Shahīd Abū ʿAbd Allāh b. ʿAlī b. Abī Ṭālib*): 289, *Tārīḫ al-Islām*, vol. V: 66–67, al-Hayṯamī., *Maǧmaʿ al-zawāʾid wa-manbaʿ al-fawāʾid*, vol. IX, bk. 37 (*Kitāb al-manāqib*), bb. 95 (*Manāqib al-Ḥusayn b. ʿAlī*), n. 15119: 220.

[101] al-Ḫawārizmī., *Maqtal al-Ḥusayn*, Part One, bb. *Fī ḫurūǧ al-Ḥusayn min Makka ilā al-ʿIrāq*: 338–339.

the killers. In Ibn ʿAsākir, Muḥammad expresses an incredulity ('even though they are believers in me?').[102] And while early concerns centred around the fate of the killer, and then the fate of the community, and in some texts too, the threat of losing the Prophet's intercession, the question here concerns the very quality of the faith of his killers. Al-Bazzār and al-Hayṯamī have al-Ḥusayn sitting on the lap of Muḥammad, who replies to Ğibrīl: "How could I not love him? He is the fruit of my heart," before Ğibrīl produces a handful of red dust.[103]

While Ibn ʿAsākir minimizes the details of the obtaining of the dust and of its qualities, for the first time Umm Salama's frustration is voiced; until now, her emotion has been bewilderment about how the boy got in, and fear that he would disturb the sleeping Prophet. However, in this text, there is no answer given her, no handing over of the dust, no glass vial. Instead, Muḥammad exits the house and goes to his companions, in Ibn ʿAsākir no longer headed by ʿAlī – unsurprising, coming from the staunch Sunnī transmitter who had little love for the Shīʿa and their claims – but by the first two caliphs, whose boldness is noted by the text.[104] These two future spiritual and political heads of the Islamic community, Abū Bakr and ʿUmar, express the same reservations about the quality of faith of those who kill al-Ḥusayn. The dust is shown them, and then disappears from the narrative, unwatched down through the years by Umm Salama. In other transmissions (al-Ṭabarānī, al-Qāḍī al-Nuʿmān, al-Shağarī, al-Hayṯamī), the event of Muḥammad going out to his companions is told is the context of ʿĀʾisha and, as noted, the names of these companions differ between Ibn ʿAsākir and the rest. Ibn ʿAsākir also offers a text from ʿĀʾisha with different details:

---

[102] al-Ḏahabī omits the 'in me' after the word believers (*muʾminīn*) as do Abū Bakr and ʿUmar at the end of Ibn ʿAsakir's narrative.

[103] al-Bazzār., *Kashf al-astār*, vol. III, bb. *Manāqib al-Ḥusayn*, n. 2640: 231, al-Hayṯamī., *Mağmaʿ al-zawāʾid wa-manbaʿ al-fawāʾid*, vol. IX, bk. 37 (*Kitāb al-manāqib*), bb. 95 (*Manāqib al-Ḥusayn b. ʿAlī*), n. 15129: 223.

[104] In al-Ṭabarānī, the they are named as ʿAlī, Abū Bakr, ʿUmar, Ḥuḏayfa, ʿAmmār and Abū Ḏarr.

> On the authority of ʿĀʾisha, who said: While the Messenger of God was sleeping, al-Ḥusayn came, crawling onto him and he pushed him away. Then I arose for some of my affairs and he was close to him. Then he woke up, weeping. I said: What is making you weep? He replied: "Ǧibrīl showed me the dust upon which al-Ḥusayn would be killed, the anger of God will be intense against the one who sheds his blood." He stretched out his hand and in it was a handful (of dust) from a plain. He said: "ʿĀʾisha, by the One in whose hand is my soul, truly it grieves me, for who is it from my community that will kill Ḥusayn after me?"[105]

Ibn ʿAsākir adds another element to his accounts, which will be taken up by numerous transmitters; that the same Umm Salama who dreams of the Prophet and witnesses angelic interventions will hear the haunting lament of the *ǧinn* over the killing of al-Husayn.[106]

Accomplished Shīʿī jurist, theologian, exegete and historian al-Rāwandī takes up a story, although in shortened form, already told by Ibn Ḥamdān, Ibn Ḥamza al-Ṭūsī and al-Baḥrānī, with al-Ḥusayn heading for Iraq and Umm Salama trying to dissuade him by quoting the prediction:

> When he had his mind set on Iraq, Umm Salama said to him: "Do not go to Iraq! I heard the Messenger of God saying: My son al-Ḥusayn will be killed in the land of Iraq, and I have dust which he gave to me in a glass vial!" He replied: "By God, so I will be killed, but if I do not go to Iraq, they will kill me anyway. If you like, I will show you the place where I will lie and the site of my companions' death!" He rubbed her face with his hand and God broadened her vision so that he could show it all to her. Then he took dust and gave some of it to her also, in another glass vial, saying: "When it overflows with blood,

---

[105] Ibn ʿAsākir., *Tārīḫ madīnat Dimashq*, vol. XIV, bb. 1566 (*al-Ḥusayn b. ʿAlī b. Abī Ṭālib b. ʿAbd al-Muṭṭalib b. Hāshim b. ʿAbd al-Manāf*): 195.

[106] Taken up also by the 8th/14th century Sunnī scholar Ǧamāl al-Dīn al-Zarandī in his *Naẓm durar al-simṭayn fī faḍāʾil al-muṣṭafā wa-l-murtaḍā wa-l-batūl wa-l-sibṭayn*, and detailed in another chapter of this book.

> know that I have been killed!" Umm Salama said: "On the day of ʿĀshūrā I looked at the two glass vials in the afternoon and they were overflowing with blood." She cried out; and on that day, one could not turn over a stone or a clod of earth but that one would find fresh blood under it.[107]

He introduces two points of interest: followed by al-Bayyāḍī, al-Iṣfahānī and al-Mağlisī, he augments the details of the mystical vision given to Umm Salama by having al-Ḥusayn rub her face with his hand, and introduces a second glass vial (taken up by al-Ḥillī al-ʿAllāma, al-Mağlisī and al-Iṣfahānī).[108] The narrative ends with the prediction coming true on the day of ʿĀshūrā, adding that under every upturned pebble or stone, blood was found.

Besides referencing Umm Salama's dream of Muḥammad with dirt on his head and his beard, Ibn Shahrāshūb retells a number of stories, including, from al-Ṭabarānī, the white dust of Karbalāʾ and from al-Ṭūsī, Ibn ʿAbbās hearing Umm Salama's cries of distress; he makes only a further brief mention of the glass vial.[109] By now, the scholars are merely repeating stories already told, occasionally shortening them, making minor changes in the details or combining the elements of more than one story into a single narrative.

---

[107] al-Rāwandī., *al-Ḫarāʾiğ wa-l-ğarāʾiḥ fī-l-muʿğizāt*, vol. I, bb. 4, n. 7: 253, al-Bayyāḍī., *al-Ṣirāṭ al-mustaqīm ilā mustaḥaqqī al-taqdīm fī-l-imāma*, vol. II, n. 6: 179, al-Mağlisī., *Biḥār al-anwār*, vol. XLV, bb. 37, n 27: 89 (cf. also vol. XLIV, bb. 37, n 2: 332), al-Iṣfahānī., *ʿAwālim al-ʿulūm wa-l-maʿārif al-aḥwāl min al-āyāt wa-l-aḫbār wa-l-aqwāl*, vol. XVII, ch. 12, bb. 4, n. 7: 157, ch. 13, bb. 1, n. 2: 181, al-Ğazāʾirī., *Riyāḍ al-abrār fī manāqib al-aʾimma al-aṭhār*, vol. I, Part One: 207–208.

[108] al-Ḥillī al-ʿAllāma., *Iṯbāt al-hudāt bi-l-nuṣūṣ wa-l-muʿğizāt*, vol. IV, bb. 15, n. 32: 46, al-Mağlisī., *Biḥār al-anwār*, vol. XLIV, bb. 37, n. 2: 332, vol. XLV, bb. 37, n 27: 89, al-Iṣfahānī., *ʿAwālim al-ʿulūm wa-l-maʿārif al-aḥwāl min al-āyāt wa-l-aḫbār wa-l-aqwāl*, vol. XVII, ch. 12, bb. 4, n. 7: 157, ch. 13, bb. 1, n. 2: 181, al-Ğazāʾirī., *Riyāḍ al-abrār fī manāqib al-aʾimma al-aṭhār*, vol. I, Part One: 207–208.

[109] Ibn Shahrāshūb., *Manāqib āl Abī Ṭālib*, vol. I, bb. *Ḏikr sayyidi-nā rasūl Allāh*: 140.

The 7th/13th century al-Shāmī, a pupil of Ibn Ṭāʾūs,[110] adds to a well-known story Umm Salama's question found in al-Kashshī and Ibn ʿAsākir; told to guard the door, and hearing loud sobbing from within, she goes in (rather than looking from the door) only to find al-Ḥusayn standing in front of Muḥammad. "By God, Messenger of God," she exclaims, "what have to come to know about him since he entered?"[111] He also returns to al-Ṭabarānī's use of 'coarse sand' to describe the dust of Karbalāʾ as he relates the angel of the rain asking permission to visit Muḥammad and, like Ibn ʿAsākir, notes that it took place on the day of Umm Salama. He takes another famous scene from Shahr b. Ḥawshab in which Ǧibraʾīl was with the Messenger of God and al-Ḥusayn with Umm Salama. The boy is crying, so she lets him go, but as soon as he seems to be approaching the Prophet, she picks him up again. Again he cries, again she lets him go and this time he goes in to Muḥammad, provoking from Ǧibraʾīl the question: do you love him?[112] Sibṭ al-Ǧawzī will take up this narrative, but making al-Ḥusayn the narrator and putting onto the lips of Muḥammad the words 'let my son be' when he hears him crying in Umm Salama's arms.[113]

> On the authority of Umm Salama that an angel asked permission of his Lord, powerful and great, to come to the Prophet who was in the house of Umm Salama. He greeted him with peace, secluded himself with the Prophet and began whispering to him. He said: "Umm Salama, guard the door for us." She said that al-Ḥusayn was with her, and while she was not paying attention, he went in to the Prophet and she followed him. The Messenger of God was turning something over and over in his hand, his eyes streaming with tears. I said: "I seek

---

110 Cf. KOHLBERG E., *A Medieval Scholar at Work: Ibn Ṭāwūs and his Library*, 1992: 302.

111 al-Shāmī., *al-Durr al-naẓīm fī manāqib al-aʾimma al-lahāhīm*, bb. 5, *Fī ḏikr al-Ḥusayn b. ʿAlī*: 536.

112 Ibid.

113 Sibṭ al-Ǧawzī., *Taḏkirat al-ḫawāṣṣ al-umma bi-ḏikr ḫaṣāʾiṣ al-aʾimma*, bb. *Ḏikr maqtali-hi*: 250.

> refuge in God from the anger of God and the anger of His Messenger!" He answered: "Neither God nor His Messenger is angry with you!" I replied: "I saw you turning something over and over in your hand, your eyes streaming with tears!" He replied: "You saw this when he came to me and said: Your son will be killed." I said: "Who will kill him?" He answered: "My community." I said: "Even though they submit themselves to the *ṣalāt*?" He answered: "Even though they submit themselves to the *ṣalāt*!" Then I said: "And in which place?" He answered: "He named for me the place in which he will be killed and showed me a handful of dust, which I am turning over and over in my hand while my eyes are streaming with tears." Umm Salama said: "I took that dust and took it away with me. When al-Ḥusayn was killed I heard the *ǧinn* lamenting over him – I had not heard them lamenting over him before that. The dust had become fresh blood."[114]

This narrative, with its abrupt change of narrator, combines a number of longstanding elements with some details that are new; Umm Salama being momentarily distracted was reported by al-Kashshī, while Ibn Abī Shayba first made mention of something unidentifiable in Muḥammad's hand. The guarding of the door is found in Ibn Ḥanbal, as is the unknown angel (although al-Shāmī adds no further clarification). What is new is the angel secluding himself with Muḥammad and whispering to him, as well as the extended dialogue in which Umm Salama has to draw out details one by one. The transmitter also introduces the lament of the *ǧinn*, and although this will be taken up in another chapter, it is of note that it is precisely their lament that causes her to notice the change from dust to blood.

The 12th/17th century Shīʿī jurist, exegete and *muḥaddiṯ*, al-Sayyid Hāshim al-Baḥrānī, in his work chronicling the miracles attributed to the twelve Imāms, reproduces two extensive texts with details drawn in and amalgamated from a number of diverse

[114] al-Shāmī., *al-Durr al-naẓīm fī manāqib al-a'imma al-lahāhīm*, bb. 5, *Fī ḏikr al-Ḥusayn b. ʿAlī*: 536–537.

sources, but into which he introduces a number of unfamiliar elements:

> On the authority of Umm Salama, who said: The Messenger of God was with me one day. A fierce heat had broken out, so he had come to my house and I spread out a mat for him, and he had thrown himself down, reclining, when al-Ḥusayn came and entered as he was lying on his back. He said: "Here, Ḥusayn!" So, he lay on his chest and began to play with him and move about on his stomach. Umm Salama said: I looked through the crack in the door; he was on his chest, playing with him.

Missing from this narrative are many of the stock details; here, Muḥammad's visit appears random rather than normative (as on 'the day of Umm Salama'), and the fierce heat (which could also be understood as Muḥammad having a fever) is an unusual addition, as if to justify why the Prophet should be lying down:

> Then I withdrew from him for an hour, and returning to the door, and I saw the Prophet, distressed, his eyes closed and on his face a type of gloom. I said (to myself): No doubt al-Ḥusayn has exceeded proper bounds with the Prophet by his youthfulness. I went to him and in his hand was something he was looking at and weeping. I said: Messenger of God, you are as dear to me as my own father and mother! May I be your ransom! How is it that I see you weeping and sorrowing? What is the news? He answered: "Ğibra'īl came down to me in this hour and informed me that this son of mine will be killed!" I said: But how and where? He replied: "After his father and his mother, in a land named Karbalā'. If you choose, I will show you a handful of its dust. He withdrew from me, and then came to me with this handful, and said: This is (some of) its dust." Then (Muḥammad) said: "Take it and keep it with you in this glass bottle; watch over it, and when you see it becoming fresh blood you will know that my son al-Ḥusayn has been killed in that hour." Umm Salama said: I did what he had told me and kept in a section of the house until the Prophet died and what happened, happened.

The mention of "after his father and his mother" alludes strongly to the prospect that Fāṭima herself must be counted among the martyrs, her death resulting immediately from the various forms of ill-treatment to which she was subject after her father's death. The narrative telescopes into a few lines an extensive period of time, from the boy al-Ḥusayn on his grandfather's chest, to the death of Muḥammad and then, thirty or so years later, the fateful departure to Iraq of an al-Ḥusayn already ostensibly fully cognizant of the vial (in this text referred to as a 'bottle') of dust:

> When al-Ḥusayn departed from Medina to Iraq, I came to him to bid him farewell, and he said: "Umm Salama, take care of the glass bottle!" So, I kept looking at it; I observed it two or three times a day, and when it was the tenth day of Muḥarram, towards noon, I took a short nap and slept a little while. I saw the Messenger of God in my dream, dishevelled and dust covered, and with dust on his head. I said: Messenger of God, you are as dear to me as my own father and mother! How is it that I see you dust covered and dishevelled? What is this dust that I see on your head and your face? He said to me: "Umm Salama, I have this night been digging the grave of my son al-Ḥusayn and the graves of his companions, and at this time I have finished with the preparation of my son al-Ḥusayn and his companions, killed at Karbalāʾ!" She awoke, dismayed and frightened, and got up and looked at the glass vial, and in it was fresh blood. She knew that al-Ḥusayn had been killed, and she said: By God, the revelation did not lie to me and the Messenger of God did not lie to me. She said: I began to cry out: O, son! O consolation of his eye! O beloved! O Ḥusayn! O loss after you, Abū ʿAbd Allāh! She said: Eventually the people gathered with me and asked: "What is the news?" and I informed them. They began to call out: "O master! O tyrannised! By God, you did not lie!" He mentioned the date of that day and it was the day al-Ḥusayn was killed.[115]

Al-Baḥrānī now introduces a further narrative, once again comprising recognizable features intermingled with fresh details:

---

[115] al-Baḥrānī., *Madīnat al-maʿāǧiz fī muʿǧizāt al-aʾimma al-aṭhār*, vol. IV, n. 271/1218: 192–194. At this point, the text drops the theme of the dream and the glass vial and turns to the lament of the *ǧinn*.

It was also reported, on the authority of Umm Salama, who said: The Messenger of God was with me one day, and while he was sleeping on the bed, crossing his leg right over left – he was on his back – al-Ḥusayn, a boy of just three years and some months came to him. When he saw him, he said: "Welcome to the consolation of my eye and the fruit of my heart!" The boy continued to draw near until he climbed onto the chest of his grandfather and stayed there. I was afraid that the Prophet was tired, and I wanted to move him from his chest, but he said: "Leave him, Umm Salama! When he wants to go down, he will go down!" Then he advised me: "Whoever harms a single hair of his, harms me!" She said: I left him and went, and when I returned, the Messenger of God was weeping. I wondered at that, after the laughter and the joy, so I approached him and said: "Messenger of God, what is making you weep? May God not cause your eyes to weep!" He was looking at something in his hand and weeping. He said: "What do you see?" I looked, and in his hand was dust, and I asked: "What is that?" He replied: "Ǧibraʾīl came to me with it this very hour and said: Messenger of God! This is mud from Karbalāʾ, the mud of your son al-Ḥusayn and his dust in which he will be buried. I have committed it to you in a glass vial, and when you see it has changed into fresh blood you will know that my son al-Ḥusayn has been killed. This will happen after me, and after his mother, his father and his brother." She said: I wept, and took it from his hand, and I set about doing what he had ordered me. It had a smell like pungent musk. The days and months had barely elapsed[116] before al-Ḥusayn departed for the land of Karbalāʾ, and my heart lamented on account of the iniquity. I went every day to observe the glass vial, and while I was doing this, suddenly, there was fresh blood in the glass vial, and I knew that al-Ḥusayn had been killed. I began to lament and weep throughout the day until night. I had no desire for food or drink or sleep, until a part of the night when drowsiness took me and I had a vision of the Messenger of

[116] In fact, more than fifty years.

> God approaching, with a quantity of dust[117] on his head and his beard. I began to dust him off him, and I wept, saying: "My soul as the ransom for your soul, how long have you neglected yourself in this way, Messenger of God? From where do you have this dust?" He replied: "This is the hour when I have finished burying my son al-Ḥusayn." Umm Salama said: I awoke, alarmed and could not stop myself from crying out: O Ḥusayn! O son! O the heart's lifeblood – until my wailing ascended and the Hāshimī and other women of Medina approached me, and said: "Mother of the faithful, what is the news?" I related the story to them and the wailing and the crying ascended and the lamenting rose – that day became like the day on which the Messenger of God died – and they walked to his grave, hearts torn and stricken[118] at the loss of the beloved.[119]

Umm Salama's profound involvement with the Karbalāʾ event does not terminate with her dreams or her private grief; she will also be witness to another, more haunting anguish, and come to the realization that the lament she is hearing on the night air is no ordinary dirge, but belongs to the dark and hidden world of the *ǧinn*.

---

117 Editor's note: In the source, 'much blood'.

118 Editor's note: In the source, 'bareheaded'.

119 al-Baḥrānī., *Madīnat al-maʿāǧiz fī muʿǧizāt al-aʾimma al-aṭhār*, vol. IV, n. 272/1219: 194–196.

Voices in the Night. A Medley of Dreams and Visions

A verse in the 7th *sūrat* of the Qur'ān issues a terse warning, not to believers alone but to humanity in its entirety, about the menace of Shayṭān: «*O Children of Adam! Let not Satan seduce you*». Viewed through the prism of mysticism, he may well be in tragic and lonely exile, the over-zealous monotheist now eternally irredeemable;[1] but

[1] The proposal of Satan as the 'desolate mystic' is found in the sphere of the Ṣūfī mystics as an attempt to reinterpret his dissent, although without necessarily redeeming him. Such arcane strands of thought are certainly found in al-Ḥallāǧ (MASON H., *Al-Hallaj*, Curzon Press, Surrey 1995: 21–22), whose Satan clings to his monotheism and his determination to bow before God alone, even in the face of disobeying a Divine ordinance, and so ends in despondent isolation. Aḥmad al-Ġazālī, younger brother of the more famous Abū Ḥāmid, expresses a similar theology (SCHIMMEL A., *Mystical Dimensions of Islam*, University of North Carolina Press, Chapel Hill 1975: 95) as does Persian mystic Farīd al-Dīn ʿAṭṭār, who envisages Satan as the perfect monotheist and lover, accepting

Shayṭān remains an antagonistic figure who looms large in the Islamic psyche. He stalks with purposeful gait through the centuries, an open enemy of mankind,[2] whose footsteps ought never to be followed,[3] causing sin and wrongdoing to seem reasonable and fair[4] and provoking forgetfulness of God.[5] It is not surprising that the Qurʾānic text labels him 'the furtive whisperer', in consequence of his tendency to withdraw into the shadows after his wicked suggestions. There, concealed from view, he is not alone, for the same verse continues: «*Indeed, he sees you, he and his tribe, from where you do not see them*».[6] This is, according to the scholars, at least in part a reference to that enigmatic group of creatures called the *ǧinn*. According to lexicographers, the root of the Arabic collective term *ǧinn* (with *ǧinnī* or *ǧiniyya* representing a single individual, male or female) gives rise to diverse meanings, but most commonly with the implication of 'concealment' or 'the confusion of intense darkness'; therefore, the word for 'garden' (*ǧanna*) as a place concealed by trees, and that for 'grave' (*ǧanan*) as a place that conceals a body, or for 'shelter' or 'shield' (*ǧunna*) by which a person is veiled or concealed.[7]

It is with the *ǧinn* that we are here concerned; those spiritual beings, concealed from the senses, interfering harmfully or helpfully, a middle class, suggests Lane, between angels and demons. The voices of the *ǧinn* are not infrequently heard; Ibn Saʿd and al-Balāḏurī, for example, mention the rumour that the death of ʿUbāda b. Saʿd was at the hands of the *ǧinn*, who are overheard

---

God's curse as a 'robe of honour': "To be cursed by Thee is a thousand times dearer to me than to turn my head away from Thee to anything else" (SCHIMMEL A., *Mystical Dimensions of Islam*, 1975: 95).

[2] Q. 2:36, Q. 12:5, Q. 17:53, Q. 35:8, Q. 36:60 et al.

[3] Q. 24:21, Q. 2:208 et al.

[4] Q. 6:43, Q. 8:48, Q. 16:63, Q. 27:24, Q. 29:38, Q. 35:8 et al.

[5] Q. 12:42, Q. 58:19, Q. 18:63, Q. 6:68, 142 et al.

[6] Q. 7:27.

[7] Cf. LANE E.W., *An Arabic-English Lexicon*, vol. II, 1968: 402–403, WEHR H., *A Dictionary of Modern Written Arabic*, 1980: 164.

boasting of what they have done,[8] al-Baġdādī reports Bashr b. al-Ḥāriṯ hearing them lamenting the death of his uncle[9] and al-Ṭabarī, Ibn ʿAsākir, Ibn Kaṯīr and Ibn Ḥağar al-ʿAsqalānī recount their mourning the death of the second Caliph, ʿUmar b. al-Ḫaṭṭāb.[10]

It is the voice of these *ğinn* that Umm Salama, and not her alone,[11] will hear on the night air, lamenting the killing of al-Ḥusayn. The reports that narrate these events are quite often repetitive and contradictory; consequently, there are several individuals or groups who are recipients of these auricular intrusions. At the head of these stands, once again, Umm Salama. In its most unadorned form, going back as far as Ibn Ḥanbal, Umm Salama reports that she heard the *ğinn* lamenting or weeping over al-Ḥusayn:[12]

---

[8] Ibn Saʿd., *Kitāb al-ṭabaqāt al-kabīr*, vol. VII, n. 3697: 274, al-Balāḏurī., *Kitāb ansāb al-ashraf*, vol. I, bb. *al-Qawl fī-l-sīrat al-nabawiyya al-sharīfa*, n. 1193: 589, al-Dāraquṭnī., *al-Muʾtalif wa-l-muḫtalif*, vol. II: 912, 935, al-Ḥākim al-Nīsābūrī., *Kitāb al-mustadrak ʿalā al-ṣaḥīḥayn*, vol. III, bk. 31 (*Kitāb maʿrīfat al-ṣaḥāba*), *Ḏikr ʿAbd Allāh b. ʿAbbās*, n. 5167: 307, al-Ḏahabī., *Siyar aʿlām al-nubalāʾ*, vol. I, n. 55 (*Saʿd b. ʿAbāda*): 277–278.

[9] al-Baġdādī., *Tārīḫ Baġdād*, vol. VII, n. 3517: 80.

[10] al-Ṭabarī., *Kitāb aḫbār al-rusul wa-l-mulūk*, vol. IV, n. 2764/1: 219, Ibn ʿAsākir., *Tārīḫ madīnat Dimashq*, vol. XLIV, bb. 5206 (*ʿUmar b. al-Ḫaṭṭāb*): 480, Ibn Kaṯīr., *al-Bidāya wa-l-nihāya*, vol. VII, bb. *Ḏikr baʿḍ mā ruʾiya bi-hi*: 140 (Ibn Kaṯīr records it as 'the women of the district' [*al-ḥayy*] rather than 'the women of the *ğinn*'), al-ʿAsqalānī., *al-Iṣāba fī tamyīz al-ṣaḥāba*, vol. III, n. 3938: 280). According to al-Dāraquṭnī, ʿĀʾisha claimed that the *ğinn* wept over ʿUmar for three days before he died (al-Dāraquṭnī., *al-Muʾtalif wa-l-muḫtalif*, vol. III: 183).

[11] Ibn al-Ğawzī notes that it was said that the *ğinn* lamented the killing of al-Ḥasan for seven days so that they were heard under the seven regions, and that the angels too all wept over him. Since this is reported in a chapter about the death of al-Ḥusayn, it is almost certainly a misprint in the text, and it is over al-Ḥusayn, rather than his brother, that they wept (Ibn al-Ğawzī., *Bustān al-waʿiẓīn wa-riyāḍ al-sāmiʿīn*, bb. 414: 262). For a description of the seven regions cf. NASR S.H., *The Islamic Intellectual Tradition in Persia*, Curzon Press, Surrey 1996: 20–21.

[12] Ibn Ḥanbal., *Kitāb faḍāʾil al-ṣaḥāba*, vol. II, bb. *Faḍāʾil al-Ḥasan wa-l-Ḥusayn*, n. 1373: 776, Ibn Abī ʿĀṣim., *al-Āḥād wa-l-maṯānī*, vol. I, bb. 36

> On the authority of Umm Salama, who said: I heard the *ğinn* lamenting over al-Ḥusayn on the day he was killed. They[13] were saying: "You killers, in ignorance, of Ḥusayn, rejoice[14] in torment and maltreatment; all the people of the heavens call down curses on you, from the Prophet and those sent, and the fallen. You have been cursed by the tongue of Ibn Dāwud, and Mūsā and the one entrusted with the gospel."[15]

Ibn Kaṯīr notes that another path, also on the authority of Umm Salama, reports verses different from these, and that 'only God knows').[16] He is quite correct; not only will a completely different set of verses be placed on the lips of the *ğinn* in Umm Salama's hearing, but the verses addressed to those who had killed al-Ḥusayn are heard in a number of other settings, by recipients other

---

(*Min ḏikri al-Ḥusayn b. ʿAlī*), n. 425: 308, al-Ṭabarānī., *al-Muʿğam al-kabīr*, vol. III, bb. *al-Ḥusayn b. ʿAlī*, n. 2862: 121, n. 2867: 122, Ibn ʿAsākir., *Tārīḫ madīnat Dimashq*, vol. XIV, bb. 1566 (*al-Ḥusayn b. ʿAlī b. Abī Ṭālib b. ʿAbd al-Muṭṭalib b. Hāshim b. ʿAbd al-Manāf*): 239–240, al-Ṭabarī., *Ḏaḫāʾir al-ʿuqbā*, bb. 9: 255–256 (adding that Umm Salama said: "It rained blood on us"), al-Ḏahabī., *Siyar aʿlām al-nubalāʾ*, vol. III, n. 48 (*al-Ḥusayn al-Shahīd Abū ʿAbd Allāh b. ʿAlī b. Abī Ṭālib*): 316, Ibn Kaṯīr., *al-Bidāya wa-l-nihāya*, vol. XI, bb. *al-Iḫbār bi-maqtal al-Ḥusayn b. ʿAlī*: 575, al-Hayṯamī., *Mağmaʿ al-zawāʾid wa-manbaʿ al-fawāʾid*, vol. IX, bk. 37 (*Kitāb al-manāqib*), bb. 95 (*Manāqib al-Ḥusayn b. ʿAlī*), nn. 15179, 15180: 234, al-ʿAsqalānī., *al-Iṣāba fī tamyīz al-ṣaḥāba*, vol. II, n. 1729: 72, *Tahḏīb al-tahḏīb*, vol. II, bb. *al-Ḥāʾ*, n. 615: 355.

[13] Feminine, plural.

[14] I have taken this as a 4th form, masculine plural imperative, used in the same sense as when, at Karbalāʾ, al-Ḥusayn is told to 'hurry' to the fire

[15] Ibn Shahrāshūb., *Manāqib āl Abī Ṭālib*, vol. IV, bb. *Fī imāmat Abī ʿAbd Allāh al-Ḥusayn*: 62, Sibṭ al-Ğawzī., *Taḏkirat al-ḫawāṣṣ al-umma bi-ḏikr ḫaṣāʾiṣ al-aʾimma*: 241, Ibn al-ʿAdīm., *Buğyat al-ṭalab fī tārīḫ Ḥalab*: 2650, Ibn Namā., *Muṯīr al-aḥzān*, bb. *Nūḥ al-ğinn ʿalā al-Ḥusayn*: 108, Ibn ʿAsākir., *Tārīḫ madīnat Dimashq*, vol. XIV, bb. 1566 (*al-Ḥusayn b. ʿAlī b. Abī Ṭālib b. ʿAbd al-Muṭṭalib b. Hāshim b. ʿAbd al-Manāf*): 240, Ibn Kaṯīr., *al-Bidāya wa-l-nihāya*, vol. XI, bb. *al-Iḫbār bi-maqtal al-Ḥusayn b. ʿAlī*: 575.

[16] Ibn Kaṯīr., *al-Bidāya wa-l-nihāya*, vol. XI, bb. *al-Iḫbār bi-maqtal al-Ḥusayn b. ʿAlī*: 575.

than Umm Salama and recited by a variety of voices. Ibn al-Aṯīr, for example, places these verses not in the mouths of the *ǧinn*, but of some of the residents of Medina,[17] while a number of transmitters write of Umm Salama hearing them spoken by a voice or voices not identified as the *ǧinn*:

> On the night al-Ḥusayn was killed, Umm Salama said: I heard a speaker saying: "You killers, in ignorance, of Ḥusayn, rejoice in torment and maltreatment. You have been cursed by the tongue of Ibn Dāwud, and Mūsā and the one entrusted with the gospel." She said: I wept…I opened the glass vial and there had begun to be blood in it.[18]

However, far more frequently, as early as al-Ṭabarī and al-Qāḍī al-Nuʿmān, the verses are disassociated from the Umm Salama narratives around Karbalāʾ, and are attributed to an unknown voice or voices, sometimes attributed to the *ǧinn*, and heard by the people of Medina.[19] A proportion of these is on the authority of ʿAmr b.

[17] Ibn al-Aṯīr., *al-Kāmil fī-l-tārīḫ*, vol. III: 441.

[18] al-Shaǧarī., *Tartīb al-amālī al-ḫamīsiyya*, vol. II, bb. *Fī ḏikr ʿĀshūrā*, n. 1800: 115, al-Ḫawārizmī., *Maqtal al-Ḥusayn*, Part Two, bb. *Fī bayān ʿuqūba qātil al-Ḥusayn*, n. 33: 107–108, al-Maǧlisī, *Biḥār al-anwār*, vol. XLIV, bb. 30, n. 34: 241, al-Iṣfahānī., *ʿAwālim al-ʿulūm wa-l-maʿārif al-aḥwāl min al-āyāt wa-l-aḫbār wa-l-aqwāl*, vol. XVII, ch. 11, bb. 6, n. 9: 128.

[19] al-Ṭabarī., *Kitāb aḫbār al-rusul wa-l-mulūk*, vol. V, n. 385: 467, al-Qāḍī al-Nuʿmān., *Sharḥ al-aḫbār fī faḍāʾil al-aʾimma al-aṭhār*, vol. III, Part Twelve, n. 1107: 167, al-Shaǧarī., *Tartīb al-amālī al-ḫamīsiyya*, vol. I, bb. *Fī faḍl al-Ḥusayn b. ʿAlī*, n. 807: 228, Ibn al-Aṯīr., *al-Kāmil fī al-tārīḫ*, vol. III, *Ḏikr maqtal al-Ḥusayn*: 301, Ibn Ṭāʾūs., *Kitāb al-luhūf fī qatlā al-ṭufūf*: 99, Ibn Kaṯīr., *al-Bidāya wa-l-nihāya*, vol. XI, bb. *al-Iḫbār bi-maqtal al-Ḥusayn b. ʿAlī*: 568, al-Mūsawī., *Tasliyat al-muǧālis wa zīnat al-maǧālis*, vol. II, Part Two, *maǧlis* 8: 372, al-Baḥrānī., *Madīnat al-maʿāǧiz fī muʿǧizāt al-aʾimma al-aṭhār*, vol. IV, Part Four, n. 254/1201: 178, al-Maǧlisī, *Biḥār al-anwār*, vol. XLV, bb. 39, n. 1: 123, vol. XLV, bb. 43, n. 6: 238, al-Iṣfahānī., *ʿAwālim al-ʿulūm wa-l-maʿārif al-aḥwāl min al-āyāt wa-l-aḫbār wa-l-aqwāl*, vol. XVII, ch. 16, bb. 3, n. 3: 391, al-Ǧazāʾirī., *Riyāḍ al-abrār fī manāqib al-aʾimma al-aṭhār*, vol. I, Part One: 244. Ibn al-Aṯīr moves the location from Medina to Karbalāʾ (Ibn al-Aṯīr., *al-Kāmil fī al-tārīḫ*, vol. III: 301).

ʿIkrima, who describes waking up in Medina the morning after al-Ḥusayn's killing to be told by an associate or a servant that in the night a group of them had heard an unknown herald calling out the verses.[20] Al-Shāmī attributes to such an unknown herald a less well-attested verse:

> It was said: I heard a reciter on the air in Medina, saying: "Let he who professes the merit of the family of Muḥammad convey our message without delay! The wicked of the Umayyads have killed the master, the best of creation, the noble one, the man in charge, son of the Chosen in heaven and its earth, grandson of the Prophet and destroyer of idols. The places of sunrise and the places of sunset wept after it; living creatures wept for him in every place. They were made to weep for the stranger to Karbalāʾ and its sands, the son of the Prophet and of the best of the women!" They came and told Umm Salama about him, and she noticed that the glass vial and become blood.[21]

Ibn Namā takes note of the disembodied nature of the voice:

> The *ǧinn* lamented over him. There was a band of the Prophet's companions, among them al-Miswar b. Maḫrama; the men listened closely to the lament and wept…on the authority of ʿIkrima, that he heard in Medina, on the night (al-Ḥusayn) was killed, a herald, whose person they could hear but not see: "You killers, in ignorance, of Ḥusayn, rejoice[22] in torment and maltreatment: all the people of the heavens call down curses

---

[20] al-Ṭabarī., *Kitāb aḫbār al-rusul wa-l-mulūk*, vol. V, n. 385: 467, Ibn Qūlawayh., *Kāmil al-ziyārāt*, bb. 29, n. 10: 197, Ibn Aʿṯam., *Kitāb al-futūḥ*, vol. V: 134, Ibn Kaṯīr., *al-Bidāya wa-l-nihāya*, vol. XI, bb. *al-Iḫbār bi-maqtal al-Ḥusayn b. ʿAlī*: 568, al-Mağlisī., *Biḥār al-anwār*, vol. XLV, bb. 43, n. 6: 238, al-Iṣfahanı., *ʿAwālim al-ʿulūm wa-l-maʿārif al-aḥwāl min al-āyāt wa-l-aḫbār wa-l-aqwāl*, vol. XVII, ch. 17, bb. 5, n. 2: 481.

[21] al-Shāmī., *al-Durr al-naẓīm fī manāqib al-aʾimma al-lahāhīm*, bb. 5 (*Faṣl fī ḏikr maqtal al-Ḥusayn b. ʿAlī*): 536.

[22] By my reading, *abshir* is the imperative of the 4th form of the verb (*abshara-yubshiru*) meaning 'to rejoice'.

> on you, from the Prophet and those sent and the fallen. You have been cursed by the tongue of Ibn Dāwud, and Mūsā and the one entrusted with the gospel."[23]

Not all transmitters follow this narrative; the verses are also placed on the lips of un unseen herald calling out from a local cemetery,[24] or simply as a voice heard from the heavens.[25] In Ibn Aʿṯam, the men carrying the head of al-Ḥusayn hear the dirge recited by an unidentified voice as they arrive in Damascus,[26] while Ibn Shahrāshūb, followed by al-Iṣfahānī and al-Mağlisī, and reporting from al-Ṭabarī, places the verses into the mouths of the angels rather than the *ğinn*.[27]

---

[23] Ibn Namā., *Muṯīr al-aḥzān*, bb. *Nūḥ al-ğinn ʿalā al-Ḥusayn*: 107–108, al-Mağlisī., *Biḥār al-anwār*, vol. XLV, bb. 43, n. 2: 235–236, al-Iṣfahānī., *ʿAwālim al-ʿulūm wa-l-maʿārif al-aḥwāl min al-āyāt wa-l-aḫbār wa-l-aqwāl*, vol. XVII, ch. 17, bb. 5, n. 12: 486.

[24] al-Qāḍī al-Nuʿmān., *Sharḥ al-aḫbār fī faḍāʾil al-aʾimma al-aṭhār*, vol. III, Part Twelve, n. 1109: 168.

[25] Sibṭ al-Ğawzī., *Taḏkirat al-ḫawāṣṣ al-umma bi-ḏikr ḫaṣāʾiṣ al-aʾimma*: 242 (who narrates that it was specifically al-Ḥusayn's killers who heard the voice), al-Mağlisī, *Biḥār al-anwār*, vol. XLV, bb. 39, n. 39: 199 (an unidentified voice from heaven).

[26] Ibn Aʿṯam., *Kitāb al-futūḥ*, vol. V: 134. Cf. also Ibn Bābawayh., *Kitāb al-amālī fī al-aḥādīṯ wa-l-aḫbār*, *mağlis* 31, n. 3: 165, Ibn ʿAlī al-Fattāl., *Rawḍat al-wāʿiẓīn wa-tabṣirat al-muttaʿiẓīn*, vol. I: 190, al-Baḥrānī., *Madīnat al-maʿāğiẓ fī muʿğiẓāt al-aʾimma al-aṭhār*, vol. IV, Part Four, n. 246/1193: 172, al-Mağlisī., *Biḥār al-anwār*, vol. XLV, bb. 39, n. 3: 155, al-Iṣfahānī., *ʿAwālim al-ʿulūm wa-l-maʿārif al-aḥwāl min al-āyāt wa-l-aḫbār wa-l-aqwāl*, vol. XVII, ch. 16, bb. 4, n. 1: 395.

[27] Ibn Shahrāshūb., *Manāqib āl Abī Ṭālib*, vol. IV, bb. *Fī imāmat Abī ʿAbd Allāh al-Ḥusayn*: 63, al-Mağlisī, *Biḥār al-anwār*, vol. XLV, bb. 43, n. 3: 236, al-Iṣfahānī., *ʿAwālim al-ʿulūm wa-l-maʿārif al-aḥwāl min al-āyāt wa-l-aḫbār wa-l-aqwāl*, vol. XVII, ch. 17, bb. 4, n. 23: 481. Ibn Ğarīr al-Ṭabarī certainly mentions the lines in his history (*Kitāb aḫbār al-rusul wa-l-mulūk*, vol. V, n. 385: 467), but places them on the lips of an unknown herald in Medina rather than of the angels. The verses are not recorded by either by Ibn Rustam al-Ṭabarī in his *Dalāʾil al-imāma* or in his *Bishārat al-muṣṭafā*, or by Muḥib al-Dīn al-Ṭabarī in his *Ḏaḫāʾir al-ʿuqbā*.

A further set of verses, with slight variations in the vocabulary used, is placed upon the lips of the *ǧinn*, specified in this instance in a number of texts as a female member of that species, and most popularly heard by Umm Salama:

> On the authority of Ḥabīb b. Abī Ṯābit, who said: Umm Salama said: I never heard the lament of the *ǧinn* since the Prophet died except for tonight, and I never dreamt of my son except when he had been killed – she had in mind al-Ḥusayn – and she said to a maid: Go out and ask. She was informed that he had been killed, and then a (female) *ǧinn* lamented: "O eye, shed tears in effort, for who will weep over the martyrs after me, over a band led by fate, to a tyrant in the possession of a servant?"[28]

According to al-Ḫawārizmī however, Umm Salama is not the first to report these words; at a place called al-Ḫuzamiyya, on the way to Karbalāʾ, an unnerved Zaynab bt. ʿAlī, who is accompanying al-Ḥusayn, informs her brother that she has heard a voice or voices calling in the night in a lament she does not understand: "O eye,

---

[28] Or, in some texts, "to a tyrant in power"; cf. al-Ṭabarānī., *al-Muʿǧam al-kabīr*, vol. III, bb. *al-Ḥusayn b. ʿAlī*, n. 2869: 122, al-Qāḍī al-Nuʿmān., *Sharḥ al-aḫbār fī faḍāʾil al-aʾimma al-aṭhār*, vol. III, Part Twelve, n. 1107: 167. Ibn Qūlawayh., *Kāmil al-ziyārāt*, bb. 29, n. 1: 189, Ibn Bābawayh., *Kitāb al-amālī fī al-aḥādīṯ wa-l-aḫbār*, *maǧlis* 19, n. 2: 139, Ibn ʿAlī al-Fattāl., *Rawḍat al-wāʿiẓīn wa-tabṣirat al-muttaʿiẓīn*, vol. I: 170, Ibn ʿAsākir., *Tārīḫ madīnat Dimashq*, vol XIV, bb. *al-Ḥusayn b. ʿAlī b. Abī Ṭālib*: 241, al-Ḫawārizmī., *Maqtal al-Ḥusayn*, Part Two, bb. *Fī bayān ʿuqūba qātil al-Ḥusayn*, n. 34: 108, Ibn Shahrāshūb., *Manāqib āl Abī Ṭālib*, vol. IV, bb. *Fī imāmat Abī ʿAbd Allāh al-Ḥusayn*: 62, Ibn al-ʿAdīm., *Buġyat al-ṭalab fī tārīḫ Ḥalab*: 2651, Ibn Namā., *Muṯīr al-aḥzān*, bb. *Nūḥ al-ǧinn ʿalā al-Ḥusayn*: 108, al-Ṭabarī., *Ḏaḫāʾir al-ʿuqbā*, Part One, bb. 9: 256, al-Hayṯamī., *Maǧmaʿ al-zawaʾid wa-manbaʿ al-fawāʾid*, vol. IX, bk. 37 (*Kitāb al-manāqib*), bb. 95 (*Manāqib al-Ḥusayn b. ʿAlī*), n. 15175: 575, al-Baḥrānī., *Madīnat al-maʿāǧiz fī muʿǧizāt al-aʾimma al-aṭhār*, vol. IV, Part Four, n. 245/1192, al-Maǧlisī, *Biḥār al-anwār*, vol. XLV, bb. 43, n. 8: 238–239, vol. LX, bb. 2, n. 3: 65, al-Iṣfahānī., *ʿAwālim al-ʿulūm wa-l-maʿārif al-aḥwāl min al-āyāt wa-l-aḫbār wa-l-aqwāl*, vol. XVII, ch. 17, bb. 5, n. 4: 482.

truly, be extravagant in effort, for who will weep over the martyrs after me, over a people whom fate drove, by decree, to the discharge of a promise?[29] A further discrepancy is that a handful of transmitters report these verses as being heard by an unspecified group of people in Medina ("Just before daybreak, the people of Medina heard the lament of the *ǧinn* over al-Ḥusayn, and from them came one female *ǧinn* saying: O eye, truly, be bathed in tears…"),[30] while some of the Shīʿī scholars provide an expanded version of the lament:

> O eye, be generous in tears and weep, for the news has turned out to be true!
>
> Weep for the son of Fāṭima, who reached the Euphrates and never returned!
>
> The *ǧinn* wept in their distress when the news of him came!
>
> Al-Ḥusayn and his band have been killed! What appalling news!
>
> Surely, I will weep for you, tormented, in the evening and at daybreak!
>
> Surely, I will weep for you as long as a vein flows and as long as the trees bear.[31]

---

[29] al-Ḫawārizmī., *Maqtal al-Ḥusayn*, Part One, bb. *Fī ḫurūǧ al-Ḥusayn min Makka ilā al-ʿIrāq*: 323–4, Ibn Shahrāshūb., *Manāqib āl Abī Ṭālib*, vol. IV, bb. *Fī imāmat Abī ʿAbd Allāh al-Ḥusayn*: 95, al-Maǧlisī., *Biḥār al-anwār*, vol. XLIV, bb. 37, n. 2: 372 al-Iṣfahānī., *ʿAwālim al-ʿulūm wa-l-maʿārif al-aḥwāl min al-āyāt wa-l-aḫbār wa-l-aqwāl*, vol. XI, ch. 25, bb. 2: 961, vol. XVII, ch. 13, bb. 1: 232, al-Ǧazāʾirī., *Riyāḍ al-abrār fī manāqib al-aʾimma al-aṭhār*, vol. I, Part One: 217.

[30] al-Shaǧarī., *Tartīb al-amālī al-ḫamīsiyya*, vol. I, bb. *Fī faḍl al-Ḥusayn b. ʿAlī*, n. 807: 228, al-Baḥrānī., *Madīnat al-maʿāǧiz fī muʿǧizāt al-aʾimma al-aṭhār*, vol. IV, n. 271/1218: 192–194, *al-Bidāya wa-l-nihāya*, vol. XI, bb. *al-Iḫbār bi-maqtal al-Ḥusayn b. ʿAlī*: 575.

[31] Ibn Qūlawayh., *Kāmil al-ziyārāt*, bb. 29, n. 11: 197, al-Baḥrānī., *Madīnat al-maʿāǧiz fī muʿǧizāt al-aʾimma al-aṭhār*, vol. IV, Part Four, n. 255/1202: 179, al-Maǧlisī, *Biḥār al-anwār*, vol. XLV, bb. 43, n. 7: 238, al-

Other individuals aside from Zaynab and Umm Salama are said to have heard the dirge; while Ibn Abī ʿĀṣim reports the words from Maymūna,[32] another transmitter traces the lines back to a woman named Laylā ("I heard Laylā saying: I heard the lament of the *ğinn* over al-Ḥusayn b. ʿAlī"),[33] but also contends that he himself heard the words:

> On the authority of ʿAlī b. al-Ḥazawwar, who said: I heard the lament of the *ğinn* over al-Ḥusayn b. ʿAlī. They were saying: "O eye, be generous in tears, for the sorrowing weep with burning and agony! O eye, sleep with its goodness distracts you from remembrance of the family of Muḥammad and lament! Their bodies passed three nights on the plateau, between wild beasts, all of them in the place of death."[34]

An entirely dissimilar lament is heard by a group of plasterers (*al-ğaṣṣāṣūn*), going out to the cemetery on the night that al-Ḥusayn is killed:

> On the authority of Abū Ḥubāb al-Kalbī, who said: I was told by the plasterers, who said: "When we were going out to the cemetery on the night when al-Ḥusayn was killed, we heard the *ğinn* lamenting him and saying: 'The Messenger stroked his brow; he had a lustre in his cheeks. His parents are from the

Iṣfahānī., *ʿAwālim al-ʿulūm wa-l-maʿārif al-aḥwāl min al-āyāt wa-l-aḫbār wa-l-aqwāl*, vol. XVII, ch. 17, bb. 5, n. 3: 482.

[32] Ibn Abī ʿĀṣim., *al-Āḥād wa-l-maṯānī*, vol. I, bb. 36 (*Min ḏikri al-Ḥusayn b. ʿAlī*), n. 426: 308, al-Ṭabarānī., *al-Muʿğam al-kabīr*, vol. III, bb. *al-Ḥusayn b. ʿAlī*, n. 2868: 122.

[33] al-Baḥrānī., *Madīnat al-maʿāğiz fī muʿğizāt al-aʾimma al-aṭhār*, vol. IV, Part Four, n. 249/1196: 174, al-Mağlisī, *Biḥār al-anwār*, vol. XLV, bb. 43, n. 13: 241, al-Iṣfahānī., *ʿAwālim al-ʿulūm wa-l-maʿārif al-aḥwāl min al-āyāt wa-l-aḫbār wa-l-aqwāl*, vol. XVII, ch. 17, bb. 5, n. 9: 485.

[34] Ibn Qūlawayh., *Kāmil al-ziyārāt*, bb. 29, n. 5: 192–193, al-Mağlisī., *Biḥār al-anwār*, vol. XLV, bb. 43, n. 13: 241.

> loftiest of the Quraysh, his grandfather the best of grandfathers'."[35]

As with all the other verses, this lament too is said to have been heard by others aside from this group of workmen. This is sometimes Abū Ḥubāb al-Kalbī himself, or a poet, or at times a nobleman who is questioned about what he and others heard:

> On the authority of Abū Ḥubāb al-Kalbī, who said: I came to Karbalāʾ, and said to man among the eminent Arabs there: It has come to me that you heard the lament of the *ǧinn*? He replied: "You will encounter neither a freeman nor a servant but that he will inform you he had heard it." He said [I said]: Inform me of what you yourself heard? He answered: "I heard them saying: 'The Messenger stroked his brow; he had a lustre

[35] al-Ṭabarānī., *al-Muʿǧam al-kabīr*, vol. III, bb. *al-Ḥusayn b. ʿAlī*, nn. 2865, 2866: 121–122, Ibn Qūlawayh., *Kāmil al-ziyārāt*, bb. 29, n. 3: 191–192, al-Shaǧarī., *Tartīb al-amālī al-ḫamīsiyya*, vol. I, bb. *Fī faḍl al-Ḥusayn b. ʿAlī*, n. 793: 217, n. 807: 228, al-Ḫawārizmī., *Maqtal al-Ḥusayn*, Part Two, bb. *Fī bayān ʿuqūba qātil al-Ḥusayn*, n. 35: 108–109, Sibṭ al-Ǧawzī., *Taḏkirat al-ḫawāṣṣ al-umma bi-ḏikr ḫaṣāʾiṣ al-aʾimma*: 242, Ibn al-ʿAdīm., *Buġyat al-ṭalab fī tārīḫ Ḥalab*: 2651–2652 (from Abū Ǧanāb), Ibn Ṭāʾūs., *Kitāb al-luhūf fī qatlā al-ṭufūf*: 114, Ibn Namā., *Muṯīr al-aḥzān*, bb. *Nūḥ al-ǧinn ʿalā al-Ḥusayn*: 108, al-Zarandī., *Naẓm durar al-simṭayn fī faḍāʾil al-muṣṭafā wa-l-murtaḍā wa-l-batūl wa-l-sibṭayn*: 223 (from Abū Ǧanāb al-Kalbī), al-Hayṯamī., *Maǧmaʿ al-zawāʾid wa-manbaʿ al-fawāʾid*, vol. IX, bk. 37 (*Kitāb al-manāqib*), bb. 95 (*Manāqib al-Ḥusayn b. ʿAlī*), n. 15176: 575, al-Mūsawī., *Tasliyat al-muǧālis wa zīnat al-maǧālis*, vol. II, Part Two, *maǧlis* 9: 459 (from Abū Ǧanāb al-Kalbī), al-Baḥrānī., *Madīnat al-maʿāǧiz fī muʿǧizāt al-aʾimma al-aṭhār*, vol. IV, Part Four, n. 247/1194: 174, n. 271/1218: 192 (a female *ǧinn* replying to the verse "O eye, shed tears…"), al-Maǧlisī, *Biḥār al-anwār*, vol. XLV, bb. 39, n. 1: 146–7, bb. 43, n. 11: 241, al-Iṣfahānī., *ʿAwālim al-ʿulūm wa-l-maʿārif al-aḥwāl min al-āyāt wa-l-aḫbār wa-l-aqwāl*, vol. XVII, ch. 16, bb. 4, n. 19: 446, ch. 17, bb. 5, n. 7: 484, al-Ǧazāʾirī., *Riyāḍ al-abrār fī manāqib al-aʾimma al-aṭhār*, vol. I, Part One: 252, 337.

> in his cheeks. His parents are from the loftiest of the Quraysh, his grandfather the best of grandfathers'."[36]

In al-Suyūṭī's *al-Ḫaṣā'iṣ*, this dirge is heard by Ḥabīb b. Abī Ṯābit and by the mother of Ibn Ǧābir al-Ḥaḍramī,[37] while Ibn Kaṯīr situates it in Karbalā',[38] and in a lengthy transmission, al-Baḥrānī proposes it as a response by a (female) *ǧinn* to the lament of a fellow-*ǧinn*, which urged the eye to be generous in its weeping:

> Another *ǧinn* answered her: "The Messenger stroked his brow; he had a lustre in the cheeks. His father is from the loftiest of the Quraysh, his grandfather the best of grandfathers. They marched against him with spears, the evilest of creatures and envoys; they killed him unjustly! Woe to them, they have dwelt in the fire of eternity." When the people of Medina heard that, they strew dust on their heads and cried out: Ḥusayn! Son of the Prophet's daughter! They went to the grave of the Messenger of God, consoling him over his son al-Ḥusayn; then they remained consoling him for three days.[39]

---

[36] Ibn ʿAsākir., *Tārīḫ madīnat Dimashq*, vol. XIV, bb. 1566 (*al-Ḥusayn b. ʿAlī b. Abī Ṭālib b. ʿAbd al-Muṭṭalib b. Hāshim b. ʿAbd al-Manāf*): 241, Ibn Shahrāshūb., *Manāqib āl Abī Ṭālib*, vol. III, bb. *Fī imāmat al-sibṭayn*: 390, al-Shāmī., *al-Durr al-naẓīm fī manāqib al-a'imma al-lahāhīm*, bb. 5, *Fī ḏikr al-Ḥusayn b. ʿAlī*: 569, al-Irbilī., *Kashf al-ġumma fī maʿrifat al-a'imma*, vol. II: 57 (who, on the authority of Abū Ḫabbāb, puts the story on the lips of a man from the Ṭayy tribe; cf. TRIMINGHAM J.S., *Christianity among the Arabs in Pre-Islamic Times*, Longman Group Unlimited, London 1979: 312), al-Ḏahabī., *Siyar aʿlām al-nubalā'*, vol. III, n. 48 (*al-Ḥusayn al-Shahīd Abū ʿAbd Allāh b. ʿAlī b. Abī Ṭālib*): 316–317, al-Maǧlisī, *Biḥār al-anwār*, vol. XLV, bb. 44, n. 15: 288.

[37] al-Suyūṭī., *al-Ḫaṣā'iṣ al-kubrā*, vol. II: 454–455. The latter hears the *ǧinn* saying: "I announce the death of Ḥusayn as a bereaved mother! Ḥusayn was a mountain."

[38] Ibn Kaṯīr., *al-Bidāya wa-l-nihāya*, vol. XI, bb. *al-Iḫbār bi-maqtal al-Ḥusayn b. ʿAlī*: 572.

[39] al-Baḥrānī., *Madīnat al-maʿāǧiz fī muʿǧizāt al-a'imma al-aṭhār*, vol. IV, n. 272/1219: 194–196. The first of al-Baḥrānī's two transmissions is probably older, by virtue of its more arcane language, as well as a change in the

A small group of transmitters report the verse entirely apart from the *ǧinn* and from the Karbalāʾ event, putting the lines instead into the mouth of an Arab who has been asking questions of al-Ḥusayn about his lineage, and who then recites the verses in homage.[40]

Scattered throughout the Sunnī and Shīʿī books is a selection of less well-attested elegies attributed to the *ǧinn* as they lament al-Ḥusayn, or to unspecified mourners. Ibn Namā records an unidentified voice in Baṣra crying out: "The arriving lances, proceeding in the direction of al-Ḥusayn to combat the revelation, are jubilant that you have been killed! But with you they have killed the *takbīr* and the *tahlīl*![41] It is as if they had killed your father Muḥammad, or Ǧibrīl!"[42] The same Ibn Namā, and al-Mağlisī after him, transmitting from Ibn al-Ǧawzī,[43] conveys words which contrast the shine on the faces of the female *ǧinn* with their sepulchral clothing: "The best of the women of the *ǧinn* weep, distressed, beat cheeks like pure dinars, and dress in black garments." The historians al-Ṭabarī, Ibn ʿAsākir and Ibn Kaṯīr narrate verses almost identical to these; but in all three cases they refer to a lament sung at the death of the

---

language used and certain strands (like the *ǧinn*) omitted in the second narration.

[40] al-Ḫazzāz., *Kifāyat al-aṯar fī-l-nuṣūṣ ʿalā al-aʾimma al-iṯnā ʿasharī*, bb. *Ma ǧāʾ ʿan al-Ḥusayn*: 234, al-Baḥrānī., *al-Inṣāf fī-l-naṣṣ ʿalā al-aʾimma*: 260, al-Mağlisī, *Biḥār al-anwār*, vol. XXXVI, bb. 43, n. 5: 385.

[41] The declarations that 'God is the greatest' (*allāhu akbar*) and that 'there is no god but God' (*lā ilāha illā llāh*).

[42] Ibn Namā al-Ḥillī., *Muṯīr al-aḥzān*, bb. *Nūḥ al-ǧinn ʿalā al-Ḥusayn*: 108, al-Baḥrānī., *Madīnat al-maʿāǧiz fī muʿǧizāt al-aʾimma al-aṭhār*, vol. IV, n. 272/1219: 194–196 (words heard by Umm Salama during a sleepless night), al-Mağlisī., *Biḥār al-anwār*, vol. XLV, bb. 43, n. 2: 235, al-Iṣfahānī., *ʿAwālim al-ʿulūm wa-l-maʿārif al-aḥwāl min al-āyāt wa-l-aḫbār wa-l-aqwāl*, vol. XVII, ch. 17, bb. 5, n. 12: 486, al-Ǧazāʾirī., *Riyāḍ al-abrār fī manāqib al-aʾimma al-aṭhār*, vol. I, Part One: 274 (a voice heard in Baṣra), 324.

[43] Apparently from Ibn al-Ǧawzī's *Kitāb al-nūr fī faḍāʾil al-ayyām wa-l-shuhūr*; but as it stands, this transmission is found in Sibṭ al-Ǧawzī's *Taḏkirat al-ḫawāṣṣ al-umma bi-ḏikr ḫaṣāʾiṣ al-aʾimma*: 242 ("The best of the women of the *ǧinn* weep, distressed, beat cheeks like pure dinars, and dress in black garments").

second Caliph, ʿUmar b. al-Ḫaṭṭāb, and while Ibn ʿAsākir keeps the lines on the lips of a female *ǧinn* ("The women of the *ǧinn* weep over you, distressed, scratching faces over you, like pure dinars…"), al-Ṭabarī and Ibn Kaṯīr put them into the mouth of unnamed (Muslim) women ("The women of the tribe will weep for you, grieving, they will weep, scratching their faces [previously] like [shining] dinars [all] pure, and wearing clothes of grief after their finery").[44] Al-Ḫawārizmī and Ibn Shahrāshūb document Saʿdā[45] bt. Mālik al-Ḫuzāʿī claiming that she heard the *ǧinn* lamenting the over al-Ḥusayn with the words: "Son of the martyr, and martyr whose uncle, Ǧaʿfar al-Ṭayyār, is the best of uncles, astonishing the burnished cutting edge, hitting you in that face of yours, and you, already covered in dust."[46]

Ibn Qūlawayh and Ibn Kaṯīr record a lament which finds its way onto the lips of a variety of people in diverse situations – Zaynab bt. ʿAlī, or one of the daughters of ʿAqīl, or ʿAlī b. al-Ḥusayn, or a bareheaded and unnamed woman from the women of ʿAbd al-Muṭṭalib, or the *ǧinn*: "The *ǧinn* wept over al-Ḥusayn b. ʿAlī

---

[44] Cf. al-Ṭabarī., *Kitāb aḫbār al-rusul wa-l-mulūk*, vol. IV, n. 2764/1: 219, Ibn ʿAsākir., *Tārīḫ madīnat Dimashq*, vol. XLIV, bb. 5206 (*ʿUmar b. al-Ḫaṭṭāb*): 480, Ibn Kaṯīr., *al-Bidāya wa-l-nihāya*, vol. VII, bb. *Ḏikr baʿḍ mā ruʾiya bi-hi*: 140. Cf. also al-ʿAsqalānī., *al-Iṣāba fī tamyīz al-ṣaḥāba*, vol. III, n. 3938: 280, al-Suyūṭī., *al-Ḫaṣāʾiṣ al-kubrā*, vol. II: 445 (without the verse as part of their lament).

[45] In other places, Saʿīda.

[46] al-Ḫawārizmī., *Maqtal al-Ḥusayn*, Part Two, bb. *Fī bayān ʿuqūba qātil al-Ḥusayn*, n. 44: 113, Ibn Shahrāshūb., *Manāqib āl Abī Ṭālib*, vol. IV, bb. *Fī imāmat Abī ʿAbd Allāh al-Ḥusayn*: 62, al-Mūsawī., *Tasliyat al-maǧālis wa zīnat al-maǧālis*, vol. II, *maǧlis* 9: 472, al-Baḥrānī., *Madīnat al-maʿāǧiz fī muʿǧizāt al-aʾimma al-aṭhār*, vol. IV, Part Four, n. 270/1217: 191, al-Maǧlisī., *Biḥār al-anwār*, vol. XLV, bb. 43, n. 3: 236, al-Iṣfahānī., *ʿAwālim al-ʿulūm wa-l-maʿārif al-aḥwāl min al-āyāt wa-l-aḫbār wa-l-aqwāl*, vol. XVII, ch. 17, bb. 8, n. 1: 498, al-Ǧazāʾirī., *Riyāḍ al-abrār fī manāqib al-aʾimma al-aṭhār*, vol. I, Part One: 275. In a second, expanded version from Diʿbil in al-Ḫawārizmī, al-Mūsawī, al-Baḥrānī, al-Iṣfahānī and al-Maǧlisī, which brands as 'donkeys' those who prohibit visits to the tomb of al-Ḥusayn, "that face of yours, already covered in dust."

b. Abī Ṭālib, saying: What will you say if the Prophet says to you; what have you, the last of the communities, done with the people of my house and my brothers and my honour after my departure, from among the prisoners and the killed, reddened with blood?"[47] One of al-Ḥusayn's aunts in Medina – although others are also reported as hearing these words – tells him that she too has heard the *ǧinn* lamenting with loud weeping for him, saying:

> The slain one of al-Ṭaff, from the family of Hāshim, subdued Qurayshī necks and they were humbled. Beloved of the Messenger of God, never immoderate, your misfortune distinguishes and goes beyond the lofty. They also said: Weep for Ḥusayn, master! Because of his killing, hair has turned white, and because of his killing you have been shaken and because of his killing the moon was eclipsed and the horizons of the sky turned red at early morning and nightfall. The sun of the countries has become dust-covered, the districts grown dark. That is the son of Fāṭima; all created things and humankind are stricken on his account. We have drawn down ignominy on his account, what is lofty cut off by peril.[48]

---

[47] Ibn Qūlawayh., *Kāmil al-ziyārāt*, bb. 29, n. 6: 193, Ibn al-Aṯīr., *al-Kāmil fī al-tārīḫ*, vol. III, *Ḏikr maqtal al-Ḥusayn*: 300, Ibn Kaṯīr., *al-Bidāya wa-l-nihāya*, vol. IX, bb. *Iḫbār bi-maqtal al-Ḥusayn*: 243, vol. XI, bb. *al-Iḫbār bi-maqtal al-Ḥusayn b. ʿAlī*: 567, al-ʿAsqalānī., *Tahḏīb al-tahḏīb*, vol. II, bb. *al-Ḥāʾ*, n. 615: 353, al-Maǧlisī., *Biḥār al-anwār*, vol. XLV, bb. 43, n. 4: 237, al-Iṣfahānī., *ʿAwālim al-ʿulūm wa-l-maʿārif al-aḥwāl min al-āyāt wa-l-aḫbār wa-l-aqwāl*, vol. XVII, ch. 17, bb. 5, n. 1: 481. Cf. also al-Ḫawārizmī., *Maqtal al-Ḥusayn*, Part Two, bb. *Fī maqtal al-Ḥusayn*: 71, 84, CLOHESSY C., *Half of My Heart. The Narratives of Zaynab, Daughter of ʿAlī*, 2018: 204–206.

[48] al-Qāḍī al-Nuʿmān., *Sharḥ al-aḫbār fī faḍāʾil al-aʾimma al-aṭhār*, vol. III, Part Twelve, n. 1108: 167–168, Ibn Qūlawayh., *Kāmil al-ziyārāt*, bb. 29, n. 8: 194–196, Ibn Shahrāshūb., *Manāqib āl Abī Ṭālib*, vol. IV, bb. *Fī imāmat Abī ʿAbd Allāh al-Ḥusayn*: 62, al-Baḥrānī., *Madīnat al-maʿāǧiz fī muʿǧizāt al-aʾimma al-aṭhār*, vol. IV, Part Four, n. 253/1200: 177–178, al-Maǧlisī., *Biḥār al-anwār*, vol. XLV, bb. 37, n. 26: 88–89, al-Iṣfahānī., *ʿAwālim al-ʿulūm wa-l-maʿārif al-aḥwāl min al-āyāt wa-l-aḫbār wa-l-aqwāl*, vol. XVII, ch. 13, bb. 2, n. 6: 316.

From al-Mağlisī come an assortment of long narratives; the first concerns an Asadī[49] man, a farmer working on the banks of the al-ʿAlqamī river in Karbalāʾ after the departure of al-Yazīd's forces and who, as part of an extended vision which includes the scent of musk and ambergris on the air and also prominently features a lion, encounters the *ğinn*:

> I began to watch until the darkness grew intense and confusing. Suddenly, the earth was filled with suspended wax candles and weeping, sobbing and a harrowing beating of chests. I made for the sounds, and behold, they were under the earth. I understood from an announcer of death among them, who was saying: "Alas, Ḥusayn! Alas, Imām!" I got goose flesh, and I drew closer to the one weeping and entreated him by God and His Messenger as to who he was. He[50] answered: "I am a woman of the *ğinn*." I said: What is your business?[51] They replied: "Every day and night, this is our ceremony of mourning for the slaughtered and thirsty al-Ḥusayn." I said: Is that al-Ḥusayn by whom the lion is sitting? They replied: "Yes, and do you know this lion?" I said: No, and they replied: "This is his father, ʿAlī b. Abī Ṭālib." I returned, and my tears were flowing down my cheek.[52]

The next, from Hind bt. Ğawn, is about a boxthorn tree outside the tent of her aunt Umm Maʿbad upon which Muḥammad discharges the water of his ablutions. In fulfilment of his prediction, the tree grows tall, with deep roots and miraculous fruit, its thorns removed by God.[53] With the death of Muḥammad, its now famous

---

[49] al-Ṭabarī and others report that it was members of the Banū Asad who had buried the bodies of al-Ḥusayn and his companions the day after ʿĀshūrā. Cf. HOWARD I.K.A., (trans.), *The History of al-Ṭabarī*, vol. XIX, 1990: 163. Cf. also Ibn Shahrāshūb., *Manāqib āl Abī Ṭālib*, vol. IV, bb. *Fī imāmat Abī ʿAbd Allāh al-Ḥusayn*: 111.

[50] The Arabic is still in the masculine form.

[51] Now in the feminine plural.

[52] al-Mağlisī, *Biḥār al-anwār*, vol. XLV, bb. 39, n. 36: 194.

[53] The description of the tree is reminiscent of the trees the prophet Ezekiel describes in Ez. 47:12 («*Fruit trees of all kinds will grow on both banks*

fruit is diminished in taste and size and the leaves fade. Thirty years later, with the death of ʿAlī, the thorns grow back and the fruits cease. With the death of al-Ḥusayn, fresh blood flows from the trunk and increasing and often unintelligible wailing is heard at the base of the tree at night, with the lament: "Son of the Prophet, son of the Trustee, the best[54] of our honourable masters." The story continues with the lament transmitted al-Ḫawārizmī and Ibn Shahrāshūb from Saʿdā bt. Mālik al-Ḫuzāʿī, who has heard the *ǧinn* singing of the burnish of the sword that struck al-Ḥusayn even as he already lay in the dust.[55]

From al-Maǧlisī comes another narrative involving five men of Kūfa who, unlike the majority of their fellow citizens, are keen to assist al-Ḥusayn, and who meet two men of the *ǧinn*. In order that the Kūfans might 'travel with foresight', one of the *ǧinn* flies off to bring news to the men:

> He disappeared for a day and a night, and when morning came, they heard a voice but without seeing anyone, and it was saying: "By God, I did not come to you until I saw him in al-Ṭaff, the cheeks dust-covered, butchered, around him young men, their chests blood-smeared, like lamps, unflagging light in the gloom. I spurred on my young she-camel so as to encounter them before they met the maidens of Paradise.[56] Al-Ḥusayn

---

of the river. Their leaves will not wither, nor will their fruit fail. Every month they will bear fruit, because the water from the sanctuary flows to them. Their fruit will serve for food and their leaves for healing»). Ezekiel's trees are miraculous in their fruits and foliage because they are nourished by the water that flows from the sanctuary of God. In the *ḥadīt*, the fruits are large, with a distinct taste and odour, and are able to satisfy thirst and hunger and increase the health and the yield of animals. The whole area becomes fertile and a place in which desert dwellers find nourishment and rest.

[54] Cf. LANE E.W., *An Arabic-English Lexicon*, vol. I, 1968: 238.

[55] al-Ḫawārizmī., *Maqtal al-Ḥusayn*, Part Two, bb. *Fī bayān ʿuqūba qātil al-Ḥusayn*, n. 44: 114, al-Baḥrānī., *Madīnat al-maʿāǧiz fī muʿǧizāt al-aʾimma al-aṭhār*, vol. IV, Part Four, n. 270/1217: 189–191, al-Maǧlisī., *Biḥār al-anwār*, vol. XLV, bb. 43, n. 1: 233–235.

[56] The word *ḫurud*, the plural of *ḫarīda*, means 'virgins'; the Arabic singular *ḥawrāʾ* (with its plural *ḥūr*) has come to mean the 'maidens of Par-

was a lamp by which to be illumined – God knows that I do not speak falsehood – delighting in chambers close to the Messenger of God, the Virgin[57] and the one who flies."[58]

---

adise', the large black pupils of whose eyes are in sharp and beautiful contrast to the whiteness of the irises and the paleness of their skin. A similar text in al-Mağlisī adds: "but divine decree prevented me, an order determined and decreed by God."

[57] Fāṭima, mother of al-Ḥusayn. The designation 'virgin' is expressed by the Arabic *al-ʿaḏrāʾ* and more frequently by *al-batūl.*

[58] The 'one entrusted' (*waṣī*) is ʿAlī b. Abī Ṭālib and the 'one who flies' (*al-ṭayyār*) Ğaʿfar b. Abī Ṭālib. A reference to ʿAlī b. Abī Ṭālib and Ğaʿfar b. Abī Ṭālib. Ğaʿfar (d. 8/629), a companion to Muḥammad and an older brother of ʿAlī, was known as *al-ṭayyār* ('the flyer') or *ḏū al-ğanāḥayn* ('possessor of wings') because after his death at the 8/629 Battle of Muʾta, Muḥammad, as he prayed and wept for him, received a vision in which Ğibrīl promised that God had given Ğaʿfar a pair of wings in place of his arms which had been cut off in battle. Cf. for e.g. al-Hilālī., *Kitāb Sulaym b. Qays*, vol. II, *al-ḥadīṯ al-awwal*: 567, Abū Miḫnaf., *Maqtal al-Ḥusayn*: 206, Ibn Furāt al-Kūfī., *Tafsīr Furāt b. Ibrāhīm al-Kūfī*, *sūrat al-Nisāʾ*: 112–113, *sūrat al-Shūrā*: 397, Ibn Bābawayh., *Kitāb al-amālī fī-l-aḥādīṯ wa-l-aḫbār*, *mağlis* 72, n. 15: 476, *Ikmāl (kamāl) al-dīn wa-itmām (tamām) al-niʿma fī iṯbāt al-ġayba wa-kashf al-ḥayra*, vol. I, bb. 24, n. 10: 264, al-Ṭabarī., *Dalāʾil al-imāma*, n. 74/470: 479, *Bishārat al-muṣṭafā*, Part Three: 115, Ibn ʿAlī al-Fattāl., *Rawḍat al-wāʿiẓīn wa-tabṣirat al-muttaʿiẓīn*, vol. II: 269, Ibn Shahrāshūb., *Manāqib āl Abī Ṭālib*, vol. II, *faṣl fī-l-iḫwa*: 189, vol. III, *faṣl fī marākibi-hi*: 233, al-Ṭabarsī., *Kitāb al-iḥtiğāğ ʿalā ahl al-liğāğ*, vol. I: 177, vol. II: 301, Ibn al-Ḥadīd., *Sharḥ nahğ al-balāġa*, vol. I, Part One: 69, vol. XI, Part Two: 118, vol. XV, Part Fifteen: 62, 182, 278–280, al-Irbilī., *Kashf al-ġumma fī maʿrifat al-aʾimma*, vol. I, Part One, n. 13: 5, n. 17: 30, al-Ḥillī al-ʿAllāma., *Kashf al-yaqīn fī faḍāʾil amīr al-muʾminīn*, Part Three, bb. 3: 192, 315, *Nahğ al-ḥaqq wa-kashf al-ṣidq*: 253, 391, al-Daylamī., *Irshād al-qulūb*, vol. II, Part Three: 320, 330, al-Mūsawī., *Tasliyat al-mağālis wa zīnat al-mağālis*, vol. II, *mağlis* 7: 316, al-Baḥrānī., *al-Burhān fī tafsīr al-qurʾān*, vol. II, *sūrat al-Anʿām*: 495, *sūrat al-Aʿrāf*: 554, *Ḥilyat al-abrār fī aḥwāl Muḥammad wa āli-hi al-aṭhār*, vol. II, bb. 16: 145, bb. 45: 401. Ibn Qūlawayh., *Kāmil al-ziyārāt*, bb. 29, n. 2: 189–191.

Al-Mağlisī relates an almost identical story from a *shayḫ* of the Banū Tamīm who claims not to have been aware of the killing of al-Ḥusayn until the night of ʿĀshūrā. He and a companion hear a similar lament, which ends:

> God bless the body enclosed by the grave of al-Ḥusayn, ally of the good, buried in chambers near to the Messenger of God and happy with the Trustee and the one who flies· We said: Who are you, may God have mercy on you? He replied: "I and my family are from among the *ğinn*. We desired to support al-Ḥusayn and console him ourselves, so we relinquished the Pilgrimage and found him killed."[59]

This is a book about encounters; asleep or awake, with angels or *ğinn* or exalted Islamic personalities returning in visions to warn, lament or chastise. All of the encounters centre around the person and fate of al-Ḥusayn; but long before his death on the field of Karbalāʾ, there was another member of Muḥammad's community glimpsing angels, and that was ʿAbd Allāh b. ʿAbbās. The texts agree that Ibn ʿAbbās was born three years before the 622 *hiğra*, so that the discrepancies (ranging from ten years to fifteen years) over how old he was when Muḥammad died in 11/632 are puzzling. He would have been thirteen at the Prophet's death, and so even younger when he first began to sight angels.[60] The double claim of

[59] al-Mufīd., *al-Amālī*, *mağlis* 38, n. 7: 320, Ibn Bābawayh., *Kitāb al-amālī fi-l-aḥādīṯ wa-l-aḫbār*, *mağlis* 3, n. 50–141: 90, al-Mağlisī., *Biḥār al-anwār*, vol. XLV, bb. 43, n. 9: 239–240, al-Iṣfahānī., *ʿAwālim al-ʿulūm wa-l-maʿārif al-aḥwāl min al-āyāt wa-l-aḫbār wa-l-aqwāl*, vol. XVII, ch. 17, bb. 5, n. 5: 483.

[60] al-Balāḏurī., *Kitāb ansāb al-ashraf*, vol. IV, bb. *ʿAbd Allāh b. ʿAbbās*: 39, al-Ḥākim al-Nīsābūrī., *Kitāb al-mustadrak ʿalā al-ṣaḥīḥayn*, vol. III, bk. 31 (*Kitāb maʿrifat al-ṣaḥāba*), *Ḏikr ʿAbd Allāh b. ʿAbbās*, nn. 6354, 6365, 6356: 656–657, Ibn ʿAbd al-Barr., *al-Istīʿāb fī maʿrifat al-aṣḥāb*, vol. III, n. 1588: 933–934, Ibn ʿAsākir., *Tārīḫ madīnat Dimashq*, vol. XXIX, bb. 3363 (*ʿAbd Allāh b. ʿAbbās*): 285, Ibn al-Aṯīr., *Usd al-ġāba fī maʿrifat al-ṣaḥāb*, vol. III, n. 3035 (*ʿAbd Allāh b. ʿAbbās*): 189, al-Ṭabarī., *Ḏaḫāʾir al-ʿuqbā*, bb. 3: 373, al-Ḏahabī., *Siyar aʿlām al-nubalāʾ*, vol. III, n. 51 (*ʿAbd Allāh b. ʿAbbās*): 332, 335, Ibn Kaṯīr., *al-Bidāya wa-l-nihāya*, vol. XII, bb. *Wa fī-hi tawaffā ʿAbd*

Ibn ʿAbbās is that Muḥammad twice invoked a blessing on him (diversely expressed in the texts) and that twice he saw Ğibrīl. The blessing that Muḥammad invokes, invariably in prayer but accompanied by rubbing the boy's head or putting his hand between the boy's shoulder blades, is that God would endow Ibn ʿAbbās with wisdom (*al-ḥikma*) and interpretation (*taʾwīl*), instruct him in religion (*dīn*), fill him with knowledge and understanding, and count him among the people of faith (*īmān*).[61]

Ibn ʿAbbās certainly claims to have seen Ğibrīl with Muḥammad. The incident is diversely narrated; in its most modest form, the boy Ibn ʿAbbās visits with Muḥammad. There is a man

---

Allāh b. ʿAbbās: 85, al-ʿAsqalānī., *al-Iṣāba fī tamyīz al-ṣaḥāba*, vol. III, n. 4779: 229–230, *Tahḏīb al-tahḏīb*, vol. V, n. 474: 276.

[61] Ibn Abī Shayba., *Muṣannaf*, vol. X, bb. 27, n. 32813: 514, nn. 32818, 32820: 515–516, Ibn Ḥanbal., *Kitāb faḍāʾil al-ṣaḥāba*, vol. II, bb. *Faḍāʾil ʿAbd Allāh b. ʿAbbās*, nn. 1560, 1561: 846, al-Buḫārī., *Ṣaḥīḥ*, vol. I, bk. 4 (*Kitāb al-wuḍūʾ*), bb. 10, n. 143: 140, vol. V. bk. 62 (*Kitāb faḍāʾil al-nabī*), bb. 24, n. 3765: 70, Muslim., *Ṣaḥīḥ*, vol. VI, bk. 44 (*Kitāb faḍāʾil al-ṣaḥāba*), bb. 30, n. [6368] 138 - (2477): 342–343, Ibn Ḥanbal., *Musnad*, vol. I, *Musnad ʿAbd Allāh b. ʿAbbās*: 266, 314, 328, 335, al-Tirmiḏī., *al-Ğāmiʿ al-ṣaḥīḥ*, vol. VI, bk. 46 (*Abwāb al-manāqib*), bb. 42, n. 3823–3824: 460–461, Ibn Saʿd., *Kitāb al-ṭabaqāt al-kabīr*, vol. II, (*Ibn ʿAbbās*): 365, 370, al-Balāḏurī., *Kitāb ansāb al-ashraf*, vol. IV, bb. *ʿAbd Allāh b. ʿAbbās*: 39–42, al-Bazzār., *Musnad*, vol. XI, *Musnad Ibn ʿAbbās*, n. 4921: 180–181, al-Ḥākim al-Nīsābūrī., *Kitāb al-mustadrak ʿalā al-ṣaḥīḥayn*, vol. III, bk. 31 (*Kitāb maʿrifat al-ṣaḥāba*), nn. 6358, 6359: 658, Abū Nuʿaym., *Ḥilyat al-awliyāʾ wa-ṭabaqāt al-aṣfiyāʾ*, vol. I, bb. 45 (*ʿAbd Allāh b. ʿAbbās*), nn. 1111–1113: 389–390, n. 1119: 391, Ibn ʿAbd al-Barr., *al-Istīʿāb fī maʿrifat al-aṣḥāb*, vol. III, n. 1588: 935, Ibn al-Ğawzī., *Ṣifat al-ṣafwa*, vol. I: 314, Ibn al-Aṯīr., *Usd al-ġāba fī maʿrifat al-ṣaḥāb*, vol. III, n. 3035 (*ʿAbd Allāh b. ʿAbbās*): 186, al-Ṭabarī., *Ḏaḫāʾir al-ʿuqbā*, bb. 3: 376/379, al-Ḏahabī., *Siyar aʿlām al-nubalāʾ*, vol. III, n. 51 (*ʿAbd Allāh b. ʿAbbās*): 334, 336–339, Ibn Kaṯīr., *al-Bidāya wa-l-nihāya*, vol. XII, bb. *Wa fī-hi tawaffā ʿAbd Allāh b. ʿAbbās*: 81–83, al-Hayṯamī., *Mağmaʿ al-zawāʾid wa-manbaʿ al-fawāʾid*, vol. IX, bk. 37 (*Kitāb al-manāqib*), bb. 155, nn. 15515, 15516 (where it is Ğibrīl, not Muḥammad, who twice invokes blessing on him; cf. also al-Ṭabarānī., *Muʿğam al-kabīr*, vol. XI, n. 11108: 80), 15517: 330, al-ʿAsqalānī., *al-Iṣāba fī tamyīz al-ṣaḥāba*, vol. III, n. 4779: 229, 230–231, *Tahḏīb al-tahḏīb*, vol. V, n. 474: 279.

with the Prophet, and when the boy, who in some texts waits for an hour before being noticed by Muḥammad (who is sometimes also portrayed as being asleep) asks who it is, he is told that it is Ǧibrīl. In more detailed accounts, the boy goes to see Muḥammad with his father al-ʿAbbās, who is perplexed that Muḥammad appears to be ignoring him. When they leave and he mentions this to his son, Ibn ʿAbbās answers that there had been a man, unseen by al-ʿAbbās, whispering to Muḥammad. They return to Muḥammad and al-ʿAbbās asks for clarification; Muḥammad asks the boy if he saw the man, and when Ibn ʿAbbās replies in the affirmative, they are told that it was Ǧibrīl. In one or two rare accounts, Ǧibrīl himself speaks, asking the identity of the boy and making a declaration about him as the 'learned man' of the community;[62] and in one report, Ibn ʿAbbās passes by Muḥammad, who is dressed in white garments, and is whispering to a man named Diḥya b. Ḫalīfa al-Kalbī. What Ibn ʿAbbās fails to realise that it is not in fact Diḥya but Ǧibrīl and so fails to greet him – he only discovers the truth when challenged by Muḥammad for his failure to acknowledge the Prophet's interlocutor.[63] Diḥya b. Ḫalīfa al-Kalbī was a companion, but Ǧibrīl also used his appearance as one of his disguises. On one

[62] Ibn Hanbal., *Musnad*, vol. I, *Musnad ʿAbd Allāh b. ʿAbbās*: 293–294, al-Balāḏurī., *Kitāb ansāb al-ashraf*, vol. IV, bb. *ʿAbd Allāh b. ʿAbbās*: 41, al-Ṭabarānī., *al-Muʿǧam al-kabīr*, vol. XII, n. 12836: 185, al-Ḥākim al-Nīsābūrī., *Kitāb al-mustadrak ʿalā al-ṣaḥīḥayn*, vol. III, bk. 31 (*Kitāb maʿrifat al-ṣaḥāba*), *Ḏikr ʿAbd Allāh b. ʿAbbās*, 6366: 660, Abū Nuʿaym., *Ḥilyat al-awliyāʾ wa-ṭabaqāt al-aṣfiyāʾ*, vol. I, bb. 45 (*ʿAbd Allāh b. ʿAbbās*), n. 1118: 391, Ibn ʿAbd al-Barr., *al-Istīʿāb fī maʿrifat al-aṣḥāb*, vol. III, n. 1588: 938, al-Ḏahabī., *Siyar aʿlām al-nubalāʾ*, vol. III, n. 51 (*ʿAbd Allāh b. ʿAbbās*): 339 (and denounced by al-Ḏahabī), Ibn Kaṯīr., *al-Bidāya wa-l-nihāya*, vol. XII, bb. *Wa fī-hi tawaffā ʿAbd Allāh b. ʿAbbās*: 84–85, al-Haytamī., *Maǧmaʿ al-zawāʾid wa-manbaʿ al-fawāʾid*, vol. IX, bk. 37 (*Kitāb al-manāqib*), bb. 155, 15518: 331.

[63] al-Ḏahabī., *Siyar aʿlām al-nubalāʾ*, vol. III, n. 51 (*ʿAbd Allāh b. ʿAbbās*): 339–340 (and denounced by al-Ḏahabī as having a weakness in the chain), al-Haytamī., *Maǧmaʿ al-zawāʾid wa-manbaʿ al-fawāʾid*, vol. IX, bk. 37 (*Kitāb al-manāqib*), bb. 155, 15519: 331.

occasion, Umm Salama too fails to recognise Ǧibrīl in the form of Diḥya because of the angel's resemblance to the man.[64]

Ibn ʿAbbās is therefore no stranger to the mystical strands that run through the faith of Islam, and his dark vision of Muḥammad in a dream is carried by numerous Sunnī and Shīʿī transmitters:

> On the authority of Ibn ʿAbbās who said: In the middle of the day I saw the Messenger of God in a dream, dishevelled and dust-covered, and in his hand a glass vial containing blood. I said: Messenger of God, you are as dear to me as my own father and mother! What is this? He replied: "This is the blood of al-Ḥusayn and his companions: I have been gathering it since that day!" He calculated that day and found that on that day, he had been killed.[65]

---

[64] Muslim., *Ṣaḥīḥ*, vol. I, bk. 1 (*Kitāb al-īmān*), bb. 74, n. [423] 271 - (167): 273, vol. VI, bk. 44 (*Kitāb faḍāʾil al-ṣaḥāba*), bb. 16, n. [6315] 100 - (2451): 312, al-Tirmiḏī., *al-Ǧāmiʿ al-ṣaḥīḥ*, vol. VI, bk. 46 (*Abwāb al-manāqib*), n. 3629: 340.

[65] Ibn Ḥanbal., *Musnad*, vol. I, *Musnad ʿAbd Allāh b. ʿAbbās*: 242, 243, *Kitāb faḍāʾil al-ṣaḥāba*, vol. II, bb. *Faḍāʾil al-Ḥasan wa-l-Ḥusayn*, nn. 1380, 1381: 778–779, n. 1389: 781, n. 1396: 784, al-Ṭabarānī., *al-Muʿǧam al-kabīr*, vol. III, n. 2822: 110, vol. XII, n. 12837: 185, al-Qāḍī al-Nuʿmān., *Sharḥ al-aḫbār fī faḍāʾil al-aʾimma al-aṭhār*, vol. III, Part Twelve, n. 1110: 168, al-Ḥākim al-Nīsābūrī., *Kitāb al-mustadrak ʿalā al-ṣaḥīḥayn*, vol. IV, bk. 47 (*Kitāb taʿbīr al-ruʾyā*), n. 8281: 553, al-Ṭūsī., *al-Amālī fī-l-ḥadīṯ*, *maǧlis* 11, n. 87–640: 314–315, al-Bayhaqī., *Dalāʾil al-nubuwwa*, vol. VI, bb. *Ma ruwiya fī iḫbāri-hi bi-qatli ibn ibnati-hi ʿAbd Allāh al-Ḥusayn*: 471, al-Baġdādī., *Tārīḫ Baġdād*, vol. I, n. 3: 142, al-Ṭabarsī., *Iʿlām al-warā bi-aʿlām al-hudā*, Part Three, bb. 2: 220, 430, al-Shaǧarī., *Tartīb al-amālī al-ḫamīsiyya*, vol. I, bb. *Fī faḍl al-Ḥusayn b. ʿAlī*, n. 773: 210, al-Ḫawārizmī., *Maqtal al-Ḥusayn*, Part Two, bb. *Fī bayān ʿuqūba qātil al-Ḥusayn*, n. 32: 107, Ibn ʿAsākir., *Tārīḫ madīnat Dimashq*, vol. XIV, bb. 1566 (*al-Ḥusayn b. ʿAlī b. Abī Ṭālib b. ʿAbd al-Muṭṭalib b. Hāshim b. ʿAbd al-Manāf*): 237, Ibn Shahrāshūb., *Manāqib āl Abī Ṭālib*, vol. IV, bb. *Fī imāmat Abī ʿAbd Allāh al-Ḥusayn*: 84, al-Shāmī., *al-Durr al-naẓīm fī manāqib al-aʾimma al-lahāhīm*, bb. 5, *Faṣl fī ḏikr maqtal al-Ḥusayn b. ʿAlī*: 536–537, Ibn al-Aṯīr., *al-Kāmil fī al-tārīḫ*, vol. III, *Ḏikr maqtal al-Ḥusayn*: 303, Ibn Abī al-

As with the dreams of Umm Salama, so too the dream of Ibn ʿAbbās is of particular note, not merely because he is highly regarded both by the Sunnī and by the Shīʿa as a transmitter, but also by reason of some of the elements his vision introduces into this genre.

Both Ibn ʿAsākir and Ibn Kaṯīr preface the dream with Ibn ʿAbbās awaking from his sleep and proclaiming the words of Q. 2:156, the *al-istirǧāʿ*: «*Lo! we are Allah's and lo! unto Him we are returning*». Then he declaims: "By God, al-Ḥusayn has been killed!" When his companions interrogate him, he tells them of his vision of Muḥammad, who is carrying a bottle of blood and who says to him: "Do you know what my community after me have done? The have killed al-Ḥusayn, and this is his blood and the blood of his companions."[66] His rhetorical question echoes the constant refrain in the visits by Ǧibrīl – "your community after you will kill him."

Dam., *al-Muḫtaṣar fī tārīḫ al-Islām*: 93, Sibṭ al-Ǧawzī., *Taḏkirat al-ḫawāṣṣ al-umma bi-ḏikr ḫaṣāʾiṣ al-aʾimma*: 241, Ibn al-ʿAdīm., *Buġyat al-ṭalab fī tārīḫ Ḥalab*, Part Six: 2635, Ibn Ṭāʾūs., *al-Tashrīf bi-l-minan fī-l-taʿrīf bi-l-fitan*, bb. 34, n. 487: 334, Ibn Namā al-Ḥillī., *Muṯīr al-aḥzān wa munīr subul al-ashǧān*: 80, al-Irbilī., *Kashf al-ġumma fī maʿrifat al-aʾimma*, vol. II, Part Three: 56, al-Ṭabarī., *Ḏaḫāʾir al-ʿuqbā*, Part One, bb. 9: 253, al-Ḏahabī., *Siyar aʿlām al-nubalāʾ*, vol. III, n. 48 (*al-Ḥusayn al-Shahīd Abū ʿAbd Allāh b. ʿAlī b. Abī Ṭālib*): 315, *Bustān al-waʿiẓīn wa-riyāḍ al-sāmiʿīn*, bb. 413: 261, Ibn Kaṯīr., *al-Bidāya wa-l-nihāya*, vol. IX, bb. *Iḫbār bi-maqtal al-Ḥusayn*: 238–239, vol. XI, bb. *al-Iḫbār bi-maqtal al-Ḥusayn b. ʿAlī*: 573–574, al-Hayṯamī., *Maǧmaʿ al-zawāʾid wa-manbaʿ al-fawāʾid*, vol. IX, bk. 37 (*Kitāb al-manāqib*), bb. 95 (*Manāqib al-Ḥusayn b. ʿAlī*), n. 15141: 225–226, al-ʿAsqalānī., *al-Iṣāba fī tamyīz al-ṣaḥāba*, vol. II, n. 1729: 71, *Tahḏīb al-tahḏīb*, vol. II, *maǧlis* 2, bb. *al-Ḥāʾ*, n. 615: 355, al-Mūsawī., *Tasliyat al-muǧālis wa zīnat al-maǧālis*, vol. II: 441, al-Suyūṭī., *al-Ḫaṣāʾiṣ al-kubrā*, vol. II: 452, al-Maǧlisī., *Biḥār al-anwār*, vol. XLV, bb. 42, n. 3: 231–232, al-Iṣfahānī., *ʿAwālim al-ʿulūm wa-l-maʿārif al-aḥwāl min al-āyāt wa-l-aḫbār wa-l-aqwāl*, vol. XVII, ch. 18, bb. 4, n. 1: 510.

[66] Ibn ʿAsākir., *Tārīḫ madīnat Dimashq*, vol. XIV, bb. 1566 (*al-Ḥusayn b. ʿAlī b. Abī Ṭālib b. ʿAbd al-Muṭṭalib b. Hāshim b. ʿAbd al-Manāf*): 237, Ibn Kaṯīr., *al-Bidāya wa-l-nihāya*, vol. XI, bb. *al-Iḫbār maqtal al-Ḥusayn b. ʿAlī*: 573–4.

Although the majority of transmitters situate the dream in the middle of the day,[67] both Ibn ʿAsākir and Ibn al-Aṯīr offer reports which modify this detail. Ibn ʿAsākir stations Ibn ʿAbbās in *al-masǧid al-ḥarām*, where he sits, anticipating news about al-Ḥusayn, and omits any reference to a dream:

> Ibn ʿAbbās was sitting in *al-masǧid al-ḥarām*, anticipating news about al-Ḥusayn b. ʿAlī, until the one coming came to him and confided something to him and he proclaimed «*Lo! we are Allah's and lo! unto Him we are returning*». We said: Abū al-ʿAbbās,[68] what has happened? He replied: "A calamity terrible for us to believe! My associate tells me that he heard Ibn al-Zubayr saying: al-Ḥusayn b. ʿAlī has been killed." We did not move until Ibn al-Zubayr came to him, offered him condolences and then departed. Ibn ʿAbbās arose and went to his house; the people went to him and offered him condolences.[69]

Conversely, Ibn al-Aṯīr records Ibn ʿAbbās as saying: "I saw the Prophet the night on which al-Ḥusayn was killed." Ibn ʿAbbās awakes the next morning and informs the local populace that day of the killing of al-Ḥusayn. Both transmitters, followed by al-Shāmī, record Muḥammad saying: "This is the blood of al-Ḥusayn and his companions which I am lifting up to God Most High."[70]

---

[67] Ibn Sīrīn notes that dreams during the day are similar to dreams at night (al-Buḫārī., *Ṣaḥīḥ*, vol. IX, bk. 91 (*Kitāb al-taʿbīr*), bb. 12: 95); such 'day visions' are found in other, more ancient cultures and civilizations, seen, for example, in the midday dream of Pharaoh Thutmose IV (d. c. 1391 BC) in which the sun god addresses him.

[68] Ibn ʿAbbās was himself the father of a firstborn son named al-ʿAbbās.

[69] Ibn ʿAsākir., *Tārīḫ madīnat Dimashq*, vol. XIV, bb. 1566 (*al-Ḥusayn b. ʿAlī b. Abī Ṭālib b. ʿAbd al-Muṭṭalib b. Hāshim b. ʿAbd al-Manāf*): 238–239. Ibn ʿAbbās goes on to highlight the *schadenfreude* of Ibn Zubayr, even in the condolences he has offered, since, as Abū Miḫnaf notes, he had, for his own political interests, encouraged al-Ḥusayn to go to Kūfa in an attempt to get him out of the way. Cf. Abū Miḫnaf., *Maqtal al-Ḥusayn*: 89.

[70] Ibn ʿAsākir., *Tārīḫ madīnat Dimashq*, vol. XIV, bb. 1566 (*al-Ḥusayn b. ʿAlī b. Abī Ṭālib b. ʿAbd al-Muṭṭalib b. Hāshim b. ʿAbd al-Manāf*): 238–239,

While Ibn Kaṯīr and al-Shāmī put into the hands of Muḥammad a glass bottle (*zuǧāǧa*), the majority use the word for a glass vial (*qārūra*), so that it makes its first appearance in the hands of Muḥammad rather than of Umm Salama. Al-Irbilī doubles the number and gives the Prophet two vials: "I saw the Messenger of God in a dream, dishevelled and dust-covered, and he had two glass vials containing blood."[71] Al-Irbilī, al-Shāmī and Ibn ʿAsākir before him, but few others beside them, also introduces the curiously extended waiting period of twenty-four days between the dream of al-ʿAbbās and the confirmation of the news of al-Ḥusayn's death – "and they did not wait for more than twenty-four days until the news came to them that he had been killed on that day and at that hour."[72] Other texts, especially those concerning Umm Salama, suggest the news arrived more speedily in Medina (the next morning, according to al-Qāḍī al-Nuʿmān and Ibn Ṭāʾūs).[73]

Ibn al-Aṯīr., *al-Kāmil fī al-tārīḫ*, vol. III, *Ḏikr maqtal al-Ḥusayn*: 303, al-Shāmī., *al-Durr al-naẓīm fī manāqib al-aʾimma al-lahāhīm*, bb. 5: 536–537. Cf. also Ibn Ṭūsī, *al-Amālī*, *maǧlis* 11, n. 87–640: 315.

[71] al-Irbilī., *Kashf al-ġumma fī maʿrifat al-aʾimma*, vol. II, Part Three, *Faṣl fī ḏikr maqtal al-Ḥusayn b. ʿAlī*: 56. For the idea of two glass vials instead of one, cf. also al-Rāwandī., *al-Ḫarāʾiǧ wa-l-ǧarāʾiḥ fī-l-muʿǧizāt*, vol. I, bb. 4, n. 7: 253, al-Ḥillī al-ʿAllāma., *Iṯbāt al-hudāt bi-l-nuṣūṣ wa-l-muʿǧizāt*, vol. III, Part Eight, n. 31: 46, al-Maǧlisī., *Biḥār al-anwār*, vol. XLV, bb. 37, n 27: 89, al-Iṣfahānī., *ʿAwālim al-ʿulūm wa-l-maʿārif al-aḥwāl min al-āyāt wa-l-aḫbār wa-l-aqwāl*, vol. XVII, ch. 12, bb. 4, n. 7: 157. Al-Haytamī seems uncertain of the content of the container: "He had a glass vial containing blood he had collected, or it contained something he had zealously sought." Cf. al-Haytamī., *Maǧmaʿ al-zawāʾid wa-manbaʿ al-fawāʾid*, vol. IX, bk. 37 (*Kitāb al-manāqib*), bb. 95 (*Manāqib al-Ḥusayn b. ʿAlī*), n. 15141: 225–226.

[72] Ibn Kaṯīr., *al-Bidāya wa-l-nihāya*, vol. XI, bb. *al-Iḫbār maqtal al-Ḥusayn b. ʿAlī*: 573–4, al-Shāmī., *al-Durr al-naẓīm fī manāqib al-aʾimma al-lahāhīm*, bb. 5: 536–537, al-Irbilī., *Kashf al-ġumma fī maʿrifat al-aʾimma*, vol. II, Part Three, *Faṣl fī ḏikr maqtal al-Ḥusayn b. ʿAlī*: 56.

[73] al-Qāḍī al-Nuʿmān., *Sharḥ al-aḫbār fī faḍāʾil al-aʾimma al-aṭhār*, vol. III, Part Twelve, n. 1106: 167, Ibn Ṭāʾūs., *al-Ṭarāʾif fī maʿrifat maḏāhib al-*

While Ibn Ṭāʾūs highlights Muḥammad's psychological state ("It has disquieted me since the day I gathered it"),[74] Ibn Shahrāshūb, for his part, emphasizes the Prophet's bedraggled state and adds the theme of litigation:

> In the report of Ibn ʿAbbās: He saw the Prophet in his dream following the killing of al-Ḥusayn, his face dusty, barefoot and weeping, hugging the opening of his shirt around himself and reciting this verse: «*Deem not that Allah is unaware of what the wicked do*».[75] He said: "I went to Karbalāʾ and collected the blood of al-Ḥusayn from the ground. It is in my protection and I am on my way to litigate with them before my Lord."[76]

If the dream of Ibn ʿAbbās is portentous, a less conventional genre, found chiefly although not exclusively among the Shīʿī transmitters, concerns dreams of torturous punishment and the recurring plea of the dreamer that he or she had nothing directly to do with al-Ḥusayn's death. The recipients of these visions are almost always soldiers from Yazīd's army, or camp followers, tradesmen and artisans who worked for the military machine. This category of dreams is dominated by four harrowing castigations: being made to drink pitch, the temporary or permanent loss of one's sight, an alteration in one's physical appearance and a loss of hope in God's forgiveness.

Al-Ṭūsī, Ibn ʿAsākir and Ibn Shahrāshūb record the first of these uncommon tales, of a man whose body odour is a clue to the crime he has committed:

ṭawāʾif, vol. I, n. 292: 203. The number twenty-four holds some significance for the recommended fast in Rağab and and Shaʿban.

[74] Ibn Ṭāʾūs., *al-Tashrīf bi-l-minan fī-l-taʿrīf bi-l-fitan*, bb. 34, n. 487: 334. This work, which is not listed by Brockelmann in his entry on Ibn Ṭāʾūs, has also been published under the title *Malāḥim wal-l-fitan (fī ẓuhūr al-ġāʾib al-muntaẓar)*. Cf. KOHLBERG E., *A Medieval Scholar at Work: Ibn Ṭāwūs and his Library*, Brill, Leiden 1992: 60–61.

[75] Q. 14:42.

[76] Ibn Shahrāshūb., *Manāqib āl Abī Ṭālib*, vol. IV, bb. *Fī imāmat Abī ʿAbd Allāh al-Ḥusayn*: 84, al-Mūsawī., *Tasliyat al-muğālis wa zīnat al-mağālis*, vol. II: 441.

> We were informed by al-Faḍl b. Zubayr, who said: I was sitting [with someone] when a man approached and sat down with him; his odour was that of pitch, so he said to him: "Have you been selling pitch?" He replied: "I have never sold it!" So he said: "Then what is that smell?" He answered: "I was one of those who was present with the army of ʿUmar b. Saʿd. I was selling them iron pegs, and when night fell, I went to bed and in my dream, I saw the Messenger of God, and ʿAlī with him: ʿAlī was giving a drink to those killed among the companions of al-Ḥusayn. I said to him: Give me a drink, but he refused. So, I said: Messenger of God, command him to give me to drink, and he replied: But you are not one of those who assisted us! I answered: Messenger of God! By God, I neither struck with a sword, not stabbed with a lance, nor pierced with an arrow, but I sold iron pegs to them! He said: ʿAlī, give him to drink, and he gave me a bowl full of pitch. I drank pitch from it, and I did not stop urinating pitch for days! Even when the urine ceased, the odour continued in my body!"[77]

The refrain "I neither struck with a sword, not stabbed with a lance, nor pierced with an arrow," or, in some texts "by God I did not fight them" reverberates through all these stories; the actual crime will, eventually, be highlighted: that this seller of nails or iron pegs, even though he did not physically fight, augmented the numbers of those arrayed against al-Ḥusayn, and is thereby guilty of his death. It creates the concept of 'guilt by association', the notion of a widely shared guilt, not restricted to those who struck a physical blow, in a sense parallel to the aspect of Shīʿī piety that enables the

---

[77] al-Ṭūsī., *al-Ṯāqib fi-l-manāqib*, bb. 6, n. 6/278: 335–336, Ibn ʿAsākir., *Tārīḫ madīnat Dimashq*, vol. XIV, bb. 1566 (*al-Ḥusayn b. ʿAlī b. Abī Ṭālib b. ʿAbd al-Muṭṭalib b. Hāshim b. ʿAbd al-Manāf*): 258, Ibn Shahrāshūb., *Manāqib āl Abī Ṭālib*, vol. IV, Part Four, bb. *Fī imāmat Abī ʿAbd Allāh al-Ḥusayn*: 58, Ibn al-Ğawzī., *Bustān al-waʿiẓīn wa-riyāḍ al-sāmiʿīn*, bb. 416: 263, Ibn al-ʿAdīm., *Buġyat al-ṭalab fī tārīḫ Ḥalab*, Part Six: 2642–2643, al-Baḥrānī., *Madīnat al-maʿāğiz fī muʿğizāt al-aʾimma al-aṭhār*, vol. IV, Part Four, bb. 3, n. 171/1118: 111.

faithful adherent to share al-Ḥusayn's struggle often simply by the desire to have fought alongside him.

In his *Maqtal*, al-Ḫawārizmī draws attention to a different crime:

> Al-Ḥasan al-Baṣrī said: Sitting with us was a distressed elder, from whom came an odour of pitch. We asked him about this, and he said: "I was among those who blocked al-Ḥusayn b. ʿAlī from the water. I saw in a dream as though the people had congregated.[78] I was stricken with a severe thirst, and looked for water, and there were the Prophet, ʿAlī, Fāṭima, al-Ḥasan and al-Ḥusayn at the Pool. I asked a drink from the Messenger of God, and he said: Give him a drink! But no one gave me a drink. He said it a second time, but no one gave me a drink. He said it a third time, and was told: Messenger of God! He was among those who blocked al-Ḥusayn from the water! So, he said: Give him pitch to drink! And I awoke, urinating pitch. I cannot even eat food without experiencing the odour of pitch from it, or drink without the taste of pitch in my mouth!"[79]

Al-Ḫawārizmī combines a number of elements to underscore not only the severity of a particular crime, and one that characterized the day of Karbalāʾ, but also the ruthlessness of the penalty; not merely banishment from life-giving waters of the Pool but being forced to drink something radically different from those vivifying waters. In Shīʿī eschatology, the Pool (*al-ḥawḍ*) is *al-Kawṯar*, the great symbol of the authority of Muḥammad and his descendants over all creation. On the Day of Resurrection, the 'day of great thirst', ʿAlī will be given authority over this Pool, to give its enlivening waters to his adherents and supporters, and to send his enemies away thirsty. This pool of *al-Kawṯar*, a concept drawn not as much from the Qurʾān as from the corpus of *aḥādīṯ*, is the concrete symbol of the prerogatives given by God to the Prophet's family. Its waters

---

[78] On the Day of Congregation (*yawm al-ḥashr*).

[79] al-Ḫawārizmī., *Maqtal al-Ḥusayn*, Part Two, bb. *Fī bayān ʿuqūba qātil al-Ḥusayn*, n. 50: 116–117.

cleanse the blood and tears of the People of the House and of all who cling faithfully to them.[80]

However, a punishment more vehement than being forced to drink pitch has its roots in earlier texts, with Ibn ʿAsākir offering the version with the sparsest detail:

> On the authority of Abū al-Naḍr al-Ǧarmī, who said: I saw a man devoid of sight and I asked him about the reason for the loss of his vision. He answered: "I was one of those who was present with the army of ʿUmar b. Saʿd. When night came, I went to sleep, and I saw the Messenger of God in a dream; in his hands was a brass vessel full of blood, with a quill pen in the blood. He came to the companions of ʿUmar b. Saʿd, took the quill pen and wrote with it between their eyes. He came to me, and I said: Messenger of God, by God I have neither struck with a sword, not stabbed with a lance, nor pierced with an arrow. He replied: Did you not increase the number of our enemies? He inserted his finger into the blood – the index and the middle finger – and reached out with them for my eyes, and when I awoke in the morning my sight was gone."[81]

---

[80] Cf. AYOUB M., *Redemptive Suffering in Islam. A Study of the Devotional Aspects of ʿAshura in Twelver Shiʿism*, 1978: 198, 200–201, CLOHESSY C., "The Face of Islām Flushed. The Karbalāʾ Event" in *Encounter*, n. 285, Pontificio Istituto di Studi Arabi e d'Islamistica, Rome, June 2002.

[81] Ibn ʿAsākir., *Tārīḫ madīnat Dimashq*, vol. XIV, bb. 1566 (*al-Ḥusayn b. ʿAlī b. Abī Ṭālib b. ʿAbd al-Muṭṭalib b. Hāshim b. ʿAbd al-Manāf*): 259. Cf. also al-Qāḍī al-Nuʿmān., *Sharḥ al-aḫbār fī faḍāʾil al-aʾimma al-aṭhār*, vol. III, Part Twelve, n. 1120: 171, n. 1123: 174, Ibn ʿAsākir., *Tārīḫ madīnat Dimashq*, vol. XIV, bb. 1566 (*al-Ḥusayn b. ʿAlī b. Abī Ṭālib b. ʿAbd al-Muṭṭalib b. Hāshim b. ʿAbd al-Manāf*): 259, Ibn Shahrāshūb., *Manāqib āl Abī Ṭālib*, vol. IV, Part Four, bb. *Fī imāmat Abī ʿAbd Allāh al-Ḥusayn*: 58, Ibn Ṭāʾūs., *Kitāb al-luhūf fī qatlā al-ṭufūf*: 80–81, Ibn al-ʿAdīm., *Buġyat al-ṭalab fī tārīḫ Ḥalab*, Part Six: 2642, Ibn Namā al-Ḥillī., *Muṯīr al-aḥzān wa munīr subul al-ashǧān*: 80, al-Irbilī., *Kashf al-ġumma fī maʿrifat al-aʾimma*, vol. II, Part Three: 57, al-Baḥrānī., *Madīnat al-maʿāǧiz fī muʿǧizāt al-aʾimma al-aṭhār*, vol. IV, Part Four, bb. 3, n. 154/1101: 83, n. 158/1105: 86, n. 167/1114: 100–101, n. 168/1115: 101–102, al-Maǧlisī., *Biḥār al-anwār*, vol. XLV, bb. 46, n. 3:

All the transmitters follow the same pattern, with a varying degree of detail. The loss of sight is portrayed in these instances as unanticipated and precipitous, leading to the questions about the cause which initiate the narrative: "A man entered the evening healthy of life and reached the morning blind," writes al-Qāḍī al-Nuʿmān, while Ibn Namā al-Ḥillī emphasizes that the sight once enjoyed by the interrogee had disappeared.[82] While in Ibn ʿAsākir the victim merely establishes that he had been present at Karbalāʾ ("present with the army of ʿUmar b. Saʿd," he notes, but with no further detail, and in Ibn Ṭāʾūs and al-Baḥrānī after him he claims nothing more than to have witnessed the killing of al-Ḥusayn), in the majority of transmitters he immediately protests his innocence ("I neither struck with a sword, not thrust with a lance, nor shot with an arrow"), before having been accused of anything. Central to the vision is the person of Muḥammad, either holding, or seated in front of, a container of blood. While Ibn Ṭāʾūs, Ibn Namā and al-Baḥrānī identify this as the blood of al-Ḥusayn,[83] in al-Qāḍī al-Nuʿmān the basin seems to contain the blood of al-Ḥusayn's killers who are themselves now being killed in retaliation.[84] While in Ibn ʿAsākir, Ibn Shahrāshūb, al-Irbilī and al-Baḥrānī the dreamer protests his innocence without provocation,[85] in most other texts he is

---

302–303, n. 5: 306, al-Iṣfahānī., *ʿAwālim al-ʿulūm wa-l-maʿārif al-aḥwāl min al-āyāt wa-l-aḫbār wa-l-aqwāl*, vol. XVII, ch. 22, bb. 4, n. 1: 624–625.

[82] al-Qāḍī al-Nuʿmān., *Sharḥ al-aḫbār fī faḍāʾil al-aʾimma al-aṭhār*, vol. III, Part Twelve, n. 1120: 171, Ibn Namā al-Ḥillī., *Muṯīr al-aḥzān wa munīr subul al-ashǧān*: 80.

[83] Ibn Ṭāʾūs., *Kitāb al-luhūf fī qatlā al-ṭufūf*: 80–81, Ibn Namā al-Ḥillī., *Muṯīr al-aḥzān wa munīr subul al-ashǧān*: 80, al-Baḥrānī., *Madīnat al-maʿāǧiz fī muʿǧizāt al-aʾimma al-aṭhār*, vol. IV, Part Four, bb. 3, n. 158/1105: 86 n. 168/1115: 101–102, al-Maǧlisī., *Biḥār al-anwār*, vol. XLV, bb. 46, n. 5: 306.

[84] al-Qāḍī al-Nuʿmān., *Sharḥ al-aḫbār fī faḍāʾil al-aʾimma al-aṭhār*, vol. III, Part Twelve, n. 1120: 171.

[85] al-Irbilī., *Kashf al-ġumma fī maʿrifat al-aʾimma*, vol. II, Part Three: 57, Ibn ʿAsākir., *Tārīḫ madīnat Dimashq*, vol. XIV, bb. 1566 (*al-Ḥusayn b. ʿAlī b. Abī Ṭālib b. ʿAbd al-Muṭṭalib b. Hāshim b. ʿAbd al-Manāf*): 259, Ibn Shahrāshūb., *Manāqib āl Abī Ṭālib*, vol. IV, Part Four, bb. *Fī imāmat Abī ʿAbd Allāh al-Ḥusayn*: 58, al-Baḥrānī., *Madīnat al-maʿāǧiz fī muʿǧizāt al-*

interrogated ("were you among those who killed al-Ḥusayn?")[86] or accused ("enemy of God, you have violated my sanctity, killed my family and have not respected my right! You did what you did!").[87] The nature of the dreamer's crime – that he increased the numbers arrayed against al-Ḥusayn – is clearly underscored by most transmitters, although in al-Irbilī he anticipates this charge and denies it before it is made ("nor did I augment their number")[88] while in al-Baḥrānī, his very origins are a problem ("are you not a Kūfan? Why did you not support my son? Why did you not answer his call?").[89]

Using either a quill pen or his finger,[90] Muḥammad then anoints or smears the eyes of the dreamer, or simply motions towards them, leading to blindness, quite patently a lesser punishment than having one's throat slit, which is apparent in a transmission from al-Qāḍī al-Nuʿmān.[91] Transmitting from Ibn Rimāḥ, al-Ḫawārizmī narrates an epic tale about a blind man:

> I met a blind man who had witnessed the killing of al-Ḥusayn. People were coming to him and asking him the reason for the disappearance of his sight. He said: "I witnessed his killing as

---

aʾimma al-aṭhār, vol. IV, Part Four, bb. 3, n. 154/1101: 83, n. 158/1105: 86, n. 167/1114: 100–101, al-Mağlisī., *Biḥār al-anwār*, vol. XLV, bb. 46, n. 3: 302–303.

[86] al-Qāḍī al-Nuʿmān., *Sharḥ al-aḫbār fī faḍāʾil al-aʾimma al-aṭhār*, vol. III, Part Twelve, n. 1120: 171, n. 1123: 174

[87] Ibn Namā al-Ḥillī., *Muṯīr al-aḥzān wa munīr subul al-ashğān*: 80, al-Baḥrānī., *Madīnat al-maʿāğiz fī muʿğizāt al-aʾimma al-aṭhār*, vol. IV, Part Four, bb. 3, n. 168/1115: 101–102, al-Mağlisī., *Biḥār al-anwār*, vol. XLV, bb. 46, n. 5: 306.

[88] al-Irbilī., *Kashf al-ġumma fī maʿrifat al-aʾimma*, vol. II, Part Three: 57.

[89] al-Baḥrānī., *Madīnat al-maʿāğiz fī muʿğizāt al-aʾimma al-aṭhār*, vol. IV, Part Four, bb. 3, n. 167/1114: 100–101.

[90] In a dream "as though the resurrection had already happened and the people were already gathered," al-Qāḍī al-Nuʿmān records one man who says that Muḥammad "put his finger into my eyes and I became blind" (al-Qāḍī al-Nuʿmān., *Sharḥ al-aḫbār fī faḍāʾil al-aʾimma al-aṭhār*, vol. III, Part Twelve, n. 1123: 174).

[91] Op. cit., vol. III, Part Twelve, n. 1120: 171.

the tenth of ten,[92] except that I did not strike or thrust or shoot. After he had been killed, I returned to my house and prayed late in the evening, and then I went to sleep. Someone came to me in my dream and said to me: Answer the Messenger of God![93] And there was the Prophet, sitting in the desert,[94] his forearms uncovered, grasping a lance and with a leather mat in front of him.[95] An angel, standing in front of him, in his hand a sword of fire, killed my companions;[96] each time he struck one of them a blow, his soul burst into flame. I approached the Prophet, knelt in front of him and said: Peace

---

[92] Possibly a reference to the soldiers around al-Ḥusayn at the moment of his death. A number of transmitters report a general reluctance, with few of the soldiers attacking al-Ḥusayn particularly eager to kill him, and holding back in the hope that this task would fall to someone else.

[93] Ibn Ṭāʾūs adds: "for he is calling you," while Ibn al-Ǧawzī, Ibn Ṭāʾūs, Ibn Namā, al-Baḥrānī and al-Maǧlisī all add: "What do I have to do with him?" and "he seized me (by my collar)" or "he pulled at me fiercely" or "he dragged me." In al-Baḥrānī, this fierce seizing hold of the dreamer is repeated and then "he rushed me along with him" (al-Baḥrānī., *Madīnat al-maʿāǧiz fī muʿǧizāt al-aʾimma al-aṭhār*, vol. IV, Part Four, bb. 3, n. 158/1105: 86).

[94] Ibn al-Ǧawzī and al-Baḥrānī read 'prayer niche' (Ibn al-Ǧawzī., *Bustān al-waʿiẓīn wa-riyāḍ al-sāmiʿīn*, bb. 415: 262, al-Baḥrānī., *Madīnat al-maʿāǧiz fī muʿǧizāt al-aʾimma al-aṭhār*, vol. IV, Part Four, bb. 3, n. 158/1105: 86).

[95] Both Wehr and Lane associate such a leather mat (*naṭʿ*) with death; it could be used as a tablecloth upon which to spread food, or as mat upon which to play chess or, in the case of executions, a place to receive the head of a person. Cf. LANE E.W., *An Arabic-English Lexicon*, vol. VIII, 1968: 3034, WEHR H., *A Dictionary of Modern Written Arabic*, 1980: 1142. Al-Baḥrānī replaces "grasping a lance" with "overcome by distress" and in another transmission adds of Muḥammad "his face reddened and frowning" (al-Baḥrānī., *Madınat al-maʿağiz fı muʿǧizāt al-aʾimma al-aṭhār*, vol. IV, Part Four, bb. 3, n. 158/1105: 86, n. 168/1115: 101–102).

[96] In Ibn Ṭāʾūs and al-Baḥrānī number these companions as nine. In al-Baḥrānī they keep coming back to life and are killed seven times (al-Baḥrānī., *Madīnat al-maʿāǧiz fī muʿǧizāt al-aʾimma al-aṭhār*, vol. IV, Part Four, bb. 3, n. 158/1105: 86).

> be with you, Messenger of God! He did not reply to me, but waited for a long time. Then he raised his head and said: ʿAbd Allāh,[97] you have violated my honour, killed my family, not respected my right, and have done what you have done! I said to him: Messenger of God, by God, I neither struck with a sword, nor thrust with a lance, nor shot with an arrow! He replied: What you say is true,[98] but you increased the multitude. Come close to me! I drew near to him, there was a basin filled with blood, and he said: This is the blood of my son al-Ḥusayn. He smeared (my eyelids) with it and I awoke, unable to see a thing since then."[99]

Referring their readers to Ibn Ḥanbal's *Faḍāʾil al-ṣaḥāba*, Ibn Baṭṭa's *al-Ibāna* and al-Dāraquṭnī's *Ǧāmiʿ*, Ibn Shahrāshūb and al-Mağlisī transmit a narrative in which the angel standing near Muḥammad plays a violent and retributive role:

> It was reported by Qurra b. Aʿyan, on the authority of his maternal uncle who said: I was with Abū Rağāʾ al-ʿUṭāridī, who said: "Do not make mention the People of the House except to speak well. A man came to us after being present at Karbalāʾ; he was cursing al-Ḥusayn, when God dropped two stars on him and his eyes became blind. ʿAbd Allāh b. Rayyāḥ al-

[97] Or, in other texts, "enemy of God" (Ibn Ṭāʾūs., *Kitāb al-luhūf fī qatlā al-ṭufūf*: 81, al-Mağlisī., *Biḥār al-anwār*, vol. XLV, bb. 46, n. 5: 306).

[98] In al-Irbili, "You lie! You took pleasure in the killing of al-Ḥusayn" (al-Irbilī., *Kashf al-ġumma fī maʿrifat al-aʾimma*, vol. II, Part Three: 57).

[99] al-Ḫawārizmī., *Maqtal al-Ḥusayn*, Part Two, bb. *Fī bayān ʿuqūba qātil al-Ḥusayn*, n. 52: 117–118, Ibn Shahrāshūb., *Manāqib āl Abī Ṭālib*, vol. IV, Part Four, bb. *Fī imāma Abī ʿAbd Allāh al-Ḥusayn*: 59, Ibn al-Ǧawzī., *Bustān al-waʿiẓīn wa-riyāḍ al-sāmiʿīn*, bb. 415: 262, Ibn Ṭāʾūs., *Kitāb al-luhūf fī qatlā al-ṭufūf*: 80–81, Ibn Namā al-Ḥillī., *Muṯīr al-aḥzān wa munīr subul al-ashǧān*: 80, al-Baḥrānī., *Madīnat al-maʿāǧiz fī muʿǧizāt al-aʾimma al-aṭhār*, vol. IV, Part Four, bb. 3, n. 158/1105: 86, n. 168/1115: 101–102, al-Mağlisī., *Biḥār al-anwār*, vol. XLV, bb. 46, n. 5: 306, al-Iṣfahānī., *ʿAwālim al-ʿulūm wa-l-maʿārif al-aḥwāl min al-āyāt wa-l-aḫbār wa-l-aqwāl*, vol. XVII, ch. 22, bb. 4, n. 1: 625.

> Qāḍī[100] asked what had blinded him and he answered: I was present at Karbalā᾽ but I did not fight. I went to sleep and I saw a formidable person, who said to me: Answer the Messenger of God! I replied: I am not able. So he dragged me to the Messenger of God, whom I found sad and holding a lance in his hand. Spread out in front of him was a leather mat and standing in front of him was an angel holding a sword of fire. He struck the necks of the people, and fire fell among them and burnt them; then they were brought to life and he killed them again. Then I said: Peace be upon you, Messenger of God! By God, I neither struck with a sword, nor thrust with a lance, nor shot an arrow! The Prophet said: Did you not increase the multitude? He greeted me with peace and took blood from a basin and smeared me with it. My eyes burned, and when I awoke, I was blind."[101]

In the landscape of Islamic eschatology, with its range of prescribed punishments, the drinking of pitch or loss of sight pales in comparison to the chastisements of the Fire, from which, says the Qur᾽ān of those condemned there, «*they will not come forth*».[102] These appalling penalties include festering water (Q. 14:16), garments of fire, boiling fluids and iron hooks (Q. 22:19, 21), fetters and chains around the neck, raging fire and choking food (Q. 73:12–13). In the Qur᾽ān, these punishments are threatened specifically against unbe-

---

[100] The name of Qurra b. Aʿyan is not diffused throughout the Shīʿī texts, but is found specifically in this story of burning eyes going blind. It may be a small play on words with the Qur᾽ānic phrase to 'gladden' or 'console' or 'cool' 'the eye' (cf. Q. 19:26, Q. 20:40, Q. 28:9, 13). The man whom Ibn Shahrāshūb calls ʿAbd Allāh b. Rayyāḥ al-Qāḍī is variously named Ibn Riyāḥ by Ibn Ṭā᾽ūs and Ibn Namā, as al-Ḥurr b. Riyāḥ al-Qāḍī by al-Baḥrānī, as al-Ḥaddā᾽ b. Rabāḥ al-Qāḍī by Ibn al-Ǧawzī, as ʿAbd Allāh b. Rabāḥ al-Qāḍī by al-Maǧlisī and as Ibn Rimāḥ by al-Ḫawārizmī.

[101] Ibn Shahrāshūb., *Manaqib al Abi Talib*, vol. IV, Part Four, bb. *Fī imāma Abī ʿAbd Allāh al-Ḥusayn*: 58, al-Baḥrānī., *Madīnat al-maʿāǧiz fī muʿǧizāt al-a᾽imma al-aṭhār*, vol. IV, Part Four, bb. 3, n. 154/1101: 83 (in much reduced form), al-Maǧlisī., *Biḥār al-anwār*, vol. XLV, bb. 46, n. 3: 302–303.

[102] Q. 5:37.

lievers, further defined as those who reject God's revelation and His messengers, as distinct from the killers of al-Ḥusayn and those associated with them (who are, in Ǧibrīl's constant refrain, members of Muḥammad's own community). Whoever the dreamer turns out to be – ironmonger or merchant, blocker of water, non-combatant soldier, transporter of heads or killer of a companion – his punishment seems to fall into an entirely different category, not delayed until the Afterlife but already begun. A third physical chastisement concerns the blackening of the face,[103] in a tale told by Ibn Bābawayh:

> On the authority of al-Qāsim b. al-Aṣbaġ b. Nubāta who said: There came to us a man from the Banū Dārim, who was among those who had witnessed the killing of al-Ḥusayn. Even though he was a handsome man and was very white, he had a very black face. I said to him: I barely recognise you because of the change of your colour! He answered: "I killed a man from among the companions of al-Ḥusayn, the white mark of prostration perceptible between his eyes, and I brought his head. Al-Qāsim said: I saw him on a horse of his, exuberant; he had affixed the head to its breast but it was hitting against its knee. He continued: I said to my father that if he had lifted the head a little, one would not have seen what the horse was doing to it. He replied to me: My son, what is being done to him[104] is worse: for he told me: I have not slept at night since I killed him, but that he comes to me in my dream, seizing me by my

[103] It is of note, in the context of the blackening of the face, that Lamoreaux records that the caliph al-Mahdī (d. 169/785) had a dream in which his face turned black, only to be told by Ibrāhīm b. ʿAbd Allāh al-Kirmānī (c. late 2nd/8th century), a famous dabbler in the meaning of dreams, that it meant the birth of a daughter (LAMOREAUX J.C., *The Early Muslim Tradition of Dream Interpretation*, State University of New York Press, Albany 2002: 25).

[104] While Ibn Bābawayh's text reads *ma yuṣnaʿu bī*, al-Maǧlisī's reads *ma yuṣnaʿu bi-hi*; the latter seems to make more sense. In his *ʿAwālim*, al-Iṣfahānī follows al-Maǧlisī. Cf. al-Maǧlisī., *Biḥār al-anwār*, vol. XLV, bb. 46, n. 8: 308, al-Iṣfahānī., *ʿAwālim al-ʿulūm wa-l-maʿārif al-aḥwāl min al-āyāt wa-l-aḫbār wa-l-aqwāl*, vol. IV, bb. 4, n. 5: 627.

> shoulder and leading me, saying: Hurry! Then he dashes along with me to Hell and flings me down and I scream."[105] The narrator went on: A female neighbour[106] of his heard this and said: "His screams stop us from sleeping at night!" He said: I went in the company of some of the youth of the city; we came to his wife and asked her. She said: "He revealed himself openly and told you the truth."[107]

Purportedly transmitting from Abū al-Farağ al-Iṣfahānī's *al-Maqātil*, al-Mağlisī repeats this story of a very handsome and pale man of the Banū Abān b. Dārim, adding that the companion he killed was al-ʿAbbās b. ʿAlī.[108] Al-Baḥrānī also tells of a man who is interrogated about his white head, which contrasts starkly with his black body and face. The man turns out to have been part of Ibn Ziyād's army and one of those who helped to transport the heads of the companions of al-Ḥusayn; he is punished not only with this physical deformity, but also, "I see in my dream that the head speaks to me all night and flings me in the Fire."[109] For his part, al-Ṭūsī moves the reader away from the field of Karbalāʾ and introduces

---

105 Al-Mağlisī substitutes 'I scream' with 'until I awake in the morning'.

106 While Ibn Bābawayh's text, like those of Ibn Shahrāshūb and al-Baḥrānī, reads 'female neighbour' (*ğāra*), al-Mağlisī transmits it as 'servant girl' (*ğāriyya*). Subsequently, Ibn Bābawayh's transmission then reads in error 'he said' instead of 'she said'.

107 Ibn Bābawayh., *Ṯawāb al-aʿmāl wa iʿqāb al-aʿmāl*: 219, Ibn Shahrāshūb., *Manāqib āl Abī Ṭālib*, vol. IV, bb. *Fī imāmat Abī ʿAbd Allāh al-Ḥusayn*, *faṣl fī āyāti-hi baʿda wafāti-hi*: 58, al-Baḥrānī., *Madīnat al-maʿāğiz fī muʿğizāt al-aʾimma al-aṭhār*, vol. IV, Part Four, bb. 3, n. 153/1100: 83, al-Mağlisī., *Biḥār al-anwār*, vol. XLV, bb. 46, n. 8: 308, al-Iṣfahānī., *ʿAwālim al-ʿulūm wa-l-maʿārif al-aḥwāl min al-āyāt wa-l-aḫbār wa-l-aqwāl*, vol. XVII, ch. 22, bb. 4, n. 5: 627.

108 al-Mağlisī., *Biḥār al-anwār*, vol. XLV, bb. 46, n. 5: 306. The editor refers the reader to *Maqātil al-ṭālibiyyīn*: 86, as well as to Ibn Shahrāshūb., *Manāqib āl Abī Ṭālib*, vol. IV, bb. *Fī imāmat Abī ʿAbd Allāh al-Ḥusayn*, *faṣl fī āyāti-hi baʿda wafāti-hi*: 58).

109 al-Baḥrānī., *Madīnat al-maʿāğiz fī muʿğizāt al-aʾimma al-aṭhār*, vol. IV, Part Four, bb. 3, n. 182/1129: 120.

into the narrative a fresh element, the story of ʿUbayd Allāh b. Yaḥyā b. Ḫāqān who becomes secretary to Hārūn al-Muʿarrī, one of the Sulṭān's commanders. Of his master, Ibn Ḫāqān says:

> His whole body was intensely white, as were his hands and his feet, but his face was intensely black, as if it were pitch, and on account of that it would burst with stinking pus. The narrator said: When we were on intimate terms, I asked him about the blackness of his face, but he refused to inform me. Then he fell ill with a sickness that would kill him. I sat down and asked him, and I noticed that he would have preferred to keep the matter secret. So, I guaranteed the secrecy, and he told me, saying: "Al-Mutawakkil sent al-Dīğaz[110] and I to excavate the grave of al-Ḥusayn and to channel water through it. When I had decided to depart and make the journey to the region, I saw the Messenger of God in a dream, and he said: Do not depart with al-Dīğaz, and do not do what you have been ordered to the grave of al-Ḥusayn. In the morning they came to

[110] Ibrāhīm al-Dīğaz receives substantial commentary in the texts as one who interfered with the grave of al-Ḥusayn, although the motif of a dream does not always occur as part of the narrative. Cf. for e.g. al-Ḫaṣībī., *al-Hidāya al-Kubrā*, bb. 13: 323, al-Ṭūsī., *al-Amālī fī-l-ḥadīṯ*, *mağlis* 11, n. 100–653: 326, nn. 100–654, 102–655: 327, Ibn Shahrāshūb., *Manāqib āl Abī Ṭālib*, vol. IV, bb. *Fī imāmat Abī ʿAbd Allāh al-Ḥusayn*, *faṣl fī āyāti-hi baʿda wafāti-hi*: 64–65, al-Mūsawī., *Tasliyat al-mağālis wa zīnat al-mağālis*, vol. II, Part Three, *mağlis* 9: 475–477, al-Ḥillī al-ʿAllāma., *Iṯbāt al-hudāt bi-l-nuṣūṣ wa-l-muʿğizāt*, vol. I, Part One, bb. 8, n. 225: 362, vol. IV, Part Four, bb. 15, nn. 13–14: 40–41, al-Mağlisī., *Biḥār al-anwār*, vol. XLV, bb. 50, nn. 2–4: 394–396, al-Ğazāʾirī., *Riyāḍ al-abrār fī manāqib al-aʾimma al-aṭhār*, vol. I, Part One: 304–305, al-Iṣfahānī., *ʿAwālim al-ʿulūm wa-l-maʿārif al-aḥwāl min al-āyāt wa-l-aḫbār wa-l-aqwāl*, vol. XVII, ch. 27, bb. 3, nn. 1–3: 724–726. As a contrast to al-Dīğaz's behaviour, al-Mağlisī transmits on the authority of Ğaʿfar al-Ṣādiq: "Whoever, in the middle of Ramaḍān, visits Imām al-Ḥusayn and, after the night prayer (*al-ʿishāʾ*) prays ten *rakʿāt* at his grave, saying in each *rakʿa*, after *al-ḥamd*, *sūrat al-tawḥīd* ten times, will not die before he sees in his dream a number of angels bringing him the good tidings of the Garden and a number of angels safeguarding him from the Fire" (al-Mağlisī., *Zād al-maʿād*, bb. 3: 121).

> impel me to make the journey; so I journeyed with them until Karbalāʾ and did what al-Mutawakkil had ordered. I saw the Prophet in a dream and he said: Did I not order you not to depart with them and not to do their work? But you did not assent, and you have done what they have done! Then he beat me and spat in my face, and my face became black as you see and my body to its first state!"[111]

Finally, there are other punishments dreamt of besides physical ones, and a handful of transmitters introduce a story that has its beginnings in Mecca:

> Al-Shaʿbī said: I saw a man clinging to the curtain of the *kaʿba* and saying: "O God, forgive me, though I do not think You will!" I asked him about his sin, and he said: "I was among those commissioned with the head of al-Ḥusayn; with me were fifty men. I saw a white cloud of light, which descended from heaven to the tent; in it was enclosed a great gathering, among them Ādam, Nūḥ, Ibrāhīm, Mūsā and ʿĪsā. Then another one descended; in it was the Prophet, Ǧabrāʾīl, Mikāʾīl and the angel of death.[112] The Prophet was weeping and the gathering wept with him. The angel of death approached and took in death forty-nine, and then pounced on me; I leapt to my feet

---

[111] al-Ṭūsī., *al-Amālī fī-l-ḥadīṯ*, *maǧlis* 11, n. 101–654: 327, al-Maǧlisī., *Biḥār al-anwār*, vol. XLV, bb. 50, n. 3: 395.

[112] Although the angel of death is mentioned once, without being named, in the Qurʾān («*Say: The angel of death, who hath charge concerning you, will gather you, and afterward unto your Lord ye will be returned*», Q. 32:11) some scholars, as noted by Nasr, see reference to a number of angels associated with death in Q. 79 (NASR S.E., (ed.), *The Study Quran*, 2015: 1469). Nonetheless, the angel of death, popularly identified with ʿIzrāʾīl and who is one of the chief angels, is important enough, as noted by Burge, to be given one of the longest chapters in al-Suyūṭī's *al-Ḥabāʾik fī aḫbār al-malāʾik*, comprising sixty-five *aḥādīṯ* (BURGE S.R., *Angels in Islam*, 2012: 137). Cf. also MACDONALD J "The Angel of Death in Late Islamic Tradition" in *Islamic Studies* 3/4 (1964): 485–519, WENSINCK A.J., "ʿIzrāʾīl" in E. van Donzel et al., (eds.), *The Encyclopaedia of Islam*, 1997: 292–293.

> and said: Messenger of God, clemency! Clemency! Because, by God, I neither complied with nor consented to his killing. He said: Alas for you, for you looked upon what was happening! I replied: Yes. He said: Angel of death, desist from taking his soul in death, because certainly, he will die one day. He let me be, and I left for this place, repenting over what I had done."[113]

As part of this lengthy *ḥadīṯ*, al-Mağlisī transmits, on the authority of Saʿīd b. Musayyib, another version of a recurring narrative, describing an incident while he was fulfilling the *ḥağğ*, that occurs as he is performing his *ṭawāf* around the Kaʿba. He sees as man

> whose hands had been cut off and whose face was like a piece of dark night. He was clinging to the curtain of the *kaʿba* and saying: "O God, Lord of this Sacred House, forgive me, though, because of the greatness of my offense, I do not suppose You will do so, even if the inhabitants of Your heavens and Your earth and all You have created made intercession for me!" Saʿīd b. Musayyib said: I was distracted, as were the people performing *ṭawāf*, until finally the people surrounded him; we gathered around him and said: "Alas for you! Even if you were Iblīs, it would not be seemly for you to despair of God's mercy![114] Who are you? What is your sin?"

The man recounts that he was a camel driver for al-Ḥusayn and had accompanied him to Karbalāʾ. During the journey, he notices and covets al-Ḥusayn's shining belt. After the Imām's death, he

---

[113] al-Ḫawārizmī., *Maqtal al-Ḥusayn*, Part Two, bb. *Fī bayān ʿuqūba qātil al-Ḥusayn*, n. 12: 99–100, al-Mağlisī., *Biḥār al-anwār*, vol. XLV, bb. 46, n. 3: 303.

[114] Alternatively, some scholars suggest that the very name Iblīs, although of disputed etymology, derives from the Arabic root *b-l-s* (in the fourth form), the connotation being that Satan has nothing to expect – *ublisa* – from God. *Balas* refers to a person of desperate character or in despair because of grief or fear, while *ablasa* means to be overcome with grief, to be desperate, to be struck with despair. Cf. PENRICE J., *A Dictionary and Glossary of the Kor-an*, Asian Educational Services, New Delhi 1995: 19, LANE E.W., *An Arabic-English Lexicon*, vol. I, 1968: 248.

hides until nightfall and then emerges, puzzled by the strange light emanating from the battlefield. Remembering the belt he so desires, he sets out to find al-Ḥusayn's body and when he does so, mutilates it, cutting off the hands in a vain attempt to retrieve the desired object, until he is interrupted by a loud quake:

> Suddenly, the earth shook and the sky trembled with great force, with weeping and shouting and a voice saying: Alas, my son! Alas, killed one, alas, my slaughtered one, alas Ḥusayn, alas, one distant from home! My son, they killed you, for they did not know you, and they forbade you a drink of water! When I saw this, I was stupefied and threw myself down among the slain, and suddenly there were three persons and a woman and creatures standing around them; the earth was filled with the figures of people and the wings of angels.

An extensive narrative follows in the form of a lament shared between al-Ḥusayn, Muḥammad and Fāṭima. In the course of the elegy, Muḥammad asks who it was cut off his grandson's hands, and al-Ḥusayn draws attention to the actions of his faithless camel driver, now hiding among the dead:

> When Muḥammad heard the words of al-Ḥusayn, he wept bitterly; then he came to me, among the dead bodies, and stood before me. He said: "What is between you and I, camel driver? You cut off the hands long kissed by Ǧabra'īl and all the angels of God and by which the people of the heavens and the earths were blessed! Was it not enough for you what the cursed did to him in ignominy and degradation?"

The camel driver than receives his punishment:

> "God blacken your face, camel driver, in this world and the Hereafter! God cut off your hands and your feet, putting you among the group which shed our blood and ventured against God!"[115] His prayer was not finished when my hands became

[115] Cf. al-Ḫaṣībī., *al-Hidāya al-Kubrā*, bb. 5: 209, al-Baḥrānī., *Madīnat al-maʿāǧiz fī muʿǧizāt al-aʾimma al-aṭhār*, vol. III, Part Three, n. 743: 83, al-Ǧazāʾirī., *Riyāḍ al-abrār fī manāqib al-aʾimma al-aṭhār*, vol. I, Part One: 281,

> paralyzed and I perceived in my face as if it were clothed in a piece of dark night. I remained in this state, so I came to this House to seek intercession, but I know that He will never forgive me.[116]

Some last sundry dreams remain; in a lengthy *ḥadīṯ*, and which fuses in one narrative a selection of features underscored in other transmissions, al-Ḫawārizmī and al-Mağlisī transmit the story of a severely crippled man (without hands, legs or eyes) who prays to be saved from the Fire. He admits to having been among those who killed al-Ḥusayn; after the death of the Imām, the man catches sight of his trousers and waistband. In a failed attempt to remove the waistband, he badly mutilates the body of al-Ḥusayn and, frightened by a sudden quake, is made to fall asleep by God there among the dead. The narrative continues:

> I saw as if Muḥammad was approaching, and with him ʿAlī and Fāṭima. They took hold of the head of al-Ḥusayn and Fāṭima kissed it. Then she said: "My son, they killed you! God kill them, who have done this to you!" He replied: "Shimr killed me and this one sleeping" – he motioned towards me – "cut off my hands!" Fāṭima said to me: "God cut your hands and feet, blind your sight and make you enter the Fire!" I awoke, and I can see nothing! My hands and my feet have dropped from me, and now nothing remains of her prayer[117] but the Fire![118]

---

al-Iṣfahānī., *ʿAwālim al-ʿulūm wa-l-maʿārif al-aḥwāl min al-āyāt wa-l-aḫbār wa-l-aqwāl*, vol. XVII, ch. 22, bb. 4, n. 8: 631.

[116] al-Mağlisī., *Biḥār al-anwār*, vol. XLV, bb. 46, n. 14: 316–319.

[117] This prayer forms part of a genre which might be termed Fāṭima's 'negative intercession', in which her pleas for justice before God on behalf of her son include a request that his killers be punished. Cf. CLOHESSY C., *Fāṭima, Daughter of Muḥammad*, 2018: 200–202.

[118] al-Ḫawārizmī., *Maqtal al-Ḥusayn*, Part Two, bb. *Fī bayān ʿuqūba qātil al-Ḥusayn*, n. 48: 115, al-Mağlisī., *Biḥār al-anwār*, vol. XLV, bb. 46, n. 13: 310–313.

As part of this lengthy *ḥadīṯ*, in which the deceased al-Ḥusayn points out his killer, al-Maǧlisī transmits another narrative, hardly identifiable but containing well-known elements. It concerns a Kūfan blacksmith in Ibn Ziyād's army, who pitches his tent on banks of the al-ʿAlqamī and makes a variety of implements for the soldiers. He is still there when al-Ḥusayn is killed, and returns home a rich man. Lying on his bed one night he sees a vision, as if the Resurrection had happened, with people surging chaotically over the earth. The narrator describes the intense thirst, a common element in Shīʿī eschatology, with people's tongues hanging out and he himself barely able to hear or to see from the heat of the sun; so thirsty that he describes how his brain appears to be boiling and how, given the choice, he would drink his own blood for relief. Suddenly, he catches sight of a bearded horseman, whose light encompasses the plain and in whose image the universe takes delight. The rider is surrounded by a crowd of thousands, every prophet and all the virtuous, the martyrs and the devout. The rider passes by like a wind or the movement of a celestial sphere. An hour passes and the narrator now sees, on a noble charger, a terrifying horseman with a face like the full moon, who, without warning, stands on his mount and signals to his companions. The narrator hears him say 'seize him' and one of them seizes hold of his upper arm as though by pincer just out of the fire, so forcibly that he feels as if his right shoulder has been torn off, and he begs him to decrease the pressure; instead, it is increased. The narrator asks the one who has seized hold of him who has given him the authority to do so:

> I said to him: Who are you? He replied: "One of the angels of the Compeller."[119] So I said: And who is that one? He replied: "ʿAlī the Valiant."[120] I said: And the one before him? He answered: "Muḥammad the Chosen." I said: And around him? He replied: "The prophets and the virtuous, the martyrs, the devout and the believers." Then I said: What I have done that

---

[119] One of the names of God (*al-Ǧabbār*); cf. Q. 59:23.

[120] The Arabic *al-karrār*, an honorific nickname given to ʿAlī at the Battle of Ḫaybar, reflecting the valiant manner in which he fought.

> he invested you with authority over me? He answered: "«*Unto Him the whole matter will be returned*»;[121] your situation is the same situation as these." I looked closely, and there was ʿUmar b. Saʿd, commander of the army and a people I did not know. There was a chain of iron around his neck and fire coming from his eyes and ears, and I was certain of perishing. The remainder of the people among them were shackled; some of them were fettered and some of them were being pulled down by their upper arm, like me. While we were walking, there was the Messenger of God whom the angel had described, sitting on a high chair – shining brightly, from pearls I think, and two men with radiant white hair on his right. I asked the angel about them, and he said: Nūḥ and Ibrāhīm. Then the Messenger of God was saying: "What have you done, ʿAlī?" He replied: "I have not missed one of the killers of al-Ḥusayn, but have brought them!" I praised God Most High that I was not one of them, and my reason returned to me. Suddenly the Messenger of God was saying: "Bring them," and they brought them to him; he began questioning them and weeping, and everyone on the plain wept for his tears, because he was saying to (each) man: "What did you do at Ṭaff, Karbalāʾ to my son al-Ḥusayn?" And he would answer: Messenger of God, I guarded the water from him, or another would say: I killed him, or another, I trampled his chest with my horse. Among them was one who was saying: I beat his ailing son. The Messenger of God cried out: "Alas, my son! Alas, the small number of helpers! Alas, Ḥusayn! Alas, ʿAlī! This is what befell you after me, people of my house! Look, my father Ādam, look my brother Nūḥ, how they have seized me from behind in my descendants!"

At this point in the vision, amidst much weeping and all those on the plain rendered speechless, a man who was a carpenter is brought forward; he claims to have done nothing more than repair a tent pole, but is nonetheless condemned to the Fire for having added to the numbers against al-Ḥusayn. As he is condemned to

[121] Q. 11:123.

the Fire, the narrator realizes that he himself will receive no immunity for not having taken part in the actually killing of al-Ḥusayn. He is brought before Muḥammad and condemned to the Fire, but wakes from his dream before being dragged there, telling his dream to everyone around him.[122]

A similar transmission has as its context a group of believers at the shrine of ʿAlī b. Mūsā al-Riḍāʾ;[123] on the day of ʿĀshūrā, a man from among them began to recite the killing of al-Ḥusayn, quoting from al-Bāqir,[124] who said: "The one whose eyes shed tears over the affliction of al-Ḥusayn, even if they are the size of a gnat's wing, God will forgive him his sins, even if they should be like the foam of the ocean." In the gathering was one man described as 'foolishly ignorant', who was persistently obstinate in refuting al-Bāqir's words. That night this man was sleeping and he saw in his dream:

> ...as if the resurrection had taken place; the people were gathered on a level plateau, «*wherein thou seest neither curve nor ruggedness*».[125] The balances were set up, the Bridge[126] extended, the reckoning started, the books were opened, the fires were kindled and the Gardens adorned. The heat became unbearable for him, so that he became intensely thirsty, and he kept looking for water but did not find it. He turned left and right, and he was at a pool, great in height and in width. He continued: I said to myself: this is *al-Kawṯar*, and indeed, in it was water, colder than ice, sweeter than sweet. At the Pool were two men

[122] al-Mağlisī., *Biḥār al-anwār*, vol. XLV, bb. 46, n. 14: 319–321. Cf. al-Iṣfahānī., *ʿAwālim al-ʿulūm wa-l-maʿārif al-aḥwāl min al-āyāt wa-l-aḫbār wa-l-aqwāl*, vol. XVII, ch. 22, bb. 4, n. 9: 633.

[123] The eighth Imam, Abū al-Ḥasan ʿAlī b. Mūsā al-Riḍā (d. 202/818).

[124] The fifth Imām, Abū Ğaʿfar Muḥammad b. ʿAlī al-Bāqir (d. between 113/732 and 124/743).

[125] Cf. Q. 20:107.

[126] The bridge (*al-ṣirāṭ*) denotes the bridge that traverses Hell. This concept abounds in the Shīʿī and Sunnī books of *aḥādīṯ*. Cf. MONNOT G., "Ṣirāṭ" in H.R. Gibb et al., (eds.), *The Encyclopaedia of Islam*, 1997, vol. IX: 670–671.

> and a woman, whose lights shone on the created beings, while their own clothing was black, and they were weeping and sorrowful. I said: Who are they? I was told: "This is Muḥammad the Chosen One, and this is Imām ʿAlī the Approved One and this is the Pure One, Fāṭima the Radiant." I said: Why do I see them dressed in black, weeping and sorrowful. I was told: "Is this not the day of ʿĀshūrā, that day of the killing of al-Ḥusayn? They are sorrowful for that reason." He said: I approached the Mistress of the women, Fāṭima, and I said to her: Daughter of the Messenger of God, I am thirsty! She looked askance at me and said to me: "You are the one who disavowed the benefit of weeping over the affliction of my son al-Ḥusayn, the lifeblood of my heart and consolation of my eye, the martyr, killed unjustly and in enmity, may God curse his killers, his oppressors and those who prevented him drinking water." The man said: I awoke from my dream terrified and appalled and asked forgiveness from God.[127]

Moving away from apocalyptic dreams and the threat of punishment, Ibn Namā recalls the dream of a Christian Byzantine official; in doing so, he not only boosts the widespread indictment of Yazīd, but also adds a polemical constituent, something which became ubiquitous in early Christian-Muslim disputatious works, frequently involving the adherent of one religious group forsaking his own creed and enlisting with the other. The text, coming from ʿAlī b. al-Ḥusayn, details a Byzantine noble and messenger of the king of the Byzantines[128] present at one of Yazīd's customary drinking

---

[127] al-Maǧlisī., *Biḥār al-anwār*, vol. XLIV, bb. 34, n. 38: 294–296. Both al-Ǧazāʾirī and al-Iṣfahānī carry this *ḥadīṯ* after al-Maǧlisī, but in the form in which al-Maǧlisī transmits it, it is untraceable in any earlier source. Cf. al-Iṣfahānī., *ʿAwālim al-ʿulūm wa-l-maʿārif al-aḥwāl min al-āyāt wa-l-aḫbār wa-l-aqwāl*, vol. XVII, ch. 20, bb. 2, n. 9: 535, al-Ǧazāʾirī., *Riyāḍ al-abrār fī manāqib al-aʾimma al-aṭhār*, vol. I, Part One: 191.

[128] Almost certainly, the reference here (*al-rūm*) is to the Byzantine king; the Byzantines, however, mostly Greek-speaking Christians, would not have referred to themselves as such, a much later term, but would have called themselves 'Romans', since they understood Byzantium as an

parties in front of the head of al-Ḥusayn. "King of the Arabs," he says, "whose head is this?" Yazīd replies: "What is it to you, whose head this is?" and the Byzantine justifies himself: "When I go back to our king, he will ask me about everything that I have seen; I would like to inform him of the story of this head and its owner so that he can share with you in joy and delight!" When Yazīd identifies the head, the Byzantine asks who the mother of the victim is and is told that she is Fāṭima, daughter of the Messenger of God. The Byzantine reacts vehemently:

> Shame on you and your religion! I have a better religion than yours! My father is of the descendants of Dāwud – between me and him there are numerous forefathers, and the Christians extol me and take up the dust of my feet as a blessing by means of my father and of the descendants of Dāwud! But you have killed the son of the daughter of the Messenger of God, and there is only one generation between him and your Prophet!

The messenger then asks Yazīd whether he has heard about the 'Church of the Hoof', and recounts the tale of a city, measuring eighty by eighty leagues[129] in the middle of an otherwise deserted ocean between Oman and China: "There is no city greater than it on the face of the earth," he tells Yazīd, this city dominated and ruled over by Christians, its exports including camphor, precious stones, and trees of aloe and ambergris. The Byzantine now turns his attention to the crux of his story:

> In that city there are many churches, but the greatest of them is the Church of the Hoof, and in its sanctuary is suspended a receptacle of gold containing a hoof. They say that this is the hoof of the donkey which ʿĪsā used to ride, and they have

---

extension of the Roman Empire. The Byzantines practiced Roman law and culture, but with a conspicuous Greek flavour.

[129] A *farsaḫ*, according to Lane's entry on this Arabicized Persian word, remains indefinable; somewhere between ten and twelve thousand cubits, or roughly three to six miles. Cf. LANE E.W., *An Arabic-English Lexicon*, vol. VI, 1968: 2369.

> adorned the receptacle with gold and silk brocade. Every year the erudite among the Christians go to it, walk around it, kiss it and lift their needs to God Most High. This is their regard and their assiduity for a donkey's hoof, alleging that is the hoof of the donkey on which their Prophet ʿĪsā used to ride! But you have killed the son of the daughter of your Prophet! God Most High will bless neither you nor your religion!

Yazīd is outraged and orders the execution of the messenger "lest he compromise me in his city!" It is at this juncture that the Byzantine reveals his dream:

> Know that last night I saw your Prophet in a dream and he said to me: "Christian, you are of the Inhabitants of the Garden!" I was astonished at his words! I bear witness that there is no god but God and that Muḥammad is the Messenger of God! Then he jumped up and ran to the head of al-Ḥusayn and pressed it against his breast, and began to kiss it and weep until he was killed.[130]

This narrative is transmitted by al-Mağlisī, but in a very altered form;[131] it is not a Byzantine Christian but rather the head of the Jewish community who approaches Yazīd, asks the identity of the head, enumerates the generations between himself and Dāwud and then converts to Islam and is killed. Al-Mağlisī then relates the story a third time,[132] again with substantially different details. Upon seeing the head, the Christian, now a merchant, tells Yazīd that he had visited Muḥammad during his lifetime with gifts of musk and ambergris. He had visited him in the house of Umm Salama, and there has seen the boy al-Ḥusayn, and had listened to Muḥammad

---

[130] Ibn Namā al-Ḥillī., *Muṭīr al-aḥzān wa munīr subul al-ashğān*: 103–104, al-Mūsawī., *Tasliyat al-muğālis wa zīnat al-mağālis*, vol. II: 398, al-Mağlisī, *Biḥār al-anwār*, vol. XLV, bb. 39, n. 1: 142–143, al-Iṣfahānī., *ʿAwālim al-ʿulūm wa-l-maʿārif al-aḥwāl min al-āyāt wa-l-aḫbār wa-l-aqwāl*, vol. XVII, ch. 16, bb. 4: 442–443, al-Ğazāʾirī., *Riyāḍ al-abrār fī manāqib al-aʾimma al-aṭhār*, vol. I: Part One: 249.

[131] al-Mağlisī, *Biḥār al-anwār*, vol. XLV, bb. 39, n. 31: 187.

[132] Op. cit., n. 36: 189–191.

cursing those who would kill him. The merchant converts to Islam in front of Muḥammad (rather than in front of al-Ḥusayn's head) but keeps his conversion a secret when he returns to Rome, (the secret conversion of Christians another prevalent theme in early Islamic polemical texts). There is no mention of a dream or of the predictions usually associated with Ǧibrīl in the house of Umm Salama.

The dreams of three disparate women, each in her own way linked, even tenuously, with the tragedy of al-Ḥusayn, bring this miscellany of visions to an end. The texts narrate that al-Ḥusayn's daughter Sukayna, imprisoned in Damascus with the other surviving women and children from Karbalā', dreams a numinous dream of five noble mounts of light, an elder on each of them, with angels encircling them and a servant walking with them. Ibn Namā relates the *ḥadīṯ* length:

> The mounts passed by, and the servant approached me, drew near to me and said: "Sukayna! Your grandfather greets you with peace." I replied: And peace upon the Messenger of God; but messenger, who are you? He answered: "One of the servants of the Garden." Then I said: Who are those elders who passed by on the noble mounts? He replied: "The first is Ādam, God's choicest, the second is Ibrāhīm, the friend of God,[133] the third is Mūsā, the one who spoke with God,[134] the fourth is ʿĪsā, the spirit of God."[135] I asked: Who is this, clutching at his beard, who falls and then rises again? He replied: "Your grandfather, the Messenger of God." So, I asked: Where are they bound? He replied: "To your father al-Ḥusayn." I approached, running in pursuit of him, to inform him what the tyrants after him had done to us, and while I was doing so, five camel litters of light drew near, with a woman in each camel litter. I said: Who are these women who have drawn near? He answered: "The first is Ḥawwā', mother of humankind, the second is Āsiya, daughter of Muzāḥim, the

[133] Title for Ibrāhīm derived from Q. 4:125 (*ḫalīl Allāh*).

[134] Title given to Mūsā (*kalīm Allāh*).

[135] Q. 4:121.

third is Maryam, daughter of ʿImrān and the fourth is Ḫadīǧa, daughter of Ḫuwaylid."[136] I asked: Who is the fifth, the one placing her hand on her head, who falls and then rises again? He answered: "Your grandmother Fāṭima, daughter of Muḥammad, mother of your father." I said: By God, I will certainly inform her of what has been done to us. I caught up with her and stood in front of her, weeping, and saying: Beloved mother, by God, they have denied our rights! Beloved mother, by God, they have eliminated our unity! Beloved mother, by God, they have regarded our women as fair game! Beloved mother, by God they have killed our father al-Ḥusayn! She said to me: "Sukayna, your cry is enough! My heart has been set on fire and has been broken! This is the shirt of your father al-Ḥusayn, which I have with me and which will not be separated from me until I meet God with it."[137] Then I awoke

---

[136] The band of heavenly visitors on camel litters is noteworthy; although unnamed in the Qurʾānic text (with the exception of Maryam), some of them are intimately connected with personalities found there. Sāra is the wife of Ibrāhīm who, insists Q. 2:135, was neither Jew nor Christian, but an upright man (*ḥanīf*). Āsiya, the daughter of Muzāḥim and wife of Pharaoh, in contrast with the unfaithful wives of the prophets Nūḥ and Lūṭ, is offered as a model of faith (Q. 66:11). Ḫadīǧa is the wife of Muḥammad. These women play an intimate role in other events closely associated with the People of the House. They serve as heavenly midwives for Ḫadīǧa as she gives birth to Fāṭima (missing from Sukayna's dream, but present in the texts of the heavenly midwives, are Kulṯūm, sister of Mūsā, and Ṣafrāʾ, daughter of Shuʿayb, the messenger to the people of Midian named in Q. 7:85, Q. 11:84, Q. 26:177 and Q. 29:36). Their names also appear in random order, together with that of Fāṭima, as the mistresses of the women of the world. In later accounts of this story in *Biḥār al-anwār*, the names change. Cf. CLOHESSY C., *Fāṭima, Daughter of Muhammad*, 2018: 62–70, 104–106.

[137] The theme of al-Ḥusayn's blood-stained shirt held before God by Fāṭima is found in a number of *aḥādīṯ*, in a moment that marks the pinnacle of her grief: "She will take the shirt of al-Ḥusayn b. ʿAlī, stained with his blood, in her hand and she will say: Lord, this is the shirt of my son. You know what was done to him." Cf. for e.g. al-Mufīd., *al-Amālī*, n. 6:

> and wanted to conceal that dream; but I told it to my family and it spread among the people.[138]

Ibn Ṭāʾūs[139] relates the same dream in a much-shortened version, while al-Mağlisī relays an account in which Sukayna repeats to Yazīd, the man who has imprisoned her, the vision she has seen:

> Sukayna bt. al-Ḥusayn said: "Yazīd, I saw a vision last night: if you would hear it from me, I will tell it to you." Yazīd replied: "Let me have what you saw!" So she said: "While I was unable to sleep and had grown fatigued from weeping, after I had made *ṣalāt* and called upon God with pleas, when my eyes were going to sleep, I saw the doors of heaven opened and I was in a light, spreading from heaven to earth; then I was with servant girls from among the servant girls of the Garden; then I was in a green garden, in which there was a castle. Then I was with five elders, who entered that castle, accompanied by a servant. I said: Servant, inform me, whose is this castle? He replied: This is your father al-Ḥusayn's, given him by God Most High, a reward for his patience. I said: And who are these elders? He answered: The first is Ādam, the father of humankind, the second in Nūḥ, prophet of God,[140] the third is Ibrāhīm, the friend of the Merciful, the fourth is Mūsā, the one who spoke with God. I said to him: Who is the fifth, who I see clutching at his beard, weeping sorrowfully among them? He said to me: Sukayna, do you not know him? I replied: No, and he said: This is your great-grandfather, the Messenger of God. Then I

130, Ibn al-Ḥadīd., *Sharḥ nahğ al-balāġa*, vol. III: 226, al-Mağlisī., *Biḥār al-anwār*, vol. XLIII, bb. 8, n. 11: 224.

[138] Ibn Namā al-Ḥillī., *Muṯīr al-aḥzān wa munīr subul al-ashğān*: 105, al-Mağlisī, *Biḥār al-anwār*, vol. XLV, bb. 39 n. 36: 194–196, n. 1: 140–141, al-Iṣfahānī., *ʿAwālim al-ʿulūm wa-l-maʿārif al-aḥwāl min al-āyāt wa-l-aḫbār wa-l-aqwāl*, vol. XVII, ch. 16, bb. 4: 440, al-Ğazāʾirī., *Riyāḍ al-abrār fī manāqib al-aʾimma al-aṭhār*, vol. I, Part One: 248.

[139] Ibn Ṭāʾūs., *Kitāb al-luhūf fī qutlā al-ṭufūf*: 109–110, al-Iṣfahānī., *ʿAwālim al-ʿulūm wa-l-maʿārif al-aḥwāl min al-āyāt wa-l-aḫbār wa-l-aqwāl*, vol. XVII, ch. 16, bb. 4, n. 19: 441.

[140] In the first version, Nūḥ is replaced by ʿĪsā.

said to him: Where do they want to go? He answered: To your father, al-Ḥusayn. I said: By God, I must meet my great-grandfather and inform him of what has befallen us! He went ahead of me, but I did not meet him, and while I was pondering, suddenly I was with my grandfather ʿAlī b. Abī Ṭālib. He was standing with his sword in his hand, and I called out to him: Grandfather! By God, your son has been killed after you! He wept, pressed me to his breast and said: Patience, daughter, for God is the One whose help is to be sought."[141]

Sukayna's dream ends with a heavenly tableau reminiscent of the dream of Jacob in the Hebrew Scriptures:

"Suddenly I was at a door that had been opened in heaven and there were angels ascending and descending to the head of my father." He said: When Yazīd heard this, he slapped his face, wept and said: "What have I to do with the killing of al-Ḥusayn?"[142]

In another report, the details of Sukayna's dream are presented in a diverse way:

---

[141] Cf. Q. 12:18, Q. 21:112.

[142] al-Maǧlisī, *Biḥār al-anwār*, vol. XLV, bb. 39, n. 36: 194–196, al-Iṣfahānī., *ʿAwālim al-ʿulūm wa-l-maʿārif al-aḥwāl min al-āyāt wa-l-aḫbār wa-l-aqwāl*, vol. XVII, ch. 16, bb. 4, n. 18: 420, al-Ṭabarsī., *Mustadrak al-wasāʾil wa mustanbaṭ al-masāʾil*, vol. III, Part Three, bb. 48, n. 3703: 327. A number of transmitters note that Yazīd ordered that the young Sukayna be seated behind his throne, in an attempt to shield her from catching sight of the head of her father and thereby "causing her kinship with Yazīd to be weakened." All of this leads Zaynab's sister Fāṭima to remark on Yazīd's kindness and Sukayna to say of Yazīd: "I never saw a disbeliever in God more charitable than Yazīd b. Muʿāwiya!" Cf. HOWARD I.K.A., (trans.), *The History of al-Ṭabarī*, vol. XIX, 1990: 169–176, Ibn ʿAsākir., *Tārīḫ madīnat Dimashq*, vol. LXIX, bb. 9353 (*Zaynab al-Kubrā bt. ʿAlī b. Abī Ṭālib b. ʿAbd al-Muṭṭalib b. Hāshim b. ʿAbd al-Manāf*): 178, Ibn al-Aṯīr., *al-Kāmil fī al-tārīḫ*, vol. II: 439, Ibn Namā al-Ḥillī., *Muṯīr al-aḥzān wa munīr subul al-ashǧān*, Part Three: 99, al-Ḏahabī., *Siyar aʿlām al-nubalāʾ*, vol. III, bb. 48: 319–320, al-Haytamī., *Maǧmaʿ al-zawāʾid wa-manbaʿ al-fawāʾid*, vol. IX, bb. 95 (*Manāqib al-Ḥusayn*), n. 15148: 227.

Then a man of brilliant colour approached us, moonlike of face and sad of heart. I said to the servant: Who is this? He answered: "Your great-grandfather, the Messenger of God!" I approached him and said to him: Great-grandfather! By God, our men have been killed, our blood shed, our women unveiled – we were transported on (camel) humps without covering and driven to Yazīd! He took me to himself and pressed me against his breast. Then he approached Ādam, Nūḥ, Ibrāhīm and Mūsā and said to them: "How do you see what my community after me has done to my son?" Then the servant said: "Sukayna, lower your voice, for you have made the Messenger of God weep!" The servant than took me by the hand and led me into the castle and behold, there were five women whose creation God has made great and whose light He has intensified. Among them was a woman of imposing character, her hair spread out and in a black dress. In her hand was a shirt smeared with blood. Whenever she stood, they all stood with her and whenever she sat, they all sat with her. I said to the servant: Who are these women whose creation God has made great. He said: "Sukayna, this is Ḥawwāʾ, mother of humankind, and this is Maryam, daughter of ʿImrān, and this is Ḫadīǧa, daughter of Ḫuwaylid, and this is Ḥāǧar and this is Sāra;[143] and this one, in whose hand is the shirt smeared with blood and who, whenever she stands, they stand with her and whenever she sits, they sit with her, is your grandmother Fāṭima the Radiant." I approached her and said to her: Grandmother! By God, my father has been killed and I have been orphaned at my young age. She pressed me to her breast and wept bitterly. All the other women wept and said to her: "Fāṭima, on the Day of Judgment God will judge between you

[143] In contraposition to the first list of Ḥawwāʾ, Āsiya, Maryam, and Ḫadīǧa.

> and Yazīd!" At that, Yazīd left her and attached no importance to her words.[144]

Yazīd, already chastened by the public rebuke he has earned from al-Ḥusayn's sister Zaynab, and supposedly distraught, at least in some narrations, by Sukayna's recital, has also to face a dream recounted to him by his wife Hind. She remains a woman hard to identify; al-Ṭabarī names Yazīd's wives as Umm Ḫālid bt. Abī Hāshim b. ʿUtba b. Rabīʿa b. ʿAbd Shams and Umm Kulṯūm bt. ʿAbd Allāh b. ʿAmīr.[145] While one of his wives, the mother of his son Ḫālid, is named as Umm Hāshim Faḫīta bt. Abī Hāshim,[146] the mother of another son, Muʿāwiya, remains unknown.[147] Hind's dream is strongly reminiscent of an incident in the Gospel of Matthew when, during the trial of Jesus, an already edgy Pontius Pilate receives a message from his wife: "Have nothing to do with that righteous man, for I have suffered much over him today in a dream."[148] This same account is recorded in the second chapter of the 'Gospel of Nicodemus', sometimes called 'The Acts of Pilate', an apocryphal text the origin of which is disputed: "Now when Pilate saw this, he was afraid, and was about to rise from his seat. But while he thought to rise, his own wife who stood at a distance, sent to him, saying, Have thou nothing to do with that just man; for I have suffered much concerning him in a vision this night." Hind's dream is far more detailed, as is Yazīd's reaction to it:

> It was reported on the authority of Hind, wife of Yazīd, may God curse him, who said: "I had taken to my bed, when I saw

---

144 al-Maǧlisī, *Biḥār al-anwār*, vol. XLV, bb. 39, n. 36: 194–196, al-Iṣfahānī., *ʿAwālim al-ʿulūm wa-l-maʿārif al-aḥwāl min al-āyāt wa-l-aḫbār wa-l-aqwāl*, vol. XVII, ch. 16, bb. 4, n. 18: 420.

145 HOWARD I.K.A., (trans.), *The History of al-Ṭabarī*, vol. XIX, 1990, n. 429: 226. Cf. al-Balāḏurī., *Kitāb ansāb al-ashraf*, vol. V, bb. *Amr Yazīd b. Muʿāwiya*: 299.

146 ULLMAN M., "Khālid b. Yazīd b. Muʿāwiya" in H.R. Gibb et al., (eds.), *The Encyclopaedia of Islam*, 1986, vol. IV: 59.

147 BOSWORTH C.E., "Muʿāwiya II b. Yazīd b. Muʿāwiya I" in H.R. Gibb et al., (eds.), *The Encyclopaedia of Islam*, 1993, vol. VII: 268.

148 Mt. 27:19.

a door from heaven that had been opened and angels descending, squadron after squadron, to the head of al-Ḥusayn and saying: Peace be with you, Abū ʿAbd Allāh, peace be with you, son of the Messenger of God! While I was thus, I looked at the cloud that had descended from heaven; in it were numerous men, and among them was a man whose colour was sparkling and his face moonlike.[149] He drew near, walking until he bent over the teeth of al-Ḥusayn and kissed them, saying: My son, they killed you, you see them, they never knew you, and they stopped you from drinking water. My son, I am your grandfather, the Messenger of God, and this is your father, ʿAlī the Approved One and this is your brother al-Ḥasan, and this is your uncle Ǧaʿfar and this is ʿAqīl, and these are Ḥamza and al-ʿAbbās. He began to enumerate the people of his house one by one. Hind said: I awoke from my dream, frightened and appalled, as a light spread out over the head of al-Ḥusayn. I set out to look for Yazīd, who had entered a darkened room and turned his face to the wall. He said: What have I to do with al-

[149] The image of the moon is used by a number of transmitters to describe Muḥammad. Certain *aḥādīṯ* tell of his face being like the moon when it is full, or like a piece of the moon (al-Buḫārī., *Ṣaḥīḥ*, bk. 61 (*Kitāb al-manāqib*), bb. 23, n. 3552: 460, Muslim, *Ṣaḥīḥ*, bk. 43 (*Kitāb al-faḍāʾil*), bb. 30, n. 6084: 190, Abū Dāwūd., *Sunan*, bk. 46 (*Abwāb al-manāqib*), bb. 8, n. 3636: 331), or that his face was like the moon whenever he was happy (al-Buḫārī., *Ṣaḥīḥ*, bk. 61 (*Kitab al-manāqib*), bb. 23, n. 3556: 461, bk. 64 (*Kitāb al-maġāzi*), bb. 80, n. 4418: 432, bk. 65 (*Kitāb al-tafsīr*), bb. 18, n. 4677: 154, Muslim, *Ṣaḥīḥ*, bk. 49 (*Kitāb al-tawba*), bb. 9, n. 7016: 156, Abū Dāwūd., *Sunan*, bk. 46 (*Abwāb tafsir al-qurʾan*), bb. 9, n. 3102: 409). Others relate that when Muḥammad was seen in the darkness of night, his face had a light 'like the first splinter of the moon' (cf. for e.g. al-Kulaynī., *al-Kāfī fī ʿilm al-dīn*, vol. I, bb. *mawlid al-nabī*, n. 20: 446, al-Ṭabarsī., *Makarim al-aḫlāq*: 24, al-Fayḍ al-Kāshānī., *Kitāb ǧāmiʿ al-wāfī*, vol. III: 904, al-Maǧlisī., *Biḥār al-anwār*, vol. XIV, bb. 8, 190). In the course of the famous *ḥadīṯ al-kisāʾ*, Fāṭima herself describes her father's face as being like the full moon (al-Iṣfahānī., *ʿAwālim al-ʿulūm wa-l-maʿārif al-aḥwāl min al-āyāt wa-l-aḫbār wa-l-aqwāl*, vol. XI, ch. 24, bb. 5: 935).

> Ḥusayn? Anguish had befallen him. I recounted the dream to him while he bowed his head."[150]

Hind bt. ʿUtba, the wife of Abū Sufyān b. Ḥarb and grandmother of the embattled Yazīd, is another who recounts a dream, with a complexity of cosmological detail that reminds of some of the dreams of Joseph recorded in the Hebrew Scriptures (Gen. 37:9). In his *Madīnat al-maʿāǧiz*, al-Baḥrānī reports the dream, with slight additions and omissions, noted by the editor, in a simpler and redacted version:

> It was reported that Hind [mother of Muʿāwiya] went to the house of the Messenger of God at daybreak. She entered, sat down next to ʿĀʾisha and said: "Daughter of Abū Bakr, I saw a curious vision, and I want to relate it to you so that you can tell it to the Messenger of God" – this was before her son Muʿāwiya entered Islam. ʿĀʾisha said [to her]: "Tell me about it, so that I can tell the Messenger of God [about it]." She replied: "In my dream I saw a sun shining over the whole world; from that sun, a moon was generated, the light of which radiated over the whole world. Then, [from] that moon, two brilliant stars were generated: the east and the west glowed by their light. While I was [thus], a dark black cloud appeared, as if it were a dark night. From that black cloud a speckled serpent was generated: the serpent crawled towards the two stars and swallowed them. The people began to weep and lamented over the two stars." The narrator said: ʿĀʾisha went to the Prophet and related the vision to him [and when] the Prophet heard her words his colour changed, and he shed tears and wept. He said: "ʿĀʾisha, I am the shining sun. The moon is my daughter Fāṭima and the two stars are al-Ḥasan and al-Ḥusayn.

---

[150] al-Baḥrānī., *Madīnat al-maʿāǧiz fī muʿǧizāt al-aʾimma al-aṭhār*, vol. IV, Part Four, bb. 3, n. 192/1139: 137–138, al-Maǧlisī, *Biḥār al-anwār*, vol. XLV, bb. 39, n. 36: 194–196, al-Iṣfahānī., *ʿAwālim al-ʿulūm wa-l-maʿārif al-aḥwāl min al-āyāt wa-l-aḫbār wa-l-aqwāl*, vol. XVII, ch. 16, bb. 4, n. 18: 422, al-Ṭabarsī., *Mustadrak al-wasāʾil wa mustanbaṭ al-masāʾil*, vol. III, Part Three, bb. 48, n. 3703: 327.

> The black cloud is Muʿāwiya, may God curse him, and the [speckled] serpent is Yazīd, may God curse him!"[151]

A final dream comes from un unidentified guardsman, one of a group of forty or fifty accompanying the head of al-Ḥusayn to Damascus. Already having twinges of conscience, his complex dream sees all the great prophets descending in support of al-Ḥusayn's head. Just as the cosmos unites in grieving over al-Ḥusayn, so in this dream all of heaven and earth gathers in a united indictment against Yazīd:

> (Yazīd) gave an order and the head was brought to the dome opposite the one in which he was drinking. He put us in charge of the head; but all of that was in my heart and sleep did not come to me in that dome. When the night came, we were again put in charge of the head. In the deep of night, I heard a sound from heaven; and then there was a herald calling out: "Ādam! Descend!" At that, the father of humankind descended with numerous angels. Then I heard a herald calling out: "Ibrāhīm! Descend!" At that, he descended with numerous angels. Then I heard a herald calling out: "Mūsā! Descend!" At that, he descended with numerous angels. Then I heard a herald calling out: "ʿĪsā! Descend!" At that he descended with numerous angels. Then I heard a tremendous noise and a herald calling out: "Muḥammad! Descend!" At that, he descended with many creatures from among the angels. The angels surrounded the dome. Then the Prophet entered the dome and took the head from it (in another report, Muḥammad sat down under the head and bent the spear so that the head dropped into the lap of the Messenger of God). He took it and went with it to Ādam and said: "My father Ādam, do you see what my community after me have done to my son?" (I got goose flesh because of that). Then Ǧabraʾīl rose and said: "Muḥammad! I am master of earthquakes! Order me to shake the earth with them

[151] al-Baḥrānī., *Madīnat al-maʿāǧiz fī muʿǧizāt al-aʾimma al-aṭhār*, vol. IV, Part Four, bb. 3, n. 138/1085: 58–60. Cf. also Ibn Shahrāshūb., *Manāqib āl Abī Ṭālib*, vol. IV, bb. *Fī imāmat Abī ʿAbd Allāh al-Ḥusayn*: 72, al-Maǧlisī., *Biḥār al-anwār*, vol. XLIV, bb. 31, n. 21: 263.

> and to let out one great cry with them in which they will be annihilated!" He replied: "No!" So, he said: "Muḥammad! Consign to me those forty guarding the head!" He said: "Do it." He began to blow at them one by one, and when he approached me, he said: "(Do) you hear and see?" The Prophet said: "Leave him, leave him. God will not forgive him." So, he left me, and they took the head, and since that night nothing was known of it.[152]

It is an eschatological vision, its stark realism far removed from the tears of the *ǧinn*. The event, once predicted by Ǧibrīl with a handful of red dust is now censured by the whole host of heaven – angels, prophets and messengers rise in fulfilment of the augural judgment pronounced over the killers of al-Ḥusayn by a disembodied voice on Medina's night air: "All the people of the heavens call down curses on you, from the Prophet and those sent and the fallen. You have been cursed by the tongue of Ibn Dāwud, and Mūsā and the one entrusted with the gospel."[153] The sounds from heaven, once the beating of an angel's wings and the whisperings of bad news, are now a roaring chorus of heavenly disapproval. But dreams may not be enough; for the God who, says the Qurʾān, «*teacheth by the pen*»,[154] will once more use the pen to write a final judgment about those who killed the grandson of His Prophet.

---

[152] al-Maǧlisī, *Biḥār al-anwār*, vol. XLV, bb. 39, n. 31: 187–188.

[153] Ibn Namā., *Muṯīr al-aḥzān*, bb. *Nūḥ al-ǧinn ʿalā al-Ḥusayn*: 107–108, al-Maǧlisī., *Biḥār al-anwār*, vol. XLV, bb. 43, n. 2: 235–236, al-Iṣfahānī., *ʿAwālim al-ʿulūm wa-l-maʿārif al-aḥwāl min al-āyāt wa-l-aḫbār wa-l-aqwāl*, vol. XVII, ch. 17, bb. 5, n. 12: 486.

[154] Q. 96:4.

Afterword

"Of all the questions you might want to ask about angels," muses poet Billy Collins, "the only one you ever hear is how many can dance on the head of a pin. No curiosity about how they pass the eternal time..."[1] Even so, Islam erupted into a world of Christian shrines and places of worship much attached to ideas, some of them heterodox, of a tangible angelic presence, and dedicated to honouring these heavenly beings who toil and intercede on humanity's behalf. As Padwick remarks: "In a world where these ideas were at work, Islam was born, and the angels have their part in its cosmogony and religious scenery."[2] The existence of angels as pure

---

[1] COLLINS B., "Questions about angels" in B. Collins, *Tasking Off Emily Dickenson's Clothes*, Picador, London 2000: 37.

[2] PADWICK C., *Muslim Devotions. A Study of Prayer Manuals in Common Use*, Oneworld, Oxford 1996: 228. As Godwin notes, the term *Angelus Occidentalis* is used for a number of species of angels found in the major monotheistic faiths, all of which share a tripartite cosmology (the division

spiritual beings is patently supported by the Hebrew scriptures (despite rejection by the Sadducees, as noted Acts 23:8) as a truth of faith, one which slipped effortlessly from there into Christian belief. Assisting and ministering to humanity (Heb. 1:14) from their inaccessible world, with a keenness and attention that the Christian scriptures suggest is their all-absorbing task (Mt. 18:10) – Schimmel takes note of Iqbal's line, "though the angels are from the magic of the spheres, their eyes are always directed towards this handful of dust"[3] – their final earthly intervention will be to summon all of humanity to judgment.

In reality, most of the Jewish and Christian knowledge of angels comes from sources outside of the canonical scriptures. In Christian theological history, for example, the four great Doctors of the Western Church,[4] Ambrose (d. 397), Jerome (d. 420), Augustine (d. 430) and Gregory the Great (d. 604) wrote comprehensively on angelology, attempting to give a glimpse of life in the heavenly realms, as did some of the great medieval mystical and scholastic theologians, like Bernard of Clairvaux (d. 1153), Peter Lombard (d. 1160) and Thomas Aquinas (d. 1274).

In the Islamic corpus there is substantially less; but even the relative dearth of Islamic texts focussing on angels does not belie the fact that, as Kassim observes, they are, in contraposition to other monotheistic faith traditions, indispensable to Islamic belief (Q. 2:177), appearing second in the list of Islamic credal articles (Q. 2:285).[5] The scarcity of written angelology in Islam is conceivably the result of the considerable Islamic emphasis on revelation, for

---

ino Earth, Heaven and Hell). Cf. GODWIN M., *Angels. An Endangered Species*, 1990: 7

[3] SCHIMMEL A., *Gabriel's Wing*, Iqbal Academy, Pakistan 2003: 204.

[4] The thirty-six or so 'Doctors' are men and women who made significant contributions to the Church through their profound understanding of the faith.

[5] KASSIM H., "Nothing can be Known or Done without the Involvement of Angels: Angels and Angelology in Islam and Islamic Literature" in F.V. Reiterer et al., (eds.), *Angels: The Concept of Celestial Beings: Origins, Development and Reception*, Walter de Gruyter, Berlin 2007: 646.

the chief importance of angels is in their function rather than in their nature. While this may be equally so in Christianity, as noted by, among others, St. Augustine, ultimately angels are, for Islam, a more essential ingredient to the divine intervention we call revelation than they are for Judaism or for Christianity.

Comparable to angels, dreams, at least in the Islamic ambit, enfold themselves virtually seamlessly into almost every aspect of human life; and, akin to angels, dreams appear to perform corresponding functions – now warning, now chastising, sometimes commiserating, sometimes commending, at other times informing or commanding. Green suggests it was the very dreams and visions of Muḥammad that announced the beginning of historical Islam, so that the Qurʾān itself may be classified as a visionary text, a point underscored also by Von Grunebaum.[6] In antithesis to the question of angels, in the case of dream interpretation the Islamic writings are substantially more voluminous than those of the Jewish and Christian corpora. Lamoureaux and Chittick provide us with the names of numerous Muslim savants and scholars who, intrigued by the role of dreams, found themselves dabbling in analysis and clarification. Ibn Sīrīn[7] was ostensibly (but seemingly erroneously) regarded as the father of Islamic dream interpretation; notwithstanding Ibn Ḫaldūn's fulsome praise and al-Buḫārī's transmitting from him the threefold classification of dreams,[8] Lamoreaux disputes whether Ibn Sīrīn ever authored a single work about deciphering

---

[6] GREEN N., "The Religious and Cultural Roles of Dreams and Visions in Islam" in *Journal of the Royal Asiatic Society*, Third Series, vol. 13, No. 3 (Nov., 2003): 287, VON GRUNEBAUM G.E. "The Cultural Function of the Dream as Illustrated by Classical Islam" in G.E von Grunebaum & R. Caillois (eds.)., *The Dream and Human Societies*, University of California Press, Berkeley 1966: 7.

[7] Muḥammad b. Sīrīn (d. 110/728: cf. GAL S. I: 102). Named by Sezgin as Abū Bakr Muḥammad b. Sīrīn al-Baṣrī al-Anṣārī (GAS I: 633–634).

[8] "Muḥammad b. Sīrīn was one of the most widely-known scholars in this and he wrote basic principles which people have passed on till this age" (Ibn Ḫaldūn., *Tarih*, vol. I: 529), al-Buḫārī., *Ṣaḥīḥ*, vol. IX, bk. 91 (*Kitāb al-taʿbīr*), bb. 26, n. 7017: 103–104.

dreams, and judges all the texts attributed to him to be inauthentic.[9] However, Ibn Sīrīn is only one of an extensive but by no means exhaustive list enumerated by the little-known al-Ḫallāl[10] in his 'The List of Dream Interpreters' (*Ṭabaqāt al-muʿabbirīn*). Others include al-Kirmānī, whose manual of the meaning of dreams is extant[11] only in fragmentary form in numerous other works like that of al-Dīnawarī;[12] and Ibn Qutayba, ostensibly the first compiler of a dream text (*ʿIbārat* [or *Taʿbīr*] *al-ruʾyā*) that is still extant,[13] as is that of al-Siğistānī.[14]

Islam is therefore not short of men and women who probed the meaning of dreams, an art seemingly as prevalent now as it was when al-Ḫallāl compiled his *Ṭabaqāt*;[15] but while the dream of

---

[9] LAMOREAUX J.C., *The Early Muslim Tradition of Dream Interpretation*, 2002: 19. Cf. also FAHD T. "The Dream in Medieval Islamic Society" in G.E von Grunebaum & R. Caillois (eds.)., *The Dream and Human Societies*, 1966: 360.

[10] al-Ḥasan b. al-Ḥusayn al-Ḫallāl (c. 4th/10th century); in his *Ṭabaqāt*, he lists about 7500 people famous as decipherers of dreams.

[11] LAMOREAUX J.C., *The Early Muslim Tradition of Dream Interpretation*, 2002: 25.

[12] Abū Saʿīd Naṣr b. Yaʿqūb al-Dīnawarī (d. after 400/1010 according to ORFALI B., "al-Dīnawarī, Abū Saʿd Naṣr b. Yaʿqūb" in K. Fleet, G. Krämer et al., *Encyclopaedia of Islam*, 3rd edition, Brill, Leiden 2008: 68–69, cf. also GAL S. I: 433) in his *Kitāb al-taʿbīr fī-l-ruʾyā*), although Orfali names the work as *al-Qādirī fī-l-taʿbīr* or *Kitāb al-ğāmiʿ al-kabīr fī-l-taʿbīr*, completed in 1009 and which quotes authors like Ibn Sīrīn and al-Kirmānī.

[13] Abū Muḥammad ʿAlī b. Muslim b. Qutayba (or Qutaybī) al-Qutabī al-Dīnawarī al-Marwazī (d. 276/889 or 270/884: cf. GAL S. I: 184). Cf. ALBERTINI T., "Dreams, Visions, and Nightmares in Islam: From the Prophet Muḥammad to the Fundamentalist Mindset" in N. van Deusen (ed.), *Dreams and Visions. An Interdisciplinary Enquiry*, Brill, Leiden 2010: 178. Orfali claims that al-Dīnawarī's is the oldest surviving authentic Arabic treatise on the interpretation of dreams: cf. ORFALI B., "al-Dīnawarī, Abū Saʿd Naṣr b. Yaʿqūb" in K. Fleet, G. Krämer et al., *Encyclopaedia of Islam*, 3rd edition, Brill, Leiden 2008: 69.

[14] Ḫallāl Abū Aḥmad Ḫalaf b. Aḥmad (d. 399/1008).

[15] EDGAR I.R., *The Dream in Islam*, Berghahn Books, 2011: 17.

Sulaymān b. ʿAbd al-Malik b. Marwān with which this book began needed the interpretation of al-Ḥasan al-Baṣrī, and the dream Umm al-Faḍl called for clarification by Muḥammad, the majority of dreams concerning al-Ḥusayn's death at Karbalāʾ are almost never enigmatic or impenetrable, or possessed of a symbolism that demands to be disentangled by some sophisticated explanation. They are characterized, instead, by a stark and unmitigated clarity.

Thomas Cahill writes amusingly and eruditely of how the citizens of Rome awoke one morning, early in the 5th century, to find the Visigoth king Alaric and his army camped outside the city. They dispatched a pair of envoys for what they imagined would be an easy negotiation, but Alaric was more cunning than they realized, and the envoys soon found themselves pleading for the city. Alaric promised to decamp as soon as his men had ransacked Rome, removing all the silver and gold, every object of value as well as every barbarian slave. The envoys were beside themselves. "But what will that leave us?" they cried. "Your lives," answered Alaric quietly. At that moment, remarks Cahill, "Roman security died and a new world was conceived."[16]

Al-Ḥusayn and his seventy-odd companions escaped with less; the murder of the grandson of Islam's prophet and his supporters was an event so inexplicably horrifying as to flush the face of Islam with shame. Nor would it be imprecise to note that at the moment of his martyrdom, a new world was conceived; the memory of the Karbalāʾ plains has embedded itself into the psyche of successive generations of Shīʿī Muslims, etching itself ever more profoundly into texts, into memories of encounters with the divine, and even into the collective subconscious of al-Ḥusayn's devotees. While the context and circumstances surrounding the last journey of al-Ḥusayn and his small party from Medina to Kūfa and their death at the hands of Yazīd's forces have been recounted often enough, the dreams that augured the event and those that ensued after the battle are not always chronicled. The commentators insist that his was a destiny preordained by God, aside from any political motives or circumstances that may have determined it; Iqbal, for example, en-

[16] CAHILL T., *How the Irish Saved Civilization*, Random House, 1996: 52–53.

visages him as the archetype of the 'warrior saint' doing battle against a purely temporal caliphate.[17] Having received from Kūfa pledges of support should he lead a revolt, the journey there was filled with unnerving reports of the capriciousness of the Kūfans, the mass of military might opposing him and the desertion of a number of his supporters. At Karbalāʾ, on the banks of the Euphrates, al-Ḥusayn and his small remnant were deprived of access to the water that flowed so abundantly nearby and finally, on the 10th day of the month of Muḥarram, were massacred by the vast opposing force. The survivors of the carnage – most of the women, including Zaynab, sister of al-Ḥusayn, as well as his young son Zayn al-ʿĀbidīn who succeeded his father as Imām, were taken captive by Yazīd's forces. The women and small children experienced significant physical and psychological agony, forced as they were to follow after the severed heads of their menfolk on the way to Yazīd in Damascus via his governor, Ibn Ziyād, in Kūfa. It was before Yazīd, that Zaynab, sometimes called 'the tongue of ʿAlī in pursuit' in homage to the oratorical skills that she had inherited from her father, began the great oral tradition that surrounds Karbalāʾ. However, the event would also be inscribed into a communal anamnesis by those who passed the dreams down to the succeeding generations.

As they progress, the dream narratives, peopled by a variety of characters, take on a vivid and increasing detail. The dust, for instance, which begins as a sign of bitter sadness on the beard and head of Muḥammad will become the dust that he turns over and over in his hand in mourning; eventually it will be afforded shape and texture, colour and odour; a clod of earth, mud or dust vibrantly red in colour, and ultimately, dust in a glass vial under Umm Salama's guardianship, which on a day and at an hour will turn to fresh blood.

There is a development not only in the character of the angel, but also in the words and gestures used by this celestial visitor. But this angel, if an angel he is, propitiously shared by the monotheistic faiths, is harder to delineate than is the Karbalāʾ dust. He makes more than one appearance in the Hebrew Scriptures, in the apoca-

---

[17] SCHIMMEL A., *Gabriel's Wing*, 2003: 167.

lyptic Book of Daniel, where he is named, and in which his own genus and species is hinted at when, in Dan. 8:17, he greets Daniel as 'O human', a term of address employed by the divine for human beings (conversely, in the Islamic texts we have studied, he always addressed Muḥammad by his name). According to Alter, his being named 'Gabriel' (meaning, in Hebrew, 'God is my strength') in the Daniel text is a feature of a late period when names were actually assigned.[18] In the ninth chapter, Daniel refers to him as 'the man Gabriel', because he has taken on anthropomorphic form, and then describes how he 'glided down in flight' (Dan. 9:21). Again, in Dan. 10:5–6 Daniel describes 'a man' who is almost certainly Gabriel, dressed in gold and linen, with a body like chrysolite and eyes like fire, arms and legs like burnished bronze and a voice like a crowd of people. Gabriel will pull Daniel, who has fainted in horror, to his feet, address him once again as 'man' and instruct him to understand the words that he, Gabriel, has been sent to speak.

He is only expressly named three times in the Qurʾān (Q. 2:97–98, Q. 66:4) and always as Ǧibrīl although, as already noted, in the corpus of *tafsīr* and *aḥādīṯ* the name varies between Ǧibrīl, Ǧabraʾīl, Ǧabrīl, Ǧabraʾil, Ǧabrāʾīl, Ǧabrayīl and Ǧabrāʾil.[19] In a manner reminiscent of Daniel, Q. 53:5–9 describes this imposing bringer of revelation as «*one of mighty powers*» and «*vigorous*» (the Arabic *mirra* conveys the sense of 'strength') who «*grew clear to view when he was on the uppermost horizon*» (an element repeated in Q. 81:23) until he hung suspended «*two bows' length or even nearer*».

The Sunnī corpus of *aḥādīṯ* provides a disparate and at times inconsistent picture of Ǧibrīl. Certainly, Ǧibrīl is seen by Muḥammad, at least twice in his original created form (insists ʿĀʾisha),[20] covered with six hundred wings,[21] at times occupying a

---

[18] ALTER R., *The Hebrew Bible. A Translation with Commentary*, vol. III, 2019: 9426.

[19] Cf. JEFFERY A., *The Foreign Vocabulary of the Qurʾān*, 2007: 100.

[20] al-Buḫārī., *Ṣaḥīḥ*, vol. VI, bk. 65 (*Kitāb al-tafsīr*), *sūrat al-Naǧm*, bb. 1, n. 4855: 322–323, Muslim., *Ṣaḥīḥ*, vol. I, bk. 1 (*Kitāb al-īmān*), bb. 77, nn. [439] 287 – (177): 282. ʿĀʾisha insists that Ǧibrīl would come to Muḥammad as a man, but on the occasion of Q. 53:8–9 he came in his

seat or a throne between heaven and earth,[22] his massive bulk filling that space.[23] More than once ʿĀʾisha describes the mechanics of the first revelation but omits any description of the being who brought it.[24] At other times, Muḥammad sees Ǧibrīl as a man (not only in his heart, as some texts insist, for there are sufficient narratives to suggest it was more than this);[25] at the 6/627 Battle of the Ditch for example, Ǧibrīl appears as a soldier, nonchalantly described by the texts as 'brushing the dust from his hair'.[26] Others do not see him: "you see what we do not see," remarks ʿĀʾisha,[27] while Umm

---

actual figure, big enough to cover the whole horizon: cf. al-Buḫārī., *Ṣaḥīḥ*, vol. IV, bk. 59 (*Kitāb badʾ al-ḫalq*), bb. 7, n. 3235: 286–287.

[21] al-Buḫārī., *Ṣaḥīḥ*, vol. IV, bk. 59 (*Kitāb badʾ al-ḫalq*), bb. 7, n. 3232: 285–286, vol. VI, bk. 65 (*Kitāb al-tafsīr*), *sūrat al-Naǧm*, bb. 1, nn. 4856, 4857: 323–324, Muslim., *Ṣaḥīḥ*, vol. I, bk. 1 (*Kitāb al-īmān*), bb. 77, nn. [432] 280 – (174), [433] 281, (in his true form with 600 wings) [434] 282: 280–281.

[22] al-Buḫārī., *Ṣaḥīḥ*, vol. IV, bk. 59 (*Kitāb badʾ al-ḫalq*), bb. 7, n. 3238: 287–288, Muslim., *Ṣaḥīḥ*, vol. I, bk. 1 (*Kitāb al-īmān*), bb. 73, n. [406] 255 – (161): 256, n. [409] 257: 257–258. The texts do not always name the angel of revelation, seated on this throne, as Ǧibrīl.

[23] al-Buḫārī., *Ṣaḥīḥ*, vol. IV, bk. 59 (*Kitāb badʾ al-ḫalq*), bb. 7, n. 3234: 286, Muslim., *Ṣaḥīḥ*, vol. I, bk. 1 (*Kitāb al-īmān*), bb. 77, n. [439] 287 (177): 282.

[24] al-Buḫārī., *Ṣaḥīḥ*, vol. I, bk. 1 (*Kitāb al-waḥy*), bb. 3, n. 3: 46–47, vol. VI, bk. 65 (*Kitāb al-tafsīr*), *sūrat al-ʿAlaq*, bb. 1, n. 4953: 401, Muslim., *Ṣaḥīḥ*, vol. I, bk. 1 (*Kitāb al-īmān*), bb. 73, n. [403] 252 – (160): 252–253.

[25] al-Buḫārī., *Ṣaḥīḥ*, vol. IV, bk. 59 (*Kitāb badʾ al-ḫalq*), bb. 6, n. 3215: 279, Muslim., *Ṣaḥīḥ*, vol. I, bk. 1 (*Kitāb al-īmān*), bb. 77, nn. [435] 283 (175), [436] 284 (176), [437] 285: 281. One text notes that Ǧibrīl experienced by Muḥammad in the receiving of revelation as a voice and a light but not seeing a visible form for seven years: cf. Muslim., *Ṣaḥīḥ*, vol. VI, bk. 43 (*Kitāb al-faḍāʾil*), bb. 33, n. [6104] 123: 197.

[26] al-Buḫārī., *Ṣaḥīḥ*, vol. IV, bk. 56 (*Kitāb al-ǧihād*), bb. 18, n. 2813: 61, vol. V, bk. 64 (*Kitāb al-maġāzī*), bb. 31, n. 4117: 269, n. 4122: 271, Muslim., *Ṣaḥīḥ*, vol. V, bk. 32 (*Kitāb al-ǧihād*), bb. 22, n. [4598] 65 – (1769): 61.

[27] al-Buḫārī., *Ṣaḥīḥ*, vol. VIII, bk. 78 (*Kitāb al-adab*), n. 6201: 123, bk. 79 (*Kitāb al-istiʾḏān*), n. 6249: 150, bk. 59 (*Kitāb badʾ al-ḫalq*), bb. 6, n. 3217: 279, vol. V, bk. 62 (*Kitāb faḍāʾil aṣḥāb al-nabī*), bb. 30, n. 3768: 74 ('you see

Salama and Ibn ʿAbbās, as already noted, are fooled into thinking that Ǧibrīl is in fact Diḥya b. Ḫalīfa al-Kalbī, a companion of Muḥammad.[28] The famous *ḥadīṯ Ǧibrīl* asserts that a number of Muḥammad's companions mistake Ǧibrīl for a man in a radiantly white garment and with pitch black hair, a traveller who shows none of the weariness of travel, and who then, having explained the fundamentals of Islam, disappears from their sight.[29] Ǧibrīl is also seen by Saʿd, who is fighting alongside Muḥammad at the 3/625 Battle of Uḥud, as Ibn ʿAbbās would see him, as a man dressed in white standing by the Prophet.[30] Abū Ḏarr hears a noise that turns out to be Ǧibrīl's voice,[31] the same voice heard by Hāǧar, mother of Ismāʿīl, in her frantic desert sojourn,[32] although another text suggests that Abū Ḏarr heard no such thing.[33]

The word 'spirit' (*rūḥ*) occurs twenty-one times in the Qur'ānic text;[34] generally, most classical commentators identify the

---

what we do not'), Muslim., *Ṣaḥīḥ*, vol. VI, bk. 44 (*Kitāb faḍā'il al-ṣaḥāba*), bb. 13, n. [6304] 91: 302.

28 al-Buḫārī., *Ṣaḥīḥ*, vol. IV, bk. 61 (*Kitāb al-faḍā'il*), bb. 25, n. 3633: 499, vol. VI, bk. 66 (*Kitāb faḍā'il al-qur'ān*), bb. 1, n. 4980: 421, Muslim., *Ṣaḥīḥ*, vol. I, bk. 1 (*Kitāb al-īmān*), bb. 74, n. [423] 271 - (167): 273, vol. VI, bk. 44 (*Kitāb faḍā'il al-ṣaḥāba*), bb. 16, n. [6315] 100 - (2451): 312, al-Tirmiḏī., *al-Ǧāmiʿ al-ṣaḥīḥ*, vol. VI, bk. 46 (*Abwāb al-manāqib*), n. 3629: 340.

29 al-Buḫārī., *Ṣaḥīḥ*, vol. I, bk. 2 (*Kitāb al-īmān*), vol. VI, bk. 65 (*Kitāb al-tafsīr*), *sūrat Luqmān*, bb. 2, n. 4777: 260–261, Muslim., *Ṣaḥīḥ*, vol. I, bk. 1 (*Kitāb al-īmān*), bb. 1, n. [93] 1 – (8): 92–95, n. [97] 5 – (9): 96–97, Abū Dāwud., *Sunan*, vol. V, bk. 39 (*Kitāb al-sunna*), bb. 16, n. 4695: 207–209.

30 Muslim., *Ṣaḥīḥ*, vol. VI, bk. 43 (*Kitāb al-faḍā'il*), bb. 10, n. [6004] 46 (2306): 160.

31 al-Buḫārī., *Ṣaḥīḥ*, vol. VIII, bk. 79 (*Kitāb al-isti'ḏān*), n. 6268: 161–162, vol. VIII, bk. 81 (*Kitāb al-riqāq*), bb. 14, n. 6444: 249, Muslim., *Ṣaḥīḥ*, vol. III, bk. 12 (*Kitāb al-zakāt*), bb. 9, n. [23041 32 – (94): 37–38.

32 al-Buḫārī., *Ṣaḥīḥ*, vol. IV, bk. 60 (*Kitāb aḥādīṯ al-anbiyā'*), bb. 9, n. 3365: 356–357.

33 al-Buḫārī., *Ṣaḥīḥ*, vol. VIII, bk. 81 (*Kitāb al-riqāq*), bb. 13, n. 6443: 247–248.

34 Four times as 'the spirit of holiness' (*rūḥ al-qudus*, Q. 2: 87, 253, Q. 5:110, Q. 16:102), three times as 'Our spirit' (*rūḥa-nā*, Q. 19:17, Q. 21:91,

'spirit' with Ğibrīl and Ğibrīl with the angelic being who descended with revelation, although the text of the Qur'ān does not construe such an identification, which in itself appears somewhat simplistic. The Qur'ān in fact does not classify Ğibrīl as either an angel or a spirit. The drawback with the word 'spirit', especially if capitalized, is that it carries the weight of Christian pneumatology. If not capitalised, the word 'spirit' could easily and justifiably refer to an angel (remembering that the word 'angel' refers to function rather than to nature) or even an angelic rank, and thus to Ğibrīl. However, where the Qur'ān speaks of God 'breathing' His spirit (in six references, Q. 21:91, Q. 66:12, Q. 15:29, Q. 38:72, Q. 4:171 and Q. 32:9), the commentators and exegetes would have to separate this 'spirit' from 'angel' and move towards a less unlikely congruence.

Of particular interest in terms of the apparent equivalence between Ğibrīl and the 'spirit' are the two Qur'ānic accounts of the disclosure of ʿĪsā's conception, comprising a single heavenly messenger in the earlier account (Q. 19:16–21) and a gathering of angels addressing Maryam, seemingly in unison, in the later account (Q. 3:42–47) uncoupling this latter passage both from Q. 19 and from the Lucan narrative in the Christian Scriptures.

In this latter narrative (Q. 3), a group of angels informs Maryam of the conception; in the same *sūrat* it is a group of angels which addresses Zakariyyā, announcing to him the birth of a son, Yaḥyā (in contraposition to the announcements of al-Ḥusayn's

---

Q. 66:12), three times as 'the angels and the Spirit' (*al-malā'ika wa-l-rūḥ*, Q. 70:4, Q. 78:38 ['the Spirit and the angels'], Q. 97:4), twice as 'My Spirit' (*rūḥī*, Q. 15:29, Q. 38:72), twice as 'the Spirit of His command' (*al-rūḥ min amri-hi*, Q. 16:2, Q. 40:15), twice as 'a Spirit from Him' (*rūḥ^un min-hu*, Q. 4:171, Q. 58:22) and once as 'the True Spirit' (*al-rūḥ al-amīn*, Q. 26:193), 'His Spirit' (*rūḥi-hi*, Q. 32:9), 'the Spirit is by command of my Lord' (*al-rūḥ min amri rabbī*, Q. 17:85), a Spirit of Our command (*rūḥ^un min amri-nā*, Q. 42:52) and the Spirit (*al-rūḥ*, Q. 17:85). Pickthall, whom I have here followed, is incorrect in his translation of *rūḥ al-qudus* as 'the Holy Spirit', and is inconsistent in his writing 'spirit' with a capital letter. In fact, the interpreters and translators who insist on spelling 'spirit' with the uppercase only add to the confusion, leading people to think this must be some sort of divine being.

death rather than birth) who, in popular tradition and parallel with al-Ḥusayn, spends only six months in the womb. In Q. 3:42–45 the angelic group addresses Maryam, making known to her the favour she has with God, instructing her in the elements of a virtuous life and announcing to her a son, albeit it in language more obscure than that used for Zakariyyā; not a son precisely but 'a word from God' who will be named, be illustrious and will be one of the *muqarribūn* – not, in this context, the angels 'drawn near' but simply 'those' drawn near. In response to the not unexpected questions asked by Zakariyyā and by Maryam, the group of angels becomes one, or at least one angel becomes the spokesperson for the group, making answer.[35]

In the earlier Qur'ānic narrative (Q. 19:19), the announcement of a son to Maryam is made by a single heavenly visitor, identified in the text as 'Our spirit' (*rūḥa-nā*). The visitor nominates himself as a 'messenger', but the appellation 'Our spirit' is repeated both in Q. 21:91 («*And she who was chaste, therefor We breathed into her (something) of Our Spirit*») and in Q. 66:12 («*And Mary, daughter of 'Imran, whose body was chaste, therefor We breathed therein something of Our Spirit*»), in which the verbal announcement by a visitor becomes an action on the part of God. Authors like Shellabear[36] suggest that in the so-called Meccan period particularly (c. 610–622), the word 'spirit' (*rūḥ*) was related to the angels, specifically Ǧibrīl, whom the very appellation seems to distinguish from all other angels (Q. 70:4, Q. 78:38 and Q. 97:4 all draw a distinction between «*the angels and the Spirit*» leading Macdonald to suggest the 'spirit' as a personality distinct from the angels).[37] As already noted, the Qur'ān never actually giving the designation 'angel' to Ǧibrīl implies that his status and function are

---

[35] ZAHNISER A.H.M., "The Word of God and the Apostleship of ʿĪsā: a Narrative Analysis of Āl ʿImrān (3): 33–66" in *Journal of Semitic Studies* XXXVII/1 Spring 1991: 101.

[36] SHELLABEAR W.G., "The Meaning of the Word 'Spirit' as used in the Koran – A Message to Muslims" in *The Muslim World*, 22 (4), 1932: 355–360.

[37] MACDONALD D.B., "The Development of the Idea of Spirit in Islam" in *The Muslim World*, 22 (1), 1932: 25–42, 22 (2): 153–168.

indeed different; it is in the corpus of *aḥādīṯ* that this supernatural being and bringer of revelation is called 'angel'.[38]

In al-Ḥusayn's case, the announcement is never made by a group of angels, but always by one who is clearly identified either by name (Ǧibrīl), or by title (such as 'the angel of the rain') or by some distinguishing characteristic (such as being described as an angel 'never sent before'). In the stories of the predictions of al-Ḥusayn's death, it is quite clearly Ǧibrīl who takes a singular role, performing distinct gestures in order to retrieve dust from Karbalāʾ; beating the ground with his hand, his fist or his wing to produce red mud, or extending his hand, or reaching into Karbalāʾ to seize a handful of its dust, or simply expanding his wing.

It would be hard to conclude that Muḥammad's experiences recounted in these dream texts were auditory rather than visual. The language used and the physicality expressed (such as Ǧibrīl handing him the dust of Karbalāʾ) suggest the very opposite; that Muḥammad saw Ǧibrīl, perhaps in a simple although unusual anthropomorphic form (he did, after all, have functional wings), while others (like Umm Salama) did not. Even al-Ḥusayn rarely if ever expresses childhood memories of actually seeing his grandfather's celestial visitor. Seldom does anyone besides Muḥammad see the heavenly messenger, even among those present at the time of the visitation (Fāṭima's tactile experience does not confirm that she saw her guests, and although sometimes it seems that Umm Salama does, this is never explicitly confirmed).

In an early visitation concerning the death of Muḥammad's son Ibrāhīm, in a narrative carried by al-Baġdādī, Ǧibrīl descended to him with 'revelation' from the Lord of the worlds. Al-Baġdādī employs the term *waḥy*, which as Madigan notes, even when addressed to prophets or messengers, does not necessarily imply scriptural revelation.[39] Nonetheless, it is of note that in attempting

---

[38] While the majority commentators easily equate Ǧibrīl with 'Our Spirit', thus making him the celestial visitor in Q. 19, it is of note that others, such as ʿĪsā, are also referred to as a 'spirit' in the Qurʾānic text (cf. for e.g. Q. 4:171).

[39] MADIGAN D., "Revelation" in Jane Dammen McAuliffe et al (eds.), *Encyclopaedia of the Qurʾān*, vol. IV, Brill, Leiden 2001: 440.

to clarify Ǧibrīl's appearance and method, others like al-Tirmiḏī take pains to separate Ǧibrīl's announcements about al-Ḥusayn from his more usual revelatory messages, to the extent of even re-identifying the angel.

The conversation between Muḥammad and the angel standing before him also grows in emotion and intensity, with Muḥammad intermittently taking the lead. In the early accounts he is a silent recipient; then he begins to express a wish to know the identity of the killers, and eventually asks to be shown the place (or the dust of the place) of the killing. Slowly too, the reader of these accounts becomes aware of the land of Karbalāʾ, which at first is hesitantly described only by certain physical elements; in an early text from al-Ḫawārizmī and Ibn Ṭāʾūs for example, Muḥammad is shown al-Ḥusayn's tomb. More frequently, it is through red dust or soil by which al-Ḥusayn's place of martyrdom is depicted. Sequentially, it is pinpointed more exactly, rather than remaining merely a place from which Ǧibrīl retrieves dust, and is named by its description as a land of distress (*karb*) and tribulation (*balāʾ*).

But at its deepest level, beyond all the details of bloodied soil and the air pulsating with beating wings, beyond the flurry of angelic movement and Umm Salama's ineffectual attempts to guard a door, beyond the proposition of the Ḥusaynian model as an indictment of iniquity and a paradigm of defiant resistance against injustice in its manifold forms, these reports detail the manner in which a very particular group people of encountered the divine. After all, the whole Muslim ethic roots itself in the conviction that the most elemental relationship in life is the relationship with God.

One might be tempted to think that these accounts of al-Ḥusayn are merely an attempt by some Shīʿī scholars to give angelic endorsement to the drama of his martyrdom. In fact, outside of the corpus of Shīʿī *aḥādīṯ* and history, they are quite patently found in the works of non-Shīʿī scholars. Nor are angelic messages about al-Ḥusayn necessarily a later interpolation; the 2nd/8th century Ibn Ṭahmān is only one of a group of scholars already alluding to them a century before al-Tirmiḏī. Even if, as noted at the very start, we choose to follow a substantial number of non-Muslim academics and regard large parts of the corpus of *aḥādīṯ* as unreliable, we still have to deal with these stories, in a basic narrative form, in the important Islamic historians, most of whom are Sunnī, so that these reports must be regarded as more than just a Shīʿī reading of history or an attempt at divine endorsement.

> In the secularized world, religious and secular history rarely coalesce, but in the great monotheistic faith traditions they do, and in Islam they are inextricably bound, running with little contention along almost parallel lines. For the secular historian, there may be no such objective reality as 'sacred history'; it has no obvious significance for secular history except insofar as secular history is affected by the way that religious groups or movements impact upon and modify the course of events. For the believer however, Jewish, Christian or Muslim, secular and sacred history journey together, since the sacred is understood as the frequent interventions and eruptions of God into the world, a collection of divine responses to earthly events. As Mahmoud Ayoub asks:

What criterion, then, must the historian, and especially the historian of religion, use in examining the various traditions purporting to relate an event of great significance for the religious life of so many people over so many centuries...? It will not do...to limit ourselves to the bare facts as we see them, because even they have to be arbitrarily chosen. Nor can we, to be sure, take all traditions to be factual data. We must, however, choose our facts, often including those facts which, while to us they do not seem historically valid, were nonetheless considered as such by the community...[40]

Mainstream Christians regard the Resurrection of Jesus as an historical occurrence, backed up at the very least by eyewitness accounts of an empty tomb and startling appearances; and yet this event does not find its way into secular history, in the way, for example, that the assassination of the Archduke Ferdinand, also an historical event supported by eyewitnesses, does. Nonetheless, Christians consistently believe in the historicity of the Resurrection, as also the Incarnation, so that we are bound to read their sacred texts not just academically but also according to the understanding

---

[40] AYOUB M., *Redemptive Suffering in Islam. A Study of the Devotional Aspects of ʿAshura in Twelver Shiʿism*, Mouton Publishers, The Hague 1978: 137.

of the religious reader; how that text forges, informs and persuades faith. The angelic announcement of an important birth or death is a fairly standard category in the scriptural traditions of the monotheistic faiths. The Annunciation narrated by Luke, for example, is regarded by exegetes as an historical narration, expressed in a genre generally held to be the announcement of a marvellous birth (either by reason of the manner of birth or of the one born), a literary genre that is well known in the Hebrew Scriptures. In those scriptures, there are several instances when a heavenly messenger announces to a woman, already advanced in age and/or sterile, that she will become a mother through a special intervention of God and counter to the laws of nature.[41]

It is unsurprising therefore, that historians like Ibn ʿAsākir and Ibn Kaṯīr should include accounts of angelic mediation in their texts; as Von Grunebaum underscores, "the objective validity of the oneiric data" is not questioned: "[T]he cognitive significance of the dream is sufficiently established and explained by the observation that 'the prophets were wont to consider dreams as revelation to them of the sacred law'."[42] Even if later Shīʿī devotees augmented the stories, adding a certain texture and depth and colour, the basic narrative remains unaltered.

Similarly, aside from purely academic motives, we have to read these texts about al-Ḥusayn – not specifically of Karbalāʾ, which easily finds its way into secular history, but the angelic announcements of his death – in the same way that religious people read them. Critical textual analysis forms a substantial and crucial part of

---

[41] Some of the best-known texts are Gen. 18:9–15 (an angelic messenger announces that the aged Sarah is to become the mother of Isaac), Jdg. 13:2–7 (an angelic messenger announces that the sterile wife of Manoah is to become the mother of Samson), I Sam. 1:1–18 (the story of Hannah and her Samuel, admittedly different in that there is no angelic visitor). In the New Testament, in the passage immediately preceding the Annunciation to Mary, an angel announces to Zechariah that his aged and sterile wife Elizabeth will conceive a child (Lk. 1: 11–22).

[42] VON GRUNEBAUM G.E. "The Cultural Function of the Dream as Illustrated by Classical Islam" in G.E von Grunebaum & R. Caillois. (eds.)., *The Dream and Human Societies*, 1966: 7.

academic life; but it is not the only or even primary reason for reading and appreciating a text. If we only read Ḥāfiẓ[43] or Wilfred Owen[44] for the purpose of critical analysis, we should fail to appreciate the cadences of great literature.

This short work is an attempt to read again the texts of encounter between humans and the divine in an attempt to catch the strains of an authentic angelic voice coming down through the years, as fresh as it was when it rang out in the house of Umm Salama.

---

[43] Ḫwāǧa Shams al-Dīn Muḥammad Ḥāfiẓ al-Shīrāzī (d. 1390), Persian poet.

[44] Wildred Owen (d. 1918), British poet.

Appendix One: The Writing on the Wall

The texts recorded in this appendix are markedly evocative of a story recorded in the Hebrew Scriptures, in the fifth chapter of the Book of Daniel. It concerns an incident during an irreligious dinner held by the Babylonian regent Belshazzar, in the course of which a hand appears and writes indecipherable words on the palace wall. With his advisors and scholars floundering, Belshazzar, upon the advice of the queen mother,[1] sends for the young Daniel, the decoder of dreams, who unlocks for him the meaning of the doom-laden words.

As it stands, the Daniel story is not without ambiguity. Belshazzar, for example, is portrayed as king and as son of Nebuchad-

[1] Rather, notes Robert Alter than the 'queen', as found in the text, who would not have had more information about Daniel than her husband the king. Cf. ALTER R., *The Hebrew Bible. A Translation with Commentary*, vol. III, W. Norton & Company, New York 2019: 9389–9390.

nezzar;[2] in reality, Belshazzar is quite clearly the eldest son of Nabonidus, the last king of the Babylonian empire, and regent for his father who was regularly absent from the city for prolonged periods. It is for this reason that all he can offer Daniel as a reward for deciphering the words on the wall is the position of third highest ruler in the kingdom, because he himself is in second place after his father, the king *in absentia.* A substantial proportion of scholars suggest that the story of Belshazzar's feast as recounted in the Hebrew Scriptures is a work of historical fiction, since it contains a series of inconsistent details. In and of themselves, the inaccuracies do not detract from the story; even if Belshazzar was never technically king, Daniel referring to him as such is consonant, for example, with Herod Antipas, who in the Gospel of Matthew (14:1, 9) is called 'king' although was only ever a governor (tetrarch). For all intents and purposes, Belshazzar was crown prince and regent of Babylon in his father's absence.

The feast story, in which Belshazzar plays a key role, holds a number of similarities with later, Islamic texts detailing the divine retribution for the ill-treatment and killing of al-Ḥusayn by members of Muḥammad's own community. In the thirty-one verses of the fifth chapter, Daniel recounts the story as follows:

> King Belshazzar gave a great banquet for his noblemen, a thousand of them, and, in the presence of this thousand, he drank his wine. Having tasted the wine, Belshazzar gave orders for the gold and silver vessels to be brought which his father Nebuchadnezzar had taken from the sanctuary in Jerusalem, so that the king, his noblemen, his wives and the women who sang for him could drink out of them. The gold and silver vessels taken from the sanctuary of the Temple of God in Jerusalem were brought in, and the king, his noblemen, his wives and the women who sang for him drank out of them. They drank their wine and praised their idols of gold and silver, of bronze

---

[2] Five times Nebuchadnezzar is called Belshazzar's father (Dan. 5:2, 11, 13, 18), and on one occasion Belshazzar is called Nebuchadnezzar's son (Dan. 5:22); however, in flexible biblical usage, the terms 'father' and 'son' could be a conventional reference to ancestors or descendants.

> and iron, of wood and stone. Suddenly, the fingers of a human hand appeared and began to write on the plaster of the palace wall, directly behind the lamp-stand; and the king could see the hand as it wrote. The king turned pale with alarm: his hip-joints went slack and his knees began to knock. He shouted for his soothsayers, Chaldeans, and exorcists. And the king said to the Babylonian sages: Anyone who can read this writing and tell me what it means shall be dressed in purple, and have a chain of gold put round his neck, and be one of the three men who govern the kingdom. The king's sages all crowded forward, but they could neither read the writing nor explain to the king what it meant.

The Islamic texts, coming both from Sunnī and from Shīʿī transmitters, situate a comparable event in a number of distinct contexts. The first concerns a group of soldiers, on their way to Damascus with the head of the martyred al-Ḥusayn:

> On the authority of Abū Qabīl, who said: When al-Ḥusayn was killed, they cut off his head and they sat down on the first leg of the journey, drinking wine and striking the head when there emerged before them from the wall an iron pen, which wrote in a line of blood: 'Does a nation who killed al-Ḥusayn hope for the intercession of his grandfather on the Day of Reckoning?' They fled, relinquishing the head, and returned.[3]

---

[3] al-Ṭabarānī., *al-Muʿğam al-kabīr*, vol. III, n. 2873: 123, al-Ḫawārizmī., *Maqtal al-Ḥusayn*, Part Two, bb. *Fī bayān ʿuqūba qātil al-Ḥusayn*, n. 28: 105–106, Ibn ʿAsākir., *Tārīḫ madīnat Dimashq*, vol. XIV, bb. 1566 (*al-Ḥusayn b. ʿAlī b. Abī Ṭālib b. ʿAbd al-Muṭṭalib b. Hāshim b. ʿAbd al-Manāf*): 244, Ibn Shahrāshūb., *Manāqib āl Abī Ṭālib*, vol. IV, bb *Fī imāma Abī ʿAbd Allāh al-Ḥusayn*: 61, al-Shāmī., *al-Durr al-naẓīm fī manāqib al-aʾimma al-lahāhīm*, bb. 5 (*Faṣl fī ḏikr maqtal al-Ḥusayn b. ʿAlī*): 570, Ibn Ṭāʾūs., *Kitāb al-luhūf fī qatlā al-ṭufūf*: 101 (omits any details of the place in which the group had stopped), Ibn Namā al-Ḥillī., *Muṯīr al-aḥzān wa munīr subul al-ashğān*: 96, al-Ṭabarī., *Ḏaḫāʾir al-ʿuqbā*, Part One, bb. 9: 248, Ibn Kaṯīr., *al-Bidāya wa-l-nihāya*, vol. XI, bb. *al-Iḫbār maqtal al-Ḥusayn b. ʿAlī*: 573 (omits any details of the place in which the group had stopped), al-Hayṯamī., *Mağmaʿ al-zawāʾid wa-manbaʿ al-fawāʾid*, vol. IX, bk. 37 (*Kitāb al-manāqib*), bb. 95

A number of texts remove these interrogative words from the context of mysterious writing on a wall and count them instead among one of the cosmic consequences of al-Ḥusayn's murder as witnessed in Jerusalem; besides blood under the stones, reddened walls and rain of blood for three days, an unknown voice is heard to say: "Does a nation which killed al-Ḥusayn hope for the intercession of his grandfather on the Day of Reckoning?" The verses go on to warn that God will forbid them the intercession of Aḥmad (Muḥammad) or Abū Turāb (ʿAlī), since they have killed "the best of those who ride mounts and the best of those from old to young."[4] Nonetheless, they are generally associated with those transporting the head of al-Ḥusayn or with a group of Muslims who find them written on a church wall. In his *Riyāḍ al-abrār*, al-Ǧazā'irī associates the words with a large group travelling after Karbalā', although a significant number of transmitters associate

(*Manāqib al-Ḥusayn b. ʿAlī*), n. 15177: 233, al-Suyūṭī., *al-Ḫaṣā'iṣ al-kubrā*, vol. II: 455, al-Baḥrānī *Madīnat al-maʿāǧiz fī muʿǧizāt al-a'imma al-aṭhār*, vol. IV, n. 180/1127: 116, al-Maǧlisī., *Biḥār al-anwār*, vol. XLIV, bb. 30, n. 4: 224, vol. XLV, bb. 39, n. 1: 125, bb. 46, n. 4: 305, al-Iṣfahānī., *ʿAwālim al-ʿulūm wa-l-maʿārif al-aḥwāl min al-āyāt wa-l-aḫbār wa-l-aqwāl*, vol. XVII, ch. 10, bb. 17, n. 3: 111, ch. 16, bb. 4, n. 19: 425, ch. 21, bb. 6, n. 1: 603, al-Ǧazā'irī., *Riyāḍ al-abrār fī manāqib al-a'imma al-aṭhār*, vol. I, Part One: 245. In his *Madīnat al-maʿāǧiz* al-Baḥrānī also records the words as an unidentified voice heard during the journey with the head: "Does a nation which killed al-Ḥusayn hope for the intercession of his grandfather on the Day of Reckoning? They have angered and doggedly opposed the Prophet, and have no dread of him for the Day of Torment. Will not God not curse the Banū Ziyād, and settle them in torment in Hell?" (al-Baḥrānī *Madīnat al-maʿāǧiz fī muʿǧizāt al-a'imma al-aṭhār*, vol. IV, n. 170/1117: 107).

[4] Ibn Qūlawayh., *Kāmil al-ziyārāt*, bb. 24, n. 2: 160, al-Baḥrānī., *Madīnat al-maʿāǧiz fī muʿǧizāt al-a'imma al-aṭhār*, vol. IV, n. 263/1210: 186, al-Maǧlisī., *Biḥār al-anwār*, vol. XLV, bb. 40, n. 6: 204, al-Iṣfahānī., *ʿAwālim al-ʿulūm wa al-maʿārif al-aḥwāl min al-āyāt wa-l-aḫbār wal-aqwāl*, vol. IV, bb. 7, n. 2: 110, vol. XVII, ch. 17, bb. 1, n. 2: 466, al-Ǧazā'irī., *Riyāḍ al-abrār fī manāqib al-a'imma al-aṭhār*, vol. I, Part One, 266. Abū Turāb ('the father of dust') is a nickname given ʿAlī by Muḥammad.

Mufaḫar b. Ṯaʿlaba with the transportation of al-Ḥusayn's head, but with different verses or no verses at all:[5]

> As for Yazīd b. Muʿāwiya, he wrote to Ibn Ziyād ordering him to transport the head of al-Ḥusayn and his companions, his women and his baggage. Ibn Ziyād summoned Mufaḫar b. Ṯaʿlaba, who greeted with peace the heads and the women, and travelled with them, as the unbelievers travel with prisoners, their faces distinct to the people of the regions. They alighted on the first leg of the journey and began to drink, when from the wall a hand emerged with an iron pen and wrote in a line of blood a verse: 'Does a nation which killed al-Ḥusayn hope for the intercession of his grandfather on the Day of Reckoning?'[6]

In a second series of transmissions, the stopping place is specified as a Christian monastery:

> On the authority of Sulaymān al-Aʿmash, who said: While I was performing *ṭawāf* in the days of the festival, a man said: "O God forgive me, although I know that You will not forgive!" I asked him the reason and he replied: "I was one of the forty who carried the head of al-Ḥusayn to Yazīd. On the way to Syria, we encamped on the first leg of our journey from Karbalāʾ at a monastery (*dayr*) of the Christians; the head was fixed on a spear and food set before us. We were eating when a line in blood was written on the wall of a monastery by a hand with

---

[5] Cf. for e.g. al-Mufīd., *al-Irshād fī maʿrifat ḥuǧaǧ Allāh ʿalā al-ʿibād*, vol. II, bb. *Tārīḫ al-Imām al-Ḥusayn*: 131, al-Ṭabarsī., *Iʿlām al-warā bi-aʿlām al-hudā*: vol. I, bb. 2: 160, Ibn Ṭāʾūs., *Kitāb al-luhūf fī qatlā al-ṭufūf*: 84–85, Ibn Namā al-Ḥillī., *Muṯīr al-aḥzān wa munīr subul al-ashǧān*: 90, al-Mūsawī., *Tasliyat al-maǧālis wa zīnat al-maǧālis*, vol. II, *maǧlis* 8: 373, al-Baḥrānī *Madīnat al-maʿāǧiz fī muʿǧizāt al-aʾimma al-aṭhār*, vol. III, n. 744: 84–85, al-Maǧlisī., *Biḥār al-anwār*, vol. XLV, bb. 39, n. 1: 124, 130, al-Iṣfahānī., *ʿAwālim al-ʿulūm wa-l-maʿārif al-aḥwāl min al-āyāt wa-l-aḫbār wa-l-aqwāl*, vol. XVII, ch. 17, bb. 4, n. 19: 425, 430.

[6] al-Ǧazāʾirī., *Riyāḍ al-abrār fī manāqib al-aʾimma al-aṭhār*, vol. I, Part One, 245.

> an iron pen: 'Does a nation[7] which killed al-Ḥusayn hope for the intercession of his grandfather on the Day of Reckoning?' We were deeply uneasy; some of us made for the hand to seize it, but it vanished, and my companions came back."[8]

In his *Iṯbat al-hudāt* al-Ḥurr al-ʿĀmilī adds: "We were deeply uneasy at this; some of us made for the hand to seize it, but it vanished, and my companions had come back to the meal when the hand reappeared and wrote, like the first time: No, by God, there is no intercessor for them; on the Day of Resurrection they will be in torment."[9] For his part, al-Baḥrānī adds in *Madīnat al-maʿāǧiz*: "My companions went to it but it vanished. Then they went back to the meal, and the pen returned and wrote: They killed al-Ḥusayn by virtue of wanton deviation; their judgment is at variance with the judgment of the Book."[10] In an extended account in *Biḥār al-anwār*, taken from al-Rāwandī, the hand disappears and then appears a second time to write: "No, by God, no one will intercede on their behalf on the Day of Judgment and they will face punishment,"

---

[7] Here, the word is 'nation' or 'community' (*umma*); in other versions, 'company' or 'group' (*maʿshar*).

[8] al-Rāwandī., *al-Ḫarāʾiǧ wa-l-ǧarāʾiḥ fī-l-muʿǧizāt*, vol. II, Part Three, bb. 14: 578, Ibn Namā al-Ḥillī., *Muṯīr al-aḥzān wa munīr subul al-ashǧān*: 96–97, al-Shāmī., *al-Durr al-naẓīm fī manāqib al-aʾimma al-lahāhīm*, bb. 5 (*Faṣl fī ḏikr maqtal al-Ḥusayn b. ʿAlī*): 562, al-Bayyāḍī., *al-Ṣirāṭ al-mustaqīm ilā mustaḥaqq al-taqdīm fī al-imāma*, vol. II, n. 8: 179 (who omits the iron pen and simply has a hand emerge from the wall and begin to write), al-Ḥurr al-ʿĀmilī., *Iṯbat al-hudāt bi-l-nuṣūṣ wa-l-muʿǧizāt*, vol. IV, bb. 15, n. 33: 46 (who also omits mention of a pen), al-Baḥrānī *Madīnat al-maʿāǧiz fī muʿǧizāt al-aʾimma al-aṭhār*, vol. IV, Part Four, n. 193/1140: 139, al-Mağlisī., *Biḥār al-anwār*, vol. XLV, bb. 39, n. 31: 180, al-Iṣfahānī., *ʿAwālim al-ʿulūm wa-l-maʿārif al-aḥwāl min al-āyāt wa-l-aḫbār wa-l-aqwāl*, vol. XVII, ch. 16, bb. 4, n. 2: 399, al-Ğazāʾirī., *Riyāḍ al-abrār fī manāqib al-aʾimma al-aṭhār*, vol. I, Part One: 167, 258.

[9] al-Ḥurr al-ʿĀmilī., *Iṯbat al-hudāt bi-l-nuṣūṣ wa-l-muʿǧizāt*, vol. IV, n. 33: 46.

[10] al-Baḥrānī in *Madīnat al-maʿāǧiz fī muʿǧizāt al-aʾimma al-aṭhār*, vol. IV, n. 193/1140: 138, al-Mağlisī., *Biḥār al-anwār*, vol. XLV, bb. 46, n. 4: 305.

then disappearing and reappearing a third time to write: "They have murdered al-Ḥusayn by an oppressive judgment, and their judgment is opposed to the judgment of the Book."[11]

The figure of the man praying without hope for mercy echoes through the stories of guilt and retribution after the death of al-Ḥusayn; in al-Rāwandī's account, al-Aʿmash interrupts his *ṭawāf* in order to approach and counsel the man whose desperate prayer he has overheard. In the ensuing conversation, the gravity of even mere association with al-Ḥusayn's death is underscored, and the account ends not on a note of mercy but on one of hopelessness:

> I was doing the *ṭawāf* of the festival when I saw a man praying and saying: "O Lord, forgive me, though I know that You will not." At that, I got up and approached him and said: You are in the sanctuary of God and the sanctuary of His messenger and these are sacred days in a great month, so do not despair of forgiveness. He replied: "My sin is great!" I said: Greater than the Tihāma mountain? He answered: "Yes!" So, I said: Comparable to the mountains of *rawāsī*?[12] He answered: "Yes. If you want, I will inform you." I said: Inform me, and he replied: "Leave the sanctuary with us," so we left.[13]

The man tells of his membership of "the accursed army, the army of ʿUmar b. Saʿd," and the subsequent events in the monastery, with the hand appearing a second time and writing: "No, by God, there is no intercessor for them; on the Day of Resurrection they will be in torment." Like al-Bayyāḍī and al-Ḥurr al-ʿĀmilī, al-Rāwandī omits mention of the pen; nevertheless, the pen hearkens

[11] al-Rāwandī., *al-Ḫarāʾiǧ wa-l-ǧarāʾiḥ fi-l-muʿǧizāt*, vol. II, Part Three, bb. 14: 578, al-Maǧlisī., *Biḥār al-anwār*, vol. XLV, bb. 39, n. 31: 184–185, al-Ǧazāʾirī., *Riyāḍ al-abrār fī manāqib al-aʾimma al-aṭhār*, vol. I, Part One: 258.

[12] The Tihāma mountains lie in south-west Saudi Arabia; the Arabic *rawāsī* is a Qurʾānic word used for mountains in general (Q. 13:3, Q. 15:19, Q. 16:15, Q. 21:31, Q. 27:61, Q. 31:10).

[13] al-Rāwandī., *al-Ḫarāʾiǧ wa-l-ǧarāʾiḥ fi-l-muʿǧizāt*, vol. II, Part Three, bb. 14: 578.

back to Q. 96:4 («*Who teacheth by the pen*»), intimating a forgetfulness of all that God has taught and a need for Him to teach again.

The mention of monasteries and monks leads inevitably into the field of Muslim-Christian polemics; a third series of texts moves the reader away from the monastery and the transportation of al-Ḥusayn's head, to a Byzantine church and a group of Muslim scholars:

> I was told by a prayer leader of the mosque of the Banū Sulaym, who said: Scholars from among us made a foray into Byzantium and found in one of their churches: 'Does a nation which killed al-Ḥusayn hope for the intercession of his grandfather on the Day of Reckoning?' Then they said: "How long is it since you found this writing in this church?" They replied: "Three hundred years[14] before the emergence of your prophet."[15]

---

[14] While most of the texts read 'three hundred years', Ibn ʿAsākir (and from him, Ibn al-ʿAdīm) in one transmission reads 'six hundred'.

[15] al-Ṭabarī., *Bishārat al-muṣṭafā*, Part Seven: 201, al-Ṭabarānī., *al-Muʿǧam al-kabīr*, vol. III, n. 2874: 124, Ibn Bābawayh., *Kitāb al-amālī fī al-aḥādīṯ wa-l-aḫbār*, *maǧlis* 27, n. 6: 131, Ibn ʿAlī al-Fattāl., *Rawḍat al-wāʿiẓīn wa-tabṣirat al-muttaʿiẓīn*, vol. I: 193, al-Ḫawārizmī., *Maqtal al-Ḥusayn*, Part Two, bb. *Fī bayān ʿuqūba qātil al-Ḥusayn*, n. 29: 106, Ibn ʿAsākir., *Tārīḫ madīnat Dimashq*, vol. XIV, bb. 1566 (*al-Ḥusayn b. ʿAlī b. Abī Ṭālib b. ʿAbd al-Muṭṭalib b. Hāshim b. ʿAbd al-Manāf*): 243, al-Shāmī., *al-Durr al-naẓīm fī manāqib al-aʾimma al-lahāhīm*, bb. 5 (*Faṣl fī ḏikr maqtal al-Ḥusayn b. ʿAlī*): 570 (who situates the church 'close to Constantinople' [al-Qusṭanṭīniyya]), Ibn al-ʿAdīm., *Buġyat al-ṭalab fī tārīḫ Ḥalab*, Part Six: 2653, Ibn Namā al-Ḥillī., *Muṯīr al-aḥzān wa munīr subul al-ashǧān*: 96–97 (who situates the church 'close to Constantinople' [al-Qusṭanṭīniyya])), Ibn Kaṯīr., *al-Bidāya wa-l-nihāya*, vol. XI, bb. *al-Iḫbār maqtal al-Ḥusayn b. ʿAlī*: 573, al-Hayṯamı., *Maǧmaʿ al-zawāʾid wa-manbaʿ al-fawāʾid*, vol. IX, bk. 37 (*Kitāb al-manāqib*), bb. 95 (*Manāqib al-Ḥusayn b. ʿAlī*), n. 15178: 233–234, al-Maǧlisī., *Biḥār al-anwār*, vol. XLIII, bb. 30, n. 3: 224–225 (who situates the church 'close to Constantinople' [al-Qusṭanṭīniyya]), al-Iṣfahānī., *ʿAwālim al-ʿulūm wa al-maʿārif al-aḥwāl min al-āyāt wa-l-aḫbār wa-l-aqwāl*, vol. XVII, ch. 10, bb. 7, n.

A number of transmitters offer variants in the details; al-Irbilī notes that the writing is in Arabic, and uses 'the Day of Return' (*yawm al-maʿād*) rather than 'the Day of Reckoning' (*yawm al-ḥisāb*). When asked, the Byzantine custodians of the church have no idea when the words were written.[16] Al-Maǧlisī transmits an account in which the words are inscribed in Byzantine Greek (*al-rūmiyya*), and the scholars have to ask someone from among the Syrians who can read the language.[17] Ibn Namā and al-Maǧlisī after him also carry a transmission which puts the writing into Himyaritic script, again leading the scholars to seek help from some Syrians in translating it.[18]

Finally, some transmitters relate this story to an unnamed Christian man:

> ʿAbd Allāh b. al-Ṣaffār, companion of Abū Ḥamza al-Ṣūfī said: We made a foray and captured prisoners. Among them was an old man from among some judicious Christians; we treated him deferentially and were friendly to him, and he said to us: "My father informed me, on the authority of his father, that they were digging a well in the country of the Byzantines, three hundred years before Muḥammad was sent to the Arabs, and they hit a stone on which was written in *al-musnad* this verse:[19]

2: 110, al-Ǧazā'irī., *Riyāḍ al-abrār fī manāqib al-a'imma al-aṭhār*, vol. I, Part One: 167.

[16] al-Irbilī., *Kashf al-ġumma fī maʿrifat al-a'imma*, vol. II: 54.

[17] Ibn Namā al-Ḥillī., *Muṯīr al-aḥzān wa munīr subul al-ashǧān*: 97, al-Maǧlisī., *Biḥār al-anwār*, vol. XLIII, bb. 30, n. 4: 224–225.

[18] Ibn Namā al-Ḥillī., *Muṯīr al-aḥzān wa munīr subul al-ashǧān*: 96–97, al-Maǧlisī., *Biḥār al-anwār*, vol. XLIV, bb. 30, n. 4: 225.

[19] In these two passages, the reference is to an ancient south Arabian script (WEHR H., *A Dictionary of Modern Written Arabic*, 1980: 507). As one of the texts notes, it is reputed to be the language of the children of Seth (Shayṯ) who lived prior to Nūḥ. (LANE E.W., *An Arabic-English Lexicon*, vol. IV, 1968: 1444). It is noted by al-Irbilī that the verse was written in the church in Arabic; cf. al-Irbilī., *Kashf al-ġumma fī maʿrifat al-a'imma*, vol. II: 54. Ibn Namā calls it the 'Himyaritic' script (Ibn Namā al-Ḥillī., *Muṯīr al-aḥzān wa munīr subul al-ashǧān*: 96–97).

> 'Does a band[20] which killed al-Ḥusayn hope for the intercession of his grandfather on the Day of Reckoning?"'[21]

Ibn Shahrāshūb records a closely related story of a man from the predominantly Christian city of Nağrān:

> Anas b. Mālik said: A man from Nağrān dug a hole, and it he found a gold tablet on which was written this verse, and after it: 'They have come to him with a deviant judgment, but their judgment was at variance with the judgment of the Book. Tomorrow, Yazīd, you will undergo punishment by the Merciful! The punishment that will be yours![22]

There are striking similarities in the Hebrew and Islamic texts; the sacred vessels, brought to Babylon from the Jerusalem Temple by Nebuchadnezzar and profoundly ridiculed during a banquet could be paralleled with the head of the martyr al-Ḥusayn, the sacrosanctity of which, seen in the numerous miracles recounted about it, is mocked by a group of soldiers. Admittedly, Belshazzar, in spite of his oppressive tyranny, was less malevolent than Nebuchadnezzar, whose wickedness is the catalyst for the story, and more on a level with the crude mockery of the soldiers carrying the head of al-Ḥusayn, who flee in fright at the appearance of the hand.[23] While the writing of the wall of the regent's palace is directed at him as an indictment of his reign, the verses seen by the soldiers and others associated with al-Ḥusayn's death are directed at a whole section of Muḥammad's community. Curiously, the 7th/13th century al-Shāmī in his *al-Durr al-naẓīm* produces a text in which the verses are ad-

---

[20] Here, the word is *ʿuṣba* ('band').

[21] Ibn Namā al-Ḥillī., *Muṯīr al-aḥzān wa munīr subul al-ashğān*: 96–97, al-Mağlisī., *Biḥār al-anwār*, vol. XLIII, bb. 30, n. 4: 224–225.

[22] Ibn Shahrāshūb., *Manāqib āl Abī Ṭālib*, vol. IV, bb *Fī imāma Abī ʿAbd Allāh al-Ḥusayn*: 62, al-Mağlisī., *Biḥār al-anwār*, vol. XLV, bb. 46, n. 5: 306, al-Iṣfahānī., *ʿAwālim al-ʿulūm wa al-maʿārif al-aḥwāl min al-āyāt wa-l-aḫbār wa-l-aqwāl*, vol. XVII, ch. 21, bb. 6, n. 6: 60.

[23] A passage in the prophet Amos (Amos 5: 19) – «*as when someone runs away from a lion only to meet a bear*») – is thought to imply Nebuchadnezzar and the less dauntless Belshazzar.

dressed directly to the ruler himself: Yazīd b. Muʿāwiya has been drinking heavily when a hand emerges from the wall in front of him and writes the verses in blood.[24] Although this relates Yazīd more closely with Belshazzar, it remains an extremely rare account, and out of step with most other transmissions. Nevertheless, in both stories, the consumption of alcohol plays a role, underlined by the Islamic texts as yet another accusation against those associated with the death of the martyr, starting with Yazīd himself; in both cases, whether soldiers eating the food of hospitality in a monastery (and thereby associating the unsuspecting monks with al-Ḥusayn's killing) or a feast in the crown prince's citadel, eating and drinking is portrayed in falsely celebratory terms which rapidly turn negative.

On both occasions, the story plays out in a public place, whether a monastery, a church or a regent's palace, and is witnessed by bystanders. The cryptic language of the writing in the halls of Belshazzar defy interpretation; in some of the Islamic texts, the writing is in a language not understood by those who read it and, as with Belshazzar's queen mother suggesting the use of Daniel, the scholars have to ask the help of local Syrians. In the end, the writing on Belshazzar's wall proves to be his end, marking the termination of his reign, his kingdom and his life.

The divine threat in the Islamic texts is one of spiritual retribution. The loss of Muḥammad's all-important intercession on that day when accounts are reckoned and lives weighed is echoed most clearly in the fateful words read out by Daniel to Belshazzar: "God has measured your sovereignty and put an end to it; you have been weighed in the balance and found wanting."

---

[24] al-Shāmī., *al-Durr al-naẓīm fī manāqib al-aʾimma al-lahāhīm*, bb. 5 (*Faṣl fī ḏikr maqtal al-Ḥusayn b. ʿAlī*): 570.

Appendix Two: Table of Sunnī and Shīʿī Arabic Sources

1st/7th century:

Shīʿī:

al-Hilālī.,[1] *Kitāb Sulaym b. Qays*

---

[1] Al-Hilālī died around the year 80/662; while some, like the Shīʿī bibliographer Ibn al-Nadīm (d. between 380/990 and 388/998) thought his the first Shīʿī work, later Shīʿī scholars are more doubtful, some thinking it a fabrication. Cf. KOHLBERG E., "Shīʿī *Ḥadīth*" in A.F.L. Beeston et al., (eds.), *Arabic Literature to the End of the Umayyad Period*, Cambridge University Press, Cambridge 1983: 301. Cf. also MODARRESSI H., *Tradition and Survival. A Bibliographical Survey of Early Shīʾite Literature*, vol. 1, Oneworld, Oxford 2003: 82/424). Considering the text's antiquity and its tenacious popularity among the Shīʿa, I am disinclined to ignore it entirely.

2ND/8TH CENTURY:

Sunnī:

al-Zuhrī.,[2] *al-Maġāzī al-nabawiyya*
Ibn Ṭahmān.,[3] *Mashyaḫat b. Ṭahmān*

3RD/9TH CENTURY:

Sunnī:

Ibn Saʿd.,[4] *Kitāb al-ṭabaqāt al-kabīr*
Ibn Abī Shayba.,[5] *al-Muṣannaf*
Ibn Rāhwayh.,[6] *Musnad*
Ibn Hanbal.,[7] *Musnad, Kitāb faḍā'il al-ṣaḥāba*
al-Kashshī.,[8] *Muntaḫab Musnad ʿAbd b. Ḥamīd*
al-Buḫārī.,[9] *Ṣaḥīḥ*
Muslim.,[10] *Ṣaḥīḥ*
Ibn Māǧa.,[11] *Sunan*

---

[2] Abū Bakr Muḥammad b. Muslim b. ʿUbayd Allāh b. ʿAbd Allāh b. Shihāb al-Zuhrī (d. 124/721: cf. GAS I: 280).

[3] Ibrāhīm b. Ṭahmān b. Shuʿba al-Ḫurāsānī Abū Saʿīd (d. c. 163/780: cf. GAS I: 92–93).

[4] Muḥammad b. Saʿd Kātib al-Wāqidī (d. 230/845: cf. GAL I: 136, GAL S. I: 208).

[5] Abū Bakr ʿAbd Allāh b. Muḥammad b. Ibrāhīm (Abī Shayba) b. ʿUṯmān al-ʿAbsī al-Kūfī (d. 235/849: cf. GAL I: 157, 516).

[6] Abū Yaʿqūb Isḥāq b. Ibrāhīm b. Muḫallad al-Ḥanzalī (Isḥāq b. Rāhwayh) (d. 237/852–3: cf. GAL S. I: 257)

[7] Abū ʿAbd Allāh Aḥmad b. Muḥammad b. Ḥanbal al-Shaybānī al-Ḏuhlī (d. 241/855: cf. GAL S. I: 309)

[8] Abū Muḥammad ʿAbd al-Ḥumayd (or ʿAbd al-Ḥamīd) b. Naṣr al-Kashshī (d. 249/865: cf. GAL S. I: 258–259).

[9] Abū ʿAbd Allāh Muḥammad b. Ismāʿīl b. Ibrāhīm b. Muġīra b. Bardizbah al-Buḫārī al-Ǧuʿfī (d. 256/870: cf. GAL S. I: 260).

[10] Abū al-Ḥusayn Muslim b. al-Ḥaǧǧāǧ al-Qushayrī al-Nīsābūrī (d. 261/875: cf. GAL S. 1: 265).

[11] Abū ʿAbd Allāh Muḥammad b. Yazīd b. Māǧa al-Qazwīnī (d. 273/886: cf. GAL S. I: 270).

Abū Dāwud.,[12] *Sunan*
al-Tirmiḏī.,[13] *al-Ǧāmiʿ al-ṣaḥīḥ*
al-Balāḏurī.,[14] *Kitāb ansāb al-ashraf*
al-Dīnawarī.,[15] *Kitāb al-aḫbār al-ṭiwāl*
Ibn Abī ʿĀṣim.,[16] *al-Āḥād wa-l-maṯānī*
al-Bazzār.,[17] *Musnad*

Shīʿī:

Ibn Muzāhim.,[18] *Waqʿat Ṣiffīn*
Rustam al-Ṭabarī.,[19] *Dalāʾil al-imāma*, *Bishārat al-muṣṭafā*
Ibn Abī Ṭāhir Ṭayfūr.,[20] *Balāġāt al-nisāʾ*

---

[12] Abū Dāwud Sulaymān b. al-Ashʿaṯ al-Azdī al-Siǧistānī (d. 275/889: cf. GAL S. I: 270).

[13] Abū ʿĪsā Muḥammad b. ʿĪsā b. Sahl al-Tirmiḏī (d. 279/892: cf. GAL S. I: 267).

[14] Abū al-ʿAbbās Aḥmad b. Yaḥyā b. Ǧābir al-Balāḏurī (d. 279/892: cf. GAL S. I: 216, GAS I: 320).

[15] Abū Ḥanīfa Aḥmad b. Dāwūd al-Dīnawarī (d. 282/895: cf. GAL S. I: 187).

[16] Ibn Abī ʿĀṣim Abū Bakr Aḥmad b. ʿAmr b. al-Ḍaḥḥāk b. Maḫlad al-Shaybānī, d. 287/900: cf. GAL S. I: 952 n. 312). While Brockelmann notes only his *Kitāb al-diyāt*, Sezgin lists seven works.

[17] Abū Bakr Aḥmad b. ʿAmr b. ʿAbd al-Ḫāliq al-Baṣrī al-Bazzār (d. 292–3/904–5: cf. GAL S. I: 258).

[18] Abū al-Faḍl Naṣr b. Muzāhim b. Sayyār al-Minqarī al-ʿAṭṭār (d. 212/827: cf. GAL S.I: 214). Brockelmann identifies him as the oldest Shīʿī historian and a lifelong inspector of market weights and measures in Kūfa – others sources (like al-Baġdādī in his *Tārīḫ Baġdād*) report that he lived in Baghdad.

[19] Abū Ǧaʿfar Muḥammad b. Ǧarīr b. Rustam al-Ṭabarī (c. 224/839: cf. GAS I: 540). As will be noted later in this text, Ibn Rustam al-Ṭabarī's dates and authorship are highly disputed.

[20] Abū al-Faḍl Aḥmad b. Abī Ṭāhir Ṭayfūr (d. 280/893: cf. GAL S. I: 210). Brockelmann transcribes the work as *Balāġat al-nisāʾ*. It is difficult to pinpoint Ibn Abī Ṭāhir Ṭayfūr's doctrinal or sectarian affiliation, since he himself in his numerous writings gives us no indication. He certainly wrote an elegy for the martyred Shīʿī agitator Yaḥyā b. ʿUmar, killed in

al-Yaʿqūbī,[21] *Tārīḫ*
al-Ṣaffār.,[22] *Baṣāʾir al-daraǧāt fī ʿulūm āl Muḥammad*

4TH/10TH CENTURY:

Sunnī:

al-Nasāʾī.,[23] *al-Sunan al-kubrā*
al-Ṭabarī.,[24] *Kitāb aḫbār al-rusul wa-l-mulūk*
al-Ḥarānī.,[25] *Tārīḫ al-Raqqa*
al-Āǧurrī.,[26] *Kitāb al-sharīʿa*
al-Ṭabarānī.,[27] *al-Muʿǧam al-kabīr*
Abū al-Shayḫ.,[28] *Kitab al-ʿaẓama*

Shīʿī:

al-Qummī.,[29] *Tafsīr*

Kūfa in 248/864 on the orders of Caliph al-Mustaʿīn, and in which he slates the Sunnī Caliphate for usurping the rights of ʿAlī and Fāṭima, but this in itself is no real proof of his being a Shīʿa. Cf. TOORAWA S.M., "Notes towards a biography of Ibn Abi Tahir Tayfur (820–893)" in *Social Sciences & Humanities and Law & Management Research Journal*, vol. I (1998), University of Mauritius, Réduit, Mauritius: 131.

[21] Aḥmad b. Abī Yaʿqūb b. Ǧaʿfar b. Wahb b. Wāḍih al-Kātib al-ʿAbbāsī al-Yaʿqūbī (d. 284/897 or 292/905: cf. GAL S. I: 405). If al-Yaʿqūbī was not, in fact, a Shīʿa, and this is a moot point, he evinces a strong Shīʿī predisposition.

[22] Abu Ǧaʿfar Muḥammad b. al-Ḥasan al-Ṣaffār (d. 290/903).

[23] Abū ʿAbd al-Raḥmān Aḥmad b. ʿAbd al-Raḥmān b. Shuʿayb al-Nasāʾī (d. 303/915: cf. GAL S. I: 269).

[24] Abū Ǧaʿfar Muḥammad b. Ǧarīr b. Yazīd al-Ṭabarī (d. 310/923: cf. GAS I: 232 and GAL S. I: 217).

[25] Muḥammad b. Saʿīd al-Qushayrī., (d. 334/945: cf. GAL. S. I: 210)

[26] Abū Bakr Muḥammad b. al-Ḥusayn b. ʿAlī al-Āǧurrī (d. 360/971: cf. GAL S. I: 274)

[27] Abū al-Qāsim Sulaymān b. Aḥmad b. Ayyūb b. Muṭayr al-Laḫmī al-Shāmī al-Ṭabarānī (d. 360/971: cf. GAL S. I: 279).

[28] Abu Muḥammad ʿAlī b. Muḥammad b. Ḥayyān al-Anṣārī al-Iṣfahānī Abū al-Shayḫ (d. 369/980: cf. GAL S. I: 347, GAS I: 200).

Ibn Furāt al-Kūfī.,[30] *Tafsīr Furāt b. Ibrāhīm*
Ibn Aʿtam.,[31] *Kitāb al-futūḥ*
Ibn Ḥamdān.,[32] *al-Hidāya al-Kubrā*
al-Masʿūdī.,[33] *Iṯbāt al-waṣiyya, Murūǧ al-ḏahab*
al-Iṣfahānī.,[34] *Maqātil al-ṭālibiyyīn*
al-Qāḍī al-Nuʿmān.,[35] *Sharḥ al-aḫbār fī faḍā'il al-a'imma al-aṭhār*
Ibn Qūlawayh.,[36] *Kāmil al-ziyārāt*
Ibn Bābawayh.,[37] *Kitāb al-amālī, Man lā yaḥḍuru-hu al-faqīh, ʿUyūn aḫbār al-Riḍā, Maʿānī al-aḫbār, Kitāb al-ḫiṣāl, Ikmāl (kamāl) al-dīn wa-itmām (tamām) al-niʿma fī iṯbāt al-ġayba wa-kashf al-ḥayra, ʿIlal al-sharā'iʿ wa-l-aḥkām*

---

[29] ʿAlī b. Ibrāhīm al-Qummī (d. 307/980).

[30] Furāt b. Ibrāhīm b. Furāt al-Kūfī (d. 310/992: cf. GAS I: 539).

[31] Abū Muḥammad Aḥmad b. ʿAlī b. Aʿtam al-Kūfī al-Kindī al-Aḫbārī (d. 314/926).

[32] Abū ʿAbd Allāh al-Ḥusayn b. ʿAlī b. al-Ḥusayn b. Ḥamdān al-Ḫaṣībī Zayn al-Dīn (d. 346/957 or 365/968: cf. GAS I. 584). I have chosen to keep al-Ḫaṣībī among the sources for this work although his transmissions are distrusted by a sizable number Shīʿī scholars. He is denounced by al-Naǧāshī as having corrupt beliefs (al-Naǧāshī., *Kitāb al-riǧāl*, n. 159: 67) and he seems to have had a substantial connection with the heterodox Nuṣayrī sect.

[33] Abū al-Ḥasan ʿAlī b. al-Ḥusayn b. ʿAlī al-Masʿūdī (d. 345/956: cf. GAS I: 333).

[34] Abū al-Faraǧ ʿAlī b. al-Ḥusayn b. Muḥammad b. Aḥmad b. al-Qurashī al-Iṣfahānī (d. 356/967: cf. GAL S.I: 225 and GAS I: 378). Modarressi notes that he was a Zaydī (cf. MODARRESSI H., *Tradition and Survival. A Bibliographical Survey of Early Shī'ite Literature*, vol. 1, Oneworld, Oxford 2003: 276.

[35] al-Nucmān b. Muḥammad b. Manṣūr b. Aḥmad b. Ḥayyūn al-Tamīmī al-Qāḍī Abū Ḥanīfa al-Shīca (d. 363/974: cf. GAL S. I: 324, where Brockelmann names the work differently).

[36] Abū al-Qāsim Ǧaʿfar b. Muḥammad b. Ǧaʿfar b. Mūsā b. Qūlūya al-Qummī (d. 369/979: cf. GAL S. I: 953).

[37] Abū Ǧaʿfar Muḥammad b. ʿAlī b. al-Ḥusayn b. Mūsā b. Bābawayh al-Qummī al-Ṣadūq (d. 381/991: cf. GAL S. I: 321 and GAS I: 544).

al-Ḫazzāz.,[38] *Kifāyat al-aṯar fī-l-nuṣūṣ ʿalā al-aʾimma al-iṯnā ʿasharī*

5TH/11TH CENTURY:

Sunnī:

al-Ḥākim al-Nīsābūrī.,[39] *Kitāb al-mustadrak ʿalā al-ṣaḥīḥayn*
Abū Nuʿaym.,[40] *Ḥilyat al-awliyāʾ wa-ṭabaqāt al-aṣfiyāʾ*
Abū Yaʿlā.,[41] *Musnad*
al-Baġdādī.,[42] *Tārīḫ Baġdād*
Ibn ʿAbd al-Barr.,[43] *al-Istīʿāb fī maʿrifat al-aṣḥāb*
al-Bayhaqī.,[44] *Dalāʾil al-nubuwwa*, *al-Ǧāmiʿ al-muṣannaf fī shuʿab al-īmān*
al-Ḥaskānī.,[45] *Shawāhid al-tanzīl li-qawāʿid al-tafḍīl*

Shīʿī:

al-ʿAyyāshī.,[46] *Tafsīr*

---

38 ʿAlī b. Muḥammad b. ʿAlī al-Ḫazzāz al-Rāzī al-Qummī (d. 381/991: cf. GAL S. I: 322).

39 Muḥammad b. ʿAbd Allāh b. Muḥammad al-Ḥākim al-Nīsābūrī b. al-Bayyiʿ (d. 404/1014: cf. GAL S. I: 276. Muḥammad b. ʿAbd Allāh b. Muḥammad al-Ḥākim al-Nīsābūrī b. al-Bayyiʿ (d. 404/1014: cf. GAL S. I: 276. Brockelmann incorrectly reports his death at 404/914 and names him al-Nīsābūrī as opposed to al-Naysābūrī, found in other texts).

40 Abū Nuʿaym Aḥmad b. ʿAbd Allāh b. Aḥmad b. Isḥāq al-Iṣbahānī (or al-Iṣfahānī) al-Shāfiʿī (d. 430/1038: cf. GAL S. I: 616).

41 Abū Yaʿlā Muḥammad b. al-Ḥusayn b. Muḥammad b. al-Farrāʾ al-Baġdādī (d. 458/1065: cf. GAL S. I: 686).

42 Abū Bakr Aḥmad b. ʿAlī b. Ṯābit al-Ḫaṭīb al-Baġdādī (d. 463/1071: cf. GAL I: 329).

43 Abū ʿUmar Yūsuf b. ʿAbd Allāh b. Muḥammad b. ʿAbd al-Barr al-Namarī al-Qurṭubī (d. 463/1071: cf. GAL S. I: 628).

44 Abū Bakr Aḥmad b. al-Ḥusayn b. ʿAlī b. Mūsā al-Bayhaqī (d. 458/1066: cf. GAL S. I: 618).

45 ʿUbayd Allāh b. ʿAbd Allāh b. Aḥmad al-Ḥaskānī al-Nīsābūrī (d. 490/1096)

46 Abū al-Naḍr Muḥammad b. Masʿūd al-ʿAyyāshī al-Sulamī (d. 401/1009: cf. MODARRESSI H., *Tradition and Survival*, 2003: 410 and

al-Mufīd.,[47] *al-Irshād fī maʿrifat ḥuǧaǧ Allāh ʿalā al-ʿibād, al-Amālī li-l-Mufīd*
al-Naǧāshī.,[48] *Kitāb asmāʾ al-riǧāl*
al-Ṭūsī.,[49] *Miṣbāḥ al-mutahaǧǧid, al-Amālī fī al-ḥadīṯ*
Ibn ʿAlī al-Fattāl.,[50] *Rawḍat al-wāʿiẓīn*
al-Shaǧarī.,[51] *Kitāb al-iʿtibār*

6TH/12TH CENTURY:

Sunnī:

Ibn ʿAṭiyya.,[52] *Muḥarrar al-waǧīz fī tafsīr al-kitāb al-ʿazīz*
al-Ḫawārizmī.,[53] *Maqtal al-Ḥusayn, al-Manāqib*
Ibn ʿAsākir.,[54] *Tārīḫ madīnat Dimashq*

Shīʿī:

al-Ṭabarsī.,[55] *Iʿlām al-warā bi-aʿlām al-hudā, Kitāb al-iḥtiǧāǧ ʿalā ahl al-liǧāǧ*

GAS I: 42). Brockelmann gives his date of death as 401/1009; Modarressi thinks the end of the 3rd/9th and beginning of the 4th/10th century.

[47] Muḥammad b. Muḥammad b. Nuʿmān al-Baġdādī al-Karḫī al-Mufīd (d. 413/1022. cf. GAL I: 188 and GAL S. I: 322).

[48] Abū al-ʿAbbās Aḥmad b. ʿAlī al-Naǧāshī (d. 450/1085: cf. GAL S I: 556).

[49] Abū Ǧaʿfar Muḥammad b. al-Ḥasan b. ʿAlī al-Ṭūsī *Shayḫ* al-Ṭāʾifa (d. 458/1066: cf. GAL I: 405 and GAL S. I: 706).

[50] ʿAlī Muḥammad b. Aḥmad b. ʿAlī al-Fattāl al-Nīsābūrī al-Farisī (c. mid-5th/11th century: cf. GAL S. I: 708).

[51] Yaḥyā b. al-Ḥusayn b. Ismāʿīl b. Zayd al-Ḥasanī al-Shaǧarī al-Ǧurǧānī (d. 499/1105: cf. GAL S. II: 1004, GAS I: 521–522)

[52] ʿAbd al-Ḥaqq b. Ġālib b. ʿAbd al-Raḥmān (d. 546/1147).

[53] Abū al-Muʾayyad Muwaffaq Aḥmad b. Abī Saʿīd Isḥāq al-Ḫawārizmī (d. 568/1172. cf. GAL S. I: 623).

[54] Abū al-Qāsim ʿAlī b. al-Ḥasan b. Hibat Allāh Ṯiqat al-Dīn b. ʿAsākir al-Shāfiʿī (d. 571/1176: cf. GAL S. I: 566).

[55] Raḍī al-Dīn Abū ʿAlī al-Faḍl b. al-Ḥasan Amīn al-Dīn al-Ṭabarsī (or al-Ṭabrisī) (d. 548/1153: cf. GAL S. I: 708). There remains a disparity among scholars as to whether someone from Ṭabristān should be called

Ibn Ḥamza al-Ṭūsī.,[56] *al-Ṭāqib fī-l-manāqib*
al-Rāwandī.,[57] *al-Ḫarā'iǧ wa-l-ǧarā'iḥ fī-l-mu'ǧizāt*
Ibn Shahrāshūb.,[58] *Manāqib āl Abī Ṭālib*
al-Shuʿayrī.,[59] *Ǧāmiʿ al-aḫbar*

7TH/13TH CENTURY:

Sunnī:

Ibn al-Ǧawzī.,[60] *Ṣifat al-ṣafwa, Bustān al-waʿiẓīn wa-riyāḍ al-sāmiʿīn, Kitab al-mawḍūʿāt*
Ibn al-Aṯīr.,[61] *al-Kāmil fī-l-tārīḫ, Usd al-ġāba fī maʿrifat al-ṣaḥāba*

---

al-Ṭabarsī or al-Ṭabrisī. I have chosen to follow Brockelmann and use al-Ṭabarsī; this notwithstanding, Bruce Fudge provides excellent argumentation for al-Ṭabrisī (FUDGE B., *Qur'ānic Hermeneutics: Al-Ṭabrisī and the craft of commentary*, Routledge, London 2014: 36). Brockelmann imputes to this author eight works, including *Iʿlām al-warā bi-aʿlām al-hudā*, *Kitāb al-iḥtiǧāǧ ʿalā ahl al-liǧāǧ*, *Makārim al-aḫlāq* and *Maǧmaʿ al-bayān fī tafsīr al-qur'ān*. It is to be noted that his authorship of *Makārim al-aḫlāq* and *Kitāb al-iḥtiǧāǧ ʿalā ahl al-liǧāǧ* is disputed. Brockelmann himself remarks that some authors attribute *Makārim al-aḫlāq* to his son, Abū Naṣr al-Ḥasan, and *Kitāb al-iḥtiǧāǧ* to Abū Manṣūr Aḥmad b. ʿAlī b. Abī Ṭālib al-Ṭabarsī. Cf. also KOHLBERG E., "al-Ṭabrisī" in P.J. Bearman et al., (eds.), *The Encyclopaedia of Islam*, vol. X, 2000: 40–41, FUDGE B., *Qur'ānic Hermeneutics: Al-Ṭabrisī and the craft of commentary*, 2014: 32–33.

56 ʿImād al-Dīn Abū Ǧaʿfar Muḥammad b. ʿAlī b. Ḥamza al-Ṭūsī (d. 560/1164: cf. GAL S. II: 969, 971).

57 Quṭb al-Dīn Abū al-Ḥusayn Saʿīd b. Hibat Allāh b. Abī al-Ḥasan al-Rāwandī (d. 573/1177: cf. GAL S. I: 624).

58 Abū Ǧaʿfar Muḥammad b. ʿAlī b. Shaḥrāshūb al-Māzandarānī al-Surrī Rashīd al-Dīn (d. 588/1192: cf. GAL S. I: 710).

59 Tāǧ al-Dīn Muḥammad b. Muḥammad al-Shuʿayrī (c. 6th/12th century).

60 Abū al-Faḍā'il Ǧamāl al-Dīn Abū al-Faraǧ ʿAbd al-Raḥmān b. al-Ḥasan ʿAlī b. Muḥammad b. ʿUmar b. al-Ǧawzī (d. 597/1200: cf. GAL S. I: 914, GAL I: 500).

Ibn Abī al-Dam.,[62] *al-Muḫtaṣar fī tārīḫ al-islām*
Sibṭ al-Ǧawzī.,[63] *Tadkirat al-ḫawāṣṣ al-umma bi-dikr ḫaṣāʾiṣ al-aʾimma*
Ibn al-ʿAdīm.,[64] *Buġyat al-ṭalab fī tārīḫ Ḥalab*
al-Ṭabarī.,[65] *Daḫāʾir al-ʿuqbā* (d. 684/1295)

Shīʿī:

Ibn al-Biṭrīq.,[66] *al-ʿUmda fī ʿuyūn al-aḫbār fī manāqib amīr al-muʾminīn, faṣl fī manāqib al-Ḥasan wa-l-Ḥusayn*
Ibn Abī Firās.,[67] *Tanbīh al-ḫawāṭir wa nuzhat al-nawāẓir*
Ibn al-Ḥadīd.,[68] *Sharḥ nahǧ al-balāġa*
Ibn Ṭāʾūs.,[69] *Kitāb al-luhūf fī qutlā al-ṭufūf, Kitāb al-iqbāl, al-Ṭarāʾif fī maʿrifat madhab al-ṭawāʾif, Kitāb al-iqbāl bi-l-aʿmāl al-ḥasana*
Ibn Namā al-Ḥillī.,[70] *Muṭīr al-aḥzān wa munīr subul al-ashǧān*

---

[61] Abū al-Ḥasan ʿAlī b. Abī al-Karam Aṯīr al-Dīn Muḥammad b. Muḥammad b. ʿAbd al-Karīm ʿIzz al-Dīn Muḥammad b. al-Aṯīr al-Shaybānī (d. 630/1233: cf. GAL I: 345).

[62] Abū Isḥāq Ibrāhīm b. ʿAlī b. ʿAbd al-Muʾmin Shihāb al-Dīn Ibrāhīm b. Abī al-Dam al-Hamdānī al-Ḥamawī (d. 642/1244: cf. GAL S. I: 588).

[63] Shams al-Dīn Aḥmad al-Muẓaffar Yūsuf b. Qizoġlū b. ʿAlī Sibṭ al-Ǧawzī (d. 654/1257: cf. GAL S. I: 589)

[64] Kamāl al-Dīn Abū al-Qāsim ʿUmar b. Aḥmad Hibat Allāh b. ʿAbd al-ʿAzīz b. Abū Garāda b. al-ʿAdīm al-ʿUqaylī al-Ḥalabī (d. 660/1262: cf. GAL I: 404–405).

[65] Muḥib al-Dīn Abū al-ʿAbbās (Abū Muḥammad Abū Ǧaʿfar) Aḥmad b. ʿAbd al-Raḥmān al-Ṭabarī al-Makkī al-Shāfiʿī (d. 684/1295: cf. GAL 1: 615).

[66] Abū al-Ḥasan Yaḥyā b. al-Ḥasan b. al-Ḥusayn b. ʿAlī al-Ḥillī al-Wāsiṭī b. al-Biṭrīq (d. 600/1203: cf. GAL S. I: 710).

[67] Abū al-Ḥusayn Warrām b. Abī Firās ʿĪsā b. Abī al-Naǧm al-Naḫāʿī al-Ashtarī (d. 605/1208, cf. GAL S. I: 709, who gives no dates).

[68] ʿIzz al-Dīn ʿAbd al-Ḥamīd b. Hibat Allāh al-Madāʾinī b. al-Ḥadīd (d. 655/1257: cf. GAL S. I: 497).

[69] Raḍī al-Dīn Abū Mūsā Abū al-ʿAbbās ʿAlī b. Mūsā b. Ǧaʿfar b. Muḥammad b. Muḥammad b. Ṭāʾūs al-Ṭāʾūsī al-ʿAlawī al-Fāṭimī (d. 664/1266: Cf. GAL S. I: 911, where this work is entitled *Kitāb al-malhūf fī qatla al-ṭufūf*).

al-Irbilī.,[71] *Kashf al-ġumma fī maʿrifat al-aʾimma*
al-Shāmī.,[72] *al-Durr al-naẓīm fī manāqib al-aʾimma al-lahāhīm*

8TH/14TH CENTURY:

Sunnī:

al-Tibrīzī.,[73] *Mishkāt al-maṣābīḥ*
al-Mizzī.,[74] *Tahḏīb al-kamāl fī asmāʾ al-riǧāl*
al-Ḏahabī.,[75] *Siyar aʿlām al-nubalāʾ*, *Taḏkirat al-ḥuffāẓ*, *al-ʿIbar fī aḫbār al-bashar muntaḫab al-taʾrīḫ al-kabīr*
al-Zarandī.,[76] *Naẓm durar al-simṭayn*
Ibn Kaṯīr.,[77] *al-Bidāya wa-l-nihāya*

Shīʿī:

al-Ḥillī al-ʿAllāma., *Iṯbāt al-hudāt*

9TH/15TH CENTURY:

Sunnī:

al-Haytamī.,[78] *Maǧmaʿ al-zawāʾid wa-manbaʿ al-fawāʾid*

---

[70] Naǧm al-Dīn Ǧaʿfar b. Muḥammad b. Ǧaʿfar b. Hibat Allāh b. Namā al-Ḥillī (d. 680/1281).

[71] Bahāʾ al-Dīn Abū al-Ḥasan ʿAlī b. ʿĪsā al-Irbilī b. al-Faḫr (d. 692/1293: cf. GAL S. I: 713).

[72] Yūsuf b. Ḥātim al-Shāmī (c. 7th/13th century).

[73] Shams al-Dīn Muḥammad b. ʿAbd al-Raḥmān al-Ḫaṭīb al-Tibrīzī al-ʿUmarī (c. 737/1336: cf. GAL S. II: 262.

[74] Abū al-Ḥaǧǧāǧ Yūsuf b. al-Zakī ʿAbd al-Raḥmān b. Yūsuf Ǧamāl al-Dīn al-Mizzī al-Quḍāʿī al-Kalbī al-Shāfiʿī (d. 742/1341.

[75] Abū ʿAbd Allāh Muḥammad b. Aḥmad b. ʿUṯmān b. Qaymāz Shams al-Dīn al-Ḏahabī (d. 748/1348: cf. GAL S. II: 45).

[76] Ǧamāl al-Dīn Muḥammad b. Yūsuf b. al-Ḥasan al-Zarandī al-Madanī al-Ḥanafī (d. 750/1349)

[77] Abū al-Fidāʾ Ismāʿīl b. ʿUmar b. Kaṯīr ʿImād al-Dīn b. al-Ḫaṭīb al-Qurayshī al-Buṣrawī al-Shāfiʿī (d. 774/1373: cf. GAL S. II: 48).

[78] Nūr al-Dīn Abū al-Ḥasan ʿAlī b. Abī Bakr b. Sulaymān b. Ḥaǧar al-Haytamī (d. 807/1405: cf. GAL II: 91, GAL S. II: 82).

al-ʿAsqalānī.,[79] *al-Iṣāba fī tamyīz al-ṣaḥāba*, *Tahḏīb al-tahḏīb*
al-Ṣabbāġ.,[80] *al-Fuṣūl al-muhimma fī maʿrifat (faḍāʾil) al-aʾimma*

Shīʿī:

al-Daylami.,[81] *Irshād al-qulūb*, *Aʿlām al-dīn fī ṣifāt al-muʾminīn*
al-Bayyāḍī.,[82] *al-Ṣirāṭ al-mustaqīm*
al-Kafʿamī.,[83] *Kitāb al-miṣbāḥ*, *al-Balad al-amīn*
al-Mūsawī.,[84] *Tasliyat al-maǧālis wa zaynat al-maǧālis*

10TH/16TH CENTURY:

Sunnī:

al-Suyūṭī[85] *al-Ḥabāʾik fī aḫbār al-malāʾik*, *al-Ḫaṣāʾiṣ al-kubrā*
al-Muttaqī al-Hindī.,[86] *Kanz al-ʿummāl fī sunan al-aqwāl wa-l-afʿāl*

Shīʿī:

al-Astarābāḏī.,[87] *Taʾwīl al-āyāt al-ẓāhira fī faḍl al-ʿitra al-ṭāhira*

---

[79] Abū al-Faḍl Aḥmad b. ʿAlī b. Muḥammad b. Ḥaǧar Shihāb al-Dīn al-ʿAsqalānī al-Kinānī al-Shāfiʿī (d. 852/1449: cf. GAL S. II: 72).

[80] Nūr al-Dīn ʿAlī b. Muḥammad al-Ṣabbāġ al-Isfāqusī al-Maġribī al-Makkī al-Mālikī (d. 855/1451: cf. GAL S. II: 224).

[81] Ḥasan b. Abī al-Ḥasan al-Daylamī (d. 840/1437: cf. GAL S. I: 261, although Brockelmann provides no dates).

[82] Zayn al-ʿĀbidīn ʿAlī b. Yūnus al-Bayyāḍī al-Nabāṭī al-ʿĀmilī (d. 877/1472: cf. GAL S. II: 133).

[83] Taqī al-Dīn Ibrāhīm b. ʿAlī b. al-Ḥusayn al-Kafʿamī (895 or 905/1498: cf. GAL S. II: 133).

[84] Adīb Muḥammad b. Abī Ṭālib al-Ḥusaynī al-Mūsawī al-Ḥāʾirī al-Karakī (d. 899/1494).

[85] Abū al-Faḍl ʿAbd al-Raḥmān b. Abī Bakr Kamāl al-Dīn b. Muḥammad b. Abī Bakr Ǧalāl al-Dīn al-Suyūṭī (d. 911/1505: cf. GAL S. II: 178).

[86] ʿAlāʾ al-Dīn ʿAlī b. Ḥusām al-Dīn ʿAbd al-Malik b. Qāḍīhān al-Muttaqī al-Hindī al-Qādirī al-Shāḏilī al-Ǧawnpūrī al-Madanī (d. c. 977/1569: cf. GAL S. II: 518).

11TH/17TH CENTURY:

Shīʿī:

Muḥammad Riḍā al-Ṭūsī.,[88] *Kanz al-daqāʾiq wa baḥr al-ġarāʾib fī tafsīr al-qurʾān*
al-Māzandarānī.,[89] *Sharḥ uṣūl al-Kāfī*
al-Qazwīnī.,[90] *al-Shāfī fī uṣūl al-kāfī*
al-Fayḍ al-Kāshānī.,[91] *Nawādir al-aḫbār, Tafsīr al-ṣāfī, al-Wāfī*

12TH/18TH CENTURY:

Sunnī:

al-ʿIṣāmī.,[92] *Simṭ al-nuǧūm al-ʿawālī*

Shīʿī:

al-Ḥurr al-ʿĀmilī.,[93] *Tafṣīl wasāʾil al-shīʿa ilā taḥṣīl masāʾil al-sharīʿa, al-Ǧawāhir al-saniyya al-aḥādīṯ al-qudsiyya, Iṯbāt al-hudāt bi-l-nuṣūṣ wa-l-muʿǧizāt*
al-Baḥrānī.,[94] *Ḥilyat al-abrār fī aḥwāl Muḥammad wa āli-hi al-aṭhār, al-Burhān fī tafsīr al-qurʾān, Madīnat al-maʿāǧiz fī muʿǧizāt al-aʾimma al-aṭhār*

---

[87] Sharāf al-Dīn ʿAlī al-Ḥusaynī al-Astarābāḏī (pupil of ʿAlī b. al-Ḥusayn b. ʿAbd al- ʿĀlī al-Karakī al-Muḥaqqiq al-Ṯānī, d. 946/1538: cf. GAL S. II: 575).

[88] Muḥammad b. Muḥammad Riḍā b. Ismāʿīl b. Ǧamāl al-Dīn al-Qummī al-Mashhadī al-Ṭūsī (c. 1059/1649: cf. GAL S. II: 582).

[89] Muḥammad Ṣāliḥ b. Aḥmad al-Māzandarānī (d. 1086/1676: cf. GAL S: II: 578), student and son-in-law of Muḥammad Taqī b. Maqṣūd ʿAlī al-Maǧlisī.

[90] Ḫalīl b. Ġāzī al-Qazwīnī (d. 1089/1678: cf. GAL S. I: 320).

[91] Muḥammad Murtaḍā Mullā Muḥsin Fayḍ al-Kāshī [Kāshānī] (d. 1090/1679: cf. GAL S. II: 584).

[92] ʿAbd al-Malik b. al-Ḥusayn b. ʿAbd al-Malik al-ʿIṣāmī (d. 1111/1699: cf. GAL S. II: 516).

[93] Muḥammad b. al-Ḥasan al-Ḥasanī b. ʿAlī b. Ḥusayn al-Ḥurr al-cĀmilī al-Mashġarī (d. 1104/1693: cf. GAL S. II: 578).

al-Iṣfahānī.,[95] *ʿAwālim al-ʿulūm wa-l-maʿārif al-aḥwāl min al-āyāt wa-l-aḫbār wa-l-aqwāl*
al-Mağlisī.,[96] *Biḥār al-anwār, Zād al-maʿād*
al-Ḥuwayzī.,[97] *Tafsīr nūr al-ṯaqalayn*
al-Ğazāʾirī.,[98] *Riyāḍ al-abrār fī manāqib al-aʾimma al-aṭhār*
Ṣadr al-Dīn al-Shīrāzī.,[99] *Riyāḍ al-sālikīn fī sharḥ saḥīfa sayyid al-sāğğidīn*

14TH/20TH CENTURY:

Sunnī:

al-Shablanğī.,[100] *Nūr al-abṣār fī manāqib āl bayt al-nabī al-muḫtār*

Shīʿī:

al-Ṭabarsī.,[101] *Mustadrak al-wasāʾil wa mustanbiṭ al-masāʾil*
ʿAbbās Qummī.,[102] *Safīnat al-biḥār*
al-ʿĀmilī.,[103] *Aʿyān al-Shīʿa*

---

[94] Hāshim b. Sulaymān b. Ismāʿīl b. ʿAbd al-Ğawād b. ʿAbd al-Raḥmān al-Ḥusaynī al-Baḥrānī (d. 1107/1695: cf. GAL S. II: 506).

[95] ʿAbd Allāh b. Nūr Allāh al-Baḥrānī al-Iṣfahānī (d. 1110/1698: cf. GAL S. II: 504).

[96] Muḥammad Bāqir b. Muḥammad Taqī b. Maqṣūd ʿAlī Akmal al-Mağlisī al-Iṣfahānī (d. 1110/1700: cf. GAL S. II: 572).

[97] ʿAbd ʿAlī b. Ğumuʿa al-Ḥuwayzī (d. 1112/1702).

[98] Niʿmat Allāh al-Ğazāʾirī (d. 1112/1702).

[99] Ṣadr al-Dīn ʿAlī b. Aḥmad b. Muḥammad Maʿṣūm al-Ḥusaynī al-Dashtakī al-Shīrāzī (d. 1120/1708–9).

[100] Muʾmin b. Ḥasan Muʾmin al-Shablanğī (d. c. 1301/1883: cf. GAL S. II: 737).

[101] al-Ḥāğğ Mīrzā Ḥusayn b. Muḥammad Taqī al-Nūrī al-Ṭabarsī (d. 1320/1902: cf. GAL S. II: 832).

[102] ʿAbbās b. Muḥammad Riḍā al-Qummī (d. 1359/1940: cf. GAL S. II: 573).

[103] Muḥsin b. ʿAbd al-Karīm al-Amīn al-ʿĀmilī (d. 1371/1952: cf. GAL S. II: 808).

BIBLIOGRAPHY

AHMADI N., "The Role of Dreams in the Political Affairs of the Safavid Dynasty" in *Journal of Shiʿa Islamic Studies*, Spring 2013, Volume VI, Number 2: 177–198.

ALTER R., *The Hebrew Bible. A Translation with Commentary*, vol. III, W. Norton & Company, New York 2019.

AYOUB M., *Redemptive Suffering in Islam. A Study of the Devotional Aspects of ʿAshura in Twelver Shiʿism*, Mouton Publishers, The Hague 1978.

BAR S., *A Letter That Has Not Been Read: Dreams in the Hebrew Bible*, Hebrew Union College Press, Cincinnati 2001.

BROCKELMANN C., *Geschichte der arabischen Literatur*, 2 vols., 3 supplementary vols., Leiden 1937–1945.

BROWN R., *The Birth of the Messiah*, Doubleday, New York 1993.

BULKELEY K., *Dreaming in the World's Religions. A Comparative History*, New York University Press, New York 2008.

BURGE S.R., *Angels in Islam*, Routledge, London 2012.

BURGE S.R., "Angels, ritual and sacred space in Islam" in *Comparative Islamic Studies*, 5 n. 2, Nov 2009: 221–245.

CHITTICK W.C., *The Sufi Path of Knowledge*, State University of New York Press, Albany 1989.

CLOHESSY C., *Half of My Heart. The Narratives of Zaynab, Daughter of ʿAlī*, Gorgias Press, New Jersey 2018.

CORBIN H., "The Visionary Dream in Islamic Spirituality" in G.E von Grunebaum & R. Caillois (eds.), *The Dream and Human Societies*, University of California Press, Berkeley 1966: 381–408.

DE LA POTTERIE I., *Mary in the Mystery of the Covenant*, Alba House, New York 1997.

EDGAR I.R., *The Dream in Islam*, Berghahn Books, Oxford 2011.

FAHD T., "The Dream in Medieval Islamic Society" in G.E von Grunebaum & R. Caillois (eds.), *The Dream and Human Societies*, University of California Press, Berkeley 1966: 351–363.

FELEK Ö & KNYSH D., (eds.), *Dreams and Visions in Islamic Societies*, State University of New York Press, Albany 2012.

GODWIN M., *Angels. An Endangered Species*, Boxtree Ltd., London 1990.

GREEN N., "The Religious and Cultural Roles of Dreams and Visions in Islam" in *Journal of the Royal Asiatic Society*, Third Series, vol. 13, No. 3 (Nov., 2003): 287–313.

GUILLAME A., *The Life of Muhammad. A Translation of Ibn Ishaq's Sirat Rasul Allah*, Oxford University Press, Oxford 2006.

HILL J., *A History of Christian Thought*, Lion Books, Oxford 2003.

JEFFERY A., *The Foreign Vocabulary of the Qurʾān*, Brill, Leiden 2007.

JONES D.A., *Angels. A History*, Oxford University Press, Oxford 2010.

KARAMUSTAFA A., *Sufism. The Formative Period*, Edinburgh University Press, Edinburgh 2007.

KASSIM H., "Nothing can be Known or Done without the Involvement of Angels: Angels and Angelology in Islam and Islamic Literature" in F.V. Reiterer et al. (eds.), *Angels: The Con-*

cept of Celestial Beings: Origins, Development and Reception, Walter de Gruyter, Berlin 2007.

KINBERG L., "Dreams and Sleep" in Jane Dammen McAuliffe et al. (eds.), *Encyclopaedia of the Qurʾān*, vol. I, Brill, Leiden 2001: 546–553

KMEID F., *Rūḥ al-qudus. A Study Based in Father Joseph Azzi's Book Bayna al-Masīḥiyya wa-l-Islām*, unpublished licentiate thesis, Pontifical Institute for Arabic and Islamic Studies, Rome 2016.

LAMOREAUX J.C., *The Early Muslim Tradition of Dream Interpretation*, State University of New York Press, Albany: 2002

LANE E.W., *An Arabic-English Lexicon*, Librairie du Liban, Beirut 1968.

LECERF J., "The Dream in Popular Culture: Arabic and Islam" in G.E von Grunebaum & R. Caillois (eds.), *The Dream and Human Societies*, University of California Press, Berkeley 1966: 365–379.

LIZZINI O., "Islamic Angelology. Revelation, Tradition and Philosophical Elaboration. Some Brief Observations" in *Encounter* n. 227, August–September 1996, Pontificio Istituto di Studi Arabi e d'Islamistica, Rome.

IBN MANẒŪR., *Lisān al-ʿarab*, 18 vols., Dār Iḥyā al-Turāṯ al-ʿArabī, Beirut 1999.

MARLOW L., (ed.), *Dreaming Across Boundaries. The Interpretation of Dreams in Islamic Lands*, Ilex Foundation, Boston 2008.

MAVROUDI M., *A Byzantine Book on Dream Interpretation. The Oneirocriticon of Achmet and its Arabic Sources*, Brill, Leiden 2002.

MEIER F. "Some Aspects of Inspiration by Demons in Islam" in G.E von Grunebaum & R. Caillois (eds.), *The Dream and Human Societies*, University of California Press, Berkeley 1966: 421–429.

MEISAMI J.S. & STARKEY P., (eds.), *Encyclopedia of Arabic Literature*, vol. I, Routledge, London 1998.

MODARRESSI H., *Tradition and Survival. A Bibliographical Survey of Early Shīʾite Literature*, vol. 1, Oneworld, Oxford 2003.

EL-MOUALLEM D.A., "For the Sake of the Infant Imām: the Development of the Errant Angel Traditions" in H. Ansari & S. Schmidtke (eds.), *Shii Studies Review*, vol. 4, issue 1–2, Brill, Leiden 2020: 108–134.

NASR S.E. et al., (eds.), *The Study Quran*, HarperOne, New York 2015.

NEIL B., "Studying Dream Interpretation from Early Christianity to the Rise of Islam" in *Journal of Religious History*, vol. 40, n. 1, March 2016: 63.

PADWICK C., *Muslim Devotions. A Study of Prayer Manuals in Common Use*, Oneworld, Oxford 1996.

POURESMAEIL E., "Seeing Allah While Dreaming: A Comparison Between Shiʿa and Sunni Beliefs" in *Journal of Shiʿa Islamic Studies*, Winter 2012, Volume V, Number 1: 65–80.

RAHMAN F., "Dream, Imagination and *ʿĀlam al-mithāl*" in G.E von Grunebaum & R. Caillois (eds.), *The Dream and Human Societies*, University of California Press, Berkeley 1966: 409–419.

REITERER F.V. et al., (eds.), *Angels: The Concept of Celestial Beings: Origins, Development and Reception*, Walter de Gruyter, Berlin 2007.

RODED R., *Women in Islamic Biographical Collections*, Gorgias Press, New Jersey 2018.

SCHIMMEL A., *Gabriel's Wing*, Iqbal Academy, Pakistan 2003.

SELLS M., "Spirit" in Jane Dammen McAuliffe et al (eds.)., *Encyclopaedia of the Qurʾān*, vol. V, Brill, Leiden 2006: 114–117.

SEZGIN F., *Geschichte der arabischen Schrifttums*, 9 vols., Leiden 1967–1972.

SIRRIYEH E., *Dreams and Visions in the World of Islam*, I.B. Tauris, London 2018.

SULAVIK A.T., *The Beginnings of Angels*, Tatra Press, New York 2014.

STEINGASS F., *Learner's Arabic English Dictionary*, 1993.

SHALIT E., "Dreams in the Old Testament" in D.A. Leeming, K. Madden et al (eds.), *Encyclopedia of Psychology and Religion*, Springer, Boston 2014.

VAN DEUSEN N., (ed.), *Dreams and Visions. An Interdisciplinary Enquiry*, Brill, Leiden 2010.

VON GRUNEBAUM G.E. "The Cultural Function of the Dream as Illustrated by Classical Islam" in G.E von Grunebaum & R. Caillois. (eds.)., *The Dream and Human Societies*, University of California Press, Berkeley 1966: 3–21.

WEBB G., "Angel" in Jane Dammen McAuliffe et al. (eds.)., *Encyclopaedia of the Qurʾān*, vol. I, Brill, Leiden 2001: 84–92.

WEBB G., "Gabriel" in Jane Dammen McAuliffe et al. (eds.)., *Encyclopaedia of the Qurʾān*, vol. II, Brill, Leiden 2001: 278–279.

WEHR H., *A Dictionary of Modern Written Arabic*, 1980.

WENSINCK A. J., *Concordance et Indices de la Tradition Musulmane*, 4 vols., 2nd edn., E.J. Brill, Leiden 1962.

INDEX OF PROPER NAMES

E

F

G

Ğ

Ġ

H

Ḥ

J